THE BODY

Social Process and Cultural Theory

edited by
MIKE FEATHERSTONE
MIKE HEPWORTH
BRYAN S. TURNER

SAGE PUBLICATIONS
London • Newbury Park • New Delhi

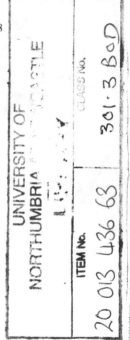

SAGE Publications Ltd
6 Bonhill Street
London EC2A 4PU

SAGE Publications Inc
2455 Teller Road
Newbury Park, California 91320

SAGE Publications India Pvt Ltd
32, M-Block Market
Greater Kailash – I
New Delhi 110 048

Published in association with *Theory, Culture & Society*,
Department of Administrative and Social Studies, Teesside
Polytechnic

British Library Cataloguing in Publication Data

The body: social process and cultural theory. – (Theory,
  culture & society).
  1. Man. Body – Sociological perspectives
  I. Featherstone, Mike II. Hepworth, Mike III. Turner,
  Bryan S. (Bryan Stanley) *1945–*   IV. Series
  304

ISBN 0–8039–8412–X
ISBN 0–8039–8413–8 pbk

Library of Congress catalog card number 90-53534

Typeset by Mayhew Typesetting, Bristol, Great Britain
Printed in Great Britain by Dotesios Ltd,
Trowbridge, Wiltshire

Theory, Culture & Society

Theory, Culture & Society caters for the resurgence of interest in culture within contemporary social science and the humanities. Building on the heritage of classical social theory, the book series examines ways in which this tradition has been reshaped by a new generation of theorists. It will also publish theoretically informed analyses of everyday life, popular culture, and new intellectual movements.

EDITOR: Mike Featherstone, *Teesside Polytechnic*

SERIES EDITORIAL BOARD
Roy Boyne, *Newcastle upon Tyne Polytechnic*
Mike Hepworth, *University of Aberdeen*
Scott Lash, *University of Lancaster*
Roland Robertson, *University of Pittsburgh*
Bryan S. Turner, *University of Essex*

Also in this series

Reproduction in Education, Society and Culture
Revised edition
Pierre Bourdieu and Jean-Claude Passeron

The Tourist Gaze
Leisure and Travel in Contemporary Societies
John Urry

Theories of Modernity and Postmodernity
edited by Bryan S. Turner

Global Culture
Nationalism, Globalization and Modernity
edited by Mike Featherstone

Consumer Culture and Postmodernism
Mike Featherstone

CONTENTS

Contributors   vii

Preface   viii

1. Recent Developments in the Theory of the Body   1
   Bryan S. Turner

2. For a Sociology of the Body: an Analytical Review   36
   Arthur W. Frank

3. On Human Beings and their Emotions: a Process-
   Sociological Essay   103
   Norbert Elias

4. On the Civilizing of Appetite   126
   Stephen Mennell

5. The Discourse of Diet   157
   Bryan S. Turner

6. The Body in Consumer Culture   170
   Mike Featherstone

7. The Midlifestyle of 'George and Lynne': Notes on a
   Popular Strip   197
   Mike Featherstone and Mike Hepworth

8. Martial Arts as a Resource for Liberal Education: the
   Case of Aikido   209
   Donald N. Levine

9. Bio-politics and Social Policy: Foucault's Account of
   Welfare   225
   Martin Hewitt

10. Genealogy and the Body: Foucault/Deleuze/
    Nietzsche   256
    Scott Lash

11. The Art of the Body in the Discourse of
    Postmodernity   281
    Roy Boyne

12. Love's Labour Lost? A Sociological View   297
    Margareta Bertilsson

13. Biographical Boundaries: Sociology and Marilyn
    Monroe   325
    Graham McCann

14. *Carmen* – or The Invention of a New Feminine Myth   339
    Dick Pels and Aya Crébas

15. The Mask of Ageing and the Postmodern Life
    Course   371
    Mike Featherstone and Mike Hepworth

16. Sociological Discourse and the Body   390
    J.M. Berthelot

Index   405

CONTRIBUTORS

J.M. Berthelot, Department of Sociology, University of Toulouse le Mirail, Toulouse, France.

Margareta Bertilsson, Department of Sociology, University of Lund, Box 114, S–22100, Lund, Sweden.

Roy Boyne, Faculty of Community & Social Studies, Newcastle upon Tyne Polytechnic, Northumberland Building, Northumberland Road, Newcastle upon Tyne NE1 8ST.

Aya Crébas, Research Associate, Universiteit van Amsterdam, Vakgroep, Sociologie en Geschiedenis, Oude Hoogstraat 24, 1012 CE Amsterdam, The Netherlands.

Norbert Elias lived in the Netherlands until his death in 1990.

Mike Featherstone, Department of Administrative & Social Studies, Teesside Polytechnic, Middlesbrough, Cleveland TS1 3BA.

Arthur W. Frank, Department of Sociology, The University of Calgary, 2500 University Drive, NW Calgary, Alberta, Canada T2N 1N4.

Mike Hepworth, Department of Sociology, University of Aberdeen, Edward Wright Building, Aberdeen AB9 2TY.

Martin Hewitt, School of Health and Human Sciences, Hatfield Polytechnic, College Lane, Hatfield, Herts AL10 9AB.

Scott Lash, Department of Sociology, University of Lancaster, Cartmel College, Bailrigg, Lancaster LA1 4YL.

Donald N. Levine, Department of Sociology, University of Chicago, Illinois 60637, USA.

Graham McCann, King's College, Cambridge.

Stephen Mennell, Department of Sociology, Monash University, Victoria, Australia.

Dick Pels, Sociologisch Instituut, Universiteit van Amsterdam, Vakgroep, Sociologie en Geschiedenis, Oude Hoogstraat 24, 1012 CE Amsterdam, The Netherlands.

Bryan S. Turner, Department of Sociology, University of Essex, Wivenhoe Park, Colchester CO4 3SQ.

PREFACE

The publication of this collection of papers is an indication of the growing interest in the sociology of the body. The majority of the papers were published in *Theory, Culture & Society* between 1982 and 1990. Three of the papers – those by Bryan Turner 'Recent Developments in the Theory of the Body', Arthur W. Frank 'For a Sociology of the Body' and Donald Levine 'Martial Arts as a Resource for Liberal Education' – have not been previously published. 'The Mask of Ageing' by Mike Featherstone and Mike Hepworth is an expanded version of 'Ageing and Old Age' which was first published in 1989.

From its very first issue *Theory, Culture & Society* has been concerned to foster interest in the Sociology of the Body as one of the crucial instances of the complex interrelations of nature, culture and society. It is also important to stress that these chapters provide an excellent illustration of the editorial policy of the journal, namely to encourage a diversity of theoretical perspectives. Here we can refer to the various influences of Foucault, Nietzsche, Elias, Douglas, Horkheimer and Adorno, Mauss, Bourdieu, Baudrillard, Goffman and feminist theorists. These theoretical perspectives are selectively drawn upon to illuminate representations of the body in a (wide) range of contexts which include: the expression of the emotions, romantic love, dietary practices, consumer-culture images of youth, fitness and beauty, martial arts, social welfare, modernism, postmodernism and old age, media images of women, and sexuality. We would not claim that this list is exhaustive; only that it provides some important representations of the contemporary sociological interest in the human body.

It is our main aim in this book to put these materials in a form which is accessible to the growing number of students and teachers who wish to study the sociology of the human body and it is the hope of the editors that both sociologists and those with broader social science and humanities backgrounds will find this material of relevance and interest.

In conclusion, the editors are pleased to express their gratitude to all the *TCS* editorial board members and associates who have helped in numerous ways with this project. We would also like to express our gratitude to Stephen Barr of Sage Publications for his unfailing support and encouragement.

Mike Featherstone, Mike Hepworth and Bryan S. Turner
Skelton

1
RECENT DEVELOPMENTS IN THE THEORY OF THE BODY

Bryan S. Turner

Anthropology and the Body

In contrast to sociology, the human body has been accorded a place of central importance in anthropology since the nineteenth century. There are at least four reasons which explain the prominence of the body in anthropology.

The first is the development of philosophical anthropology, and the issue of the body in relation to an ontology of Man, (the word 'Man' is deliberately employed here to indicate a gendered understanding of humanity, and the probability that classical social science was itself gendered or indeed, to invent a verb, bodied). Historically speaking, anthropology has been more inclined to pose questions about the universal essence of humanity, because anthropology in the context of European colonialism was forced to address the problem of human universals (of ontology) in relation to variations and differences of social relationships. The ontological centrality of human embodiment consequently emerged as a focus of universality. The fact of human embodiment (or more technically the fact that humanity is in evolutionary terms a warm-blooded mammal, a species being) gives rise to certain problems which must be satisfied in order for Man to survive. In particular, it raises the question: what range of social and cultural arrangements are minimally necessary for human survival and reproduction? These basic constraints produced a limited range of options for humanity in the stage of primitive evolution in terms of social structure in relation to a precarious food supply (Glassman, 1986). In nineteenth-century anthropology, in Marxism and philosophy we can detect a convergence on questions of universals in human origins. For example, the research of Lewis Henry Morgan into ancient society, the Iroquois confederation and primitive systems of classification was influential in part because it supported the theory of a common human ancestry (Kuper, 1988). In summary, the body played a part in early anthropology, because it offered one solution to the problem of social relativism. It is possible in philosophical anthropology to trace a line of development in the history of ideas from Ludwig Feuerbach's sensualism (Kamenka, 1970) to the materialism of Sebastian Timpanaro (1975).

We can consider a second stream in anthropology, also related to this quest for an anthropology which was fundamentally concerned with the relationship between culture and nature. This line of development can be framed in the question: granted that humanity has a common point of origin in its mammalian species-being, what constitutes the point of disjunction between nature and culture? In short, what is Man? This question directs our attention to the origins of social science as such. Certainly Herodotus' history of human manners, for example, can be regarded as an early contribution to this anthropological question because he clearly addressed the issue of conventionality versus universality. The answers to this ancient question have of course been highly variable, ranging from the model of Man as a tool-bearing animal through to, in the case of Nietzsche (1980), the concept of man as an animal with a memory (that is, self-consciously situated in history).

From our point of view, the answers which are particularly persuasive are those which have conceptualized the disjunction between Man and nature in terms of certain prohibitions, especially on unrestrained or indiscriminate sexuality. Thus, the incest taboo is often represented as evidence of a fundamental discontinuity between the natural world of animality and the cultural world of humanity. While explanations of incest taboos have given rise to endless disputes amongst anthropologists, the existence of such a taboo has often been taken as evidence of the fact that human social behaviour rests more on the cultural regulation of actions which become institutionalized than it does on instinctual controls. Social life required prohibitions, but these social requirements were achieved at a necessary psychic cost. The incest taboo provided Freud with what we might call 'the elementary forms of neurotic life'. In *Totem and Taboo* (1950), Freud argued that he had discovered a certain 'agreement between the mental lives of savages and neurotics'. This view of taboo controls became the basis of a philosophical tradition which established a series of contradictions between body and soul; instinctual gratifications and social regulations; and sexuality and civilization.

This theoretical orientation was particularly important in the anti-capitalist romanticism of the German *Lebensphilosophie* tradition of the George Circle, especially in the writings of Ludwig Klages, such as *Vom kosmogonischen Eros* (1963), a study of eros and ecstacy going back to the foundations of human society. In addition, the symbolist poet Stefan George developed a theory of human character which he analysed in terms of three dimensions: *Leib* (body), *Geist* (spirit) and *Seele* (soul) (Bowra, 1959). This trichotomous paradigm of human nature proved an indirect influence on the development of what came to be known as 'phenomenological anthropology', which played an important role in the theoretical evolution of the social sciences, especially in Germany and the Netherlands (van Peursen, 1961). One can find, for example, elements of this perspective in the influential sociology of Arnold Gehlen (1988). From Nietzsche, Gehlen borrowed the basic notion of man as an unfinished creature or a 'not yet determined animal' (*noch nicht festgestelltes Tier*). Because Man is an unfinished biological creature who is not at home in nature, he requires the protective canopy of institutions and culture for shelter from dangerous environmental threats during the process of socialization (Berger and Kellner, 1965). The very embodiment of Man makes him nostalgic. This view of culture (especially language and religion) as a kind of 'relief' (*Entlastung*) created the theoretical basis for the philosophical anthropological perspective in Peter L. Berger and Thomas Luckmann's notion of 'reality as a social construction' (Berger and Luckmann, 1967).

There was, of course, yet another line of development through evolutionism to anthropology, which contributed to the study of the human body, especially in the Victorian period, namely social Darwinism. Broadly speaking, three key ideas were adopted by social scientists from Darwinian biology (Burrow, 1970: 114–15). The first was that human beings are essentially a part of nature, rather than outside it. Secondly, Darwinism was used to provide an account of racial differences and finally the doctrine of natural selection was converted into a theory of 'the survival of the fittest' to explain social change. These Darwinistic assumptions were and are clearly controversial, and 'physical anthropology' was rather slow to develop as a specialized sub-branch of mainstream anthropology. However, Darwin's theory of the expression of emotions in humans proved influential in the development of anthropology. In this tradition we might also include the work of Konrad Lorenz on aggression (1966) and more recently the (somewhat popular) contributions of Desmond Morris in *The Naked Ape* (1967) and *Man Watching* (1977), or Robert Ardrey's *The Territorial Imperative* (1971). In a more serious vein, there has been the development of sociobiology (Wilson, 1975), which attempts to discover and to explain 'human universals' in terms of human genetic inheritance. Although these traditions contributed greatly to the scientific development of ethnography and ethnology, the application of biological theories to social relationships has been at best unimpressive (Hirst and Woolley, 1982). The predominant and most substantial theoretical trend in mainstream anthropology has been to focus attention on culture. In this respect, the work of Alfred L. Kroeber, such as *Anthropology* (1923) and *The Nature of Culture* (1952), were crucial in shaping the orientation of both anthropology and sociology to the centrality of the cultural in the constitution of the human.

In conclusion, sociology has inherited three fundamental propositions from this tradition. First, human embodiment creates a set of constraints (for example, how to reproduce successfully, given a mammalian genetic inheritance with limited possibilities and the limits of physical ageing), but equally important the body is also a potential which can be elaborated by sociocultural development. In western philosophy and theory, therefore, the body appears simultaneously as constraint and potential. Secondly, there are certain contradictions between human sexuality and sociocultural requirements. This paradox was beautifully expressed by Gaston Bachelard who observed that 'Man is a creation of desire, not a creation of need' (1987: 16). Thirdly, these 'natural' facts are experienced differently according to gender, again a classificatory system which lies ambiguously across the nature/culture division as a social principle.

The question of the body as a classificatory system has been fundamental to the anthropological vision of Mary Douglas (1970, 1973); the main theme of her whole work is the human response to disorder in which may be included risk, uncertainty and contradiction. The principal response to disorder is systematic classification: the creation of ordered categories which both explain disorder and restore order. (The principal medium of classification has been historically the human body itself.) Although Douglas does not appear to provide an explicit explanation of why the body rather than some other alternative medium is the principal code, we may assume that the body is the most ubiquitous, natural and, also self-consciously adopting a body metaphor, a ready-to-hand source of allegories of order and disorder. (The idea that the body is the central metaphor of political and social order is in fact a very general theme in sociology and history (Barkan, 1975; Kantorowicz, 1957; MacRae, 1975; O'Neill, 1985).)However, Douglas was able to use the idea of the body's boundaries as a metaphor of the social system to explain a wide variety of cultural patterns (from Old Testament dietary rules to modern organizational behaviour); more importantly, she made the cultural analysis of the body a central issue in anthropological theory itself.

Alongside Douglas's anthropology, we should also note that there is a growing *oeuvre* of historical and theological work on how Christ's body became first a fundamental metaphor of the Church and subsequently a model of early mercantile corporations and political institutions. It was R.H. Tawney who, for example, noted how the functions of the parts of the human body were employed as a theory of society in a state of equilibrium in *Religion and the Rise of Capitalism* (1926). The argument is that the body (its health, dispositions, status, histories) is taken as substantial evidence of the spiritual status of the insubstantial soul; the skin becomes a window on the soul. The ascetic regulation of the body is a necessary practice for the management of the life of the spirit (Turner, 1983: 116). These religious practices were, according to Foucault, the origin of the western apparatus of Truth.

Finally, anthropology, rather than sociology, developed a theory of the body (or at least a strong research interest in the body) because in pre-modern societies the body is an important surface on which the marks of social status, family position, tribal affiliation, age, gender and religious condition can easily and publicly be displayed. While it is obviously the case in modern societies that bodily displays (dress, posture, cosmetics) are crucial for indicating wealth and life-style, in pre-modern societies the body was a more important and ubiquitous target for public symbolism, often through decoration, tattooing and scarification (Brain, 1979; Polhemus, 1978). The use of body symbolism may also be associated with the fact that in pre-modern societies status differencès of an ascribed nature (between age cohorts and sexes) were both more rigid and more obvious. The rite of passage between different social statuses was, as a result, often indicated by ritual transformation of the body, often involving some mutilation. While contemporary societies clearly have rituals which employ the body as a mechanism to display some change of status, for example in degradation ceremonies (Garfinkel, 1956), such ritualism is generally less prevalent or important in contemporary urban industrial societies. Tattooing has become part of fashion rather than a necessary aspect of religious culture or the stratification system. However, it is still the case that, for example among young men, tattooing is a mark of social membership within an urban 'tribe'.

Classical Sociology

It has been argued that, while classical sociology failed to generate a genuine sociology of the body, in nineteenth-century anthropology the question of the body was important in early theories of ritual, cosmology and social structure. We have considered four reasons which may explain the importance of the body in anthropological theory. In explaining the failure of sociology to explore similar theoretical possibilities, we can now run this argument in reverse. First, classical sociology around the figures of Max Weber, Georg Simmel, Ferdinand Tönnies, Emile Durkheim, and Karl Mannheim was concerned with the similarities between industrial capitalist societies rather than the differences between human beings over long evolutionary periods. In short, sociology asked a specific and precise question: what are the defining characteristics of urban, industrial society? If sociology had a more general, philosophical question, it may have been: how can humanity survive such a problematic, alien and anomic environment?

From the perspective of German sociological theory, it was generally assumed that industrial society would converge towards a rationalized, bureaucratic and alienated social order, in which the stability of rural life would be fractured by class conflicts, and the family and the Church would gradually be replaced by more public, rational and instrumental institutions. The question of the ontological status of social actors remained submerged, and in so far as classical social theorists turned to such issues, they defined the human actor in terms of agency, which in practice meant the rational choice of ends in terms of either criteria of utility or of general values. It was an economic framework which thus dominated early sociological preoccupations with matters of utility, commodities and equilibrium. The development of a voluntaristic framework of action in sociology was achieved via an exchange with institutional economics (Parsons, 1934). It was, at least initially, difficult to incorporate the 'as yet undetermined animal' of German life philosophy into such a model, because economics was more concerned with the material production of goods rather than with the reproduction of bodies.

With the possible exception of Vilfredo Pareto, the biological conditions of action were relatively unimportant in the construction of a science of action. In part, we can see the development of sociology as a somewhat hostile reaction to Darwinistic evolutionism, eugenics or biologism. Thus, when Weber defined the basic types of social action, there was little room for the biological conditions of action or for the idea of the 'lived body'. Structural-functionalism was strongly influenced by Kroeber's theory of culture (Kroeber and Parsons, 1958). In the subsequent elaboration of the voluntaristic theory of action by Talcott Parsons, the fact of human embodiment was first relegated to the conditions of action, although later Parsons recognized, but did not fully develop, the idea of an organic subsystem or level of action (Parsons, 1977). In attempting to establish the analytical foundations of sociology, Weber, Pareto and Parsons took economics and law as models for the formulation of the basic notions of actor, action, choice and goals. Consumer choice, which in principle could have produced a theory of the embodiment of the social actor via the idea of consumer needs and wants, remained largely underdeveloped in economics and sociology. Economic science focused on technical problems, such as the marginal utility of goods. The issue of human embodiment was similarly not immediately convertible into juristic preoccupations with notions of legal liability. Thus, whereas the body had entered anthropology at the fundamental level of ontology, sociology, partly by evolving theoretically along the notion of rational economic action, never elaborated a sociology of the body.

While anthropology concerned itself with the question of culture/nature, in sociology the question which occupied the same theoretical space was the issue of historicity: how do societies enter history? It was this Hegelian question concerning the emergence of societies into historical self-consciousness which dominated Marxism. In dialectical materialism, societies develop through various stages of production, but in capitalism this socioeconomic development is transformed in scale and capitalism drags the dormant and stagnant societies of Asia and Africa into global consciousness. Following Habermas's analysis in *The Philosophical Discourse of Modernity* (1987), we can date this project of modernity as a question about history from the publication in 1784 of Kant's 'Idea for a Universal History from a Cosmopolitan Point of View'. The problem (what is nature?) which had shaped anthropology was thus excluded from sociology:

> Sociologists have, on the whole, energetically denied the importance of genetic, physical and individual psychological factors in human social life. In so doing, they have reinforced and theorized a traditional Western cultural opposition between nature and culture. Social relations can even be conceived as a *denial* of nature. (Hirst and Woolley, 1982: 23)

This issue is given prominence in Norbert Elias's discussion of the emotions in this volume. It is with the postmodernist critique of the rational project that the question of the body is, so to speak, brought back into the historical question in the form of a debate about the relationship between desire and reason. The critique of reason as emancipation has resulted in an interest in the body, both as a source of opposition to instrumental reason and as the target of the colonization of the everyday world by the public arena of (male) reason. However, through most of its short history, sociology has been fundamentally a historical enquiry into the conditions for social change in social systems; it never successfully posed the question of the body as a historical issue.

It was previously argued that anthropology developed an interest in the body because the body acts as a classificatory system. The body (with its orifices, regular functions, reproductive capacity, environmental adaptation and its organic specificity) proved a 'natural' resource for social metaphoricality: the head of state, the body politic, and corporate culture. In industrial societies, while these body metaphors are still present, they are less obvious and direct. Sovereign power, which once resided in the body of the king and queen became more abstract, dispersed and impersonal with the rise of the modern state and its bureaucratic civil service, its regular army, and division of powers. In the nineteenth century, social analysis often used medical discourse to describe the social problems of an urban, industrial environment: social medicine, which regarded all social problems in terms of social pathology, gave rise eventually to the idea of a medical police force (Rosen, 1979). The language of positivistic medical science also entered modern sociology via Durkheim's version of functionalism (Hirst, 1975) and via the impact of L.J. Henderson on the early work of Parsons (Barber, 1970). However, the entry of the body into sociological theory through early forms of functionalism (especially on the basis of the so-called organic analogy) was possible once the body had been translated into an organic system, that is, a system of energy input and output mechanisms. Sociologists were thus able to draw rather obvious comparisons between organic systems equilibrium and the equilibrium of the social system in relation to its environment. The organic analogy which was a feature of Herbert Spencer's evolutionism was an important component of social theory in Europe in the late nineteenth century (Timasheff, 1957).

We can regard action theory in Weberian sociology as a reaction against some aspects of evolutionism; Weber's distinction between action and behaviour subsequently became an essential feature of the sociological repertoire. The consequence of these theoretical developments was that the notion of the 'lived body' in phenomenological and existential traditions in philosophy was lost to sociology (Levin, 1985). The result was that the body as the organic system was either allocated to other disciplines (such as biochemistry or physiology) or it became part of the conditions of action, that is, an environmental constraint. The body thus became external to the actor, who appeared, as it were, as a decision-making agent.

The further theoretical result is that sociology did not exhibit much interest in the idea of the body as a classificatory system of modern industrial societies. In anthropology, there had been an important theoretical development in which it was realized that the classification of societies into families, clans and tribes provided the basis for classification generally, and that there was an important relationship between classificatory principles in grammar and those in society. These developments were an important background to the work of Durkheim and Mauss on *Primitive Classification* (1963). Another important development in anthropology was made by research into the classificatory symbolism of the left and right hand. While organic asymmetry is common in human beings, asymmetry has been developed as a major classificatory principle: left-handedness for example, is the sign of women, of weakness and of evil (Hertz, 1960). If we regard these developments as the beginnings of an anthropology of knowledge, then we can compare how sociologists treat classificatory systems in the sociology of knowledge.

The most influential contributions to the sociology of knowledge have typically taken social stratification as the primary code of classification. For example, Karl Mannheim's *Ideology and Utopia* (1960) conceptualized society as a dominant class which employed ideology to legitimize its position and a subordinate class which was attracted to a variety of utopian visions of reality. In similar fashion, Stanislaw Ossowski saw class theory as a version of traditional views of 'the spatial metaphors of the vertical stratification of social classes' (1963: 19). In sociology, the debate about consciousness, knowledge and ideology (or the 'superstructure' in the language of Marx's preface of 1859 to *A Contribution to the Critique of Political Economy*) was dominated by a Marxist legacy from Gramsci on hegemony, Lukács on reification, Raymond Williams on literary analysis, or more recently by the work of the Birmingham Centre for Contemporary Cultural Studies on working-class oppositional culture. The metaphors of social reality which were analysed by sociologists were not in terms of left and right hand, or of bodily pollution, but in terms of spatial metaphors of rank. It was not until feminist theory (especially through the writing of Luce Irigaray, Julia Kristeva or, in an earlier generation, Simone de Beauvoir) began to change the direction of social theory by bringing gender more prominently into an understanding of the social processes of classification that the issue of organic differentiation and its sociological import commanded sociological interest. The questions of age and generation have also been somewhat neglected in mainstream sociology as aspects of the system of social stratification by ascriptive criteria despite the fact that Mannheim had, for example, devoted considerable attention to the question of generation as a principle of rank. However, contemporary sociologists are now much more sensitive to the fact that the classifications of social status depend significantly on the ways in which the body is presented in social space. In one of the most influential studies of social class and aesthetic taste, Pierre Bourdieu has argued that:

> Taste, a class culture turned into nature, that is, *embodied*, helps to shape the class body. It is an incorporated principle of classification which governs all forms of incorporation, choosing and modifying everything that the body ingests and digests and assimilates, physiologically and psychologically. It follows that the body is the most indisputable materialization of class taste. (1984: 190)

In recent developments in social theory there has been an important re-evaluation of the importance of the body, not simply in feminist social theory, but more generally in terms of the analysis of class, culture and consumption. Of course, in recent social theory the work of Erving Goffman was significant in alerting social theorists to the role of the body in the construction of a social person. For Goffman, the body formed an implicit foundation of his theories of stigma, face-work, embarrassment and social self, although it was characteristic of Goffman's work as an ethnography of social life that a specific theory of embodiment was never produced. However, there is clearly a Goffman legacy in modern symbolic interactionism which has, more than most other theoretical traditions in sociology, regularly produced a sociological awareness of the symbolic significance of the body to the interactional order. Whether these developments can be sustained and produce a substantial redirection of social thought remains an open issue. For example, despite Anthony Giddens's involvement in the development of a theory of structuration which, among other things, attempts to overcome the traditional divisions in social theory (such as action and structure), he has to date paid little attention to the issue of embodiment apart from some commentary in *The Constitution of Society* (1984) on time and the body.

His recent textbook on sociology has a brief discussion of 'body language' in the context of an analysis of micro-social behaviour (Giddens, 1989: 91–4).

The Secret History of the Body in Social Theory

Before turning to specific features of modern social change which have brought the question of the body into sharper focus in social theory, it is important to keep in mind the fact that, in certain theoretical and philosophical traditions, the importance of human embodiment had not been forgotten; in other traditions of social theory, the human body remained submerged as a potent but somewhat disguised issue. For example, contemporary criticism of modernism typically draws inspiration from the work of Friedrich Nietzsche, partly because in Nietzschean philosophy we notice that the body is crucial to understanding the dilemmas of modernity (Stauth and Turner, 1988a). Some aspects of this issue are further explored by Scott Lash, Chapter 10 in this collection. Nietzsche's attempt to bring the body back into the debate about aesthetics was in fact a highly complex critique. In social terms, it was a protest against the conformity, powerlessness and puritanism of the German middle class, especially the *Beamtenbürgertum* (small-town officials, teachers, minor civil servants and local professionals). In the aftermath of the French Revolution, the German middle class had looked towards education as the principal mechanism of social reform, and in particular they came to regard aesthetic education as an alternative to revolutionary politics (Bendix, 1977). This class, which became the *Bildungsbürgertum* (the cultivated or educated middle classes), looked towards classical Greece as the model of virtue, education, freedom and self-restraint.

Nietzsche launched a two-pronged attack on this German middle-class culture. First, he showed that aesthetic experience had more in common with sexual ecstacy, religious rapture or the frenzy of primitive dance than it did with the quiet, individualistic contemplation of a work of art in a spirit of disinterested, rational enquiry. The sensual and erotic response of the body rather than the neutral enquiry of the mind was the core of all artistic experience. Nietzsche had looked towards Wagnerian opera as a mechanism for transforming values, but came eventually to condemn Wagnerianism as an hallucination of gestures. Secondly, Nietzsche attacked the conventional

Hellenism of the German middle class who believed that tranquillity and stability were the primary qualities of the ancient world. In *The Birth of Tragedy* Nietzsche showed that Greek values were originally the products of Dionysian intoxication rather than rational speculation. The two principal institutions of the Greek world – competitive games and the rhetorical competitions of political engagement in the polis – were based on interpersonal violence. He concluded that the German race was degenerate, because it had sublimated sexuality and violence under the civilized facade of religion and morality. Nietzsche's views were not only influential among the George Circle, where they were critically received, but they had a lasting impact on, for example, Walter Benjamin's account of the evolution of drama in his *Ursprung des deutschen Trauerspiels* (1955).

There is much dispute about the philosophical function of Nietzsche's references to biology and physiology. What appears beyond dispute, however, is Nietzsche's criticism of Socratic rationality as a perspective (or way of life) which obscured the importance of emotion and feeling in the human perception of reality. In order to restore this emotionality (the reality of touch, taste and the senses), Nietzsche ascribed a singular importance to artistic creativity as a simultaneously political and therapeutic activity. Art reawakened the sense of rapture which had been lost to modern, individualized, disciplined Man. Artistic regeneration was an important antidote to the growth of nihilism and negativity in modern culture against which Nietzsche saw his task as the revaluation of values. He attacked all such no-saying philosophies, of which Socratism and Protestantism were primary examples. These no-saying philosophies not only undermined genuine values, but also contributed to the neurosis of the modern personality. A yes-saying world-view appeared to require an affirmation of the life of the body.

Nietzsche saw the relationship between culture and nature in terms of a dialectic. Every epoch in the history of human evolution, by which Man transforms nature by technology, is also a period in which the nature of Man is transformed. Each period then gives rise to a (physical) ideal of Man, a special characterology which is also and simultaneously a new body. Although this theory may look like a version of social Darwinism in which the survival of the organism is the outcome of a complex exchange between genetic structure, reproduction and environment, Nietzsche rejected Darwinism as false scientific optimism. For Nietzsche, modern society had brought about, not the survival of the fittest, but the survival of the most degenerate. What was in fact required was a new species of Man, an *Ubermensch*, and art was one major mechanism for this work of creation.

It is not until recently that the general, rather than the specific, impact of Nietzsche on western social theory has been fully acknowledged. The relationship between Nietzsche's view on the sublimation of strong passions and Freud's theory of sexuality and neurosis are now quite evident. The intellectual legacy of Nietzsche in the philosophy of Heidegger, Foucault and Derrida has been perhaps more explicit, self-conscious and deliberate (Lash, 1984; Megill, 1985). For sociology, it is interesting to note that recent interpretations of Weber have made the relationship between Nietzsche, Weber and Foucault appear to be one of convergence. For example, Wilhelm Hennis (1988) has argued that the central question or theme in Weber's sociology as a whole was an enquiry into what forms of life world or life orders (*Lebensordnungen*) produced what type of character or personality. In short, Weber's historical sociology was a study of characterology. His ethical anxiety was that the life orders of capitalism, which were a legacy of ascetic Protestantism, were producing people who were merely cogs in a machine, heartless bureaucrats and soulless officials. This class of men was precisely the group whom Nietzsche had also condemned as 'despisers of the body': theologians, philistines, state officials and nationalists. In Foucault, there is a parallel theme that the modern epoch was inaugurated by the discovery of a new regime of surveillance (the panoptic system) which has produced the useful and the disciplined body (Turner, 1982). The modern state, however, depends not only on these localized, dispersed and decentralized practices of regulation, but also on the fact that civilized man has learned a battery of internal techniques of self-mastery and restraint. These technologies of the self grew out of and presuppose a complex array of technologies of the body (Martin et al., 1988).

There is a common theme in this type of social theory. Man has been wrenched from the natural world by the creation of civilized societies which require institutional regulations of violence (especially the control of sexuality). The growth of civilization requires simultaneously the restraint of the body and the cultivation of character in the interests of social stability. This account is one version of the Hobbesian problem of order. But civilization is often bought at a cost. The growth of instrumental rationality as the main principle of rationalization requires the suppression of desire, but is also the wellspring of art, imagination and creativity. Civilization is in this respect a self-destructive and self-defeating process. The decline, decay and degeneration of the human species is the unintended outcome of social peace. This cultural nihilism is expressed on the individual level by neurosis.

There are many versions of this account of the contradiction of civilization and nature. In the work of Norbert Elias, it is one theme in the civilizing process (Elias, 1987; Mennell, 1987), although the Elias version does not carry the pessimism associated with 'the prophets of extremity' (Megill, 1985). In Marxism, the 'natural man' (the species-being) is destroyed by the division of labour, individualism and alienation typical of the capitalist mode of production, but there is also the promise of restoration in communism, which resolves the fragmentation of man by the destruction of private property and the reduction of the division of labour. The conflict between mind and body represented in mental and manual labour can be overcome (Sohn-Rethel, 1978). So it is not surprising that we find a similar version of the nature/civilization contradiction in the Frankfurt School and the critical theorists.

In *Dialectic of Enlightenment*, there is a very clear statement of this principle:

> Europe has two histories: a well-known, written history and an underground history. The latter consists in the fate of the human instincts and passions which are displaced and distorted by civilization. . . . The relationship with the human body is maimed from the outset. (Adorno and Horkheimer, 1979: 231)

Adorno and Horkheimer go on to argue that Christianity and capitalism have joined forces to declare that work is virtuous, but the body is flesh and the source of all evil. The love–hate relationship with the body dominates modern culture. This critical view of the body in relationship to the demands of capitalism was subsequently developed and elaborated by Herbert Marcuse. The work of Marcuse can be seen as an attempt to bring about a reconciliation of Marxism and Freudian psychoanalysis (Jay, 1973). For example, in *Eros and Civilization* (1969), Marcuse argued that, whereas in simple societies a certain degree of sexual repression might be necessary in order to secure minimal requirements of economic reproduction, capitalism had produced huge economic surpluses, based on its technological supremacy. In such a situation there was also a surplus sexual repression, because capitalism could achieve social control via sexual regulation. The challenge to capitalism could be channelled through sexual liberation, because a release of libidinal power would directly threaten the ascetic regulation of the population.

Although Marcuse came to be identified with the student protest movement and the radical critique of American culture, his perception of a contradiction between instrumental rationality in which Christian asceticism and capitalist production requirements were fused and sexuality was certainly not unique. In *The Cultural Contradictions of Capitalism*, Daniel Bell (1976) argued that the modernist project of rationality had become increasingly overwhelmed by 'porno-pop culture' in which the instinctual replaced all other cultural principles. Bell thus anticipated much of the subsequent discussion of postmodernism in social science by arguing that we had entered a visual culture which was post-literate; that aesthetics had become the main justification for life; that elite values would be undermined by the democratization of life through mass culture; and that public values could no longer be validated, given the polytheism of values in contemporary society. The apocalyptic writings of Norman O. Brown in *Life Against Death* (1959) and *Love's Body* (1966) were an index of the new mood: one road to salvation was through Dionysian sexuality. In an earlier period, Wilhelm Reich's theories of the orgasm and the sexual revolution were equally important in locating opposition in sexual liberation (Poster, 1978; Rycroft, 1971).

One feature of oppositional writing in social theory has involved a rediscovery of de Sade. Foucault's analysis of sexuality in *The History of Sexuality* (1981) clearly depended on this re-evaluation of de Sade in the development of western sexuality. Philosophical interest in de Sade has, however, been quite widespread, for example in Roland Barthes *Sade/Fourier/Loyola* (1977), Simone de Beauvoir *Must We Burn Sade?* (1962),

Jacques Lacan 'Kant avec Sade' (1971) and Angela Carter *The Sadeian Woman* (1979). The body as the seat of desire, irrationality, emotionality and sexual passion thus emerged, especially in French social theory, as a central topic in oppositional writing, as a symbol of protest against capitalist rationality and bureaucratic regulation. One important representative of this tradition of (romantic) opposition was Georges Bataille.

We can see much of the intellectual development of the last 150 years as a response to, and often rejection of, the system of Hegelian philosophy. Certainly we can regard Kierkegaard, Schopenhauer and Nietzsche as representing in some sense existential rejections of Hegel's idealism. Nietzsche in particular was a philosopher against systems. If we therefore treat Kant and Hegel as inaugurating the modernist project in western philosophy, postmodernism is, however distantly, a contemporary version of the rejection of the Hegelian idealist system. It is important to see Habermas's defence of modernity and rationality as a contemporary defence of Hegel through a revised version of Marxism. In *The Philosophical Discourse of Modernity* Habermas indicates the validity of this interpretation when he argues that, whereas Horkheimer and Adorno in *Dialectic of Enlightenment* undertook a protracted struggle with Nietzsche, Heidegger and Bataille 'gather under Nietzsche's banner for the final confrontation' (Habermas, 1987: 131). In *Eroticism* (1987), Bataille celebrated excess, transgression and sensuality against the bourgeois virtues of order, regulation and work.

There is thus a broad theme in western social theory, which posits a contradiction or opposition between nature and culture. But we should not suggest that the expression of this theme was entirely coherent, or that there were no variations on this theme. For example, it is important to keep in mind that Foucault wanted to distance himself partly from such an interpretation of the centrality of sexuality. He complained that he had been 'given the image of a melancholic historian of prohibitions and repressive power. . . . But my problem has always been on the side of another term: truth' (Foucault, 1988: 111). Quite simply, 'Sexuality is the truth of desire' (Lemert and Gillan, 1982: 80). Foucault did, however, want to show that, in addition to histories of economics and politics, 'it was also possible to write the history of feelings, behaviour and the body' (Foucault, 1988: 112). Similarly, while we can read Elias through a Freudian paradigm, Elias is not opposed to the civilization process, because he also regards civilizational controls as beneficial to individual development. Weber also predominantly argued that one had to face sexual constraint realistically and seriously as necessary to social stability, although it has also been suggested that Weber on some occasions showed a sympathy for the erotic doctrines of the Otto Gross Circle (Schwentker, 1987). Despite these distinctive variations, it is clear that western thought has been profoundly influenced by the dichotomies: body/soul and nature/culture.

The Social Context of the Sociology of the Body

Having argued that, with the exception of anthropology, an analysis of the body has been absent from mainstream theory, we have described an oppositional tradition from Schopenhauer to Foucault in which the body has been central to social theorizing as a critique of capitalist rationality, the Christian concept of moral restraint or of exploitative sexual relations within the patriarchal family. With the growing popularity of Foucault, the revival of interest in Nietzsche, and the continuing importance of Heidegger, in recent years there has been a deluge of books on the body, which is discussed in this collection by Arthur W. Frank. We cannot understand this development in social theory without some analysis of the broad social changes which have brought the body into prominence. In this introductory discussion, we consider a number of major social changes which help us to understand, or at least situate, current developments in social theory. These changes include the growth of consumer culture in the postwar period, the development of postmodern themes in the arts, the feminist movement and finally what Foucault (1981) has called 'bio-politics' (within which we will include the demographic changes in the structure of human populations with the greying of industrial societies, the AIDS crisis and the politics of pollution).

In the late nineteenth century it was possible for radical 'decadent' artists and philosophers to rock the bourgeois world by celebrating sexuality (especially deviant sexual behaviour) over the virtues of middle-class society. In the 1920s artistic protests against bourgeois morality were still possible. *Der Dada* announced the end of art and the equation of Dada with politics. In the 1930s the surrealistic creations of Magritte were equally shocking, blending the fictional and the factual within a psycho-analytical vision of the unconscious in art. However, the ability of oppositional art to shock society has diminished during the development of the twentieth century. The reasons for this are complex, but they have been briefly summarized by Habermas (1987: 215) who comments that 'there is nothing left to profane in modernity'.

What has changed? First, the entire moral apparatus of bourgeois capitalism with its religious (if hypocritical) condemnation of sexual pleasures has largely collapsed with the disappearance of Christian puritanical orthodoxy and authority. In some respects, this change has taken place because of the erosion of competitive capitalism based on a disciplined labour force and heavy industrial production for a world market. The increasing importance of service industries has been associated with the decline of the traditional working class and with changes in life-style emphasizing consumption and leisure. The reduction in the length of the working week, compulsory retirement and a greater emphasis on the positive value of sport and recreation has meant that conventional wisdom relating to the work ethic and the heroism of toil has progressively become irrelevant. These changes are a rather minor feature of the democratization of culture and morality by the growth of mass consumption.

The consequences of post-industrialism and post-Fordism are extremely important for our general argument regarding the incorporation of oppositional cultures within consumerism. In addition to the commercial and consumerist interest in the body, there is a new emphasis on keeping fit, the body beautiful and the postponement of ageing by sport (Featherstone, 1982); it is difficult to see how a bohemian life-style could be shocking, given the commercialization of sexuality and the eroticism of the average advertisement for cigarettes and soft drinks. Once more many of these developments were clearly anticipated by Bell in *The Cultural Contradictions of Capitalism*, which argued that there was an important tension between the declining ascetic values of the workplace and the increasing importance of sensibility and hedonism arising out of leisure. It is interesting that perhaps one of the most shocking artists of the late twentieth century is Francis Bacon who, as it were, attacks modern consciousness by representing the body as diseased meat, as Roy Boyne explains in this collection. The consequence is that it is difficult to see how it is possible to have an avante-garde in modern society (Bürger, 1984) any more than it is to have high and low culture (Stauth and Turner, 1988b). So the struggle between modern and postmodern culture also represents a struggle between different wings of the art world for control over what is normatively acceptable. One consequence has been that different representations of the body become critical not only to artistic theory but also to popular culture.

A second major development leading, in my view, to an increasing interest in the body is the outcome of changing relations between the sexes. Feminist criticism of the subordinate position of women in society eventually created a much greater sensitivity towards gender/sexuality/biology on the part of social theorists. Feminism has generated a range of theoretical questions in which the analytical and political status of the human body has one more become critical (Suleiman, 1986). Because sexual inequality appears to be basic to all forms of human society, feminist criticism casts doubt on the ability of Marxism to explain phenomena like patriarchy and sexism, since sexual inequalities appeared to be as profound in socialist as in capitalist societies. If this is the case, how can these fundamental structures of gendered stratification be explained?

This question creates a dilemma within feminist theory. If the problem is social, then there is no essential or ontological difference between men and women; indeed, it is conceivable that the whole division between men and women could disappear. Gender inequality is socially constructed. However, there are some radical feminists who would not like the existing divisions between men and women to disappear because, they would argue, there are fundamental differences between the sexes in personality, values, attitudes and life-styles. One explanation for these fundamental differences is that men and women have different bodies, and that their relationship to the world, via the experience of childbirth for example, are fundamentally different, if not incompatible. Because we as human beings possess different types of bodies, it is possible to achieve greater equality between the sexes, but differences will not, cannot, and for some theorists should not, be eradicated. These debates raised in a fundamental way the status of the body in relation to nature and culture (Rosaldo and Lamphere, 1974). In political and legal terms, one can see how these theoretical and ideological battles were fought out in debates around menstrual tension in relation to legal responsibility, or paternity rights for men in relation to the demands of continuous employment, or parenting rights in the case of divorce.

We have seen how in the history of romanticism and critical theory the body and the liberation of sexuality were important oppositional themes in the evolving critique of capitalism. From the perspective of contemporary feminism, it is possible to argue that these oppositional postures were both masculine and privileged. There was little interest in the care of children in debates about sexual liberation. It is not clear whether sexual liberation actually included women, or whether the liberation of women would be fundamentally different from that of men. Nietzsche's view of women and sexuality was notoriously ambiguous (Schutte, 1984). Once more we see an interesting dilemma in feministic theories. If sexual liberation is in fact both adolescent and patriarchal, then feminism should oppose prostitution, pornography and other forms of commercialized sexuality in which women are normally targets of male violence and exploitation. But the oddity of this position is that it puts radical feminists in the same camp as Mary Whitehouse and the conservative wing of the Christian Church. The evaluation of pornography by feminist theory thus becomes a critical issue in relation to the general political orientation of women (Faust, 1981). The problem is that once the dominant culture utilizes erotic sexuality for consumerist promotion, it is difficult for an oppositional culture to adopt a political stance which does not appear to be mere moralizing. In a longer historical perspective, the prostitute has often appeared to be a figure of criticism, because her very existence is an accusation of the patterns of 'normal' sexuality.

The third set of factors which has brought the question of the body into central political prominence is the demographic transition. The greying of human populations has become a matter of international political and economic concern, because the economic implications for the labour market, retirement costs, medical provision and housing of the ageing are seen to be negative (Markides and Cooper, 1987). It is useful to see the issue of ageing within the broader context of modern medical changes generally. The ageing of the population is partly, but not wholly, a consequence of improvements in medical provision, following improvements in the standard of living. The increase in life expectancy is one dimension of a wider scenario which includes artificial insemination, heart transplants, micro-surgery and advances in pharmacology. The impact of scientific high-technology medicine has raised difficult philosophical and ethical problems: who ultimately has legal ownership of parts of human bodies? What is the role of the state in protecting the sick and elderly from unwarranted medical experimentation? Can we measure or identify 'unnecessary surgery'? What is death? The consequence of these scientific developments has been to resurrect many ancient philosophical dilemmas about the relationship between the body, consciousness, existence and identity in the context of contemporary high-technology medicine. Finally, these developments are further complicated by the HIV and AIDS crisis, because, apart from the economic burden of AIDS sufferers on the health budget, these epidemics of the late twentieth century have once more raised problems of moral responsibility in relation to the etiology of major disease. These developments in modern medicine have fundamental implications, therefore, for what it is to have or to be a body. The identity problems of *Robocop* in relation to his body/machine is a futuristic statement of contemporary medical technology in relation to the reproduction of bodies (Kroker et al., 1989: 137–8).

Power/Sexuality

It is clear that some of the essays in this collection (especially the contributions of Boyne, Hewitt, Lash and Turner) have been either directly or indirectly influenced by the philosophical and genealogical studies of Foucault into power/knowledge. Foucault's work has and can be interpreted in many different ways (Cousins and Hussain, 1984; Dreyfus and Rabinow, 1982; Hoy, 1986; Lemert and Gillan, 1982). In this introduction I have, for reasons that are perfectly obvious, focused on the issues of the body, sexuality and truth in Foucault's work. Foucault himself of course also gave a very strong warrant for such an interpretation. He has written, commenting on materialism in Marxism, 'I wonder whether, before one poses the question of ideology, it wouldn't be more materialist to study first the question of the body and the effects of power on it' (Gordon, 1980: 58).

Foucault was especially interested in the construction of both a micro-politics of regulation of the body and a macro-politics of surveillance of populations. These preoccupations with body and population as 'the two places around which the organisation of power over life was deployed' (Foucault, 1981: 139) led Foucault into the study of nineteenth-century medical and disciplinary changes as responses to the peculiar problems of urban control, particularly in France. He claimed that the 'great demographic upswing in Western Europe' (Gordon, 1980: 171) made knowledge of 'population' an essential feature of the regulation of urban space. This interpretation may be regarded as a 'sociologization' of Foucault's work on discipline, prisons, clinics and asylums, but Foucault himself towards the end of his life recognized a parallel between his interest in discipline and the carceral society and Adorno's concept of 'the administered society' (Jay, 1984: 22). In short, a sociological orientation to Foucault's work is not illegitimate as an interpretative strategy.

Placing Foucault within a sociological and historical context, it is possible to argue that the rational disciplines of the body and populations were responses to the urban crises of the late eighteenth and nineteenth centuries, but the origins of these disciplines can be found in Protestant asceticism, medical regimes, military organization and architectural structures. These controls over populations were associated with the rise of demography and town planning, while the regulation of the internal and external body required the intervention of psychology, clinical medicine and criminology (Turner, 1984).

The 'crisis' in nervous illnesses in the late nineteenth century produced a cluster of conditions – anorexia, agoraphobia, anorexic hysteria, virgin's disease, or various wasting diseases – which can be interpreted as symptomatic of changes in the relationship between the sexes, between public and private space, between the family and the economy within the context of the growing dominance of medicine over moral issues. A number of writers have analysed these disease categories as a social control problem (Brumberg, 1988), but we can also locate these socio-medical debates within the context of a *fin de siècle* cultural crisis around the idea of nihilism and decadence.

The 'problem' of female sexuality was an issue within the general question of sexuality, especially male homosexuality. Thus, it is possible to identify the rise of an analysis of the peculiarities of the nervous, fragmented, decadent body in

Europe as part of a broader cultural *fin de siècle* complex which included the anti-Semitic struggles of Austria (Oxaal et al., 1987), Freudian psychoanalysis, the tortured electric bodies of Egon Schiele, the Dionysian art of Austrian Saga society (McGrath, 1974), the decadent poetry of Baudelaire, and the general sense of nihilism. This cultural complex has been regarded by Buci-Glucksmann (1984) as a form of late baroque in which the female body becomes a symbol of cultural crisis. If this comment opens up a plausible interpretation of the emergence of the sexualized body of the 1890s, it also suggests a view of the (re)discovery of the body in the 1980s and what we may call the politics of anxiety. The body has once more become apocalyptic given the threat of chemical warfare, the destruction of the natural habitat, the epidemic of HIV and AIDS, the greying/declining populations of northern Europe and the apparent inability of national governments to control medical technology or medical costs. We are surrounded by a new set of military metaphors relating to AIDS (Sontag, 1989). These political anxieties, as one could expect, have been reproduced in sociology in terms of apocalyptic theories of the body invasions (Kroker and Kroker, 1987).

Fin de Siècle Bodies

We are probably prone to consider our age not only as uniquely special but also as unmatched in the pervasiveness and depth of its crisis. Our age is struck forcefully and self-consciously by its modernity, its secularization and its nihilism. Perhaps the conflict between the modernists and the postmodernists should be seen precisely in the context of such global crises, namely that it is no longer clear that dependence on human rationality will be sufficient in principle to respond to these global crises, precisely because there is the suspicion that the crises are actually produced by the same instrumental rationality. There is now the widespread suspicion that global disasters such as the holocaust are not an abnormal or perverted digression in the unfolding of western rationality, but in fact the primary and ordinary illustration of instrumental rationalism in practice (Bauman, 1989).

Given the doom that threatens to engulf us, it is hardly surprising that social philosophers have increasingly turned to Nietzsche for a perspective on our apocalyptic times. We appear to have exactly that combination of neurosis, nihilism and cultural despair that in the last century produced the fatalism of Schopenhauer, the visionary politics of Sorel, or the celebration of decadence in Baudelaire. As H. Stuart Hughes (1959) argued in his now somewhat neglected masterpiece on European intellectual history between 1890 and 1930 (*Consciousness and Society*), it is not only reason, but the very foundations of a civilized society, which have been brought into question by military struggles, by anti-Semitism and racism, and by the fragmentation and alienation of life in urban, industrial societies.

The crisis of Europe in the 1890s was focused on and acted out in Paris, Berlin and Vienna. It was perhaps in the melting-pot of the Habsburg Empire that most of the themes of the twentieth century were most profoundly conceived: the analysis of the subconscious and the role of the irrational in collective life, the quest for nationalism as a basis for political identity, the notion that reality is merely an effect of particular grammatical structures, and the notion that perhaps the solution to the ethnic and cultural fragmentation of modern society can be sought in a radical reconstruction of *Gemeinschaft*. We have merely to think of the intellectuals produced in Vienna – Mahler, Freud, Wittgenstein, Klimt – to realize that the late nineteenth-century crisis of the Austrian Empire was in many respects the flashpoint of the modern conflagration; it also produced Theodor Herzl, and it was in Vienna that the young Hilter was horrified by the sight of ethnic diversity, of Poles, Hungarians, Czechs, Croats, Serbs and above all the 'eternal mushroom' (*Spaltpilz*) of Jews. The other images of the modern crisis came from Berlin as described by Simmel in his essays on the tragedy of culture and from Paris as sketched out in Walter Benjamin's notes *Das Passagen-Werk* (1982).

For a great variety of reasons, therefore, the 1990s already have, more in the medical than in the chronological sense, a terminal quality. We have moved into the era not only of postmodernity but of post-industrial society, post-Marxism, and post-Fordism. It already appears that Marxism, as the science of the crisis of early capitalism, is close to extinction, since the reality which its core conceptual apparatus sought to understand has largely vanished. For example, the organized, urban working class in western capitalism is in decline in absolute and relative terms. With that decline there has been a profound change in the politics and culture of the everyday world of capitalism (Gorz,

1982; Touraine, 1971; Turner, 1988). At least it is not clear how or whether organized communism can survive the erosion of party authority in Poland, Yugoslavia and Hungary, the ethnic violence of the Balkan states of the Soviet Union, the organized brutality of the events in Tiananmen Square, the revelations of party corruption in Cuba and Siberia, or the economic collapse of Eastern Europe.

Perhaps we have already moved into the era of *Fin-de-siècle Socialism* (Jay, 1988) but, while conservative politicians and theorists might incautiously and naively gloat, it is clear that the resulting political instabilities will also rock the West with earthquake-like force. While the modern theoretical crisis may be a crisis of Marxism, it is not clear yet who will have to pay the price of the demise of Stalinism (Holton and Turner, 1989). Although conservative analysts have derived, privately or other- wise, comfort from the departure of Eric Honecker from power in the German Democratic Republic, the prospects of German reunification may have a devastating impact on the long-term peace of Europe. We are forced to live in interesting times.

Although other commentators may tend to regard themselves as peculiarly privileged to live at this particular conjuncture in the unfolding of world history (in the sense that we have a Hegelian consciousness of ourselves as modern, at the cutting edge of the global process), already we begin to detect a parallel with the 1890s. As social theorists we have in any case a special empathy with this period. It was the decade of the 1890s which produced sociology as an organized discipline rather than a pipe- dream of St Simon and Comte. It was sociology (with its enquiry into suicide and anomie, rationalization and bureaucracy, aliena- tion and factory life, the peculiar characteristics of the mass culture of city life, in fact into urbanism as a way of life, and the characterology of capitalism) which more than any other social science discipline prefigured many of the philosophical debates of the twentieth century. Sociology became an essential component of the modern *Angst*.

However, having entertained the possibility that other people in other epochs might have imagined themselves in a global context of crisis, perhaps we should follow this further in search of parallels and analogies. What other epoch was conscious of a 'world' crisis, of impending doom, of the crisis of social control, urban decay, and of a sense that the very foundations of reality might be in question? The answer is the baroque culture of the crisis of absolutism (in Spain, France, Germany, central and southern Europe), especially in the first half of the seventeenth century. Baroque culture followed the Protestant Reformation as an attempt to win the hearts and imaginations of the people in the interests of a hierarchical and authoritarian power bloc, which sought to stabilize Europe against total collapse, or more exactly to defend the old order against individualism, Protestantism, commercial urban power, against the notion that the social order could be based on a social contract and against the mass, which had been created by a flood of peasants entering European cities.

The baroque mentality saw the world as a constructed environment, and was correspondingly fascinated by time, death, ruins, decay, decadence, and the circumstantiality of phenomena (Maravall, 1986). Its characteristic figures and themes were Hamlet (in the graveyard scene), *The Anatomy of Melancholy* of Robert Burton, Leibniz's *Monadology* and the theodical doctrine of the best of all possible worlds (Turner, 1981: 142–76), and the paintings of Velasquez. Let us consider, for example, Leibniz's doctrine of the fundamental substances of the universe, namely the monads. The whole system of the universe is made up of an infinite number of monads, which reflect the universe and which contain its potential (the notions of Perception and Appetition in Leibniz's terminology). In short, the Monads are a system of mirrors which reflect the universe. The *Monadology* expressed simultaneously a philosophical and aesthetic baroque principle. Thus, 'Le monde est à la fois un miroir de miroirs, un livre des livres, et un univers esthetique de formes-forces en equilibre/ desequilibre permanent' (Buci-Glucksmann, 1986: 79). While the baroque period regarded itself as modern, in fact its aesthetic principles often anticipated postmodern themes. If this interpretation of Leibniz is correct, then the doctrine of the monads embraces the idea of the textuality of reality, or more precisely of the centrality of optics – and therefore of perspectivism – in the technological apparatus by which the world is appropriated, but only by a gaze (Jay, 1986).

The crucial issue about the baroque mentality, however, is that it was modern, or more accurately regarded itself as modern. While baroque has the superficial characteristics of conservatism as a guided culture directed towards the conservation of a hierarchical, authoritarian society, baroque elites used techniques of control (the stimulation of the senses, the creation of a culture of spectacle, the manipulation of mass markets, the erection of an architecture of display) which required new attitudes, orientations and assumptions, and thus 'The people of the Baroque, finally judged themselves and their epoch to be "modern"' (Marvall, 1986: 145).

The baroque ideologues had a real sense of the mass, and its capacity for manipulation as a force both for change and order. It is not surprising that the baroque is a culture of effects (Miller, 1949). Gianlorenzo Bernini (1598–1680), who was initially influenced by Michelangelo, the Antique, and Caravaggio, eventually came to be the master of baroque effects in which the space between the artwork and the spectator is broken. His sculpture of the *Ecstasy of S. Teresa* on the altarpiece of S. Maria della Vittoria is a stunning example of baroque sensuality, indeed eroticism. Bernini produced an aesthetic of erotic illumination as the medium by which God enters the world (Buci-Glucksmann, 1986: 100–1). Here we have sensual effect and affect, combined into the spiritual service of the Church. In baroque religious art, the orgasm of the body is brought into play against the barren hygienic churches of northern, Protestant Europe. It was a spiritualization of the sensual body in the service of both spiritual development and political control.

But why dwell on the baroque? As Buci-Glucksmann (1984) has argued in *La raison baroque*, we can discover wonderful parallels between the culture of crisis in the seventeenth century, the nihilism of Baudelaire at the end of the nineteenth century, the 'sociological' writing of Benjamin on contemporary art and the 'primitive' symbolism of Paul Klee. The baroque provides a distinctive insight into the dilemmas and questions of the late twentieth century. We may list these issues briefly.

First, there is a common breakdown between high and low culture, which brings into question the role of the artist in society, but more generally the role of the intellectual. In the high art of baroque we always find kitsch – in Bernini's *S. Teresa*, in Poussin's *Pastoral*, and in Velazquez's public art. In mobilizing affects, the baroque artists challenged the high/low distinction by mixing various traditions and styles. Secondly, there is a strong sense of contrivance, of constructionism and artifice. The idea of permanent 'natural order' was challenged. The baroque artists were, as Benjamin noted in his study of German tragic drama, fascinated by the ruin, both constructed and natural, as a noble allegory of the melancholic dimension of human existence (Benjamin, 1955: 155–60). Thirdly, there was a form of perspectivism, which blended, for the sake of affects and effect, sacred and secular themes. By bringing the sensual to the forefront of effects in order to break down the space between art-object and subject-spectator, the baroque transformed the human body into rippling, creamy, palpable flesh. Caravaggio (1571–1610) placed such emphasis on huge, fleshy, bloated peasant bodies that his commissioned works were often rejected by the Church authorities for their lack of decorum. His impact on the work of Rembrandt (in the *Anatomy Lesson of Dr Tulp*, or *A Woman Bathing in a Stream*) was considerable, but in the Protestant countries of northern Europe the influence of baroque was subdued for example in the work of Vermeer (1632–75) of Delft. The full impact of baroque in terms of scale, colour and quality can be best seen in the mythological representations of Rubens (1577–1640), for example the *Rape of the Daughters of Leucippus* or the *Judgment of Paris*. In these paintings one has, not the austere beauty of classicism, but the use of women of bourgeois background to exhibit a virtual delirium of flesh. Another example, but in a rather different idiom, is the work of Velazquez (1599–1660), whose painting of Pope Innocent X is extraordinarily successful in capturing the sensual, threatening, saturnine features of his face. These leading artists of baroque used the body to achieve exceptionally vivid mass effects. It is only appropriate that one of the most exciting artists of the twentieth century, Francis Bacon (Boyne, 1988), should return to the face of Innocent X to destroy its ontological security through the screaming of a mouth.

I have suggested a certain parallel between the baroque and the postmodern mentality which I have attempted to illustrate briefly by reference to the mass culture of urban seventeenth-century societies and by arguing that baroque sought its mass effects through exciting the senses. Baroque ceilings drip with pink, abundant flesh. It can be objected of course that in terms of economics and politics it would be perverse to press this comparison too far. While such a note of caution might have a *prima facie* value, it appears to me that the parallel can be defended. One feature of political life in both baroque and contemporary life is the centralization of power in large bureau-cracies. Absolutist power depended on policies of mercantilism, which required state intervention to regulate international trade through the control of exchange rates. One consequence was the centralization of power and the emergence of what we may call decisionism. Although it would be simply wrong to argue that the western capitalist world is based on absolutism, the growth of large political bureaucracies has made representation in modern democracies a key issue. Effective democratic participa-tion in the European Parliament is simply not possible, and the modern citizen is often reduced to a spectator rather than a participant. Spectator democracy might in this sense be the modern version of baroque decisionism.

If a comparison of the baroque age and postmodernism is plausible, then we might start asking whether there will be a post-postmodernism? At the tail end of baroque, the middle classes turned away from large public spectacle and rococo flourished briefly as a pretty style of interior decorations. The great regal displays of public baroque were converted into pleas-ing scenes of *fates d'amour* by Jean Watteau (1684–1721). We may recall that Weber has argued that there were a number of possible responses to the fragmentation, alienation and rationalization of society. These cultural responses included a return to conventional religion, the serious calling to politics, the eroticism of Otto Gross, or the cultivation of a personal interior life, which resembled Troeltsch's conception of mysticism and which would have to be played quietly, or *pianissimo*. Perhaps the dilemmas and the challenges of postmodernism in our age will be psychologically too demanding and too dangerous; in this event, perhaps postmodern baroque will be replaced by the privatization of the social, which has been described by Robert Bellah and his colleagues in *Habits of the Heart* (1985). The public will be turned into an arena of organized opinions and privatized sentiments. A rococo individualism and a culture of sentimentality might be a fitting, if depressing, conclusion to the debate between modernism and postmodernism.

References

Adorno, T. and Horkheimer, M. (1979) *Dialectic of Enlightenment*. London: Verso.
Ardrey, R. (1971) *The Territorial Imperative*. London: Collins.

Bachelard, G. (1987) *The Psychoanalysis of Fire*. London: Quartet Books.

Barber, B. (1970) *L.J. Henderson on the Social System*. Chicago: University of Chicago Press.

Barkan, L. (1975) *Nature's Work of Art: the Human Body as Image of the World*. New Haven: Yale University Press.

Barthes, R. (1977) *Sade/Fourier/Loyola*. London: Jonathan Cape.

Bataille, G. (1987) *Eroticism*. London: Marion Boyars.

Bauman, Zygmunt (1989) *Modernity and the Holocaust*. Cambridge: Polity Press.

Beauvoir, S. de (1962) *Must We Burn Sade?* London: John Calder.

Bell, D. (1976) *The Cultural Contradictions of Capitalism*. London: Heinemann Educational.

Bellah, Robert N., Madsen, Richard, Sullivan, W.M., Swidler, Ann and Tipton, Steven M. (1985) *Habits of the Heart: Individualism and Commitment in American Life*. Berkeley: University of California Press.

Bendix, R. (1977) 'Province and metropolis: the case of eighteenth-century Germany', in J. Ben-David and T.N. Clark (eds), *Culture and its Creators. Essays in Honour of Edward Shils*. Chicago and London: University of Chicago Press. pp. 119–49.

Benjamin, W. (1955) *Ursprung des deutschen Trauerspiels*. Frankfurt am Main: Suhrkamp.

Benjamin, W. (1982) *Das Passagen-Werk*. 2 vols. Frankfurt am Main: Suhrkamp.

Berger, P.L. and Kellner, H. (1965) 'Arnold Gehlen and the theory of institutions', *Social Research*, 32: 110–15.

Berger, P.L. and Luckmann, T. (1967) *The Social Construction of Reality*. London: Allen Lane.

Bertilsson, M. (1986) 'Love's labours lost? A sociological view', *Theory, Culture & Society*, 3(2): 19–35 (reprinted in this volume).

Bourdieu, P. (1984) *Distinction: a Social Critique of the Judgement of Taste*, London: Routledge & Kegan Paul.

Bowra, C.M. (1959) *The Heritage of Symbolism*. London: Macmillan.

Boyne, R. (1988) 'The art of the body in the discourse of postmodernity', *Theory, Culture & Society*, 5(2–3): 527–43 (reprinted in this volume).

Brain, R. (1979) *The Decorated Body*. London: Hutchinson.

Brown, N.O. (1959) *Life Against Death: the Psychoanalytic Meaning of History*. Middletown: Wesleyan University Press.

Brown, N.O. (1966) *Love's Body*. New York: Random House.

Brumberg, J.J. (1988) *Fasting Girls: the Emergence of Anorexia Nervosa as a Modern Disease*. Cambridge, MA: Harvard University Press.

Buci-Glucksmann, C. (1984) *La raison baroque, Baudelaire à Benjamin*. Paris: Editions Galilee.

Buci-Glucksmann, C. (1986) *La folie du voir, de l'esthetique baroque*. Paris: Galilee.

Bürger, P. (1984) *Theory of the Avant-garde*. Minneapolis: University of Minnesota Press.

Burrow, J.W. (1970) *Evolution and Society: a Study in Victorian Social Theory*. Cambridge: Cambridge University Press.

Carter, A. (1979) *The Sadeian Woman: an Exercise in Cultural History*. London: Virago.

Cousins, M. and Hussain, A. (1984) *Michel Foucault*. New York: St Martin's Press.

Douglas, M. (1970) *Purity and Danger: an Analysis of Concepts of Pollution and Taboo*. Harmondsworth: Penguin Books.

Douglas, M. (1973) *Natural Symbols: Explorations in Cosmology*. Harmondsworth: Penguin Books.

Dreyfus, H.L. and Rabinow, P. (1982) *Michel Foucault. Beyond Structuralism and Hermeneutics*. Brighton: Harvester Press.

Duerr, H.P. (1988) *Nacktheit und Scham: der Mythos vom Zivilisationsprozess*. Frankfurt am Main: Suhrkamp.

Durkheim, E. and Mauss, M. (1963) *Primitive Classification*. London: Routledge & Kegan Paul.

Elias, N. (1987) 'On human beings and their emotions: a process-sociological essay', *Theory, Culture & Society*, 4(2-3): 339-61 (reprinted in this volume).

Elias, N. (1988) 'Was ich unter Zivilisation verstehe. Antwort auf Hans Peter Duerr', *Der Zeit*, 25, 17 June.

Faust, B. (1981) *Women, Sex and Pornography*. Melbourne: Melbourne House.

Featherstone, M. (1982) 'The body in consumer culture', *Theory, Culture & Society*, 1(2): 18-33 (reprinted in this volume).

Featherstone, M. and Hepworth, M. (1983) 'The midlifestyle of "George and Lynn"', *Theory, Culture & Society*, 1(3): 85-92 (reprinted in this volume).

Foucault, M. (1981) *The History of Sexuality, Volume One: an Introduction*. Harmondsworth: Penguin Books.

Foucault, M. (1987) *The Use of Pleasure: the History of Sexuality, Volume 2*. Harmondsworth: Penguin Books.

Foucault, M. (1988) *Politics, Philosophy, Culture. Interviews and Other Writings 1977-1984*. New York and London: Routledge.

Fox, R.A. (1976) *The Tangled Web. The Structure of Disorder in the Anatomy of Melancholy*. Berkeley: University of California Press.

Freud, S. (1950) *Totem and Taboo*. London: Routledge & Kegan Paul.

Garfinkel, H. (1956) 'Conditions of successful degradation ceremonies', *American Journal of Sociology*, 61: 420-4.

Gehlen, A. (1988) *Man, his Nature and Place in the World*. New York: Columbia University Press.

Giddens, A. (1984) *The Constitution of Society: an Outline of the Theory of Structuration*. Cambridge: Polity Press.

Giddens, A. (1989) *Sociology*. Cambridge: Polity Press.

Glassman, R.M. (1986) *Democracy and Despotism in Primitive Societies* 2 vols. New York: Associated Faculty Press.

Gordon, C. (1980) *Michel Foucault, Power/Knowledge. Selected Interviews and Other Writings 1972-1977*. Brighton: Harvester Press.

Gorz, A. (1982) *Farewell to the Working Class: an Essay on Post-industrial Socialism*. London: Pluto Press.

Habermas, J. (1987) *The Philosophical Discourse of Modernity*. Cambridge: Polity Press.

Hennis, W. (1988) *Max Weber: Essays in Reconstruction*. London: Allen & Unwin.

Hertz, R. (1960) *Death and the Right Hand*. New York: Cohen & West.

Hirst, P.Q. (1975) *Durkheim, Bernard and Epistemology*. London: Routledge & Kegan Paul.

Hirst, P. and Woolley, P. (1982) *Social Relations and Human Attributes*. London: Tavistock.

Holton, R.J. and Turner, B.S. (1989) *Max Weber on Economy and Society*. London: Routledge.

Hoy, D.C. (ed.) (1986) *Foucault, a Critical Reader*. Oxford: Basil Blackwell.

Hughes, H. Stuart (1959) *Consciousness and Society: The Reorientation of European Social Thought 1890-1920*. London: MacGibbon & Kee.

Jay, M. (1973) *The Dialectical Imagination: a History of the Frankfurt School and the Institute of Social Research 1923-50*. London: Heinemann Educational.

Jay, M. (1984) *Adorno*. London: Fontana.

Jay, M. (1986) 'In the Empire of the Gaze: Foucault and the denigration of vision in twentieth-century French thought', in David Couzens Hoy (ed.), *Foucault, a Critical Reader*. Oxford: Basil Blackwell. pp. 175-204.

Jay, M. (1988) *Fin-de-siècle Socialism*. New York and London: Routledge.

Kamenka, E. (1970) *The Philosophy of Ludwig Feuerbach*. London: Routledge & Kegan Paul.

Kantorowicz, E. (1957) *The King's Two Bodies*. Princeton, NJ: Princeton University Press.

Klages, L. (1963) *Vom kosmogonischen Eros*. Bonn: Bouvier.

Kroeber, A.L. (1923) *Anthropology*. New York: Harcourt.

Kroeber, A.L. (1952) *The Nature of Culture*. Chicago: University of Chicago Press.

Kroeber, A.L. and Parsons, T. (1958) 'The concepts of culture and of social system', *American Sociological Review*, 23: 582-3.

Kroker, A. and Kroker, M. (1987) *Body Invaders. Panic Sex in America*. Don Mills, Ontario: Oxford University Press.

Kroker, A., Kroker, M. and Cook, D. (eds) (1989) *Panic Encyclopedia. The Definitive Guide to the Postmodern Scene*. London: Macmillan.

Kuper, A. (1988) *The Invention of Primitive Society, Transformations of an Illusion*. London: Routledge.

Lacan, J. (1971) 'Kant avec Sade', in *Écrits 11*. Paris: Editions de Seuil.

Lash, S. (1984) 'Genealogy and the body: Foucault/Deleuze/Nietzsche', *Theory, Culture & Society*, 2(2): 1-18 (reprinted in this volume).

Lemert, C.C. and Gillan, G. (1982) *Michel Foucault: Society Theory and Transgression*. New York: Columbia University Press.

Levin, D.M. (1985) *The Body's Recollection of Being: Phenomenological Psychology and the Deconstruction of Nihilism*. London: Routledge & Kegan Paul.

Levin, D.M. (1988) *The Opening of Vision: Nihilism and the Postmodern Situation*. London: Routledge.

Lorenz, K.Z. (1966) *On Aggression*. London: Methuen.

McGrath, W.J. (1974) *Dionysian Art and Populist Politics in Austria*. New Haven and London: Yale University Press.

MacRae, D.G. (1975) 'The body and social metaphor', in J. Benthall and T. Polhemus (eds), *The Body as a Medium of Expression. An Anthology*. New York: Dutton. pp. 59-73.

Mannheim, K. (1960) *Ideology and Utopia*. London: Routledge & Kegan Paul.

Maravall, J.A. (1986) *Culture of the Baroque: Analysis of a Historical Structure*. Manchester: University of Manchester Press.

Marcuse, H. (1969) *Eros and Civilization*. London: Sphere Books.

Markides, K.S. and Cooper, C.L. (eds) (1987) *Retirement in Industrialized Societies. Social, Psychological and Health Factors*. Chichester: John Wiley.

Martin, L.H., Gutman, H. and Hutton, P.H. (1988) *Technologies of the Self, a Seminar with Michel Foucault*. London: Tavistock.

Megill, A. (1985) *Prophets of Extremity: Nietzsche, Heidegger, Foucault, Derrida*. Berkeley: University of California Press.

Mennell, S. (1987) 'On the civilizing of appetite', *Theory, Culture & Society*, 4(2–3): 373–404 (reprinted in this volume).

Miller, Alec (1949) *Tradition in Sculpture*. London: Studio Publications.

Morris, D. (1967) *The Naked Ape*. London: Jonathan Cape.

Morris, D. (1977) *Man Watching. A Field Guide to Human Behavior*. New York: Abrams.

Nietzsche, F. (1980) *Untimely Meditations. Four Essays on the Advantage and Disadvantage of History for Life*. Indianapolis: Hackett.

O'Neill, J. (1985) *Five Bodies: The Human Shape of Modern Society*. Ithaca and London: Cornell University Press.

Ossowski, S. (1963) *Class Structure in the Social Consciousness*. London: Routledge & Kegan Paul.

Oxaal, I., Pollack, M. and Botz, G. (eds) (1987) *Jews, Antisemitism and Culture in Vienna*. London: Routledge & Kegan Paul.

Parsons, T. (1934) 'Some reflections on the nature and significance of economics', *Quarterly Journal of Economics*, 48: 511–45.

Parsons, T. (1977) *Social Systems and the Evolution of Action Theory*. New York: Free Press.

Pels, D. and Crébas, A. (1988) '*Carmen* – or the invention of a new feminine myth', *Theory, Culture & Society*, 5(4): 579–610 (reprinted in this volume).

Polhemus, T. (1978) *Social Aspects of the Human Body*. Harmondsworth: Penguin Books.

Poster, M. (1978) *Critical Theory of the Family*. New York: The Seabury Press.

Rosaldo, M.A. and Lamphere, L. (eds) (1974) *Woman Culture and Society*. Stanford, CA: Stanford University Press.

Rosen, G. (1979) 'The evolution of social medicine', in H.E. Freeman, S. Levine and L.G. Reeder (eds), *Handbook of Medical Sociology*. New Jersey: Prentice Hall. pp. 23–52.

Rycroft, C. (1971) *Reich*. London: Collins.

Schutte, O. (1984) *Beyond Nihilism: Neitzsche without Masks*. Chicago: University of Chicago Press.

Schwentker, W. (1987) 'Passion as a mode of life: Max Weber, the Otto Gross Circle and eroticism', in W.J. Mommsen and J. Osterhammel (eds), *Max Weber and his Contemporaries*. London: Allen & Unwin. pp. 483–98.

Sohn-Rethel, A. (1978) *Intellectual and Manual Labour, a Critique of Epistemology*. London: Macmillan.

Sontag, S. (1989) *AIDS and its Metaphors*. New York: Farrar, Strauss & Giroux.

Stauth, G. and Turner, B.S. (1988a) *Nietzsche's Dance. Resentment, Reciprocity and Resistance in Social Life*. Oxford: Basil Blackwell.

Stauth, G. and Turner, B.S. (1988b) 'Nostalgia, postmodernism and the critique of mass culture', *Theory, Culture & Society*, 5(2-3): 509-26.

Stauth, G. and Turner, B.S. (forthcoming) 'Ludwig Klages and the origins of critical theory', *Theory, Culture & Society*.

Suleiman, S.R. (ed.) (1986) *The Female Body in Western Culture*. Cambridge, MA: Harvard University Press.

Tawney, R.H. (1926) *Religion and the Rise of Capitalism*. New York: Harcourt Brace.

Timasheff, N.S. (1957) *Sociological Theory, its Nature and Growth*. New York: Random House.

Timpanaro, S. (1975) *On Materialism*. London: New Left Books.

Touraine, A. (1971) *The Post-Industrial Society, Tomorrow's Social History: Classes, Conflicts and Culture in the Programmed Society*. New York: Random House.

Turner, B.S. (1981) *For Weber. Essays on the Sociology of Fate*. London: Routledge & Kegan Paul.

Turner, B.S. (1982) 'The discourse of diet', *Theory, Culture & Society*, 1(1): 23-32 (reprinted in this volume).

Turner, B.S. (1983) *Religion and Social Theory: a Materialist Perspective*. London: Heinemann Educational.

Turner, B.S. (1984) *The Body and Society: Explorations in Social Theory*. Oxford: Basil Blackwell.

Turner, B.S. (1988) *Status*. Milton Keynes: Open University Press.

van Peursen, C.A. (1961) *Lichaam-Ziel-Geest, inleiding tot een fenomenologische anthropologie*. Utrecht: Erven J. Bijleveld.

Wilson, E.O. (1975) *Sociobiology. The New Synthesis*. Cambridge, MA: Harvard University Press.

2

FOR A SOCIOLOGY OF THE BODY: AN ANALYTICAL REVIEW

Arthur W. Frank

An Analytical Theory of the Body

Sociology and the Body

How would the course of sociology have run differently if Mead's (1970) classic work had been titled, 'Body, Self, and Society'? What if Durkheim had analyzed suicide from the perspective of the embodied act of turning a living body into a dead one, or if Weber had privileged changes in uses of and attitudes toward the body as he formulated the nexus of Protestantism and capitalism?

The point is not only 'what if?' (since the topics of these classics remain open to contemporary rewriting), but rather 'why not?' What was there in the formulation of the enterprise of sociology which continues to inhibit attention to the body as the 'rock bottom' unit of social explanation? The non-body bias of sociology may be crystallized most clearly in Parsons's use of Freud to develop a theory of how society's norms become internalized as individuals' personal need-dispositions, thus effectively disembodying (and desexualizing) the super-ego. In contemporary theory the body remains silent. In the work of Anthony Giddens the unconsciousness receives more play than embodiment. Greater space for the body exists in Randall Collins's 'interaction ritual chains' (see Frank 1989), perhaps due to the influence of Pierre Bourdieu (1977, 1978, 1984), who may be the most prestigious contemporary theorist who does give explicit consideration to the body. Bourdieu in turn is influenced by Erving Goffman standing in a tradition which, in that respect, is more social anthropological than sociological. It was the anthropologist Marcel Mauss, not his sociological uncle and sometimes collaborator Durkheim, who introduced 'body techniques' into modern social scientific consideration (Mauss 1979; but on professional obstacles Mauss encountered while writing this paper, see Duden 1989, p. 527).

In the earlier review of recent literature on the body (Frank 1990), I tried to show sociology being overtaken by a proliferation of publications on the body in other disciplines: social history, clinical practice in psychiatry and psychoanalysis, anthropology, and cognitive science and philosophy. The attempt of that paper was simply to display the range of work and suggest that sociology must join the rest of academic discourse in affording centrality to the body. To that end, the literature was divided into substantive categories, which were: the *medicalized* body (Fisher 1986, Herzlich and Pierret 1987, Kleinman 1988, Murphy 1987, Silverman 1987, and Zola 1982); the *sexual* body (Gregor 1986, Kroker and Kroker 1987); the *disciplined* body (Bell 1985, Freund 1983, Gold 1987, Hepworth and Featherstone 1982, Hochschild 1983, Kupfermann 1979, Martin et al. 1988, and Schwartz 1986); and *talking bodies* (Johnson 1987, Lakoff 1987). This literature was considered with some reference to the social theoretical framework proposed by Bryan Turner (1984), but for the most part issues were allowed to proliferate without a significant attempt at integration.

The subtitle of that paper was 'A Decade Review,' since I also made no pretension of considering such classic works as Mauss (1979), the psychoanalytic tradition, Norbert Elias (1978), phenomenological philosophy (Merleau-Ponty 1962, Sartre 1966), Goffman (1959, 1963, 1967, 1971, 1976), Mary Douglas (1966, 1973), or Ernst Kantorowicz (1989). This neglect is perpetuated in the present chapter, though more contemporary material is included. The essential difference here is that rather than organize the literature on the body within categories of convenience reflecting substantive topics of consideration, I now discuss the literature within a theoretical framework which is both original and analytical, presented as complementary to Turner's (1984) typology.

This chapter begins by reviewing the intellectual background which has produced the current interest in the body. The most significant theoretical typologies of the body, Turner (1984) and Feher (1989), are then summarized with some critique of Turner.

Based on this critique, my own theoretical typology of the body is proposed. The four types of body usage developed within this 'action theory of the body' provide the next four sections. The conclusion, which is the final rationale for creating such a theory, considers the relation of the body to ethics.

Why a chapter such as this one makes such a gesture toward theory is by no means self-evident. The advantage of avoiding analytical theory when writing about the body is exemplified by the most significant publications to appear since the earlier review was written, the three volume *Fragments for a History of the Human Body* edited by Michel Feher with Ramona Naddaff and Nadia Tazi (1989a, 1989b, 1989c). These volumes are certainly the most extensive compendium of historical and cross-cultural source materials on the body available in English. It is hard for the reader to imagine what could displace them not only for information presented, but also for elegance of publication. But even 'fragments' need some organization, which requires theory. I will consider Feher's theory below. The present point is that Feher and his colleagues have organized a maximum of material on the basis of a minimum of meta-theory. The epigram for the writing style of the papers could be Jean Starobinski's (1989, p.353) suggestion 'that the most fruitful generalizations are those arising from fairly precise studies of limited topics.' Why not listen to Starobinski?

The preliminary defense of an analytical schema is that if the generalizations from fairly precise studies are to be most fruitful, they must be gathered up and given some organization in which certain interconnections are specified, at least as topics for further investigation. The problem of theorizing is to remember that in gathering up some generalizations and interconnections, others are being neglected. If the study of the body teaches us anything, it is that the proclaimed determinacies of one theoretical moment (whether that moment is medical, artistic, political, or social theoretical) usually signify little more than the imminence of that system's collapse into a wholly different order of things. Leaving this rationale for theory incomplete – perhaps only the theory itself can justify itself – I turn to the body as topic.

Why Bodies Now?

There are some cynical reasons which account disturbingly well for the resurgence of interest in the body. Starobinski (1989, p. 353) quotes Paul Valéry's notebook entry, 'Somatism (heresy of the end of time), Adoration, cult of the machine for living.' Starobinski then asks, 'Have we come to the end of time? The heresy anticipated by Valéry has almost become the official religion.' Less cynically, does our concern with the body represent the beginning of a new basis of post-Enlightenment ethics? Feher introduces the *Fragments* with a call for an 'ethics of the body' (1989, p. 12). The formulation of such an ethics will, in the conclusion of this chapter, be taken as a stronger reason than that proposed above for doing analytical theory about bodies.

This ethics can be introduced by contrasting Valéry's cynicism about Somatism with Françoise Héritier-Augé posing the magisterial question, 'Can one say that male domination is *universal*? If so, what is the *origin*, the explanation for this fundamental inequality between the sexes?' (1989, p. 282). Her answer, to be discussed below, depends on conditions of embodiment. The conditions are never absolutes, but embodiment is defined by societies and cultures as a principal means by which domination is practised and rationalized. Does our inquiry into the body mark Valéry's end of time exhaustion, or the beginning of a new ethical impulse to demystify domination?

Current interest in the body as topic of investigation seems to have three proximate sources, which can be roughly labelled as modernism, postmodernism, and feminism.

The *modernist* impulse is divided between a post-Enlightenment positivism and, alternatively, a spirit of fragmentation, flux and uncertainty (which may or may not be counter-Enlightenment). In the positivist attitude the body is knowable, and this knowledge provides some grounding. This modernist will-to-truth can be feminist as well as it can affiliate with any other politics: Héritier-Augé's paper is one example of the attempt to know the body. It is the elusive quarry she chases down to its social origins in hunter-gatherer societies where, in Durkheimian tradition, she seeks in the most primitive case some fundamental truth of social organization.

Positivist enlightenment can be juxtaposed to Marx's classic epigram of modernity, 'all that is solid melts into air.' Here is the other of the Janus-faces of our present attitude toward the body: the body is both the privileged site of the modernist will-to-truth and the equally privileged site of the equally modernist display of cultural relativity, if not relativism. Studies also use the body to demonstrate the relative constructedness of cultural beliefs and social organizations; see particularly the studies of the construction of sexual bodies, e.g., Boswell's (1980) historical-empirical deconstruction of the concept of what is 'natural' in the use of bodies.

The modernist conflict between the body as constant in a world of flux, and the body as the epitome of that flux, is carried forward in the *postmodern*. Here also two styles are readable. There is the high-theoretical postmodernism of the body theories found in Roland Barthes (e.g., 1985), Jacques Lacan (1977, 1982), Gilles Deleuze and Felix Guattari (1983), Michel Foucault (1978, 1979, 1980, 1986, 1988) and Jean Baudrillard (1988a). A reaction may be setting into this high-theoretical postmodernism. We can see emerging in the *Fragments* volumes what may be called an empirical or a minimalist postmodern style. The writers of the *Fragments* essays seem to have taken seriously Jean-François Lyotard's (1984) injunction against 'grand narratives.' Extending Starobinski's suggestion, quoted above, they not only seek generalizations through 'fairly precise studies of limited topics,' but often break off their considerations of these topics just when generalization seems possible. The high theoretical influence continues to be evident less in conceptual apparatus than in style. The snap-shot juxtaposition of historical moments through which Foucault frames his analysis in *Discipline and Punish* is a technique employed and extended in articles (e.g., Marin 1989, Schwartz 1989) which then refuse recourse to master concepts (e.g., Foucault's 'discipline' or 'panopticism').

Modernism, then, provides both an impetus to study the body, which is the need for some constant in a world of flux, and a problematic of that body: far from becoming a constant, it was subsumed into the flux. Postmodernism provides a style of minimalist empiricism which, resting on the tacit assumption that the reader shares specific resources of high theory, is neither so minimal nor so empirical. *Feminism* has provided a specific research problem. Kantorowicz's (1989) theory of the body as a principle of social-political organization (see Dupont 1989, Le

Goff 1989) has resolved itself into the more concrete question quoted above from Héritier-Augé, which I paraphrase as this: How have their respective conditions of bodies allowed males to dominate women? Moreover, how is this domination not just a principle of social organization, but perhaps *the* foundational principle of the organization?

Héritier-Augé's (1989, p. 295) conclusion, presented after considerable and compelling data, proposes fertility as a dual principle of social organization and domination: 'So it is not sex but the capacity for fertility that makes up the real difference between male and female, and male domination, which we must now attempt to comprehend, is ultimately the control, the appropriation of a woman's fertility when she is fertile.' There are other responses. Klaus Theweleit's (1987, 1989) disturbing study of images of and attitudes toward women and sexuality among German soldiers between the world wars proposes darker responses to the question of domination. The present point need only be that feminism now sets much of the theoretical and empirical agenda.

Bringing bodies back in is, as a theoretical and empirical research program, made thinkable and imperative by the practical political program of women bringing themselves back in. A provisional response to sociology's traditional neglect of the body is simply that it was a male sociology. This sociology has reflected a male domination which first naturalizes the capacities of bodies and then, legitimated by this naturalization, denies any domination at work in it, i.e., each does according to her or his 'natural' endowments. The debate over whether Marx and Engels do more than assimilate women to a gender-neutral model of capitalist domination is beyond the scope of this chapter. Within the corpus of sociology proper, only Georg Simmel (1984) in his published work and Max Weber in his personal encouragements (Weber 1975) seem to have recognized the differential situation of women and only Simmel considered how theory would look different from a feminist perspective. At the other extreme, Durkheim's (1978) arguments against divorce (see also Jones 1986, p. 101) seem to recognize the differential subordination and even suffering of women, but to accept these as simply necessary to the higher demands of social order.

As Mary O'Brien's (1989) work underscores most simply but clearly (though see also Benhabib and Cornell 1987, Smith 1987), bringing women into sociological theory begins with a recognition of women's differential conditions of embodiment. Sociology's minimal recognition of any embodiment effectively mystifies this difference and the domination it entails. For men, social 'reproduction' refers to abstract conditions of culture and social organization, and these abstractions become privileged in sociology's definition of its theoretical concerns. Even in a theorist sympathetic to the body such as Mead, the privileged sensory capabilities are hearing oneself and seeing the other. Bodily contact with objects is increasingly left behind as mankind, and theory, progress. The culmination of society-building is the achievement of the significant symbol, which *is* an achievement, but its theoretical privilege leads subsequent theorizing away from the symbol's embodiment in bodies recognizing other bodies. O'Brien's work leads to the argument that for women, reproduction takes as its locus the potential of the woman's own embodied experience of birth, whether the specific woman chooses to have that experience or not. What has remained mystified in the male sociological abstraction of reproduction is the organization of societies around male appropriations of the products of female reproductive experience (see also Rousselle 1989), which is to say, in general, kinship (Héritier-Augé 1989). Male legitimation of this appropriation in turn requires the theoretical (and then practical) relegation of embodiment to a residual physiological constraint on social organization.

The sociology of the body understands embodiment not as residual to social organization, but rather understands social organization as being about the reproduction of embodiment. Embodiment is anything but a neutral constant in social life, representing instead the political principles of class (i.e., in Bourdieu) and gender domination. On the questions of domination and appropriation hang much of the story of society. Feminism has taught us that that story both begins and ends with bodies.

Typologies of the Body
The only attempt to provide systematic theory of the body is that proposed by Bryan Turner in *The Body and Society* (1984), one of the two sociology books devoted specifically to the body (see also O'Neill 1985). Turner develops earlier work of Featherstone (1982) into a four cell structure relating bodies to society (see

Table 2.1 *Turner's 'societal tasks' model*

	Populations	Bodies	
Time	Reproduction	Restraint	Internal
	Malthus	Weber	
	Onanism	Hysteria	
	Patriarchy	Asceticism	
Space	Regulation	Representation	External
	Rousseau	Goffman	
	Phobia	Anorexia	
	Panopticism	Commodification	

(modified from Turner 1984, p. 91)

Table 2.1). The columns represent populations and individual bodies, and there are two sets of rows, one dimension referring to populations and the other to individuals. With regard to populations, the rows are time and space, as the principles by which populations can be ordered. With regard to individual bodies, the rows are internal and external.

Turner thus develops a typology in which the body is considered from the perspective of society, looking down as it were. As he states it, 'the thesis is that the classical Hobbesian problem of order can be re-stated as the problem of the government of the body' (Turner 1984, p. 2). Turner will later (1984, p. 90) move to a 'neo-Hobbesian version of the body,' but he continues to understand the body as presenting a 'problem of government' for society. The tacit functionalism of these presuppositions is made explicit in Turner's next statement, in which he fills in the cells of his matrix. 'Every society,' he writes, 'is confronted by four tasks . . .' (Turner 1984, p. 2). Again, this construction invites the reader to view the body from the perspective of the society, society's tasks, its problems of government.

The four cells are then filled in as follows. With regard to populations in time, the task is *reproduction*. With regard to populations in space, the task is *regulation*. With regard to the individual body's interior, society's task is *restraint*. With regard to the body's exterior, the social task is *representation* (Turner 1984, pp. 2, 41, 90 ff.). Turner is rewriting Hobbes less than he is rewriting Parsons. Each 'task' is a kind of functional prerequisite of society with regard to bodies, or as Turner writes (1984, p. 91), 'every social system has to solve these four sub-problems.'

Turner's typology goes on to specify a dominant *theorist* of each societal task, a paradigmatic *disease* in which bodies break down under society's imposition of the task, and an institutional *subsystem* in which society manages each task. The full typology is presented in Table 2.1

The nature of the institutional subsystems (patriarchy, asceticism, panopticism, and commodification) should make it evident that Turner is following Parsons in his form of theorizing but not in content. What we have may be a functionalism, but it is a critical one, informed not only by Marxist but also by feminist and Foucauldian analyses. Turner's typology allows him to theorize how both critical Marxisms and feminisms have underestimated the functional requirement of commodification. The needs for workers not only to produce, but also to consume, has enhanced the possible formation and effect of oppositional movements. In specifying the structural necessity of these opposi-tional movements, Turner (1984, p. 175; 1987, p. 233) aligns Walter Benjamin with Foucault, responding to the absence of an explicit political philosophy in the latter. His arguments also complement much of what will be said below about Baudrillard.

In my own research, Turner's categories prove highly robust in their capacity for ordering empirical materials about the body in society. One reason for this robustness is that the categories can be considered not only as Parsonian functional prerequisites for society *about* bodies, but also as problems *of* bodies themselves, albeit within a differently understood matrix space.

Reproduction is not only a societal prerequisite with regard to populations, it is at least equally and perhaps primarily a task of bodies themselves to work out the terms in which they will or will not reproduce. Ultimately it is only bodies which reproduce themselves. Society can set conditions for this reproduction, but it cannot itself reproduce bodies. Similarly, the individual body must work out terms of regulating its external behavior. This is closely affiliated with, but not quite the same as the body restraining its internal workings, that distinction being as old as Jesus's extension of sin from performance of the overt act to a desire to perform a forbidden act. Before, restraint was simply regulation; as the Christian entered into a different relationship to his or her body, restraint became something different from, and more than, regulation. The distinction will be carried forward in psychoanalysis, in which restraint of the fantasy may be as much a topic as regulation of overt behavior. Finally there is representation, which is as much an issue of how one chooses to represent one's own body as it is of how society provides for bodies to be represented. Thus what we have in Turner's categories are not only four tasks which a society must solve with regard to bodies, but also four problems which a body must solve to be in society.

I will return to Turner's typology in the next section. Prefatory to that, Feher's (1989) organizational scheme for the *Fragments* books also deserves consideration. The three volumes of the *Fragments* are organized on three axes. Part One is most clearly organized on what Feher calls the *vertical axis* on which the human body, at the top, aspires to the divine, and at the bottom, is reduced to the animal or the machine. Bodies are constructed with regard to some cultural ideal: 'what kind of body do these same Greeks, Christians, Jews, or Chinese endow themselves with – or attempt to acquire – given the power they attribute to the divine? . . . what exercise [should one] do in order to resemble a god physically or to commune sensually with him. Should one strive to maintain one's vigor . . .; or should one, on the contrary, expose the flesh to suffering . . .?' (Feher 1989, p. 13). At the bottom of the axis is the animal and the machine, images of which are understood to contaminate the human body by their similarities. The human fear is that of being pulled 'in the direction of animals and automatons' (1989, p. 14).

The articles in Part One can be read smoothly from beginning to end, top to bottom, or reversed, from the boy as mimicking the automaton to the body as representing the god. The axis of Part Two does not provide for quite the same organization of materials. Feher (1989, p. 14) calls this the 'transversal' axis, 'how the "inside" relates to the "outside."' Thus an interior soul is made exterior through the face or gesture. But the interior/exterior relation involves more of a hermeneutic recursion than a simple projection. Thus Feher recognizes that 'the singularity of the emotions [are] immanent in the ceremonies that produce them. Not that the transports of love are artificial; but they do not exist outside a certain setting, this is, a stylization of movements and poses' (1989, p. 14). The person does not so much 'have' a soul or certain emotions as one produces these in the medium of the body, whether the activity of that medium is saintly asceticism (Bynum 1989) or the rituals of courtly love (Nelli 1989).

The articles as a collection do not have quite the tightness of organization around this axis as those in Part One have, but the accumulation of empirical materials makes its point nevertheless. Bodies do not naturally 'have' interiors and exteriors. Rather these interiors and exteriors are what ethnomethodologists would have called practical accomplishments, and they exist in complex relations of mutual constitution. Constituting the body involves the practical work of formulating an inside and an outside, and developing a bodily practice in which inside and outside reproduce each other. Thus, to gloss Nelli's argument about courtly love in terms which risk oversimplifying the historical reality, the exterior of the Lady's body inspires certain interior feelings in the Lover, which then condition his exterior behavior (as verification of these interior feelings), which in turn affect her interior love for him, reflected (and verified) in her exterior deportment, and so on.

Part Three has no axis at all, the primary topic being how the body and its organs become endowed with metaphorical functions. Again, a complex hermeneutic of body and society is involved. The theme here is 'the fate of bodies [to be] assigned a pivotal position in perpetuating life or maintaining the social order' (Feher 1989, p. 16). These fates involve the sacrifices not only of captives and slaves (Duverger 1989) but also of kings (de Heusch 1989). The contribution of the articles is to demonstrate that organicist metaphors not only naturalize a particular social order (thought they clearly do that, see Le Goff 1989). Equally important, 'the application of organic metaphors to politics actually has the reciprocal effect of producing political or at least antagonistic metaphors for organic life: rivalries between head, heart, and liver within the organism, or even more strikingly, between male and female seeds within the embryo' (Feher 1989, p. 16). The papers tell more of the legitimation and domination purposes of body constructions, but at other historical moments these same constructions open an oppositional discourse which may be explicitly feminist (Héritier-Augé 1989), more generally reformist (Laqueur 1989b), or spiritual (Marin 1989).

People construct and use their bodies, though they do not use them in conditions of their own choosing, and their constructions are overlaid with ideologies. But these ideologies are not fixed; as they are reproduced in body techniques and practices, so they are modified. The 'government of the body' is never fixed but always contains oppositional spaces. Thus medieval holy women were able to use body techniques of asceticism to create a political status for themselves which the ideology of their time did not, at first, seem to provide (see the discussion of Bell 1985 below). Feher's most important idea may be the emphasis on the body being perpetually reconstituted in processes which are each hermeneutic: the body's interior to its exterior, the relation of male to female, of body to state, and so forth. In these oppositions, neither term is fixed, but each mutually constitutes the other. The body is process, a hermeneutic recursion of oppositions which are themselves in perpetual reconstitution. The constitution of the body is a history of oppositions, but as Laqueur puts it (1989a, p. 102), 'if structuralism has taught us anything, it is that humans impose their sense of opposition on a world of continuous shades of difference and similarity.' The oppositions are haunted by these shades, and eventually must be replaced by new oppositions, which will be haunted none the less. The government of the body is never more than a provisional ordering.

How, then, can we construct a theory of the body in a way which remains open to this hermeneutic process with its perpetual degradation of the oppositions which constitute the body within that theory?

Action as Embodiment
The problem which I have implied with regard to Turner's typology can now be made explicit. Turner begins with the body as a functional problem for a society. As I have suggested, his categories can be applied beyond this functional perspective, but the perspective continues to limit his work as a general theory for the sociology of the body. I propose instead to begin with how the body is a problem *for itself*, which is an action problem rather than a system problem, proceeding from a phenomenological orientation rather than a functional one. If the theoretical objective is to move from body to self to society, Turner's typology would represent the final, societal level of

theorizing. Theorizing about society may culminate in Turner's categories, but these categories must first be postulated not as abstract needs of a 'society,' but rather as deriving from the body's *own* problems of its embodiment within a social context.

Bodies alone have 'tasks.' Social systems may provide the context in which these tasks are defined, enacted, and evaluated, but social systems themselves have no 'tasks' (see Haines 1988, p. 164). The theoretical problem is to show how social systems are built up from the tasks of bodies, which then allows us to understand how bodies can experience their tasks as imposed by a system. What Feher contributes to such a theory is the need to be hermeneutic; specifically, the recognitions that bodily oppositions (e.g., surface/interior, sacred/polluting) can only be *continua*, not dichotomies, and that bodily and social reproduction is not linear but proceeds recursively.

What I propose, following Giddens (1979, 1984; see also Haines 1988) but not too far, is a structuration theory of the body and society, only the beginning of which can be presented in this chapter. Theory needs to apprehend the body as both medium and outcome of social 'body techniques,' and society as both medium and outcome of the sum of these techniques. Body techniques are socially given – individuals may improvise on them but rarely make up any for themselves – but these techniques are only instantiated in their practical use *by* bodies, *on* bodies. Moreover, these techniques are as much resources *for* bodies as they are constraints *on* them; constraints enable as much as they restrict. In one of his more elliptical phrases Goffman (1981, p. 74), after extensive rehearsal of all of the constraints to which speakers orient in natural conversation, concludes, 'there is no box.' He ends the book by demonstrating talk is nothing but boxes, but the point is that speakers *use* these boxes as much as they are boxed in by them. Much of what follows in the present chapter applies this lesson to bodies.

Modifying Giddens's (1984) central concepts of structure and system, I suggest that bodies exist among discourses and institutions. *Discourses* imply cognitive mappings of the body's possibilities and limitations, which bodies experience as already there for their self-understanding. Like Weber's types of rationality (traditional, charismatic, etc.), these mappings form the normative parameters of how the body can understand itself. These parameters are, to be redundant about an important point, not fixed limits but fluid resources, not necessarily requiring specific bodily techniques but providing for variation and improvisation of these techniques. Part of what a theory must account for are which orientations to the body provide for what degree of improvisation, in practice. Parameters can always be improvised upon, but depending on the orientation to the body, this possibility may or may not be grasped, and if grasped will be used to different ends.

Discourses only exist as they are instantiated in on-going practice or retained by actors as 'memory traces' (following Giddens 1984, p. 337). *Institutions*, on the other hand, have a specificity within both space and time. A discourse can only be spoken or enacted; it is nowhere but in that act or speech. An institution is a physical place where one can go, which may or may not be there any longer. But then a relation of mutual elaboration sets in, since institutions are constituted in and through discourses, and discourses are instantiated and modified in institutional sites. The point of a sociology of the body is not to theorize institutions prior to bodies, but to theorize institutions from the body up. Rather than postulating more about institutions now, it is preferable to let them emerge from the actions of bodies, even though that emergence is beyond the limits of this chapter. Still, because the theory is based on a recursive structuration, we must recognize institutions from the beginning, since the actions of bodies are already oriented to institutional contexts.

Bodies, of course, do not emerge out of discourses and institutions; they emerge out of other bodies, specifically women's bodies (see O'Brien 1989). Thus the *corporeality* of bodies is the third dimension of their constitution. Bodies too exist within space and time, as physiologies. But 'physiology' is at any given time produced in a discourse which seeks some 'truth' of bodies, and the history of physiology proves only that this truth may be redefined without apparent limit. Empirical bodies do have real limits. Beyond the relative discourse of physiology, corporeality remains an obdurate fact. There is a flesh which is formed in the womb, transfigured (for better or worse) in its life, dies and decomposes. Thus what I am calling 'the body' is constituted in the intersection of an equilateral triangle the points of which are *institutions*, *discourses*, and *corporeality*. A brief example may set this relation in order.

One of the more fascinating topics in the social history of the body is ascetic practices, particularly fasting, among medieval holy women (Bell 1985; Bynum 1987, 1989). More will be said about this example later, but here it can suggest the constitution of the body between institutions, discourses, and corporeality. The institution is the medieval church, as it existed at that time, in particular places. The discourses, which in this example as in most are necessarily plural, include the doctrines of that church – what acts, for example, were regarded as reflections of sanctity and where was the boundary between sanctity and self-indulgence – but also include discourses of medieval marriage and the place of wives, mothers, and women in that society. There were also discourses of politics, folk beliefs, and even commerce, the latter taking us back to the construction of being a medieval wife (relevant since many of the fasting saints had tried and rejected lives as wives and mothers).

Against this complex of discourses stands the corporeality of the body, posing in this example the question of how much self-punishment and deprivation it will bear. How much it apparently did bear, if we are to believe the documents from the period, leads Caroline Bynum to ask the fascinating question of whether corporeality itself can be regarded as a constant. Her consideration of medieval accounts of 'stigmata, incorruptibility of the cadaver in death, mystical lactations and pregnancies, catatonic trances, ecstatic nosebleeds, miraculous inedia [sic], eating and drinking pus, visions of bleeding hosts' as well as the fundamental phenomenon of how long these bodies supposedly survived virtually without food, leads her to venture the conclusion that 'The body, and in particular the female body, seems to have begun to behave in new ways at a particular moment in the European past.' 'The body itself,' she concludes (1989, p. 171), 'may actually have a history.' Not only are institutions and discourses in flux, but so also corporeality may be less than constant.

The example also underscores that bodies are used purposefully by the consciousness within them, and more about the strategic use of the body by medieval holy women will be written below. Although the recursive development of self from body is beyond my present scope, the progression to the self must be through the body as consciousness of itself. The theoretical jump of language to 'embodied consciousness' should not hypostatize the latter term: embodied consciousness is always a body conscious of itself. The theoretical task is to describe the dimensions of this consciousness.

Following Mead, I suggest that the body becomes most conscious of itself when it encounters resistance (see Joas 1985), which is to say, when it is in use, acting. I propose four questions which the body must ask itself as it undertakes action in relationship to some object. These questions then provide the four continua within which types of body usage may be conceptualized.

First, there is a dimension of *control*. The body must ask itself how predictable its performance will be. Writing of the Greeks, Jean-Pierre Vernant (1989, p. 32) describes their epic characters 'represented as being perfectly sure of their powers.' What makes them heroes is that their bodies are utterly predictable to them, while for us mortals the body's performances present some greater degree of contingency. We may know what we want the body to do, but 'it' retains some contingent will of 'its' own. This contingency is found in Mead's 'I' and in Freud's parapraxes. Bodies always align themselves somewhere on the continuum between god-like assurance and the embarrassment of the Freudian slip. 'This *My Body*,' writes Paul Valéry (in Starobinski 1989, pp.398–9), 'obeys or disobeys, favors or obstructs our designs. . . .'

Second, the body must constitute itself on a dimension of *desire*. Here the question is whether the body is lacking or producing. Vernant (1989, p. 23) describes the Greek opposition of the body which is marked 'with the seal of limitation, deficiency, incompleteness . . . that makes it a sub-body' as opposed to the body of 'corporeal plenitude, a super-body, the body of the gods.' As in each dimension, this one has what we can call, after Marshall McLuhan, its flip-point, or the moment at which one end of the continuum resolves back into the other. Luc De Heusch (1989, p. 387) refers to the body of the African king as 'an illusory producing machine.' The king's body produces the fertility of the tribe. It equally produces its own desires, which run to excess. This body is denied nothing, until at the culmination of its excess it is mocked and ultimately sacrificed. The king appears alternatively naked or in costume, in a perpetual alternation of lack and productivity, the sub-body and the super-body. Consumer culture makes the problem of desire acute. Hillel

Schwartz (1989, p. 416) describes the nineteenth-century ideology of the department store at the flip-point of lack and production: 'no desire is unfulfillable and . . . no desire can be fully satisfied.'

Third, the body must have some sense of its *relation to others*. Does the body relate to itself as monadic and closed in upon itself, or as dyadic, existing in relation of mutual constitution with others? Writing of Melanesian body culture, Bruce Knauft suggests a distinction between a traditionally closed western body and an open Melanesian body: 'In Western culture, the importance of transaction . . . in the consitution of the self is a late annex to knowledge. In Melanesia, by contrast, it is a fundamental axiom of being that self and body are transactionally constituted through social relationships and through beliefs in spiritual forces' (1989, p. 203). The medieval holy woman, at least as reconstructed by hagiographers, lived in the monad of a closed body in which, as Bynum (1989, p. 175) writes, sin arose 'from within the woman's body' and had to be dealt with on the surface of that body, alone. The dyadic body, as described by Knauft, understands itself as a medium through which self and other are connected. As we will see in the literature, however, this dyadic relation can be one of domination and force as often at it can be open and communicative.

Fourth is the dimension of the *self-relatedness* of the body. Does the body consciousness associate itself with its own being, particularly its surface, or dissociate itself from that corporeality? The attitude of dissociation is exemplified by Gnosticism: 'The body as a "garment" was a widely used metaphor in Antiquity. Gnostic writers, too, often made use of the image, to underscore the disassociation of the person from the physical body' (Williams 1989, p. 136). To borrow Weber's phrase, the Gnostic was in but not of his body.

The contemporary adolescent can exemplify the opposite attitude of association: 'The adolescent girl, unlike her brother, feels her relationship to others mediated through her body, and particularly her clothes, which serve the ambiguous purpose of covering and revealing at one and the same time. Adolescence, furthermore, is a phase when girls are more sensitive than ever to their appearance. The merest glance can provoke a blush, and the girl feels helpless, as if her protective covering had been torn aside' (J. Cohen, quoted in Beaune 1989, p. 470). This passage was published in 1966. We can mute its sexism by suggesting that insofar as 'the girl' may differ from 'her brother,' it is because the body of each is constituted within respectively different discourses of adolescence. In, for example, his athletic performances (or when he first dresses in a locker room), he no less than she may be *of* his body as well as *in* it, but society naturalizes his embodiment as it alienates hers.

The medieval holy woman exemplifies the flip-point of self-relatedness. In her mystical lactations and stigmata, she is associated with her body as the site of the conjunction with the body of Christ, for whom she lactates and whose sufferings she bears. Her self-mortifications, descriptions of which strain the modern reader's credibility no less than the other 'miracles,' mark an equal dissociation from the body as 'it' which had to be mortified. The Gnostic lived no less on the flip-point of dissociating from the body as a cruel imposition 'devised in desperate malice by invisible monsters,' from which the Gnostic could only hope to be rescued, and associating with it as 'the best *visible* trace of the divine in the material world' (Williams 1989, p. 130; also 136). The prevalence of these flip-point examples means that no theory based on a typology of ideal types will ever capture the richness of the empirical world. Or, in Schwartz's (1986, p. 109) phrase, which any general theory should hold as epigrammatic, 'The truth was a mess.'

These four dimensions (control, desire, other-relatedness, and self-relatedness) then generate a matrix of four cells, which provide the section headings for the remainder of this chapter. These are: the *disciplined* body, the *mirroring* body, the *dominating* body, and the *communicative* body. The full discussion of how each type fits into an ideal typical space on each continuum is described in the respective sections below. I want to emphasize that these types represent styles of body usage. As the body responds to all four of the questions of its object relatedness (e.g., is it predictable or contingent, etc.), a typical style of body usage emerges. To write of 'the disciplined body' is to suggest a typical style of how the body is experienced and deployed. Of course empirical bodies will not stay long with one type of usage; again, the truth is a mess. But the objective is to generate heuristic guides through which to order empirical behaviors and understand something of their flips and relations.

For bodies themselves, there is no Hobbesian 'order problem,'

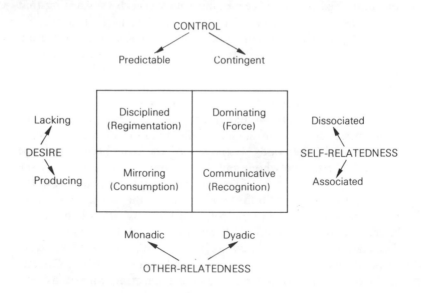

Figure 2.1   *A typology of body use in action*

rather there are only action problems: how predictable am I, do I lack or produce, am I associated or dissociated from my corporeal body, and am I monadic or dyadic toward others? Each ideal type of body usage resolves these problems in its respective medium of activity, which is its mode of action. For the disciplined body, this medium is the *regimentation*, the model of which is the rationalization of monastic order. For the mirroring body, the medium is *consumption*, the model of which is the department store. For the dominating body, the medium is *force*, the model of which is warfare. For the communicative body, the medium is what can loosely be called *recognition*, models of which may be shared narratives, dance, caring for the young, the old, and the ill, and communal ritual.

The dimensions of action problems, the types of bodily activity, and the typical media are presented in Figure 2.1.

The Disciplined Body
The 'disciplined body' describes a style of body use and body-to-object relatedness which, in its ideal typical form, is based on the

following responses to the questions of control, desire, self-relatedness, and other-relatedness.

With regard to control, the disciplined body makes itself *predictable* through its regimentation. So long as the regimen is followed, the body can believe itself to be predictable; thus being predictable is both the medium and outcome of regimentation. That this predictability may reflect an unconscious fear of the body's real contingency is probable, but so long as the technique of the regimen is successful, the disciplined body can regard itself as predictable to itself. Whatever it unconsciously fears about itself, the disciplined body consciously knows itself as predictable; what else can discipline be but predictability? When internal discipline can no longer neutralize the threat of its own contingency, the disciplined body may turn to domination, enforcing on the bodies of others the control it cannot exercise over itself.

With regard to desire, the disciplined body understands itself as *lacking*. What it lacks is itself; the regimentation does not remedy this lack, but it can forestall total disintegration. In the practice of the regimen, the body is able to recognize itself as being: the soldier comes to know himself as being in his drill, the ascetic in her or his self-mortification. George Vigarello (1989, p. 152) states that in the sixteenth century, 'posture indirectly reveals a person's "inner depths."'

For discipline to be sustained, the sense of lack must remain conscious. One device for sustaining the consciousness of lack is for the disciplined body to place itself in some hierarchy (military, monastic or other), in which it is perpetually, and to itself justifiably, subordinated. Thus subordination is a medium and outcome of lack. The lack justifies the subordination, which in turn reproduces the lack. When in consumer culture the disciplinary regimens of diet and fitness do effectively remedy the sense of lack, there is a shift to the mirroring body.

The other-relatedness of the disciplined body is *monadic*, as the body becomes isolated in its own performance even if, as in military drill (Foucault 1979), the body performs among others. In drill unlike communal ritual, the disciplined body may be among others, but it is not *with* them. The disciplined body is, in Weber's sense, a virtuoso in the practice of the regimen. When such a body comes out of itself and does relate to others, the mode of that relation will predictably be force, since the disciplined body can only relate to others by projecting its regimen upon them. At this point there is a flip into domination.

Finally on the dimension of self-relatedness, the disciplined body is *dissociated* from itself. The ascetic can tolerate the degradation of her or his body because she or he only observes that body; the ascetic is in but not of the body. Recursively, the objective of mortification practices or military training is to cultivate an attitude of dissociation. Part of the discipline is to cease to feel the body's pain or hunger as one's own. Dissociation fashions the body to be what Parsons called 'instrumental' while an attitude of association creates the body along Parsons's 'consummatory' axis.

With regard to the body, an instrumental attitude involves the body's consciousness dissociating itself from that body's surface, and then by extension, dissociating itself from any empathy with the experienced body of the other. As Mark Elvin (1989, p. 317) writes of what revolutionary discipline does to bodies, 'This body is a remarkable all-purpose tool and weapon, hardened in a training that removes the old supportive physical affection and toughened by constant tests.' Unable to receive affection, it will be equally unable to give it.

The theorist of the disciplined body is Foucault. Foucault perpetually redefined the nature of his project, but by the time of his participation in the seminars at the University of Vermont in 1982 (Martin et al. 1988), Foucault understood himself as investigating the interface 'between the technologies of domination of others and those of the self' (Martin et al. 1988, p. 19). Foucault seems to have reached the idea that a theory of domination must begin with the body dominating itself. From an extensional societal perspective we may see domination as imposed, but to understand its effectiveness, we must also understand this domination as chosen. Bodily domination is never imposed by some abstract societal Other; only bodies can do things to other bodies. Most often, what is done depends on what bodies do to themselves.

This domination of self proceeds by what Foucault called 'truth games,' a term curiously combining Nietzschean intent and Wittgensteinian language. Truth games are discourses (e.g., economics, biology, psychiatry, penology, or as discussed above, physiology) which are 'related to specific techniques that human beings use to understand themselves' (Martin et al. 1988, p. 18).

Although most of the papers in Martin et al. describe truth games in the medieval church, we can hear a truth game just as well in the ideology of the dieter: 'Imprisoned in every fat man a thin one is wildly signalling to be let out' (Cyril Connolly, c. 1942, quoted in Schwartz 1989, p. 407). The thin man inside is the truth, the scale becomes the daily truth game, and the diet the disciplinary regimen. The trade name of the first American home bathroom scale is, appropriately, the Detecto (Schwartz 1989, p. 449). The truth game is always a contest: Detecto versus the weighed body. But the game cannot be won. Detecto can only determine if the body is continuing to play, game without end. Diet is clearly a truth game. The question to which we will have to return is whether this particular truth game is based on a disciplined body.

Why do people play truth games? As we recollect Foucault at increasing distance after his death, the desire of human beings 'to understand themselves' may emerge as the central presupposition of his philosophical anthropology, just as the notion of 'technologies' may form the core of his institutional analyses. To be human is to believe in the possibilities of one's own truth, and the truth of others. Power is less abstract than Foucault sometimes presents it to be. In its embodied form, power takes its volition from each person's search for his or her own truth. Power is productive as it recursively elaborates the self which seeks itself. Technologies then draw on this energy, often turning power back on the individual in ways that generate resistances. But what is being resisted is what, on some level, the body itself has instituted.

Sometimes the will-to-truth emerges as a technique of domination. In the introductory volume to *The History of Sexuality*, the metaphor of this domination through truth seeking is Prince Mangogul's ring from Diderot's *Les bijous indiscrets* (Foucault 1978, p. 77). In this quasi-pornographic novel, the Prince has a magic ring which has the power to compel others to tell their sexual secrets. Participation in the truth game is thus compelled by the Other, as a kind of rape in which the victim is forced to play. The problem with such a truth game as a model of social power is that she who is subject of the truth game is, to rephrase Garfinkel's famous charge against Parsons, a 'discourse dope.' What is difficult to theorize is how players can be dominated but not be dopes.

In Foucault's middle work such as *Discipline and Punish* bodies are compelled through disciplines, and truth is only one legitimation for the imposition of these disciplines. The regimen is the truth, and the practice of the regimen is the truth game, contested on the site of the body. The problem for the theory was whom to place in the persona of Prince Mangogul; who compels? The answer in *Discipline and Punish* is the principle of panopticism, which takes on a kind of Durkheimian *sui generis* force. The theory thus tends toward a hypostatization of 'social control,' rendered less vague than it actually is by the details through which Foucault presents it (see Hoy 1987 for similar lines of criticism).

As Foucault's later interest turns to sexuality, the categories of 'discipline' and 'care' become difficult to disentangle. Care of the self is a regimen, but is it a discipline? Truth seems to change from being a legitimation by the Other to being a 'legitimate' motivation of the self. Had Foucault lived longer, my prediction is that he would have attended more to the viable possibilities (rather than the mock-heroic failures of Pierre Rivière and Herculine Barbin) of oppositional spaces within truth games and disciplines. Disciplines not only make bodies productive in terms defined by some other, whether king or factory owner. Disciplines can also be used by bodies themselves to achieve productive ends of their own. But to the extent that these bodies choose a monadic relation to others, trying to achieve productive ends through discipline will perhaps inevitably be a contradictory pursuit.

The limits of strategic behavior by the disciplined body are best exemplified by the case described above of medieval holy women. Rudolph Bell is clearest in understanding their fasting and self-mortification practices as 'one aspect of the struggle by females striving for autonomy in a patriarchal culture' (1985, p. 86). This struggle begins in the women's families, before they embrace the religious life. Many came from relatively prosperous families, with whom they broke over the demand for marriage or remarriage. Between religious discourse and the discourses of marriage and feminine submission, an oppositional space was opened up, which it was the genius of these women to exploit strategically.

When the parents of Catherine of Siena tried to marry her off against her will, Catherine turned to ascetic fasting. What she defined as divinely inspired, her parents interpreted as temporal rebellion. In the contest for the truth of her action, Catherine won by defining it as being for their welfare. 'Catherine not only forgave them but contracted to save them as well' through her fasting. Her fast was defined as a compact with God in which he was to reward Catherine with her parents' salvation. Whatever God's attitude toward this compact, its effect within the family was to render her the most powerful player in the family game: 'Once the pact was made, to yield to [her parents'] entreaties would be to damn them forever, and she loved them too much to do that. By her agreement with God the rebellious and troubled Catherine suddenly gained total power over [her parents], power in the next world that enabled her to defeat them in all struggles on earth' (Bell 1985, pp. 40–1).

Fasting could only be a power play because it was also a Foucauldian truth game. As a truth game, it was also a contest not just of corporeality with itself. Again, the body is formed not just by corporeality, but this together with discourses and institutions. Within the institutional church's discourse of medieval theology, the contest was whether the source of the inspiration to fast was divine or demonic. The relevant institution, the church, was ambivalent. Individual fasting women were venerated as saints, but the general attitude toward fasting was negative. Thus the motivation for fasting was subject to constant interrogation. Fortunately for later scholars, this interrogation took the partial form of diaries and journals which both the women and their confessors were required to keep as one aspect of their confessional practice. Thus confessional practice can be considered a technology of the self in its own time, and for those who come later, data.

What the truth game made crucial was not the behavior of fasting, but its motivation, and motivation remains crucial to the disciplined body. The *vitae* of the holy women, Bell (1985, p. 152) writes, 'even as they extol an individual who was in God's grace . . . serve to remind confessors of all the false steps and errors that women fall into.' Here we reach the essence of the truth game: 'Unless she is inspired purely by the divine, and only male clerics seem able to ascertain this, her piety is not only useless but dangerous.' As the Middle Ages became the Renaissance, institutions changed their discourses. Danger came to predominate over piety: 'the inspired wisdom of female mystics . . . comes to be replaced with charges of heresy.' In more theoretical terms, the institution closed the discursive loophole which afforded bodies a power which that institution was not prepared to allow them.

As important as institutions and discourses are, we cannot leave out corporeality. Many of the women died of their disciplinary practices. Others achieved some degree of institutional status. Catherine herself became a confidante of the Pope and a major political power of her time. Her corporeality allowed her to pay the enormous physical cost of her resistance and live to enjoy its rewards. But the issue of cost is not only corporeal pain; it is also collusion. This disciplined resistance only ended by reproducing the patriarchal discourse which had driven the women to resist. In his epilogue to Bell's book, the clinician William Davis notes the paradox of any opposition which proceeds within a prescribed discipline: the church fathers 'did not have to enforce their domination via suspicions of demonic possession or complicated formulas for beatification. The [women] saints themselves were unknowingly supporting their cultural values by equating bodily purity with essential holiness . . . the women who struggled to express their sense of self by becoming holy did so in a way that reinforced a male interpretation of female psychology' (quoted in Bell, 1985, p. 185). Catherine of Siena did not really resist the social order of her time, she simply used discipline to cut herself a better deal within that order.

Bodies pursue ends which are their own, but in so doing, they reproduce structures which require further resistance. Bodies discipline themselves, but they do so within institutions and discourses which are not their own. Thus we have the paradox that resistance will often reproduce that which it initially opposed. That individuals would perpetually seem to be seduced by this paradox is no great surprise, if we remember that resistance in the individual case is always about that individual's own situation, so long as the body remains monadic and dissociated. It is in these fundamental qualities of closure, as well as its sense of lack and its need to be predictable, that the disciplined body is constituted. Within these qualities the body can still be strategic, but its strategies will be limited by its qualities.

The contemporary regimens are those of care: the disciplines of confession and mortification now find their analogues in diet and exercise (Green 1986; Hepworth and Featherstone 1982; Schwartz 1986, 1989). But how analogous are these practices? Care can still represent a truth game, and its techniques can form a regimen, but with the 'disciplines' of care we move to a body which is associated with its surface, and producing rather than lacking. The difference between care and discipline can only depend on how the practices are undertaken; once again, the truth is a mess.

Disciplined bodies continue to exist, but perhaps at present most of these bodies are found closer to the flip-points of other body styles. Those for whom the need for self-discipline must be projected out assume the style of domination over others. And there are those for whom discipline of the body becomes its care. As consideration turns to the mirroring body, it will be clear that consumption has its regimens, but these are not disciplinary regimentation.

The Mirroring Body

The mirroring body remains *predictable*, but for different reasons from those of the disciplined body. The disciplined body achieved predictability through practising its regimen; its predictability had the cost of its effort. The mirroring body finds itself to be predictable as it reflects that which is around it. The medium of the mirroring body is consumption; based on consumption, the body becomes as predictable as the objects made available for it. It is predictable in the way fast food is; its epigram might be that of the American hotel chain which advertised the cross-country homogeneity of its rooms with the slogan, 'No surprises.'

The other-relatedness of the mirroring body remains *monadic*, again for different reasons. Where the disciplined body was closed in the virtuosity of its practice, the mirroring body is open to an exterior world, but monadic in its appropriation of that world. As the disciplined body gained power over others in order to pursue its own virtuosity, the mirroring body constitutes its objectives in its own self-reflection. Even as the body itself mirrors these objects, the objects are always already seen as mirroring the body. Other objects are all 'pre-assimilated' to the body. One size fits all, and all fits the one body. Consumption thus cannot mean 'use' in the classic Marxist sense, but rather the endless assimilation of the world's objects to one's own body, and of one's own body to the world's objects. The institutional structures of consumer society are designed to facilitate this mutual assimilation.

In the world of the mirroring body, projection and introjection take place in seamless reciprocity. The body is monadic in that nothing in the world challenges its consciousness of itself. Julia Kristeva (1989, p. 239) quotes one of Dostoyevsky's characters saying, in contemplation of Holbein's painting *The Body of the Dead Christ in the Tomb*, 'That picture . . . that picture! Why, some people may *lose their faith* by looking at that picture?' People then had a faith which was embodied and could be undermined or strengthened by images of embodiment. Holbein, unlike for example Philippe de Champaigne (pictured in Marin 1989, p. 420), does not depict Christ almost lifting off the cross, his dying body light as it seems to be already leaving earth in favor of heaven. Philippe de Champaigne gives us faith that out of suffering can come resurrection. Holbein shows the crucified Christ as a mortified, thoroughly human body, locked in the horizontal space of a grave from which it will not emerge. His image had the power to challenge faith by causing a radical reassessment of embodiment. The mirroring self could never respond as Dostoyevsky's character did (any more than a faith embodied in discipline could be challenged). Its monadic closure denies the challenge of an image outside of itself. Outside of the mirror of its own body, there is no reality. Consumption is the monadic reproduction of the body through its assimilation of a world which exists only for its own assimilation.

If the disciplined body made itself predictable against an unconscious fear of its own contingency, the mirroring body is endlessly *producing* desires in order to keep its lack unconscious. The mirroring body finds its paradigmatic medium of activity in consuming, but consumption is less about actual material acquisition than it is about producing desires. The paradox of the mirroring body's consumption is that it need not, as it were, be consummated. As the body sees the object it immediately aligns itself in some fit with that object; its desire is to make the object part of its image of itself. Thus the object becomes a mirror in which the body sees itself reflected, but only (unlike Dostoyevsky) on its own terms.

Consumer culture then shortens the time and space between

desire and consummation. For the ultimate mirroring body, it is enough simply to walk through the shopping malls, to see what is there, perhaps to 'try on some things.' The object need not be purchased because it has already been consumed in the initial gaze, and there will be a new object next month, if not next week. What counts is the endless producing and reproducing of desire, of the body in the world's image and the world in the body's image. A North American cable television station broadcasts nothing but still images of objects which can be purchased by telephone. People call the station to talk about their purchases. A recent cartoon shows men sitting at a bar, watching this station. Each says to the next, 'Shopping has replaced baseball as the national pastime, pass it on.'

The mirroring body is *associated* with its own surface in the mythological sense of Narcissism. Eric Alliez and Michel Feher write (1989, p. 61), 'The narcissistic soul, in love with its own body, wishes to become united with it.' This body as surface exists in order to be decorated. The mirroring body is that described by Valéry (1989, pp. 399–400) as 'the body on which materials, ornaments, armor sit. . . . It knows no pain, for it reduces pain to a mere grimace.' Pain becomes a grimace not out of ascetic or warrior dissociation, but because in the mirroring form of association, the sign is purely an image, having no referent in a feeling. Having learned itself through advertising, the mirroring body sees the grimace as a sign of an occasion for drug taking. Pain signifies the grimace; the grimace signifies consumption, not embodied pain.

This body 'goes little farther than the view of a surface' (Valéry, pp. 399–400). It is 'without knowledge of his inner organization.' The medieval holy women were obsessed with pus, body fluids, and excretions. Whatever they knew or did not know of the inner organization of the body, they sought some connection to it. For the mirroring body its inner organization is like a closed circuit appliance: only authorized personnel may open it, which means the rest of us need not concern ourselves with what is inside.

Theoretical consideration of the mirroring body runs from Jean Baudrillard to Pierre Bourdieu. Baudrillard's 'selected' writings (1988a) of most relevance to social scientists have only recently become available to English-speaking readers in a convenient collection by a publisher with major distribution capabilities. As edited and introduced by Mark Poster, his work reads as less diffuse and obscure than it has previously appeared. Although his influence among the arts community has already waxed and waned (see Hughes 1989), his social scientific vogue may be yet to happen, or perhaps even in social science the duration from desire to consummation may be shortening. The new edition of his work may signal his end, not his beginning.

Baudrillard's simplest insight may be his most powerful. As Poster (Baudrillard 1988a, p. 1) describes it, Baudrillard 'found that the productivist metaphor in Marxism was inappropriate for comprehending the status of commodities in the post-war era.' Baudrillard has attempted to move theory from a model in which the body reproduces itself by externalizing objects in labour, to one in which it reproduces itself by internalizing objects in consumption. What are now produced are desires which are signs, not material objects. Desire can only operate on objects by turning them into signs. The commodity is less a real thing than it is a sign of itself, because it is the sign we desire.

Poster's (Baudrillard 1988a, p. 3) summary is elegant: Baudrillard 'indicates how consumer objects are like hysterical symptoms; they are best understood not as a response to a specific need or problem but as a network of floating signifiers that are inexhaustible in their ability to incite desire.' For the mirroring body, these 'hysterical symptoms' are no longer sources of suffering but have become sites of pleasure. Ideas like this give Baudrillard's writing what even his more hostile critics recognize as an eerie sense of rightness. Post-Marx and post-Freud, the shopping mall is the dream site in which the reader is forced to admit that he or she has indulged an hallucinatory fantasy, and felt at home.

In his travel book *America* Baudrillard (1988b) provides numerous evocations of the mirroring body. In describing the body's mania for consumption, the significations of its presentations, its production of desires within its monadic enclosure (epitomized by the Walkman), he is superb. The monadic body characterizes itself when the speaker refers to him or herself as being 'into' whatever. 'This "into,"' Baudrillard writes (1988b, p. 35) 'is the key to everything. The point is not to be nor even to *have* a body, but to be into your own body. Into your sexuality, into your own desire. Into your own functions, as if they were energy differentials or video screens. The hedonism of the "into". . . .'

But then this insight becomes an undifferentiated hostility to any embodied activity. Baudrillard is most hostile to joggers and particularly marathon runners. In his vision the New York Marathon 'has become a sort of international symbol of such fetishistic performance, of the mania for an empty victory, the joy engendered by a feat that is of no consequence' (1988b, p. 20). Ultimately the marathon is 'a form of demonstrative suicide' for Baudrillard (1988b, p. 21). The marathon runners seek only to prove to themselves that they exist; they are, like graffiti, 'free publicity for existence' (Baudrillard 1988b, p. 21).

There are insights here too, but Baudrillard is limited by the disembodiment of his own vision. His eyes see scenes without the rest of him being embodied in these scenes. He is the remote control video probe from another world, seeing but never inquiring, incapable of joining in. Baudrillard can only see the marathon as mass suicide because for him bodily association can only be monadic, never dyadic. He cannot perceive the marathon as, in the full sense of the pun, a human race. He cannot hear runners talking to each other, much less drawing energy from their communal effort. Instead he sees only monads. He is not wrong, only limited. In an urban space which denies embodiment, running a marathon may be 'publicity for existence,' but the action involved is less advertising, as Baudrillard calls it, than resistance. It is a communal ritual of shared embodiment, constituted in moments of shared intimacy of a sort which urban life rarely allows.

Baudrillard's problem is that he has no *Verstehen* for the embodiment which is being preserved and achieved, seeing only 'an empty victory.' What victory of bodies would, for him, be full?

Bodies, in Baudrillard's world, are ultimately assimilated to the general condition which he calls hyperreality. If the real becomes 'that for which it is possible to provide an equivalent representation' – in other words, we only acknowledge the real in its image – then the hyperreal is 'that which is always already reproduced' (Baudrillard 1988a, pp. 145–6). In this stoned Saussurian world, there are no referents. As I read Baudrillard, bodies no longer exist, at least in the terms I have called corporeality. As the body enters hyperreality, the anchor of corporeality is cut away. Eventually the body reaches the condition which Baudrillard (1983, p. 133) calls 'the schizo': 'It is the end of interiority and intimacy, the overexposure and transparence of the world which traverses him without obstacle. He can no longer produce the limits of his own being, can no longer play nor stage himself, can no longer produce himself as a mirror. He is now a pure screen, a switching center for all the networks of influence.' What I am calling the mirroring body has not yet reached this point; it can still produce itself as a mirror, it has boundaries. The schizo is the flip-point at which the mirroring self leaves my typology of embodied action, because the body is abandoned totally. Here we reach Baudrillard's writings on death, which I find the most unreadable parts of his work in their romantic indulgence; but perhaps these are the limits of my own embodied critical facilities.

If the mirroring body has not yet become Baudrillard's schizo, its endless simulation of what are already simulations denies it any praxis. Poster (Baudrillard 1988a, p. 4–5) summarizes Baudrillard's political development: 'from a position of firm leftism he gradually moved to one of bleak fatalism.' Although Bourdieu seems to share many of Baudrillard's presuppositions about the centrality of consumption, his analysis retains a modernist emphasis on the determining variable of social class and the praxis of demystifying class relations. Thus it remains possible to speak of domination with Bourdieu's world, while for Baudrillard 'no one is dominating, nothing is being dominated and no ground exists for a principle of liberation from domination' (Baudrillard 1988a, p. 6). To quote this statement out of context trivializes Baudrillard's argument, but it suggests the problem which his work presents for critical theory. Baudrillard presents not a critique of the mirroring body, but an analysis from that subject position.

For Bourdieu (1977, 1978, 1984) domination remains, but it must be reconceptualized in a world of consumption. Domination is now mediated by taste. The capacity of dominant groups to reproduce themselves, and to legitimize this reproduction, depends on their capacity to define what a society holds in distinction. To be dominant is to be able to determine that what a society values as having distinction will be those same qualities which members of that group are able to display, thus reproducing their own domination as legitimated 'distinction.' It is no longer ownership of the means of production which provides domination – the joint stock company was already giving Marx problems on that issue – but socially recognized taste, as the capacity to determine terms of distinction.

The key concept in class reproduction is what Bourdieu calls 'habitus,' which is the member's internalization, as natural, of the tastes of his or her class. The lower the class, the more habitus seems somewhat naively Durkeimian. The member is disposed to like that which she or he has grown up having, and by displaying these tastes, continues to mark her or himself as a member of that class. Among higher classes habitus involves more of a praxis in its naturalization. A taste which is cultivated must be presented as natural. Georges Vigarello's (1989, p. 156) description of the training of Renaissance nobility describes their habitus: 'Excellence should in no way show the care which leads to it. It should truly become second nature. The nobleman should carry it as a sign of his breeding.' In the contemporary class system, even 'breeding' may be effaced. Excellence should be carried as a natural inclination. Today, no less than in the Renaissance, the body 'is heavily laden with demonstrative value' (Vigarello, 1988, p. 156). It is through this value that class position can be reproduced. The 'matter of lineage' is no less present, but is now legitimated as other capacities, principally for Bourdieu, academic achievement.

For Bourdieu, domination seems largely a question of appropriation denying its existence. If there is an upper-class ideology, it is that there is no ideology. Featherstone (1987, p. 122) describes Bourdieu's position: 'society is not conceived as being held together by a dominant ideology which produces a common culture. On the contrary while legitimate taste achieves hegemony and recognition, different classes and class fractions pursue tastes which are a reflection of their particular position determined by type and volume of [cultural] capital.' Thus we are brought back to the body, which is now the body of the habitus, reflecting its particular class position.

Classes reproduce themselves by their members' internalization and display of certain tastes, which then mark only some for distinction. At the foundation of these tastes is the body. Taste 'is *embodied* being inscribed onto the body and made apparent in body size, volume, demeanour, ways of eating and drinking, walking, sitting, speaking, making gestures, etc.' (Featherstone

1987, p. 123). Empirical investigation can then proceed with a number of body-oriented research projects, for example sport: 'Whereas the working-class men may engage in gymnastics to develop a *strong* body, the new middle class seek to produce a *healthy* or slim body' (Featherstone 1987, p. 129). In either case, however, the body is mirroring a habitus, either to reproduce its original class position or, since there is definitely mobility in Bourdieu's scheme, it is attempting to mirror another class presentation even if it lacks the habituated dispositions to act in those ways. A working-class person can redevelop his or her body along middle-class lines, but she or he will not necessarily be disposed to do so. Even the disposition for mobility may be a matter of habitus.

The body in Bourdieu becomes a form of capital, sometimes referred to specifically as 'physical capital' (Bourdieu 1978, p. 832). and other times within the more general term 'cultural capital.' Cultural capitals exist preeminently for reinvestment. Marriage selection and employment are two media of this reinvestment, the spouse or the job then becoming a further form of capital. Thus the Bourdieuian body is associated in its self-consciousness, predictable in its tastes, producing in its capitals, and monadic in its demonstrative value. As it mirrors its habitus, it reproduces the society which it comprises.

Between the disciplined and the mirroring body the flip-point was when the disciplines gave way to care, and regimentation to consumption. The flip-point between the mirroring body and the communicative body will be when the boundaries of the body are open. As healthist pursuits are described by Hepworth and Featherstone (1982), bodies seek only to mirror images they have already internalized. In their diets and exercises, and even more in their cosmetic surgeries, these bodies remain closed in the endless reproduction of their own images. But when Harvey Green concludes his social history of health and exercise in America with the suggestion that fitness activity may reflect 'an expression of the desire for community and emotional bonding in a culture of men and women alone' (1986, p. 323), he suggests an openness of the body to others. Such bodies are not trying to reproduce an image from within a closed self-reflection. Rather they are open to recognizing the others as different but attractive. Before discussing this communicative body, however, we must return to the level of lack and dissociation, and the dominating body.

The Dominating Body

Thomas Gregor, whose observations of sexual domination among the Mehinaku people of the Amazon will be discussed below, writes of these people, 'Even though male identity and men's house culture are not immediately in danger of collapse, the cost of maintaining the facade runs high. The price the men pay is in anxiety: fear of their own sexual impulse and fear of women' (1986, p. 115). Two observations which inform the consideration of the dominating body can be immediately derived from this quotation. First, dominating bodies are, at least in the literature, exclusively male bodies. Hence it is impossible to consider the dominating body without also questioning the construction of the masculine body. Second, among the four dimensions of embodiment, what counts preeminently for dominating bodies is their sense of lack, characterized by Gregor as anxiety and fear. The dominating body's response to its sense of its own contingency, its dissociated self-relatedness, and especially its dyadic other-relatedness are all configured by lack. Hence to theorize the dominating body is to entertain the relation of masculinity and lack.

The other essential difference between consideration of the dominating body and the other bodily styles is the literature itself. To think about disciplined, mirroring, and communicative bodies it is necessary to do a kind of academic *bricolage* of empirical fragments written from a variety of perspectives and of theories which have a scope going well beyond the body. The dominating body, however, is the topic of what may be currently the preeminent work on bodies, Klaus Theweleit's two volume *Male Fantasies* (1987, 1989; original publication 1977, 1978). No other work combines so much empirical and theoretical material, which is both the richness and the problem of *Male Fantasies*. The volumes are less a book than an archive; in its diffuseness *Male Fantasies* sometimes seems to be a text only in the sense of being bound together.

Theweleit's original core of materials is by and about the German Freikorps. This was first an official army unit formed at the end of the First World War to fight 'Bolsheviks' (and trade unionists) along Germany's eastern border. When their official mandate ended, many continued the fight as a vigilante force. Many of those left alive ended up in the SA and SS, some of the latter becoming concentration camp commandants during the Second World War.

This core of materials then expands to include other sources from the period between the world wars, and ultimately the whole problem of fascism is implicated. Parallel to the text, though rarely having any direct reference to it (and never commented on), are hundreds of illustrations, photographs, movie stills, comics, and art reproductions. These are by no means limited to the 1920–40 time period. The visual material provides a counterpoint to the written text which both expands its concerns and decenters its specificity. Finally there are extensive theoretical excurses on psychoanalytic theory (Freud, Reich, Mahler, Balint), Deleuze and Guattari, Elias Canetti, Mary Douglas and Norbert Elias. When the theoretical excursus on Elias leads to an extended empirical sub-excursus on the construction of the female body (1987, p. 325 ff.), the reader can only wonder what in these books is an excursus; much more than the Freikorps or even fascism is involved.

The effect of such a decentered text is intensified for the non-German reader by *Male Fantasies* being written from within both an authorial subject position and an historical frame of reference which are preeminently German and do not always translate. It might have been most useful if the English edition had included extra footnotes explaining more of the history of the period which Theweleit simply assumes his readers know. The sense that I was missing many of the references intensified the decentering effect of the text.

But even if one knew the history behind the materials, it would remain difficult to sustain a stable sense of what Theweleit is doing; the book is 'about' so much. His author's endnote suggests the massiveness of the project finally overwhelmed him, and it overwhelms the reader. Rather than quibble over a need for editing, it may be best to take the text's effect as part of its message. To desire as a reader to 'control' an argument which is 'linear' in its statement and 'stripped' of extraneous discussions is to want to dominate that text and be able to use it as a resource to dominate other texts. *Male Fantasies* resists any will to textual domination. It may be a tool kit for future theory, but it cannot be appropriated as a weapon. To use the period metaphors that Theweleit analyzes, the reader must enter its mass, and be taken along with its flood. To fear the mass and the flood is to share the mind-set of the Freikorps. Reflexively, I found that my problems with *Male Fantasies* could be constructed as reflecting precisely the male will to domination which the text deconstructs. That may be rationalization for a work which remains unmanageable in its diffuseness, but why do we want to 'manage' texts?

So to discuss dominating bodies is to discuss Theweleit, but no discussion of Theweleit can do more than nibble around the edges of his work. I will seek only to appropriate enough to display the complementarity between the theory developed in this chapter and the argument of *Male Fantasies*. As stated above, the essential quality of dominating bodies is the construction of their desire as *lack*. Theweleit takes his initial formulation of lack from the psychoanalyst Michael Balint's theory of the 'basic fault,' which derives from a crisis in the process of separation-individuation from the mother. What Theweleit finds most significant is Balint's emphasis on 'an exclusive two-person relationship' (the *dyadic* constitution of the body), that the relationship does not [yet] 'take the form of a conflict,' and that the body 'assumes . . . the form of a mistake in the basic structure, a fault, a lack that demands to be compensated for' (1987, p. 207). The conflict comes later, as Theweleit writes: 'The acts of murder the soldiers enter into, for pleasure and to counteract fear, likewise strike me less as defenses against the threat of castration than as attempts to compensate for the fundamental lack of which Balint speaks' (1987, p. 208).

Thus when a dyadic other-relatedness is combined with a fundamental sense of lack, the body turns to domination of that other. The other becomes a 'subhuman' who is 'a human of the nether regions, a person who is human even [sexually] below' (1987, p. 399). But the other is no less necessary even if subhuman. For the dominating body, 'someone or other had to die so that they could live' (1987, p. 209). The dominating body needs to seek out others, as subhuman enemies which it can fight, and through the fighting, live. For the Freikorps soldiers, 'The only real thing was fighting. (You couldn't be a man without fighting, and being a man was the only way of being alive.) When there is no more fighting, no more being a man, life ceases and everything (the man, the world) becomes a pulp' (1987, p. 395).

This 'pulp' or 'bloody mass' becomes both the medium and outcome of domination. Theweleit summarizes his consideration of the gaze of what he calls the 'soldier male:' 'The real source of terror is the light they themselves cast onto reality. As if magnetically attracted, their eyes hunt out anything that moves. The more intense and agitated the movement, the better. When they spot such movement they narrow their eyes to slits (defense), sharpen their vision of it as a dead entity by training a spotlight on it (deanimation), then destroy it, to experience a strange satisfaction at the sight of this "bloody mass." Their writing process works in exactly the same way' (1987, p. 217). What this review must necessarily abridge is the basis of such summary passages in Theweleit's extensive quotations from Freikorps diaries, journals, some letters, and considerable novels written by themselves and others about their experience. Like medieval holy women, the Freikorps' technology of the self included a literary component which left a rich source of materials; horrible, but nonetheless rich.

The dominating body's quality of *contingency* can be suggested more briefly. The world of the dominating body is a world of warfare, which is always contingent. The Freikorps soldiers are not epic heroes, sure of their own power. They are as threatened as they are threatening, and threatened by themselves as much as by others. The need to dominate the other is a need to control the projection of the internal contingency which threatens them. The 'movement' referred to above, which must be destroyed, is contingent; only its reduction to 'bloody mass' renders it predictable. But unlike the stable predictability achieved by the disciplined body through regimentation, the dominating body is perpetually threatened by new contingencies, new movement, and ultimately, new life which must be reduced to the 'bloody mass.'

The dominating body must be *dissociated* from itself in order to punish and absorb punishment. The paradigm of this dissociation is what Theweleit calls the 'prohibition' that 'bodies cannot know themselves.' '[T]he despot was the only one who could (theoretically) use his body in any way he pleased.' Again, this argument resolves into lack: 'The authority of rulers is implanted into subjects' bodies in the form of a lack in overflowing (a prohibition against using what *belongs* to you). These subjects have always experienced their lack of social power as a lack of power over specific areas of their own bodies. The body must not become too familiar, "known"; it must be an object and source of fear' (1987, p. 414). Theweleit goes on to discuss

Adam and Eve as the paradigm of this enforced institution of lack, creating dissociation of the body from itself. Ultimately, dissociation from the body is fear of its inner 'dark territories' (1987, p. 415). The sense of the body as a dark territory, fearful and forbidden, is prerequisite to being a warrior, since to fight is to turn this dark power outward. The soldier male's darkness is his strength, though this power remains contingent since it is never really his.

The dissociated, contingent body can only become the warrior body, the body which can only exist with itself by dominating. Once domination has been adopted as a style of bodily usage, the body itself is reproduced in the medium of force and becomes incapable of other action forms of relatedness. Theweleit summarizes the construction of the dominating body as warrior: 'The soldier male is forced to turn the periphery of his body into a cage for the beast within. In so doing, he deprives it of its function as a surface for social contact. His contact surface becomes an insulated shield, and he loses the capacity to perceive the social corpus within which his insulated body moves. . . . A man [so] structured craves war, because only war allows him to achieve identity with his alien, "primitive," "bestial" interior, while at the same time avoiding being devoured by it' (1989, p. 22).

Domination thus becomes medium and outcome of the warrior body: 'What seems to hold the masculine-soldierly body together is his compulsion to oppress the body of another (or bodies, or the body in his own body). His relation to the bodies he subordinates is one of violence and, in extreme cases, of murder' (1989, p. 87).

Before moving to some of Theweleit's conclusions, a short break from the Freikorps may be useful, though hardly refreshing. An easy explanation of their behavior is that their lack is a sexual deprivation, and their aggression is a project of frustration. Gregor's Mehinaku observations suggest such thinking is too simple. Among the Mehinaku domination is, to use Lévi-Strauss's terms, cool rather than hot. Freikorps domination destroys, utterly. Mehinaku domination provides for and achieves reintegration, though the order of bodies which is reintegrated is one in which male domination has been guaranteed.

In many aspects of their culture, the Mehinaku present an almost idyllic society. Families show affection, initiations involve minimal brutality, tribal rivalries are resolved through wrestling matches rather than war. Less idyllic is their organization of work on the basis of gender, with men estimated to spend three and a half hours a day in productive labour, compared to women's seven to nine hours (Gregor 1986, p. 24). It is interesting to compare these estimates with those of Héritier-Augé, who argues (1989, p. 298) that in hunter-gatherer societies, women 'occasionally' contribute more than seventy percent of food supplies though 'the real prestige accrues to the role of hunter.' But however unequal this gendered division of labour may be, it is accepted by Mehinaku women, among whom work is communal and even eroticized (Gregor 1986, pp.83–4).

Most idyllic of all is Mehinaku sexuality. The Mehinaku have a playfully libertine attitude toward couples meeting each other in the bushes, where most of the sexual activity seems to take place (the men and women sleeping separately for the most part). This libertine attitude still operates within some boundaries of verbal discretion so Gregor could not gather precise data, but his estimate is that during the period of his field work, 'the thirty-seven adults were conducting approximately 88 extramarital affairs' (1986, p. 35). Thus when we turn to Mehinaku male violence, a sexual frustration hypothesis hardly seems appropriate. Consensual sex is simply too available.

The darker side of Mehinaku life is the use of sexuality as a method of male domination. The sexual division of the social order is sustained not only by traditional tales, rituals, and exercises in folklore; it is sustained explicitly by gang rapes. The rapes are infrequent, but their possibility is a constant topic of communal gossip and fear of rape is omnipresent in women's nightmares. Their infrequency does not diminish their importance but may, on the contrary, increase their impact.

In the men's house, which women cannot enter, there are kept the sacred flutes, which women are not allowed to see. On certain occasions the flutes are taken out into the main village square and played. The occasions are known in advance, and part of the ritual is for women to hide in their huts. Should a woman happen into the village and see the flutes, she is dragged into the bush and raped. The horror of this rape is threefold. Although they go about naked, the Mehinaku women walk and sit so that the labia are kept out of sight. Part of the rape is the display of the women's genitals to the men. Second, the

Mehinaku, for all their sexual liaisons, consider sexual fluids degrading, and the rape victim is smeared with semen. Third, some men with whom sexual relations would be taboo due to incest or other prohibitions participate in the rape. 'In the distorted logic of rape, however, the shame is that woman's, and somehow she must live with it' (Gregor 1986, p. 103). After the rape the woman takes a ritual bath and is reintegrated into the group, but as Gregor writes, the shame remains.

Again, rape is not that frequent, but frequency hardly matters. What is more important is selectivity. The men can choose to ignore some women who accidently see the flutes, or they may entrap others. Thus rape is a constant background to other interactions. Male wrestling, on the one hand a non-violent form of dispute resolution, is also practised in a milieu of sexual innuendo. This innuendo is not only homoerotic, but also frames the wrestling as a display of ultimate male power. Thus what Gregor calls 'phallic aggression' pervades Mehinaku life.

The Freikorps soldiers are, significantly, not rapists. They take pleasure in flogging women, even to death, but rape would have been 'defilement' (see Theweleit 1987, p. 421 for the Freikorps horror of contact with women). A temporary seduction (1987, pp. 184–7) can only be rectified by the execution of the offending woman. To rape the woman would be to give them a victory, since their evil is precisely to incite male desire. Instead of being raped, women must be annihilated. Theweleit (1987, p. 180) quotes a Freikorps novel: 'With their screams and filthy giggling, vulgar women excite men's urges. Let our revulsion flow into a single river of destruction. A destruction which will be incomplete if it does not also trample their hearts and souls.'

Theweleit's conclusions are diffused throughout his work and difficult to summarize without rehearsing more of his theoretical sources than space permits. The following points can be made, and then briefly related to a contemporary example, lest the phenomenon of the Freikorps, like that of the Mehinaku, be considered too exotic to be of present relevance.

The Mehinaku example, where rape is clearly an act of domination through violence, without reference to sexual desire, complements the Freikorps who abjure rape in favor of beating and murder. What is involved in both is what Theweleit (1987, p. 370) calls 'the persistence of female sacrifice.' The need for this sacrifice has been suggested above: someone has to die so that someone else can live (Theweleit 1987, p. 209). The female is constructed as other, from the nether regions; it is she (like homosexuals) who remains human 'even below' (1987, p. 399), which is to say she is human (and worth killing) even in a sexual position in which the male would be defiled and she is therefore also subhuman (thus being legitimate to kill). What defiles the soldier male is the body's fear of its dissolution into the mass, the flood, the slippery fluids which are woman. 'The soldier male's most intense fear is his fear of dissolution' (Theweleit 1989, p. 40) or of 'total annihilation and dismemberment' (1987, p. 205).

Ultimately the soldier male's hatred is of life itself, as productive and contingent. 'The monumentality of fascism,' Theweleit writes (1987, p. 218), 'would seem to be a safety mechanism against the bewildering multiplicity of the living. The more lifeless, regimented, and monumental reality appears to be, the more secure the men feel. The danger is being alive itself.' And those who most fear being alive make the best soldiers.

The ultimate question for Theweleit would seem to be the source of the lack which motivates domination. Here he rejects classical psychoanalytic explanations making Oedipal conflicts central and opts instead for a social explanation, based generally on the work of Deleuze and Guattari (1983). The contrast of the two perspectives is summarized as follows: 'And so, the story doesn't go; because he couldn't take possession of the mother, he subjugated the Earth to himself (Freud). It goes: because he wasn't allowed to use the Earth and produce, he went *back* to his mother. In this scheme of things, "incestuous desire" is not primary desire at all, but a form that Desire assumes because of the repression to which it is subject in society' (1987, p. 213).

Another telling of the story involves the society instituting within the body the dark territories referred to above. Theweleit (1987, p. 414) gives the biblical story of Adam and Eve a kind of post-Gnostic retelling as 'a failed revolution [told] from the victor's standpoint. For attempting to put into practice their slogan "Our bodies belong to us," the rebels were sentenced to a life of forced labor in the sweat of their brows. "Your bodies belong to your ruler!" was the response.' The 'prerequisite . . . for ideological assault' is to install a condition of lack in bodies. 'Installing dark territories, sources of terror and anxiety, in and on people's own bodies and the bodies of those they desired' creates the 'fear and uncertainty, of people's feeling that there were many places within themselves that no one could enter – neither they themselves, nor anyone else. Those were the territories occupied by the gods, the police, laws, Medusas, and other monsters' (1987, p. 415).

A brief contemporary observation may stifle any optimistic sense that these struggles lie behind us; rather they lie ahead. At present, those who most loudly dare to proclaim 'Our bodies belong to us!' are women who favor a position of choice on the issue of abortion. They do not favor abortion, only choice; the woman's body belongs to her and to her alone. Those who oppose them, rejecting choice, are notable in several respects. If not exclusively male, they seem exclusively male led, at least in Canada. A far more specific observation is that anti-choice demonstrators identify themselves by carrying signs with pictures of aborted fetuses on them. Some live fetuses are shown, but the placard image of choice (for anti-choice) are predominantly dead fetuses. Their fascination – to call it fetishism is underdetermined by observation – with these pictures suggests two issues elucidated by Theweleit.

First, those who call themselves 'pro-life' choose to present themselves not with images of living children (presumably the best advertisement for not aborting), but with images which reduce life to 'pulp' or 'bloody mass.' Choice, of course, is an acceptance of contingency; anti-choice defends itself against 'the bewildering multiplicity of the living.'

Second, these pictures, whether of living or aborted fetuses, isolate the fetus from the womb in which it exists. The woman, through whose labour the baby is produced (see O'Brien 1989) is literally out of the picture. Male appropriation of female fertility is nothing new (see Héritier-Augé 1989, p. 279). Theweleit presents a Nazi text typical of their ideology of making birth masculine: 'It (nationalism) is more than just one idea among others. . . . It is the surest route to the material being that gives birth to new forms in every century. And we have seen that there are still men who can create after the fashion of the warrior.' As Theweleit (1989, p. 88) glosses the passage, 'what is excluded from procreation is femininity; over and above this, there is an absence of any process of fertilization. Men create the future, the Führer, power, and the *Reich* – totalities . . .' (1989, p. 88). Such thinking represents what Mary O'Brien calls 'the tyranny of the abstract' (1989, p. 45 ff.) and the critique of such thinking must be a fundamental task of the sociology of the body.

The end of the feminist pro-choice movement may be the end of all failed revolutions since Adam and Eve tried to claim control of their own bodies. One version of this end is depicted in Margaret Atwood's dystopian novel *The Handmaid's Tale* (1985).

It may be that the abortion issue is, as O'Brien describes it, 'a clash between two opposing abstractions, the emptied perceptions of Right and an equally empty ideology of pure life' (1989, p. 28). She argues instead that the real issue, from which abortion 'deflects our attention,' is reproductive technology as male control of reproduction (1989, pp. 30–1). What is abrogated by turning living birth into technology is the female body. 'In their birthing potential,' O'Brien writes (1989, p. 28), 'women unify nature and history in a way not accessible to masculine experience.' The claim to unify nature and history (within the abstraction of 'nationalism') is precisely what underlies the Nazi appropriation of birth as male, quoted above. Whether abortion choice or reproductive technology, the capacity of the body to claim itself for itself remains the issue.

Why is domination so exclusively a style of the male body? If lack is, as Theweleit claims, socially instituted, why do women not adopt the warrior Freikorps style? Answers will continue to be suggested; here is Héritier-Augé (1989, p. 298) making the best argument I have found: 'What man values in man, then, is no doubt his ability to bleed, to risk his life, to take that of others, by his own free will; the woman "sees" her blood flowing from her body . . . and she produces life without necessarily wanting to do so or being able to prevent it. In her body she periodically experiences, for a time that has a beginning and an end, changes of which she is not the mistress, and which she cannot prevent. It is in this relation to blood that we may perhaps find the fundamental impetus for all the symbolic elaboration, at the outset, on the relations between the sexes.' From this observation it would be possible to begin the whole argument over again: from the experience of blood comes a different response to contingency, a different form of self-relatedness, a different alignment of desire, a different construction of the dyad.

The last, sad word on domination can be given to one of the Freikorps writers, pronouncing his own epigram and epitaph: 'Only now do we recognize how little at home we are within ourselves' (quoted by Theweleit 1987, p. 243).

The Communicative Body

The disciplined, mirroring, and dominating bodies could be discussed on a level of empirical description. The communicative body is less a reality than a praxis. I seek not ideal types of the communicative body, but rather to idealize approximations of that which is itself an ideal. Thus in the present discussion this chapter moves in the direction of the ethics of the body suggested by Feher.

To evoke the other styles of body usage ideal typical representatives were readily available: the ascetic holy woman, the consumer or the warrior. Locating the communicative body as a social type is more difficult. It would be possible to look back historically; Mikhail Bakhtin's (1984) Rabelaisian bodies could serve as types of the communicative body. I choose instead to look forward and search for the emergence of the communicative body in the aesthetic practices of dance and performance and the caring practices of medicine. The essential quality of the communicative body is that it is a body *in process* of creating itself. Theory cannot describe such a body, nor can it prescribe it. The task is rather to bring together fragments of its emergence.

The dimensions of the communicative body should be familiar by now. What counts is how the value of each changes in their reconfiguration. The body's contingency is no longer its problem but its possibility. Héritier-Augé, in the passage quoted above (1989, p. 298), connects women's (re)production with the contingency of their bodies: 'she produces life without necessarily wanting to do so or being able to prevent it.' The woman can neither prevent nor be the mistress of her periodicity. Thus women's embodiment can teach them to live with contingency, to make it their potential (as opposed to a male ideology which calls it a 'curse'). Male sexuality may be no less contingent (although the technology of penile implants, rendering erections utterly predictable, flourishes), but as many have observed, the erection is centred on its own desire. Woman's contingency links her to another who might be: as lover or child, mother or daughter. The contingency of male sexuality initially presents itself as monadic; that of female sexuality as dyadic.

It is when contingency and dyadic other-relatedness intersect with a desire which is producing and a self-relatedness which is associated that dyadic relations need no longer be dominated and contingency is no longer responded to as threatening. Dyadic contingency becomes the body's potential to realize itself diffusely. Desire is producing, but unlike the mirroring body, the communicative body's desire is for dyadic expression, not monadic consumption. It produces itself not as a surface mirroring all around it, but as an expressiveness recreating a world of which it is part. Whether it produces joy, sorrow, or anger, it uses itself to express these. This expression takes the form of dyadic sharing. In the further contingency of this sharing, the body has the potential for more diffuse realization. Diffusion is no longer the threat of dissolution but the various possibilities of pleasure and expression.

The body's association with itself is no longer a mirroring, but is a realization. What is realized is simply the body itself, producing itself, recursively, through the variations of a life which is no longer appropriated by institutions and discourses but is now the body's own. The body continues to be formed among institutions and discourses, but these are now media for its expression. For the communicative body institutions and discourses now enable more than they constrain, while in the other body styles the opposite balance prevailed.

Dance appealed to me as one site at which communicative bodies might be found. Dance is producing in its expressiveness, and the dancer must be associated with her or his body. Dance evolves through the contingency of the body (see Levin 1985, p. 360, n.16), this contingency being dance's source of change and inspiration. Most important, dance is communal. Dyadic relation with others who join in the dance implies an associatedness which goes beyond one's own body and extends to the body of the other(s). Finally dance may be no more a metaphor for the sexual joining of bodies than sex may be a metaphor for dance.

In Judith Lynne Hanna's *Dance, Sex and Gender* (1988), however, bodies may or may not be communicative. We can find an ideal of dance, but then we are plunged back into a reality in which this ideal is rarely reached. The book tells less than might be useful about what it feels like to be dancing the dances Hanna describes. Her method is content analysis of scenarios, not interviews with performers. But the advantage is that she tells a good deal about the institutional gender constraints within which the discourse of dance is formulated.

Hanna describes dance as focussing 'awareness on the body' in order to be 'both expressive and communicative' (1988, p. 13). In one of the few bits of interview data, she quotes a member of an all-male (straight and gay) dance workshop speaking of dance's ability to produce self-realization in its expressiveness: 'We struggle to share our vulnerabilities as well as our strengths.' This could be fairly standard 'sensitivity group' talk, except that in its context it is embodied. The vulnerabilities and strengths are, in the first instance, physical ones of bodies performing at their own and each others' limits. Thus the dyadic nature of dance is synergistic. Another dancer says, 'The impact of several men dancing in a group can be overwhelming: our size, our smell, our presence . . .' (1988, p. 138).

But as in the consideration of the Mehinaku, the idyll is short lived. Hanna (1988, p. 128) quotes a dance insider referring to the 'enforced infantilism' of dancers in ballet schools. 'Despite notable exceptions,' Hanna writes (1988, p. 246), '*backstage*, males tend to be managers of companies and theatres, artistic directors, and choreographers who determine the rules, hierarchical chains of command . . . and general working conditions' (see also 1988, p. 121). Although Hanna continues to maintain that dance can be an occasion for challenging gender hierarchies, the institutional pattern she reports is that of men pushing out women either by achieving a greater celebrity as performers (1988, p. 144 ff.) or by taking over companies founded by women (1988, pp. 127–8).

At its worst, dance is the imposition of male fantasies on the female body. Hanna (1988, p. 128) quotes the autobiography of the ballerina Gelsey Kirkland, writing of the great George Balanchine: 'He halted class and approached me for a kind of physical inspection. With his knuckles, he thumped on my sternum and down my rib cage clucking his tongue and remarking, "Must see the bones." . . . He did not merely say, "Eat less," He said repeatedly, "Eat nothing."' Other reports confirm that Balanchine 'expected his dancers to treat him like God' (1988, p. 128), but this attitude hardly distinguished him from other choreographers.

Nor, finally, does Hanna encourage us to think of dance's institutional sexism as an aberration of capitalism. She quotes anthropological reports of traditional dancing which also has the function of affirming 'the sharp line of demarcation between men and women and the avowed inferiority of the latter' (1988, p. 51, see also 85). If there is an emerging ideal of a communicative body in dance, it is found not by going backward toward traditional dance, but by going forward to postmodern dance. Hanna (1988, p. 134) quotes the dancer Eleanor Luger expressing the communicative body potential she finds in dance: 'What I have experienced in my own dancing, is trying to tie up movement with one's own image as a woman.' The potential for this kind of experience seems far more richly realized as dance has evolved into performance art.

Those who are thoroughly depressed by Theweleit, and find too little comfort in Hanna, can turn to Henry Sayre's *The Object of Performance* (1989) for a book which matches Theweleit in theoretical sophistication and approaches him in richness of empirical materials. Students of the body will find Sayre opens up postmodern art as an area of investigation, and through his empirical materials provokes a rereading of postmodern theorists such as Derrida and Deleuze for their relevance to the body. The basic story is this: while men have taken over conventional dance to reap its financial benefits, women have moved into performance art as a medium in which they can achieve greater autonomy and express feminist concerns which remain suppressed in institutional dance (see Hanna 1988, pp. 139–40 for the denial of lesbianism in dance, even as gay dancers were using dance to give artistic expression to their sexual orientation).

The category of performance artist, despite the commercial success of Laurie Anderson, remains marginalized and even suppressed. Carolee Schneemann writes in her piece *Interior Scroll*: 'he told me he had lived with/ a "sculptress" I asked does/ that make me a "filmmakress?"/ Oh no he said we think of you/ as a dancer' (quoted in Sayre 1989, pp. 66 and 90). Sayre describes performances such as *Interior Scroll* in far more detail than I am able to, and with pictures. To fragment the performances further by suggesting details would only trivialize them. Moreover, my objective is not aesthetic criticism but sociology. With whatever aesthetic consequences, performance effaces the boundary between art and social theory. What gives this 'performance social theory' its power is that the performer enacts it on the site of her body. Thus 'praxis,' which has become a hollow word in its overgeneralization, takes on new meaning as the embodiment of theory in communal performance.

The lines quoted above from *Interior Scroll* are about the power of men to keep women in subordinate categories of embodiment. Of the performance works described by Sayre, Schneemann's stand out as the praxis most relevant to the ideal of the communicative body. Quoting from her own writing, Sayre (1989, pp. 96–7) describes Schneemann's work '*Eye Body* was a conscious attempt on her part to use her body not as an object but "as a primal, archaic force,"' an almost pure vernacular expression. She felt compelled, she says, 'to "conceive" of my body in manifold aspects which had eluded culture around me.' A partial gloss on this praxis is provided in Sayre's comment (1989, p. 81) on the writer Kathy Acker. 'It is as if, suddenly, something seems to be writing itself through Acker. She becomes a *medium*, a voice through which culture speaks, and not a particularly attractive culture at that. Acker's work operates along the same edge which defines the ambiguous zone of pornography itself, a zone that threatens and undermines society at the same time that it is the fullest expression of society's unspoken desires.'

In the praxis of Schneemann's performances, she self-consciously uses her body as a medium to reflect this 'not particularly attractive culture' which women find their bodies formulated (see Kirkland's quotation, above) to reflect. By purposefully taking this reflection on herself, making herself the subject of all that society does to women's bodies, she theorizes resistance and bodily freedom. The intentionality of her performance deconstructs an ideology of the female body which only works so long as it is unspoken and imposed. Or so she seeks to do. Necessarily she also puts herself in 'the ambiguous zone of pornography itself.' Sayre writes (1989, p. 170): 'In 1974 she defended her use of the naked body in her work by saying that she intended "to break into the taboos against the vitality of the naked body in movement, to eroticize my guilt-ridden culture and further to confound this culture's sexual rigidities." She wonders, near the end of *Fresh Blood*, "IF BLOOD WERE A

MENTAL PRODUCT WOULD IT BE ACCEPTABLE?"'
(capitals in original). In these words we have the feminist critique
of male abstraction.

Fresh Blood is of particular present interest because
Schneemann's description of her intent in that piece echoes so
literally the essay quoted above by Héritier-Augé (1989, p. 298),
although any reciprocal knowledge of the two works is unlikely.
Fresh Blood 'is about the difference between "reactive male
mythologies" in which "men wound each other" to spill blood,
"blood revenge, blood lust, bad blood between them, blood
brothers" and the "blood nourishment" of the female, "the
proportionate periodicity of menstrual blood"' (Sayre 1989,
p. 169).

What emerges is nothing less than a feminist praxis of the
body: an embodied theory of embodiment. Again from *Fresh
Blood*: 'Early on I felt that the mind was subject to the dynamics
of its body. The body activating pulse [in painting] of eye and
stroke, the mark signifying event transferred from "actual"
space to constructed space [on the canvas]. And that it was
essential to dance, to exercise before going to paint in order *to
see better*' (quoted in Sayre 1989, p. 170). Just as Héritier-Augé
can gloss the earlier passage as being about the male tendency to
domination, so this passage could be glossed by the philosophical
work on mind/body connection presented by Mark Johnson
(1987) and George Lakoff (1987). A non-feminist version of the
same insight is found in papers by Donald Levine (1984, and ch.
8, this volume) on Aikido training as an aspect of liberal arts
education. Exercise and thought recursively create the possibility
for each other, and either without the other is deprived.

What makes these glosses inadequate (important as they are in
their own terms) is what makes Schneemann's work a praxis,
which is its distinctively feminist element of anger. Society is not
merely unattractive, it is deformative to women's bodies. As any
woman knows, and men are beginning to realize, Kirkland's
quotation describing her treatment by Balanchine could be
reproduced any number of times in any setting. Schneemann is
angry on a number of levels, and that is the dynamic of her
praxis. Male writing on the body, including my own, always falls
flat. Between disgust (at the Freikorps, for example) and utopian
promise, praxis remains missing because the only praxis males

can conceive of involves 'spilling blood.' But the only praxis of the body must be embodied. By embodying her anger in her art and making it a performance, Schneemann keeps her praxis from becoming a will to domination, which is why something new may come out of it. Her performance mediates play and anger, the hurt and joy of her woman's body. At least in the ideal of such a performance – and possibly Sayre's book is better than the real thing, which is a distinctly postmodern possibility – the communicative body is realized.

As Sayre describes performance art pieces, they seem to have a common theme of the body seeking to break out of codes in which it cannot express itself and find self-expression in a code of its own invention. That this code can only have the duration of the piece may create some of the aesthetic tension. This process is not unlike illness, although that may be my own projection on performance art. In illness also, the body finds itself progressively unable to express in conventional codes. Sometimes, with the right kind of support, it creates a new code, but this code too may have a terminal duration.

In his autobiography *The Body Silent*, the anthropologist Robert Murphy describes the loss of his capacity to express through his body. Murphy was growing increasingly paralyzed as the result of a benign tumor in his spinal cord. 'The quadriplegic's body can no longer speak a "silent language" in the expression of emotions or concepts too elusive for ordinary speech, for the delicate feedback loops between thought and movement have been broken. Proximity, gesture, and body-set have been muted, and the body's ability to articulate thought has been stilled' (Murphy 1987, p. 101). Thought, no longer capable of being embodied, turns inward as pure cognition: '. . . the thinking activity of the brain cannot be dissolved into motion, and the mind can no longer be lost in an internal dialogue with physical movement. . . . My thoughts and sense of being alive have been driven back into my brain, where I now reside' (1987, p. 102).

More, perhaps, than he realizes, this disembodiment of his thoughts may affect Murphy's relationships to others. He describes his relationship to his wife and caregiver as becoming mediated by his physical dependency, which generates a positive feedback loop of mutual annoyance: 'Since I know she is overburdened, I generally hesitate to ask for things and feel slightly guilty about bothering her – a guilt that becomes added to that caused by my damaged body. As a result, I am especially sensitive to the tone of her response. . . . Does that slight inflection say, "What in hell does he want from me now?" . . . In my disabled mindset . . . I pick up the right cues but I alter and magnify them, interpreting a small note of fatigue as major resentment. . . . My voice often anticipates a possibly negative reaction, and, by so doing, sometimes begets it' (Murphy 1987, pp. 213–14). The end result is a relationship of which, at its worst, Murphy writes (1987, p. 199), 'we are both held in thrall by my condition – we are each other's captives.'

The Freikorps soldiers feared their own dissoluton as a fantasy; Murphy lives with his as a reality. 'Paralysis,' he writes (1987, p. 223), 'engages its victims directly in the battle against dissolution.' But Murphy's response is fundamentally different from that of the dominating body. He is able to mourn the 'estrangement from others, from one's own body, and ultimately from one's self' (1987, p. 223). In his writing he is able to take a meta-position to his dissolution and create new forms of relatedness, these perhaps more embodied than he realizes. Having lost one level of expressiveness, he creates another.

This same loss of the capacity for embodied expressiveness is described by Irving Zola, a sociologist partially paralyzed as a result of polio compounded by an auto accident. In *Missing Pieces* (1982) Zola describes a week he spent in a Dutch residential facility, the village of Het Dorp. To participate in the life of Het Dorp, Zola removes his leg braces, with which he can walk, and takes up life in a wheelchair. He is not passing as a resident but he does assume their physical level. In the community of his fellow disabled Zola begins to recollect his own life, but forging a narrative is difficult. 'I remember, however, but fragments of a story, for there is no special world of the handicapped, and herein lies another major problem in telling the story. There are several reasons for this lack' (1982, p. 206). My present interest is less in these reasons than in the lack, which is not only physical but narrative as well.

Zola's time in Het Dorp is spent exchanging stories with the other residents about their lives. Several years later, back in his academic position in Boston, these stories have their effect: 'Working more and more with people who had disabilities, one day I finally recognized that the pain I often felt was not merely empathy for their situation, but was really part of my own' (1982, p. 241). The communal dialogues at Het Dorp, continued in groups in Boston, engage Zola in 'a continuing effort to reclaim what I had lost' (1982, p. 214), and as in Murphy's case, the writing of a book provides the performative occasion for this reclamation.

Both their stories are about living in the fundamental conditions of the ill body: lack, dissociation, contingency, and monadic self-relatedness. It is not a condition which fits my diagram (Figure 2.1), thus demonstrating that any theory must have its residual categories. But it is being residual to society, not to theory, which troubles Murphy and Zola. Their writing is a producing desire for recognition, a remedy to lack. There are, then, two kinds of ill: those who remain in this condition of being residual to society and captives of their condition, and those who achieve interpersonal recognition, through some combination of their own efforts and the care of others.

Recognition is the medium of the communicative body. The performance artist seeks not just the attendance of an audience but their recognition. In the same mode, the ill want not only to be cared for in their physical needs, but to be recognized in their condition, or, for this condition to be recognized as fully human. One of the essential lessons of psychiatrist and anthropologist Arthur Kleinman's *The Illness Narratives* is that a central task of the physician, perhaps *the* central task, is to assist the ill person in creating, out of illness, a narrative. This narrative must be shared with others, at minimum with the physician. Its objective is to render coherent the contingency and lack involved in illness.

Kleinman is evocative of the ill person's experience of contingency and lack in her or his body: 'It menaces. It erupts. It is out of control. One damned thing follows another. . . . The fidelity of our bodies is so basic that we never think of it – it is the certain grounds of our daily experience. Chronic illness is a betrayal of that fundamental trust. We feel under siege: untrusting, resentful of uncertainty, lost. Life becomes a working out of sentiments that follow closely from this corporeal betrayal: confusion, shock, anger, jealousy, despair' (1988, pp. 44–5).

However the physician responds to the corporeal disease, what is fundamental to the response to illness is what Kleinman calls the 'process of narratization' in which the ill person is allowed and encouraged to turn this 'it' which imposes itself on his or her life into a story which he or she tells. 'Telling this tale is of great significance. . . . For the care giver what is important is to witness a life story, to validate its interpretation, and to affirm its value. Most of us figure out our own thoughts by speaking them to the persons whose reactions are as important as our own' (1988, p. 50). Thus Kleinman prescribes as clinical practice what Murphy and Zola discover in their texts. When illness is told, its lack becomes producing, and as desire becomes producing, contingency becomes possibility.

The ill body has its own communicative potential, to which Kleinman may be the most attentive of clinicians and theorists. 'For the seriously ill,' he writes (1988, p. 55), 'insight can be the result of an often grim, though occasionally luminous, lived wisdom of the body in pain and the mind troubled.' This insight can then become communal: 'For family members and practitioners, moral insight can emerge from the felt experience of sympathy and empathy. It is this particular sense that I take to be the inner moral meaning of chronic illness and care.'

The strongest clinical example of this power of narratization may be a transcribed dialogue Kleinman presents between a young man dying of cancer, Gordon Stuart, and the family physician helping him to die at home as he wished. The physician summarized his death: 'He was no less angry, not accepting in the end, but he kept his sense of irony, his way with words. He seemed to grow into whom he wanted to be. His death confirmed his life' (quoted in Kleinman, 1988, p. 149). If the communicative body is the body in the process of creating itself, the physician's phrase, 'He seemed to grow into whom he wanted to be,' describes that process. Instead of his anger leading to violence (often, in the case of the ill, against the self), it remained expressive.

Not only does the ill body have the potential to become communicative in new ways, the caregiver too can realize her or his body in a new relation to the other. Kleinman writes of care in terms which are evocative of the ideal of religious experience: 'a willingness to help bear the burden of the lived experience of suffering' (1988, p. 161). Against a medical system which, he clearly recognizes, reproduces care as a commodity (see 1988, pp. 258, 265), Kleinman presents a detailed format for the physician or other caregiver to develop a 'mini-ethnography' (1988,

p. 230 ff.). What it amounts to is a technique to facilitate the skill of eliciting narratives.

Narratives are essential not only to the coherence of our own bodies and lives. They are no less essential to the mutual recognition on which relations with others are grounded (for the fullest phenomenological explication, see the writings of David Carr 1986a, 1986b). Among the ill, as among performance artists, narratives are fundamentally embodied. Of his transcription of the dialogue between Gordon Stuart and his physician, Kleinman (1988, p. 147) notes, 'Throughout the interview, Mr. Stuart is wracked by bouts of coughing. There is a rattling sound in his chest, and he wheezes. His voice is faint but clear. He breaks off, then begins anew. I've made no attempt to enter these resonant physical emblems of death in this selection from the transcript.' Kleinman's editorial decision was sound, but it must be remembered that the omitted 'resonant physical emblems' are what embody the narrative and give it its particular force. In the same sense of embodiment, the dancer who was quoted above discussing a group sharing vulnerabilities tells a narrative which could be mundane outside of the physical context of bodies being projected through space into one another's arms, trusting each other against threat of injury.

What communicative bodies are about is the capacity for recognition which is enhanced through the sharing of narratives which are fully embodied. What is shared is one body's sense of another's experience, primarily its vulnerability and suffering, but also its joy and creativity. It is when narratives are spoken from the experience of the body that they can be shared most readily. O'Brien's (1989) 'tyranny of the abstract' is the detachment of narrative from the body. The further narrative gets from the body of the teller, and the further the teller is from feeling at home in her or his body, the more dangerous that narrative becomes. Specifically, the more it becomes a language of appropriation. But this term takes us into our final consideration, which is how a sociology of the body can assist an ethics of the body.

The communicative body remains an ideal, elusive to descriptions, evoked only in idealizations. A line from the performance artist Eleanor Antin (quoted in Sayre 1989, p. 164) can serve as closing epigram: 'I'm learning. I know one when I see one. That's the first step. Rome wasn't built in a day.'

From Analytical Theory to Ethics

Devising analytical theory is not, at present, an activity which can be taken for granted as interesting or valid. A sympathetic critic of analytical theory writes, 'If sociological theory can be revitalized, it will require that we abandon the modernist project of providing analytical foundations, at least as a chief task of theory' (Seidman 1989, p. 636). Most sociologists would agree, although for a diversity of reasons. In the face of such opposition, why suggest an analytical theory as the basis of a sociology of the body?

The simple reason is that such a theory is proposed not as the 'chief task' for a sociology of the body, but only as a prerequisite necessary for the theorist's orientation to the mass of fragmented materials which the study of the body presents. Although I have presented my theory in quasi-Parsonian fashion (pattern variables resolving into a four-cell typology), the differences are more significant than the similarities. First, the 'pattern variables' are not dichotomous choices but continua. Second, and following this, the cells are ideal types which are analytically separable only in isolated moments of their existence in real time and space. Third, the culminating type, the communicative body, is more an idealization than an ideal type. Thus forth and most important, the typology is *not* designed to serve as a 'basis for continuing research.' Research has and will proceed well enough without an analytical theory. What we need theory for is to coalesce fragmentary research so that, in Feher's words (1989, p. 12), 'we can define more precisely the current boundaries of an ethics of the body.'

It is this goal of an ethics of the body which must inform a sociology of the body, just as the empirical findings of a sociology of the body are the only foundation on which an ethics can be based. For a sociology of the body, the body is not merely a substantive topic reference which categorizes an otherwise disparate collection of studies. Rather the body is both the scandal of social theory and its *aporia*, 'a problem or difficulty arising from an awareness of opposing or incompatible views on the same theoretic matter . . . giving rise to systematic doubt' (Webster's *Third International*). The scandal is that despite the incompatible views members of society hold on the body, and the violences resulting from those incompatibilities, there has been so little systematic doubt raised by social theorists about how bodies are to be sustained and enhanced in society.

The sociology of the body argues for the reconceptualization of social theory. The grounding of theory must be the body's consciousness of itself, and this grounding has been the objective of this chapter. Only on this grounding can theory put selves into bodies and bodies into society. At the level of society, the fundamental reorientation of perspective for a sociology of the body is that *there is no 'social order' problem*. To think of 'society' having a 'social order' problem is more tyranny of the abstract. Bodies certainly have problems among other bodies, but the point is to hold onto the fundamental embodiment of those problems rather than allowing the problems to be abstracted from the needs, pains and desires of bodies.

What exist are bodies, which have their own internal contingencies and live in an environment which is more contingent still in its effect on them. When bodies encounter each other, there is a problem of aligning individual contingencies and coping with new mutual contingencies which arise in the interaction. This is a problem of order, but that word suddenly places us looking down on bodies, instead of experiencing what are their own problems of contingency and alignment. I prefer instead to think of the problems as those of communication. Not the social 'ordering' of bodies, but individual bodies 'coming to terms' with each other is the foundational topic (see Habermas 1986, 1987, though the complementarities with that usage of communication have yet to be specified).

Although I have theorized discourses and institutions only in the barest terms, bodies are the foundation of both as well as their product. Discourses exist and are reproduced only through bodies and their techniques. Part of the enormous contribution of George Lakoff (1987) and Mark Johnson (1987) (see also Lakoff and Johnson 1980) is to put language back into the body, and to compel us to understand speech as embodied. Institutions are only formed through the labor of bodies, and are only reproduced through this labor. These bodies are real, lived experiences, and institutions cannot be understood apart from those experiences. Lakoff's and Johnson's accomplishment with regard to speech may find its closest analogue in the sociology of institutions in Goffman (1961), though focussing analysis on the body is not the declared principle of that text.

If the body is the subject of sociology, theory becomes possible insofar as the theorist shares that embodiment. A sociology taking its orientation from the embodiment of its practitioners as well as that of its 'subjects' can make its epigram the line of the performance artist Martha Rosler, 'This is a work about how to think about yourself' (quoted in Sayre 1989, p. 83). And so all our sociological works should be, lest we fall in abstraction. The best safeguard for theory is that offered by Theweleit (1987, p. 219): 'The science of human beings should learn to renounce such [abstract] distinctions and learn to introduce others, for instance, distinctions based on modes of production or degrees of aliveness. "Living," "dying," and "killing" are distinctions that are more adequate to reality, easier to make, and more useful (but more dangerous).'

My ranting against abstraction hardly means that the sociology of the body can avoid complexity. We are not in bodies simply, as is illustrated by the complex embodied texts of performance artists and the equally complex embodied texts of medieval holy women (who may be less the anorexics of their day, as Bell [1985] suggests, and more the performance artists of their time). Here is a complex text: 'I am in my body, as other people are in their cars,' says Laurie Anderson (quoted in Sayre 1989, p. 150), suggesting the further strange loops which the body in consumer culture presents. But for all the complexity of her text, it, like Schneemann's and Theweleit's and Kleinman's, retains the body as its fundamental point of reference. What grounds the textual complexity are such realities as suffering and the joy of movement. Just as anger is no impediment to communication, so complexity is no justification for becoming abstracted from the body.

As the sociology of the body seeks to inform an ethics of the body, the research suggests two substantive issues as paramount. These are contingency and appropriation.

The issue of contingency is whether people who have taken places in the institutions they create can tolerate what Theweleit calls the bewildering diversity of life. Simply reading the body literature is an exercise in self-criticism of the routinization of one's habitus. I found myself forced to recognize my own boundaries of pollution, of taste and distinction (in Bourdieu's terms), and of my own slipping into hyperreality, which is the most troubling of all.

The boundary of the hyperreal is the point at which my body exists only in images of it, these images being based only on other images. In hyperreality the body fades into its own simulation, which is to say, into a cognitive dream of embodied perfection. The technology of hyperreality is coming (see Brand 1987), and a Luddite response is wholly inappropriate. But we must also see the danger of a new domination. As in the old domination, the issue remains the tolerance for contingency. In the perfection of the simulation, that which does not fit the image must be disallowed, or in Baudrillard's language (1988a, p. 124), 'ex-terminated.' The danger of hyperreality is the denial of the contingency of the lived body; this denial is the will to exterminate.

The boredom and occasional tastelessness of performance art have the purpose of posing the question of how diffusely we can allow our embodied selves to be realized. Beyond that is a more fundamental issue: how much of bodies can we tolerate? Can I take off my body's armor, deconstruct the images in which I have constructed my body, and enter, however provisionally, a different code which is an embodied anti-discourse, even as it discourses? Illness poses much the same question in more direct terms: can I allow myself to recognize the suffering of the other? Can I accept what that other's bodily contingencies have imposed on it as being possibilities also for my own body? Can I find terms of shared humanity with an other (which may be the otherness of my own ill body) who threatens my healthy image of myself and my fundamental need to trust this health as my body's 'natural' condition? These are the basic ethical questions of contingent embodiment. A contribution of theory may be to juxtapose settings which practitioners would regard as disparate. Performance art's use of high tech as embodied play might teach health workers how to remain focussed on an ill body which is increasingly absorbed into the hyperreality of medical high tech. Performance art can be read diffusely for its lesson on how to use technology, as it does, without becoming hyperreal. Theory can guide such a reading.

Appropriation has not been an explicit topic of this chapter until now, but it has always loomed in the background. Medieval holy women were resisting the appropriation of their bodies for purposes of commercial alliance through marriage and child production, though they did so at the cost of allowing their

bodies to be appropriated differently. Consumption is a willingness to be appropriated. The consumer thinks he or she appropriates the commodity, while it appropriates its consumer. The
dominating body seeks to appropriate everything, fascism being
world-historical appropriation. Only the communicative body
abjures appropriation, or such is its ideal.

Perhaps what is most alive in Marx, as articulated by Elaine
Scarry (1985), is his outrage at capitalism's appropriation of the
body. Capitalism first uses up the worker's body in her or his
labor and then appropriates the product of that labor. Alienation
lives, in production and in consumption. Techniques of appropriation do change, however much the process remains the same.
Much appropriation in the 'information age' takes place by
redesignating the products of embodied labor as 'technology,' a
word which immediately endows these products with a kind of
non-personal genesis.

'Reproductive technologies' is a term which ex-terminates the
woman through whose embodied labor (O'Brien 1989) that reproduction takes place. Relegated to being one aspect of a hyperreal
'technology,' the laboring woman is both denied and colonized.
My own university started an 'Office of Technology Transfer' for
marketing what they call 'intellectual property.' Thus embodied
creativity in intellectual labor becomes a 'technology,' the
'transfer' of which ex-terminates the source of production in the
body of the person. Computers facilitate the mystification of
'intellectual property' by the printed illusion that the work has
sprung directly from the circuitry (just as the ownership of the
means of production once mystified the labor which created the
product). As I write this my shoulders and neck grow stiff from
the posture which the labor imposes on my body and my eyes
want to close; these are the 'resonant physical emblems' which are
ex-terminated as embodied writing becomes 'information
technology' ready to be 'transferred.'

At the extreme the appropriation of whole bodies themselves
continues. In Canada during the summer (1989) in which this
chapter was written, the daily headlines told how the ex-lovers of
two women were awarded court injunctions preventing these
women from obtaining legal abortions. One injunction was finally
overturned only at the Supreme Court level (Daigle v. Tremblay).
For some weeks then, the country watched while a woman's body
was legally appropriated by the State; enjoined by a male,

contested by male lawyers before a predominantly male tribunal. As powerful as it was in itself, what happened to these women should also serve as a reminder of the other routine daily appropriations of men's and women's bodies in work places which continue unnoticed (Freund 1983; see also my comments on Hochschild 1983 in Frank 1990).

The most subtle appropriations are those in which, as Theweleit described it, dark territories are inscribed in the body, to which that body itself is denied entry. There remain, in bodies, 'territories occupied by the gods, the police, laws, Medusas, and other monsters' (Theweleit 1987, p. 415). The womb is only the most newsworthy of these territories. It is only the current site, though an eternally privileged one, on which the rebellion under the slogan 'Our bodies belong to us' opposes a colonizing despotism. Again, these colonizations are complex. Foucault (1978) showed us most clearly that despotism can wield the carrot of pleasure as readily as the stick of fear.

Men's bodies may be appropriated as well as women's, but appropriation is not gender neutral either. Women's bodies are appropriated more often and more completely. The appropriation of men's bodies may be equally violent, but there are differences we are only beginning to observe and can hardly articulate (see Messner 1988). These differences may be one source of bias in Foucault's relegation of domination to technologies of the self; perhaps, and only perhaps, it is more of a male construction to understand body violences as mediated by self-understandings.

The most significant problem with any general typology of the body is its guise of gender neutrality. At some point one theory does not fit all. A sociology of the body is not feminism, as I understand that term. Men cannot be feminists, which rests on an embodied understanding only women can share (see O'Brien 1989, pp. 27–8). But men do share embodiment with women, however differently. There can be a sociology of the body, although one of its on-going tasks will be to sort out gendered difference.

Ultimately there would be no ethics of the body, but rather all ethics would take the body as its fundamental point of departure. Thus also there would be no sociology of the body, but rather the fundamental embodiment of social action would ground all sociology. The reason is simple: only bodies suffer. Only by a studied concentration on the body can we bear adequate witness to this suffering. Only an ethics or a social science which witnesses suffering is worthy of our energies or attention.

The body exists between birth and death. It comes to be in order to cease to be. It is not an entity, but the process of its own being. To make a process observable we need fixed reference points, and so I have proposed an analytical theory. If that theory enhances our appreciation of the body's contingency, and helps us to recognize and eliminate appropriations of the body, then the theory too will have merged into the process.

Note

This chapter would not have been written without the suggestions and constructive criticism of Mike Featherstone and Bryan Turner. My thinking on matters of theory has been enhanced by Valerie Haines, whose last-minute reading of the manuscript improved it as much as the little time I gave her permitted. Catherine Foote has taught me what I know of process and practice; she also labored hard editing the final manuscript. My debts to David Carr and Dorothy Smith go beyond the few citations to their work, though they are free to disclaim responsibility. My thanks to all; distortions remain reflections of my embodiment, not theirs.

Partially Annotated Bibliography

This bibliography has been prepared as an aid to research and thus contains sources not mentioned in 'For a Sociology of the Body.' Some of these are given a brief annotation. Books discussed in Frank (1990) are not annotated, nor are anthologies. Articles from the three volumes of Feher, Naddaff, and Tazi, editors, *Fragments for a History of the Human Body, Part One, Part Two and Part Three*, are cited as *Fragments* One, Two and Three. Only those papers referred to above are given individual entries. Readers are also referred to Duden (1989) for a partially annotated bibliography (about 1,000 items) containing extensive non-English-language sources.

Alliez, Eric and Feher, Michel (1989) 'Reflections of a Soul', in *Fragments* Two.
Atwood, Margaret (1985) *The Handmaid's Tale*. Toronto: McClelland and Stewart.
Bakan, David (1968) *Disease, Pain & Suffering: Toward a Psychology of Suffering*. Boston: Beacon Press. The psychology of suffering considered from a spiritual perspective, including a major interpretation of the Book of Job.
Bakhtin, Mikhail (1984 [1965]) *Rabelais and His World*. Bloomington: Indiana University Press.
Banner, Lois W. (1983) *American Beauty*. Chicago: University of Chicago Press. A cultural history of American ideals of beauty and bodily perfection, with considerable material on the history of popular ideas of health; complements Green and Schwartz.
Barthes, Roland (1976) *Sade/Fourier/Loyola*. New York: Hill and Wang.

Barthes, Roland (1985) *The Grain of the Voice, Interviews 1962–1980*. New York: Hill and Wang.

Bataille, Georges (1984 [1962]) *Death and Sensuality*. Salem, New Hampshire: Ayer Company. A *locus classicus* of postmodernism, emphasizing transgression.

Baudrillard, Jean (1983) 'The Ecstasy of Communication', in Hal Foster (ed.), *The Anti-Aesthetic: Essays on Postmodern Culture*. Port Townsend, Washington: Bay Press.

Baudrillard, Jean (1988a) *Selected Writings*. Mark Poster (ed.). Stanford: Stanford University Press.

Baudrillard, Jean (1988b) *America*. London: Verso.

Beaune, Jean-Claude (1989) 'The Classical Age of Automata: An Impressionistic Survey from the Sixteenth to the Nineteenth Century', in *Fragments* One.

Bell, Rudolph M. (1985) *Holy Anorexia*. Chicago: University of Chicago Press.

Benhabib, Seyla and Cornell, Drucilla (eds) (1987) *Feminism as Critique*. Minneapolis: University of Minnesota Press.

Bologh, Rosalyn Wallace (1987) 'Max Weber on Erotic Love', in Sam Whimster and Scott Lash (eds), *Max Weber, Rationality and Modernity*. London: Allen and Unwin.

Boswell, John (1980) *Christianity, Social Tolerance, and Homosexuality: Gay People in Western Europe from the Beginning of the Christian Era to the Fourteenth Century*. Chicago: University of Chicago Press.

Bourdieu, Pierre (1977) *Outline of a Theory of Practice*. Cambridge: Cambridge University Press.

Bourdieu, Pierre (1978) 'Sport and Social Class', *Social Science Information*, 17(6): 819–40.

Bourdieu, Pierre (1984) *Distinction: A Social Critique of the Judgement of Taste*. Cambridge, MA: Harvard University Press.

Brand, Stewart (1987) *The Media Lab: Inventing the Future at MIT*. New York: Viking. A journalistic account of the people creating the post-postmodern cyborg body. Brand provides the specifics of Baudrillard's hyperreality.

Bynum, Caroline Walker (1987) *Holy Feast and Holy Fast: The Religious Significance of Food to Medieval Women*. Berkeley: University of California Press.

Bynum, Caroline Walker (1989) 'The Female Body and Religious Practice in the Later Middle Ages', in *Fragments* One.

Callwood, June (1986) *Twelve Weeks in Spring*. Toronto: Lester & Orpen Dennys. A first-person account of participation in a 'team' caring for a terminally ill woman, allowing her to die at home.

Callwood, June (1988) *Jim: A Life With AIDS*. Toronto: Lester & Orpen Dennys. Written from 'Jim's' notes, this account of AIDS centers on the body, rather than on politics.

Caplan, Pat (ed.) (1987) *The Cultural Construction of Sexuality*. London: Tavistock.

Carr, David (1986a) 'Narrative and the Real World: An Argument for Continuity', *History and Theory*, 25(2): 117–31.

Carr, David (1986b) *Time, Narrative, and History*. Bloomington: Indiana University Press.

Crimp, Donald (1988) 'AIDS: Cultural Analysis/Cultural Activism', *October*, 43:

3–16. An essay not only about AIDS but the construction of illness and bodies in general.

Deleuze, Giles and Guattari, Félix (1983) *Anti-Oedipus: Capitalism and Schizophrenia*. New York: Viking.

Douglas, Mary (1966) *Purity and Danger: An Analysis of Concepts of Pollution and Taboo*. London: Routledge and Kegan Paul.

Douglas, Mary (1973) *Natural Symbols*. New York: Vintage.

Duden, Barbara (1989) 'A Repertory of Body History', in *Fragments* Three.

Dupont, Florence (1989) 'The God-Emperor's Other Body', in *Fragments* Three.

Durkheim, Emile (1978 [1906]) 'Divorce by Mutual Consent', in Mark Traugott (ed.), *Emile Durkheim: On Institutional Analysis*. Chicago: University of Chicago Press.

Duverger, Christian (1989) 'The Meaning of Sacrifice', in *Fragments* Three.

Elias, Norbert (1978 [1939]) *The Civilizing Process, Volume 1. The History of Manners*. New York: Urizen.

Elvin, Mark (1989) 'Tales of *Shen* and *Xin*: Body-Person and Heart-Mind in China during the Last 150 Years', in *Fragments* Three.

Featherstone, Mike (1982) 'The Body in Consumer Culture', *Theory, Culture & Society*, 1(2): 18–33 (reprinted in this volume).

Featherstone, Mike (1987) 'Leisure, Symbolic Power, and the Life Course', in J. Horne et al. (eds.), *Leisure, Sport and Social Relations*. Sociological Review Monograph 33.

Featherstone, Mike (1989) 'Postmodernism, Cultural Change and Social Practice', in D. Kellner (ed.), *Postmodernism/Jameson/Critique*. Washington: Maisonneuve Press.

Featherstone, Mike and Mike Hepworth (1989) 'Ageing and Old Age: Reflections on the Postmodern Life Course', in B. Bytheway et al., *Becoming and Being Old*. London: Sage.

Feher, Michel (1989) 'Introduction', in *Fragments* One.

Feher, Michel, Naddaff, Ramona, and Tazi, Nadia (1989a) *Fragments for a History of the Human Body, Part One*. New York: Zone.

Feher, Michel, Naddaff, Ramona, and Tazi, Nadia (1989b) *Fragments for a History of the Human Body, Part Two*. New York: Zone.

Feher, Michel, Naddaff, Ramona, and Tazi, Nadia (1989c) *Fragments for a History of the Human Body, Part Three*. New York: Zone.

Fisher, Sue (1986) *In the Patient's Best Interest*. New Brunswick, NJ: Rutgers University Press.

Foucault, Michel (1978) *The History of Sexuality, Volume 1*. New York: Pantheon.

Foucault, Michel (1979) *Discipline and Punish*. New York: Vintage.

Foucault, Michel (1980) *Power/Knowledge: Selected Interviews & Other Writings, 1972–1977*. New York: Pantheon.

Foucault, Michel (1985) *The Use of Pleasure*. New York: Vintage.

Foucault, Michel (1986) *The Care of the Self*. New York: Pantheon.

Foucault, Michel (1988) *Politics, Philosophy, Culture: Interviews and Other Writings, 1977–1984*. New York: Routledge, Chapman and Hall.

Frank, Arthur W. (1989) 'Symbolic Interaction or Interaction Ritual?', *Symbolic Interaction*, 12(1): 71–5.

Frank, Arthur W. (1990) 'Bringing Bodies Back In: A Decade Review', *Theory, Culture & Society*, 7(1): 131–62.

Freund, Peter E.S. (1983) *The Civilized Body: Social Domination, Control, and Health*. Philadelphia: Temple University Press.

Gallagher, Catherine and Laqueur, Thomas (eds) (1987) *The Making of the Modern Body: Sexuality and Society in the Nineteenth Century*. Berkeley: University of California Press.

Giddens, Anthony (1979) *Central Problems in Social Theory*. Berkeley: University of California Press.

Giddens, Anthony (1984) *The Constitution of Society*. Berkeley: University of California Press.

Gilman, Sander L. (1988) *Disease and Representation*. Ithaca: Cornell University Press.

Girard, René (1977) *Violence and the Sacred*. Baltimore: Johns Hopkins University Press. Often cited, and disagreed with, on the nature of sacrifice.

Goffman, Erving (1959) *The Presentation of Self in Everyday Life*. New York: Doubleday Anchor.

Goffman, Erving (1961) *Asylums*. New York: Doubleday Anchor.

Goffman, Erving (1963) *Stigma: Notes on the Management of Spoiled Identity*. Englewood Cliffs, NJ: Prentice-Hall.

Goffman, Erving (1967) *Interaction Ritual*. New York: Doubleday Anchor.

Goffman, Erving (1971) *Relations in Public*. New York: Basic Books.

Goffman, Erving (1976) *Gender Advertisements*. New York: Harper Colophon.

Goffman, Erving (1981) *Forms of Talk*. Philadelphia: University of Pennsylvania Press.

Gold, Penny Schine (1987) *The Lady & the Virgin: Image, Attitude, and Experience in Twelfth-Century France*. Chicago: University of Chicago Press.

Gregor, Thomas (1986) *Anxious Pleasures: The Sexual Lives of an Amazonian People*. Chicago: University of Chicago Press.

Green, Harvey (1986) *Fit for America: Health, Fitness, Sport and American Society*. Baltimore: Johns Hopkins University Press.

Habermas, Jurgen (1986) *Autonomy and Solidarity: Interviews*. Peter Dews (ed.). London: Verso.

Habermas, Jurgen (1987) *The Theory of Communicative Action, Volume 2, Lifeworld and System: A Critique of Functionalist Reason*. Boston: Beacon Press.

Haines, Valerie (1988) 'Social Network Analysis, Structuration Theory, and the Holism-Individualism Debate', *Social Networks*, 10: 157–82.

Hanna, Judith Lynne (1988) *Dance, Sex and Gender*. Chicago: University of Chicago Press.

Hepworth, Mike and Featherstone, Mike (1982) *Surviving Middle Age*. Oxford and New York: Blackwell.

Héritier-Augé, Françoise (1989) 'Semen and Blood: Some Ancient Theories Concerning Their Genesis and Relationship', in *Fragments* Three.

Herzlich, Claudine and Pierret, Janine (1987) *Illness and Self in Society*. Baltimore: Johns Hopkins University Press.

Heusch, Luc de (1989) 'The Sacrificial Body of the King', in *Fragments* Three.

Hochschild, Arlie (1983) *The Managed Heart: Commercialization of Human Feeling*. Berkeley: University of California Press.

Hoy, David Couzens (1987) *Foucault: A Critical Reader*. Oxford: Blackwell.

Hughes, Robert (1989) 'The Patron Saint of Neo-Pop', *The New York Review of Books*, 36(9): 29–32.

Joas, Hans (1985) *G.H. Mead: A Contemporary Re-examination of his Thought*. Cambridge, MA: MIT Press.

Johnson, Diane and Murray, John F. (1988) 'AIDS Without End', *New York Review of Books*, 35(13): 57–63.

Johnson, Mark (1987) *The Body in the Mind: The Bodily Basis of Meaning, Imagination, and Reason*. Chicago: University of Chicago Press.

Jones, Robert Alun (1986) *Emile Durkheim: An Introduction to Four Major Works*. Newbury Park, CA and London: Sage.

Kantorowicz, Ernst H. (1989) *The King's Two Bodies: A Study in Medieval Political Theology*. Princeton: Princeton University Press.

Kleinman, Arthur (1988) *The Illness Narratives: Suffering, Healing & the Human Condition*. New York: Basic Books.

Knauft, Bruce M. (1989) 'Bodily Images in Melanesia: Cultural Substance and Natural Metaphors', in *Fragments* Three.

Kristeva, Julia (1989) 'Holbein's Dead Christ', in *Fragments* One.

Kroker, Arthur (1984) 'Power in Reverse Image: The Paradigm Shift of Michel Foucault and Talcott Parsons' in John Fekete (ed.), *The Structural Allegory*. Minneapolis: University of Minnesota Press. A major and often neglected study, with particular relevance to each theorist's concept of the body.

Kroker, Arthur and Kroker, Marilouise (eds & introductions) (1987) *Body Invaders: Panic Sex in America*. Montreal: New World Perspectives.

Kroker, Arthur, Kroker, Marilouise, and Cook, David (1989) *The Panic Encyclopedia*. Montreal: New World Perspectives. The Krokers' publishing project takes embodiment seriously. Influenced by Baudrillard but without his sense of resignation, this is an excellent source on 'mirroring' bodies.

Kupfermann, Jennette (1979) *The MsTaken Body*. London: Robson Books.

Lacan, Jacques (1977) *Écrits: A Selection*. New York: Norton.

Lacan, Jacques (1982) *Feminine Sexuality*. Juliet Mitchell and Jacqueline Rose (eds). New York: Norton.

Lakoff, George and Johnson, Mark (1980) *Metaphors We Live By*. Chicago: University of Chicago Press.

Lakoff, George (1987) *Women, Fire, and Dangerous Things: What Categories Reveal about the Mind*. Chicago: University of Chicago Press.

Laqueur, Thomas (1989a) 'Amor Veritis, vel Dulcedo Appeletur', in *Fragments* Three.

Laqueur, Thomas (1989b) 'The Social Evil, the Solitary Vice and Pouring Tea', in *Fragments* Three.

Le Goff, Jacques (1989) 'Head or Heart? The Political Use of Body Metaphors in the Middle Ages', in *Fragments* Three.

Levin, David Michael (1985) *The Body's Recollection of Being*. London: Routledge and Kegan Paul. A phenomenological and spiritual meditation on the body, mostly from a Heideggerian perspective; extensive quotations on the body from a variety of sources.

Levine, Donald N. (1984) 'The Liberal Arts and the Martial Arts', *Liberal Education*, 70(3): 235–51.

Lyotard, Jean-François (1984) *The Postmodern Condition: A Report on*

Knowledge. Minneapolis: University of Minnesota Press.

Marin, Louis (1989) 'The Body-of-Power and Incarnation at Port Royale and in Pascal OR of the Figurability of the Political Absolute', in *Fragments* Three.

Martin, Luther H., Gutman, Huck, and Hutton, Patrick H. (eds) (1988) *Technologies of the Self: A Seminar with Michel Foucault*. Amherst: University of Massachusetts Press.

Mauss, Marcel (1979 [1936]) 'Body Techniques', in *Sociology and Psychology: Essays*. London: Routledge and Kegan Paul.

Mead, George Herbert (1970 [1934]) *Mind, Self, and Society*. Chicago: University of Chicago Press.

Merleau-Ponty, Maurice (1962) *Phenomenology of Perception*. London: Routledge and Kegan Paul.

Messner, Michael (1988) 'When Bodies Are Weapons: Masculinity and Violence in Sport'. Unpublished paper, Program for the Study of Women and Men in Society, University of Southern California. Reports research in progress on sport as a site for the construction of 'dominating bodies' and the relation of masculinity to domination.

Murphy, Robert F. (1987) *The Body Silent*. New York: Henry Holt.

Nelli, René (1989) 'Love's Rewards', in *Fragments* Two.

O'Brien, Mary (1989) *Reproducing the World*. Boulder, San Francisco and London: Westview Press.

O'Neill, John (1985) *Five Bodies*. Ithaca: Cornell University Press.

Pagels, Elaine (1988) *Adam, Eve, and the Serpent*. New York: Random House. Describes Christianity's conflicts over the body in the first centuries. Essential to the religious formulation of the body.

Patterson, James T. (1987) *The Dread Disease: Cancer and Modern American Culture*. Cambridge, MA: Harvard University Press.

Peters, Edward (1985) *Torture*. New York: Blackwell. Forms of torture suggest how an age formulates bodies, particularly in relation to truth.

Roche, Maurice (1988) 'On the Political Economy of the Lifeworld: A Review of John O'Neill's *Five Bodies*', *Philosophy of the Social Sciences*, 18(2): 259–63.

Rousselle, Aline (1989) 'Personal Status and Sexual Practice in the Roman Empire', in *Fragments* Three.

Sacks, Oliver (1984) *A Leg to Stand On*. New York: Summit Books. A first-person account of an accident leading to the temporary loss of any feeling in one leg. A major meditation on the holism of embodiment.

Sartre, Jean-Paul (1966) *Being and Nothingness*. New York: Simon and Schuster.

Sayre, Henry M. (1989) *The Object of Performance*. Chicago: University of Chicago Press.

Scarry, Elaine (1985) *The Body in Pain*. New York: Oxford University Press.

Schwartz, Hillel (1986) *Never Satisfied: A Cultural History of Diets, Fantasies, and Fat*. New York: Free Press.

Schwartz, Hillel (1989) 'The Three Body Problem and the End of the World', in *Fragments* Two.

Seidman, Steven (1989) 'The Tedium of General Theory', *Contemporary Sociology* 18(4): 634–6.

Shorter, Edward (1985) *Bedside Manners*. New York: Simon and Schuster. A popular history of medicine, with an emphasis on its formulation of the body it treated.

Silverman, David (1987) *Communication and Medical Practice*. London: Sage.

Simmel, Georg (1984 [1911]) 'Female Culture', in Guy Oakes (ed.), *Georg Simmel: On Women, Sexuality, and Love*. New Haven: Yale University Press.

Smith, Dorothy (1987) *The Everyday World as Problematic: A Feminist Sociology*. Toronto: University of Toronto Press.

Sontag, Susan (1978) *Illness as Metaphor*. New York: Vintage.

Sontag, Susan (1989) *AIDS and Its Metaphors*. New York: Farrar, Straus, and Giroux.

Starobinski, Jean (1989) 'The Natural and Literary History of Bodily Sensation', in *Fragments* Two.

Suleiman, Susan Rubin (ed.) (1986) *The Female Body in Western Culture*. Cambridge, MA: Harvard University Press.

Theweleit, Klaus (1987 [1977]) *Male Fantasies, Volume 1: Women, Floods, Bodies, History*. Minneapolis: University of Minnesota Press.

Theweleit, Klaus (1989 [1978]) *Male Fantasies, Volume 2: Male Bodies: Psychoanalyzing the White Terror*. Minneapolis: University of Minnesota Press.

Turner, Bryan S. (1984) *The Body and Society*. Oxford: Blackwell.

Turner, Bryan S. (1987a) 'The Rationalization of the Body: Reflections on Modernity and Discipline', in Sam Whimster and Scott Lash (eds), *Max Weber, Rationality and Modernity*. London: Allen and Unwin.

Turner, Bryan S. (1987b) *Medical Power and Social Knowledge*. London: Sage. Revises medical sociology from an embodied perspective, with particular emphasis on Foucault.

Valéry, Paul (1989) 'Some Simple Reflections on the Body', in *Fragments* Two.

Vernant, Jean-Pierre (1989) 'Dim Body, Dazzling Body', in *Fragments* One.

Vigarello, Georges (1989) 'The Upward Training of the Body from the Age of Chivalry to Courtly Love', in *Fragments* Two.

Weber, Marianne (1975 [1926]) *Max Weber: A Biography*. New York: John Wiley.

Williams, Michael A. (1989) 'Divine Image – Prison of Flesh: Perceptions of the Body in Ancient Gnosticism', in *Fragments* One.

Zaner, Richard (1981) *The Context of Self: A Phenomenological Inquiry Using Medicine as a Clue*. Athens: Ohio University Press. A critical review of the literature on the body in phenomenological philosophy.

Zola, Irving Kenneth (1982) *Missing Pieces*. Philadelphia: Temple University Press.

3

ON HUMAN BEINGS AND THEIR EMOTIONS: A PROCESS-SOCIOLOGICAL ESSAY

Norbert Elias

I

Psychological and biological studies of human emotions, in the vast majority of cases, are concerned with structural aspects of human emotions which they share with what are thought to be emotions of non-human species. The process-sociologist's concern with human emotions, by contrast, centres on *both* characteristics of human emotions which they share with those of non-human species *and* others which are uniquely human and without parallel in the animal kingdom. I hasten to add that the attention to be given here to the union of animalic and uniquely human characteristics of human emotions does not imply any disregard of the evolutionary continuity linking humans to their non-human ancestors. It does, however, represent a determined break with a tradition of long-standing which induces human biologists and psychologists either to disregard or to blur structural differences between human emotions and those of non-human species as far as we know them. Discussions about the functional union of characteristics which humans share with other species and those uniquely human are still rare.[1] Such discussions could be useful. For a measure of consensus about the concept of human beings underlying theories of emotions and, beyond them, theories of human sciences generally, are a major requisite of advances in these fields.

As things are, one can observe in human sciences two opposite tendencies. Some of them focus attention on properties which humans share with other species, thus legitimizing their claim to the status of natural sciences. Ethology and some schools of psychology are in the forefront here. Human sciences of this type usually remain indifferent to the evolutionary innovations characteristic of the human species, including those to which humanity owes its emerging mastery over most animal species. Representatives of these sciences usually select as relevant what they regard as unvarying natural human characteristics, preferably those which humans share with other species. Their approach, in other words, is monistic and reductionist.

The second set of human sciences, among them almost all social sciences as well as those which used to be called 'moral sciences' or *Geisteswissenschaften*, are concerned with objects which are usually seen as not belonging to nature. But apart from this negative diagnosis, the ontological status of these non-nature objects and their relationship to nature remain unclear. Many of the basic uncertainties of these human sciences are due to this fact. They treat their subject matter as something set apart from nature, as something to be explored entirely on its own. They are thus in effect dualistic and isolationist. But their dualism is hidden and unacknowledged. Most of these sciences, history and sociology among them, are concerned with aspects of human life which are uniquely human, which in other words are, or are due to, evolutionary innovations. They distinguish humanity from other species. As a rule, however, these human sciences remain more or less indifferent to the problem encountered here. They do not ask how these uniquely human properties are connected with those which humans share with other species such as birth and death. Their representatives may not entirely fail to take note of the fact that human beings have properties in common with non-human beings. References to the human body may represent an attempt at acknowledging that fact. But even in such cases no attempts are made to bridge the gap, to discover the hinge connecting nature with what may be seen as non-nature. Thus sociologists may see the body as a topic of interest. But the prevailing routines of analytical isolationism make it easy to treat the body as a topic of sociological research set apart from other topics, perhaps as the subject matter of a specialism. There does not seem any need to explore the links connecting aspects of humans perceived as body, with other aspects perhaps perceived as disembodied. On a larger scale too, human sciences of this type tacitly work with the image of a split world. The division of sciences into natural sciences and others not concerned with nature reveals itself as a symbolic manifestation of an ontological belief — of the belief in a factually existing division of the world. By and large it is a hidden belief rarely mentioned in scientific discussions or subjected to scientific scrutiny, thus escaping the need to justify itself. This type of human science usually takes the image of a dual world for granted. What are in fact different but wholly inseparable aspects of human beings are thus treated — if they become objects of scientific research — as if they existed in isolation from each other. Thus the question as to which unique biological characteristics of human beings make history possible has hardly been a talking point among historians. Nor have the distinguishing characteristics and the relationship of biological evolution and social development been a frequent point of discussion among sociologists. The term evolution is at present used indiscriminately with reference to both. How culture, rationality, knowledge, conscience and other similar aspects of human beings fit into the well-established theory of an evolutionary descent of humans is anybody's guess. While human sciences with a monistic bent tend to overemphasize the similarities and to ignore the differences between human and non-human beings, those with a dualistic perspective continue, often without much reflection and in an undeclared way, an age-old tradition which suggests an absolute divide between nature and non-nature straddled by human beings.

Both tendencies suffer from an inability to understand the nature of processes. They are still trapped by a powerful conceptual heritage which forces people to represent in static terms sets of events that can be recognized and understood only if they are perceived as parts or aspects of processes, as events in a condition of continuous structured flux. Processes, however, have structural properties unfamiliar to those accustomed to the use of static concepts. Among them is the observable propensity of some types of processes for combining continuity and innovation. There are many examples of processes which in a steady movement, from time to time, lead to the emergence of novel structures without precedent in their earlier phases. The apparent strangeness of some of the properties of long-term processes, moreover, is sometimes increased by the fact that observers born into a later stage of such a process may have difficulties in reconstructing the sequence of antecedent phases because all living representatives of these phases have irretrievably vanished, and may have left few if any traces.

In the case of human beings a long line of their direct biological ancestors have in fact become extinct. Rather late in the day, humans themselves now try to prevent any further extinction of species. At an earlier stage of their existence they were probably less charitable. The disappearance from the living of all the various emergent hominid groups except one may have been due, at least partly, to survival struggles among these groups themselves. Whatever the reason, the fact that the only hominids still living can no longer see and meet with living representatives of the sequence of stages in the course of which, step by step, their own species formed itself and intermediaries disappeared — all this now plays a significant part in the difficulties human beings have with their own self-image, and in coming to grips with the fact that they are like and yet also unlike other animals. That living representatives of their more immediate ancestors might ever come to light is now highly unlikely. At present, even lifeless relics of their direct biological ancestors are few and far between. The study of living apes is often used as a substitute for that of humanity's real evolutionary forebears. But the living apes belong to a fairly early collateral line of the direct human ancestry. Their study can be misleading; it can divert attention from the need for constructing, at least by way of hypothesis, models of the missing phases of the evolutionary process — models which can indicate their structure and direction and thus help to explain which evolutionary innovations gave the living species their advantage.

It is not without significance that in this case, as in that of other evolutionary processes which look like a breakthrough to a new mode of living, the intermediary stages have disappeared. Something similar appears to have happened in the case of other highly innovatory transformations, for example, in those of sea- into land-animals or of reptiles into birds. Very few living representatives of intermediary stages are left in the first case, none in the second. It may well be that in such cases later products of an evolutionary process reach a kind of perfection within their own setting, a superiority over their predecessors which leads to their victory over them in a long-term survival struggle, and eventually to the extinction of the earlier forms.

In all previous cases, however, representatives of the more successful innovatory organization underwent a process of *biological differentiation*; they divided into a great number of different species no longer able to interbreed, which exploited their novel capacities by filling their living space to the last corner. Thus the archetype (or types) of four-legged land animals evolved into a host of different four-legged species, filling all the different niches of the earth's continents which offered them a living. Similarly the archetype birds, two-legged and winged, branched out into a great multitude of different species of birds adapted to all parts of the earth and air accessible to them. They too are no longer able to interbreed. Human beings in contrast had acquired a highly innovatory natural equipment which enabled them to adapt to a very great variety of conditions on earth and to procure a living there *without* any major biological differentiation, *without* the division into a great number of different species. Mountain Gurkhas can intermarry with lowland Britons, Chinese with Americans. In the case of humans, the same species adapted itself to vastly different conditions on earth mainly by means of a *social differentiation*, while biological variations never affected the sameness of the species. Humans filled the earth by learning from experience and by handing on knowledge from one generation to another. They adapted themselves to new surroundings with the help of a sequence of social transformations: that is, transformations in the form of a social development, and without further evolutionary transformations breaking the biological unity of their species. The distinct biological characteristics which enabled human beings to learn from experience, to transmit knowledge between the generations and to change their group life according to new demands in a great variety of ways, deserves closer attention.

It is possible that even in the long run one may never be able to do more than work out and improve hypothetical models of the actual process in the course of which living beings with the unique characteristics of humans made their appearance on earth. Human emotions can serve as a useful, though not the only, point of departure for this reconstruction work. The following text offers a set of hypotheses about the distinguishing characteristics of human emotions and thus of human beings compared with other species. It represents a fairly coherent theoretical framework for the study of emotions, with some preliminary models indicating missing links of the still hidden evolutionary process which led to the emergence of the living species of humans.

II

What I have to say about human emotions is centred on a number of hypotheses about human beings. They are all interconnected although they do not all belong to the same level of synthesis. I shall mention them by and by as I go along. The first hypothesis is one of the most crucial, most fundamental in terms of a theory of human beings. It also shows in a nutshell how one may set about recreating in the form of a theoretical model aspects of the evolutionary process leading up to the present type of human beings. Such a process model can provide possible answers to the problem mentioned before: how can the fact that the human species has certain unique characteristics be reconciled with the continuity of the evolutionary process?

The first hypothesis is quite simple; it may seem obvious. Many animals combine with their equipment of unlearned behaviour a capacity for learning behaviour. Even an earthworm can learn. So of course can apes; they can remember individual experiences and steer their behaviour accordingly. But in the case of earthworms the scope for learning is exceedingly limited. The conduct of animals at these earlier stages of the evolutionary process, though even there traces of learning may be detected, is in the main programmed genetically; it is species-specific and unvarying. Even in the case of apes, though their capacity for learning is vastly superior to that of most other animals, it is still very limited compared with the natural learning capacity of human beings. Even in the case of apes, the balance between mainly learned and mainly unlearned forms of conduct is still heavily weighted in favour of the latter; and the same can presumably be said of the feeling components of their emotions.

My first hypothesis is simply that *as a species human beings represent an evolutionary breakthrough*. In all other cases, although the scope for learning in relation to the scope for unlearned conduct has been growing during the pre-human phases of the evolutionary process, the unlearned genetic programme of reactions always remained dominant. The blind hit-and-miss inventiveness of the evolutionary process often works very slowly. Steering conduct mainly with the help of learned knowledge offers a species biologically equipped for it very great advantages over all species whose behaviour is largely governed by innate mechanisms. It is astonishing enough that a biological equipment for learning evolved at all. From very small beginnings it gradually gained greater weight. But in all pre-human forms of living, steering of conduct with the help of individually made and remembered experiences remained subordinate to unlearned forms of steering conduct. In the case of the human species living at present it is my hypothesis that the balance of power between learned and unlearned conduct took a new turn. For the first time in the evolutionary process, mainly learned ways of steering behaviour became clearly and unmistakably dominant in relation to mainly unlearned ways. One day it may perhaps be possible to equate this breakthrough to the dominance of learning with that of cerebral dominance. Whichever way one looks at it, this is an example of process continuity going hand in hand with the uniqueness of some structural characteristics of the process representatives. The consequences of this evolutionary breakthrough were far-reaching.

One can show it best with the help of a second hypothesis. It is equally simple, but not always clearly stated. One can present it in one sentence though it requires elaboration: Human beings not only *can* learn far more than any other species, they also *must* learn more. Like other living forms, human beings have a repertoire of unlearned ways of behaviour. They, however, have become softened and weakened to such an extent that human beings can neither orientate themselves in their world nor communicate with each other without acquiring a great deal of knowledge through learning. Thus, during a long stretch of its pre-human phases, the evolutionary process with regard to learning retains its direction towards the growth of the learning capacity; but humans were the first and, as far as is known, the only type of living beings where unlearned forms of steering conduct became subordinate to learned forms. Moreover, the new balance of power did not leave the latter unchanged. Some, though not all, unlearned forms lost their genetic rigidity, in the case of humans. They became more malleable, and in a number of cases even merged with learned forms. In fact the learning potential of humans had grown to such an extent that they, and they alone, came to be totally dependent on learned forms of knowledge for their dominant form of communication and for their orientation in the world. To be sure, humans like other living forms remained biologically equipped with unlearned types of behaviour and, among them, of communication. Smiling, groaning, crying in pain are examples. But these unlearned types of communication have become functionally so much weakened in the case of humans that a growing-up person who for some reason had to rely on them alone would remain outside the human pale. Human beings not only can, but also must learn from others a pre-existing language of a specific society. They must learn it not only in order to communicate with others, but also in order to become fully functioning individual human beings. The same picture emerges if one examines the means of orientation. In the human case, innate and species-specific means of orientation have almost disappeared. Human beings depend for their orientation in the first place on the learning of a pre-existing social fund of knowledge. Without it they cannot even find their food or distinguish between food that tastes fine but is poisonous, and healthy food that tastes indifferently. Without acquiring a fairly large social fund of knowledge they cannot survive nor simply become human. They are in fact biologically constituted in a way which makes it possible as well as necessary for them to orientate themselves by means of learned knowledge.

It would be easier to understand the distinct relationship of unlearned and learned characteristics in the human case if the routines of thinking were not so strongly shaped by the two alternative tendencies mentioned before, by a reductionist monism and an isolationist dualism. In the case of the former the uniqueness is lost, in the case of the latter the continuity. On the face of it the old nature–nurture controversy has been dead and buried for at least thirty years. But beneath the ashes its fire continues to smoulder sustained by the analytical passion for presenting as disconnected what is in fact connected, as existing in isolation what is in fact interdependent. Thus knowledge and, indeed, everything acquired by humans through learning is widely regarded as non-nature — if not as *anti*-nature. Nature is equated with immutability and innateness, and thus conceptually isolated from what is changeable and learned. And what is changeable and learned is classified as culture, society, or other representations of what is regarded as not natural. Yet how could human beings learn anything, if they were not by nature, that is biologically, equipped for it?

The problem encountered here is not always stated as clearly as it deserves: *in the human context the concept of nature has to be re-defined*. Perhaps one can start from the demonstrable fact that it is possible to distinguish between two types of structures which deserve to be called natural. There are, on the one hand, structures which are completely inaccessible to change as a result of stored and remembered experiences — that is, as a result of learning. There are also, on the other hand, natural human structures which remain dispositions and cannot fully function unless they are stimulated by a person's 'love and learn' relationship with other persons. The presence of such structures is most obvious in the case of young children. But the fact that the presence of human structures which remain dormant unless they are awoken by the relationship with other persons makes itself most strongly felt and is perhaps most obvious in childhood, does not denote their total absence at other ages in the life-cycle. The general thesis is, as one may remember, that humans not only can but must learn in order to become fully functioning human beings.

Take as example people's vocal apparatus. No human being could learn the complicated sound patterns of a human language without being biologically equipped for that task. Without doubt a child's vocal apparatus is initially used entirely for the production of unlearned pre-language sounds and a number of pre-language sounds remain with humans throughout their life. They are, like the more innately fixated means of communication of animals, highly spontaneous and fairly rigidly bound to the internal or external situation of animals or humans who produce these signals. In the case of humans, even these can come gradually under conscious control and be modified through learning when people grow up. In small children, however, one can still observe how the more animalic and species-specific sounds are gradually overlaid as a means of communication. They become gradually overlaid by, and lose their supremacy to, a totally different communications system, communication by means of a language which existed before the child was born, which the child has to learn from its elders through a relationship which involves affects and emotions as much as intellect, a love-and-learn relationship. Language can be used in relative detachment from a person's internal and external situation. What one can still observe in every child may well be regarded as an abbreviated replica of an evolutionary sequence. A child's learning of a language is made possible by the intertwining of two processes: a biological process of *maturation* and a social process of *learning*. Everybody who watches with open eyes day by day a child's progress with the production of words and sentences can hardly fail to notice how closely this learning process is bound up with the process of biological maturation and growth. One cannot make experiments with human children; but there is a good deal of evidence which suggests a further enlargement of the hypothesis that human nature makes learning both possible as well as necessary. In early childhood the human organism, through a process of biological maturation, is, as it were, made ready for the patterning of speech centre and vocal apparatus through the learning of a social language. It is not enough, moreover, that a child learns to produce the sound patterns of a social language; it must learn at the same time, and is able to learn to remember and thus to understand the social meaning associated in the society concerned with these sound-patterns if they are produced by others. A child's learning of a language would be entirely without function if it were confined to the child's own capacity for speaking it, and not at the same time to the child's capacity for understanding the social meaning of the sound pattern produced by others. Learning a language means learning a two-way traffic.[2]

This example has considerable theoretical significance not only for the study of human emotions but for that of human beings generally. The dovetailing of a biological process of maturation and a social process of learning in a human child brings to light the hinge connecting human nature with human society, human culture and other aspects of what is traditionally set apart from nature as a second world existing in isolation from it, or alternatively reduced to the non-human levels of nature. I have mentioned before the evolutionary change, especially in the steering of conduct, during which the balance of power between learned and unlearned properties changed from the subordination to the dominance of the learned forms with regard to the steering of conduct. The relationship of unlearned pre-language sounds and learned language patterns in the case of humans, or that of the intertwining of an unlearned process of maturation and of a social learning process, show in greater detail what this change in the balance of learned and unlearned characteristics implies.

Learning, accumulating experiences, acquiring knowledge — they are all based on the utilization and patterning of natural structures. But that is not all. One can enlarge the hypothesis that humans must learn by adding that in all likelihood specific forms of knowledge must be acquired, specific experiences passed through at the right time — that is, the right time in terms of the biological process they undergo. No doubt humans possess a natural potential for learning throughout their lives. But there is some evidence which suggests that some experience must be passed through, some types of knowledge learned by a person early in life, when the natural process of maturation creates as it were the strongest possible natural disposition for learning them. The capacity for speaking and for understanding a language is one of the several instances of this kind. That of loving and responding to love is another, the capacity of regulating oneself according to learned social standards, of controlling one's drives and emotions, a third. The enlargement of the second hypothesis put forward here implies it is not enough to say that humans are by nature so constituted that they must learn and learn a great deal in order to become fully functioning human adults. Their natural constitution also makes it imperative that they acquire some types of knowledge, that they have some specific experiences at the right time and, one may add though one cannot enlarge on it here, in the right manner. A great deal of unorganized knowledge, so far without theoretical synthesis, suggests for example that if the natural potential for speaking and understanding a language is not utilized, if the speech-producing and speech-receiving centres are not activated and patterned by a love-and-learn process, say from the sixth month onward — that is, during the period at which a maturing child is most ready for learning a language (and much else besides) — then it becomes more and more difficult to learn a language at the later stages of a person's life. For obvious reasons one cannot make planned experiments with human children. But unplanned experiments are made occasionally. Sooner or later some of them may yield evidence for or against the 'right time hypothesis' and its corollary the 'right manner hypothesis' represented here by the term 'love-and-learn' process.

The conception of a biological process covering the readiness and even the need for impregnation and organization in terms of a social learning process has consequences not only in practical but also in theoretical terms. It helps to close the gap which a long-standing tradition has established between the world of nature and the human world. It suggests that natural evolution has produced process dispositions which remain dormant, perhaps stunned, unable to realize their functional potential, unless they are activated by a 'love-and-learn' process. But the functional dependence between two types of processes, the biological and the social, is reciprocal. No learning processes are independent of unlearned or natural processes and structures. In the case of human adults the steering of conduct generally can never be attributed to either nature or to nurture alone. It is always the result of an intimate interweaving of learned and unlearned processes. We may assume that the child's biological process of maturation is as much dependent on the social 'love-and-learn' process as the latter on the former.

The way in which in a child's life the process of maturation and that of learning a language dovetail into each other has an exemplary significance. By learning a language a child becomes integrated into a specific human group. That a process characteristic of human nature, and *unlearned*, helps to prepare the way for a person's close integration in a group can serve as a reminder that in the human case a strong biological disposition links nature and group life. One can only surmise that unlearned dispositions preparing the human child for the acquisition of learned bonds with a specific group in terms of a language and, indeed, of the patterns of self-regulation as well, must at some earlier stages of the evolutionary process have had a particularly high survival value. No doubt the same can be said of the apes' disposition to live in groups, but in all other cases the social life of living beings is based only to a very small extent on learned and to a very large extent on unlearned or innate means of communication. That in the human case a learned form of communication, a language, surpasses by far in its social import-ance the communication by means of unlearned signals has far-reaching consequences. It is at the root of a condition which accounts for the fundamental difference between human and ani-mal societies. That the capacity for communicating by means of unlearned signals dominates the social life of non-human forms of living, while the scope for variations of unlearned signals through learning (which does indeed exist) is comparatively small, symbol-izes the high rigidity of animal societies. It implies that societies at the pre-human level — small, local variations apart — are always species-specific. Animal societies only change if the biological spe-cies itself changes in the course of an evolutionary process. The fact that humans are bonded to each other by means of a learned language, as well as learned varieties of emotion and conscience, accounts for one of the most striking differences between animal societies and human societies. In contrast to all animal societies, human societies can change without biological changes of those who form them. They can undergo development or have, as we say, a *history* without any change in their genetic makeup.

The dominance of learned over unlearned characteristics in hu-mans provides a biological framework for a social development which can occur without any biological changes, that is to say, independently of the process of evolution. The two concepts refer to processes which are different in kind. At present they are fre-quently confused. It has become customary to use the term indis-criminately for both. Some people present social development in the monistic manner as part of the unitary biological process. Others, dualistically, present biological evolution on the one hand and social development under the name of history on the other as totally distinct and totally isolated from each other, without giving any thought at all to the problem of *the hinge*, to the question of their connection with each other. What I have tried to do here is just that: I have intended to indicate the nature of the hinge. Starting from the postulate that humans not only can but *must* learn in order to become fully human I have clarified the problem of the hinge. The biological propensity of humans for learning provides the answer. Without the changeability as well as the factual changes of what can and what has to be learned, without changes in knowledge including language changes, social development would not be possible. The *biological* dominance gained by learned forms of steering experience and conduct over unlearned forms of conduct links irreversible evolution to reversible development. Learned knowledge can be forgotten. The large human potential for forms of orientation and communication acquired through learning which is part of human nature also constitutes the hinge between nature and society, nature and culture, and in consequence between natural and social sciences.

All aspects of what is called the human personality — all aspects of the overall organization of a person's experiences, attitudes and conduct in relation to self and non-self persons and objects — are derived from the intimate merging of unlearned and learned processes. According to the old convention, human nature and learning, human nature and human society, or human biological evolution and human social development had to be considered either as two ontological fields existing separately and independently from each other, or as manifestations of relatively undifferentiated and unitary nature like those of non-human species. In contrast, it follows from the hypotheses I am advancing that the task is instead to find out more about the way the uniquely large unlearned human potential for learning, uniquely large compared with other forms of living, is activated and patterned by the learning process itself. One discovers soon enough that the relationship between natural and social process is not always the same. So far I have used as my main example a type of human communication — oral and auditory communication — where unlearned modes of expressing feeling such as groaning or crying in pain very obviously play a subsidiary part, and a less emotional form — communication by means of learned language — has gained supremacy. One can easily overlook the fact that learning a language presupposes a highly specific unlearned biological structure which for all we know, though species-specific, may leave room for individual differences. But the language itself imprinted on natural organs, brain centres and vocal/auditory apparatus is a wholly learned way of sending and receiving messages. It may change considerably within one and the same society, in a time-span rather too short for equally considerable biological changes.

But the situation is not quite the same if one considers other forms of human communication usually classified as emotions, such as smiling.

My third hypothesis, in this context, is that *no emotion of a grown up human person is ever an entirely unlearned, genetically fixated reaction pattern*. Like languages, human emotions result from a merger of an unlearned and a learned process. Recognition of this fact can be obscured in a variety of ways. It may be of help to indicate at least one of them. It also shows that academically the term emotion has not quite the same meaning as that which it has in everyday life, for instance when one says 'this person is rather emotional about this or that'. In that case the *feeling* component of emotions is placed in the centre. Feeling is not always clearly seen as at least one of the indispensable components of human emotions. The research strategy of many schools of psychology is legitimation of research in human psychology through animal experiments. As it is difficult to make reliable statements about the feelings of animals, a research strategy which only considers similarities and fails to consider the evolutionary dissimilarities between the emotions of human and non-human beings is bound to run into difficulties.

As a brief introduction to the problem of human emotions one can, broadly speaking, distinguish three component aspects in all of them: a behavioural component, a physiological component and a feeling component. English, French, German and many other languages possess an extremely rich vocabulary with the help of which members of these societies can converse about their own as well as other people's emotions. They provide a rich material for psychosociological study of emotions, all the more so as the shades of feeling represented by the emotion vocabulary of different languages, the degree of differentiation as well as a spectrum of feelings covered by the vocabulary of different peoples vary considerably. This is a rich field of research for those courageous enough to undertake comparative studies and ask unconventional questions — for instance why the feeling vocabulary is more differentiated in one country than in another. It would be rather foolish to suggest that people who make use of the possibility to communicate feelings to each other talk about nothing. Differences in the vocabularies of different peoples also confirm the hypothesis that learning plays a part in the feeling component of emotions. Animals, however, have no possibility of communicating any feeling experience to us with the help of a language. In their case, human study is confined to observations about the behavioural and, in some cases the physiological component of emotions. But the fact that we cannot rely on any verbal evidence for the feeling component of emotions in the case of animals in no way justifies the assumption that in their case such feeling experiences do not exist.

III

Human beings have evolved within a world which consists of other existences apart from themselves. Each human being therefore is made by what we call nature for life in company and in relation with a great variety of existences, some friendly, some hostile, some inanimate, some animate, and some of the latter are human. Accordingly most attributes and properties of a human being have functions which can only be understood if one considers people's relationships with existences other than themselves. The function of a stomach can only be understood if one considers that for a continued existence a person requires materials and energy from sources outside. A person's lungs would be without function if there were no air around the earth, the eyes useless without a sun and the legs without the firm earth.

Emotions too have a function for human beings in their relations with other existences. Broadly speaking emotions have three components, a somatic, a behavioural and a feeling component. A well known example is the fight- and flight-reaction. The experience of danger elicits a more or less automatic reaction pattern which puts the whole organism into a different gear. It has an obvious survival value. It prepares an organism for strong and fast movements, for the two great alternatives needed in order to cope with physical danger, for fight or for flight. There is a somatic component. Digestion may be slowed down, the heart may beat faster. There is a motor component. More blood is pumped into the skeletal muscles making arms and legs ready for fight or flight. And there is a feeling component usually described as fear or rage. To some extent humans share this reaction pattern with non-human species. However, there are also marked differences. In the case of animals, including apes, the behavioural component of a fear or rage syndrome is comparatively stereotyped; it is cast into a fairly rigid species-specific mould. In the case of humans it is capable of far greater diversification in accordance with different situations and different antecedent experiences. Moreover, in the human case we know about the feeling component of a fear or rage reaction because humans are able to verbalize their feelings. They can communicate them to each other and to themselves by means of a learned language. Animals cannot do that. If human observers find that a non-human species in case of danger shows behavioural and perhaps also somatic reaction patterns akin to those of humans in a danger situation, they tend to conclude that members of that species also have the same feeling experience as humans have in a similar situation. Since in the case of animals verbalization is lacking, this is a conjecture. One is probably right to assume feeling experiences of some kind akin to those of humans in the case of apes and other higher mammals. There is some reason to think that birds have strong if highly stereotyped feeling experiences. But as one descends the evolutionary ladder one enters a relatively little known territory. Have fish any feelings? Or the busy ants? At present one cannot tell. In case of danger the behavioural component of an alarm reaction may still be recognizable as such. Even at these levels animals may still struggle wildly and behave as if they were afraid. But about the feeling component of this reaction pattern nothing is known. Research in that field is still rare. Experts in that field are often given more to a flat identification of humans with animals, animals with humans, than to a clear account of evolutionary difference. Thus a series of postulates representing a programmatic introduction to a psycho-evolutionary theory of emotion begins with the categorical statement: 'The concept of emotion is applicable to all evolutionary levels and applies to animals as well as to humans.'[3] One of the following postulates (postulate 4) refers to the fact that 'the forms of expressions of emotions' may differ in different species. This gives the impression that the behavioural component, the visible 'expression', may change while the term emotion, as that which is being expressed, appears to refer to the feeling component. Does this statement suggest that at different levels of the evolutionary process the feeling component remains the same while the behavioural changes? One cannot tell. References to different levels of the evolution may give rise to the expectation of a clear statement about the distinguishing characteristics of emotions at different evolutionary levels, akin to that which I am seeking to make here. However, the psycho-evolutionary theory quoted before provides no clear statement about the relationship and the structural differences between emotions at different levels of the evolutionary process. As a variant of monistic reductionism the example is informative. Differences between species and thus their emotions are mentioned, but essentially presented as structureless divergences, hence of little theoretical relevance. What is similar at different levels, and thus also similar in the case of human and animal emotions, is placed at the centre of the theory, what is different at the margin. One has to consider emotions at a very high level of abstraction in order to attribute their essentials to amoebae and jellyfish as well as to human beings.

The routinely used term 'expression of emotions' invites reflection. What possible functions can it have for living beings to express emotions? And what actually is it that is being expressed? The routine answer is that it is an emotion which behaviour expresses. Used in that sense the term emotion appears to become identified with its own feeling component. The conclusion is a little startling. In connection with a fear or rage syndrome it is as a rule clearly recognized that the three components are equivalent. One could say that the feeling component like the somatic component prepares for action, but the behaviour itself has an obvious survival function appropriate to a specific situation. It would be odd to conceptualize fight or flight as expressions of an emotion, thus giving the impression that these forms of behaviour have no other function than that of expressing fear or rage.

This is a major source of confusion in the study of emotions. Inadvertently the term emotion, even in professional discussions, is used with two different meanings. It is used in a wider and in a narrower sense at the same time. In the wider sense the term emotion is applied to a reaction pattern which involves the whole organism in its somatic, its feeling and its behavioural aspects, as exemplified by a fear reaction. In that sense the syndrome of an emotion is seen as a reaction pattern which has a clearly recognizable function in a specific situation. In its narrower sense the term emotion refers to the feeling component of the syndrome only. By presenting the related behaviour component as an expression of an emotion, or in other words of feeling, one tacitly attributes to feeling a master position, perhaps a causal function, while by describing the behaviour as expression one places it in a dependent or derivative position, perhaps even making it merely an effect. The term 'expression of an emotion' does not include any obvious reference of either emotion or expression to any particular situation nor does it invite further questions about the function of either emotion or its expression. Nor, as a rule, is it found necessary to explain what function it has for an organism to give expression to feelings. In this narrower sense the term emotion is representative of a human self-image according to which the true self of a person is hidden deep inside — one cannot be quite sure inside of what.[4] What shows itself on one's 'outside', for instance on one's face, is merely a derivative or else an 'expression', and often not a true or even a distorted expression, of what one is inside. A common-sense concept of emotion, representing a popular but quite inadequate image of human beings, has thus slipped into the professional language of research into emotions.

IV

A useful way of approaching the problem of human emotions, and indeed the wider problem of the relationship between the human and other species, is to take a closer look at the human face. It is clearly related to, and has some features in common with, animal faces and yet it is also very different from them. Its unique characteristics can serve as a reminder of the singularity of human beings. It has a special significance for the study of human emotions which is often overlooked. The face is one of the chief instruments for indicating their feelings with which human beings are endowed by nature, that is, as a result of an evolutionary process. One may well be inclined to say that the human face expresses emotions. But as soon as one asks what can have possibly been the evolutionary function which led from the far more furry and rigid faces of our animal ancestors to the naked and far more mobile faces of human beings, one is set on the road to discovery. It becomes easier to explain the transition from the faces of older mammals to those of humans if one does not try to consider the human individual in isolation. It can only be understood in terms of the evolution of groups. Consideration of the possible evolutionary function of means of communication in the form of languages already indicates the high survival value which better and better natural equipment with a highly differentiated communication system must have had for human ancestral groups during some stages of hominid evolution. But communication by means of languages, which are wholly learned and the exclusive possession of a particular group, can probably be regarded as the attainment of a relatively late phase of hominid evolution. In the course of that evolution the face too became a major instrument of communication. The face evolved into a signalling board. The signals and thus the messages which people could give each other by means of their faces were considerably less versatile, considerably more stereotyped than members of a group could give each other through speaking, and listening to, the common language of their group. Furthermore, face to face communication was, and still is to a much higher extent than language communication, genetically fixated or unlearned, though it can now be greatly modified by means of a deliberate use of the unlearned face signals. It is also true that individual experiences can settle down in a face. However, as learning has a far more restricted scope in face communication compared with language communication, one probably has to regard it as an older form of communication. Its close links to feelings point in the same direction. But it also shows the decisive role which the better attunement of individuals to each other by means of a more finely adaptable natural equipment — adaptable to a greater variety of situations — played in the evolution of hominids.

A rather different picture of emotions emerges from these considerations of the possible function of the ancestral face formation process. Consider one of the best known face signals, the smile. The somatic component is not yet clear. The feeling- and behaviour-components are more obvious. In its primary form where it can be regarded as unlearned and spontaneous, a person's smile seems to indicate to another person friendly feelings and a readiness for friendly action. One can speculate, for example, that in a period in which violence in the approach of a man to a woman was perhaps more frequent, a man's smile and a woman's responding smile facilitated the approach to each other. Whether or not that was the case, the example can make some contribution both to the question of the function of the feeling component and to that of the behavioural component in an emotion syndrome. The feeling component prepares a person for a specific type of action. It can also reinforce an action already under way. In the case of a smile the behavioural component has the function of communicating the 'set' of a human being in relation to another, the way he or she feels like acting in relation to others. Apes have some homologous signals but in their social life whole-body postures play a far greater part as social signals. By comparison with them face signals and vocal signals play a subsidiary part in group communication. The human face compared with an ape face is, as it were, the living evidence of the greater role, compared with whole-body movements, which facial behavioural components assumed in the human group life. The innateness of such signals indicates once more that in the human case nature and society are closely interrelated. In non-human cases not only the sender of a message but also the receiver must have a natural propensity for reading the signal in the same sense as the sender. One can perhaps expect a horse to react to a human voice. But one cannot expect it to react to human face signals in the sense which they have for humans themselves. The horse's own capacity for giving face signals is almost nil. Go in a lion's den with a smile and see what happens. Even gorillas may misunderstand or not understand at all, for their facial vocabulary is different.

One has to be human in order to read the signals of human faces properly. The capacity for both giving face signals and perceiving them has an innate — that is to say species-specific — plastic core which in every particular case is capable of being re-modelled through learning in varying degrees. Face signals such as the smile also show very graphically that the evolutionary process has fashioned human beings in such a way that what we call their 'nature' prepares them for a life in groups. In the course of this process, life with each other — and, in particular, signals designed to probe each other's intention in anticipation of the enactment of conduct, and thus also signals such as the smile which are capable of allaying suspicion and fear — must in the life of our ancestors have helped to temper frictions and to make a more differentiated life with each other possible.

As we find it today, moreover, a face signal such as the smile, with its peculiar blend of learned and unlearned aspects, can perhaps be regarded as a record of an evolutionary process of which so far no other records have come to light. I have introduced earlier the concept of balance and interplay between learned and unlearned forms of steering behaviour. If one applies that theoretical concept to the empirical study of the smile, it becomes easier to clarify some of its aspects which remain hidden as long as one persists with the antithetical use of such terms as 'nature' and 'nurture', of learned and unlearned properties of people.

Both the vocal-auditory mode of human communication and the visual face signal mode acquire their present adult form through the mobilization and patterning of an unlearned propensity by means of learning. But in the case of the vocal-auditory type of communication the need for mobilizing the unlearned potential through learning is far greater, the receding of unlearned patterns and the dominance of learned patterns far more pronounced, than in the case of the face-signal forms of communication. The smile is a telling example. In the case of a young baby the smile is wholly innate; it is spontaneous and very closely associated with a specific condition of the young organism itself as well as its relationship with other human beings. As human beings grow older the wholly innate form of a smile is greatly weakened and becomes much more malleable, that is modifiable in connection with antecedent as well as immediate experiences. One may still feel a slight tendency to smile back at a smiling face: even a frontal picture of a horse's face with seemingly raised corners of his mouth may be spontaneously perceived as a friendly gesture, as intimation of a smile or perhaps of incipient laughter! Moreover, superimposed upon very weak traces of an inborn tendency to give or to receive a smiling signal is, in the present human species, an extensive capacity for utilizing the ancient innate signal more deliberately in connection with a social process of learning which may be different in different societies. And the core of the smiling emotion both in its feeling and its behavioural component in the case of an adult is much more malleable than it is in its baby form. It can be deliberately used to convey to others a rich variety of shades of feeling. It can be a hesitant, a withdrawn, a broad, a triumphant, a supercilious and even a hostile smile. And yet in all these cases a learned and deliberate steering of conduct merges with an unlearned form of steering one's face muscles.

In all varieties of the smile, one encounters the social and individual diversification of an old innate facial signal. If one tries to read the present constellation as a record of an evolutionary process, a possible sequence of events suggests itself. At the present stage of our knowledge it is not unreasonable to assume that the capacity of humans for a more differentiated use and thus also the greater plasticity of the smiling signal, its greater submission to the dominance of learned impulses, represents a relatively late evolutionary stage. What is at present the baby form of a smile, a smile that is wholly unlearned, quite rigid in its pattern, spontaneous and closely bound to a specific situation, is the late remnant of a form of smiling and thus of a form of intra-species communication which at some earlier stage was a common form of communication not only of infants, but of adults too. For the unlearned baby smile with its unyielding automaticity and rigidity, its firm bonding to specific situations, resembles more closely the dominant form of communication in animal groups. Its softening resembles the transition from the dominance of unlearned to that of learned steering of conduct. If one knows how to read it, one may well find here, in one's own face, a record of the evolutionary extension of cortical control.

V

The next step which suggests itself is a closer look at the manifestations of this extension, at the consequences of the tilting of the balance between learned and unlearned forms of steering conduct in favour of the former. The ruling convention of knowledge enforces a conceptual representation of the results of this process in non-processual terms. The best known example of this is the representation of the controlling agencies, whose biological substratum has evolved in the course of this process and which develop through learning in the life of each individual, as unlearned if invisible and intangible organs with names such as 'reason' or 'conscience'.

As one may see, this chapter represents in certain respects a reorientation of one's approach to the problems of human emotions. A tradition of long-standing has made it appear as self-evident that aspects of human beings such as emotions can be studied in isolation, that is without reference to the human beings as a framework where fear, joy and other emotions have their place and their function. I have tried to indicate that the study of emotions must remain unproductive as long as their connection with other aspects of human beings is not clearly taken into account. In the case of human beings unlearned emotional impulses are always related to a person's learned self-regulation, more specifically to learned controls of emotions. The chargeable balance between emotional impulses and emotion-controlling counter-impulses shows itself in a person's movements, in their gestures and in their facial expressions which are signals by means of which people communicate involuntarily or with intent the condition of the self-regulation of their emotions to other human beings. The term expression obscures the social, the communicative function of facial and other movements. Pointing out the inadequacy of the routinely used concept of 'expression of emotions' is the second focus of the re-orientation suggested here. Thus, finally, emotions and the related movements have a function within the context of a person's relationship with other persons and in a wider sense with nature at large. Emotions and the related movements or 'expressions' are, in short, one of the indications that human beings are by nature constituted for life in the company of others, for life in society.

Notes

I am very grateful to Dr Stephen Mennell for reading this text and suggesting significant improvements.

1. Julian Huxley, *The Uniqueness of Man*. London: Chatto & Windus, 1941.

2. One remembers the many experiments aimed at making apes speak. They were almost invariably concerned with a one-way traffic only, with attempts at making the ape produce sound patterns of a human language. Less attention was given to the question whether apes can understand the language sound pattern produced by other apes.

3. R. Plutchnik 'A General Psycho-Evolutionary Theory of Emotions' in L. Plutchnik and H. Kellerman (eds) *Emotion: Theory, Research and Experience*. New York, 1980, p. 8.

4. See the remarks on the long dominant mode of thinking in terms of *homo clausus* in the 1968 Preface to N. Elias *The Civilizing Process*, Vol. I. Oxford: Basil Blackwell, 1978, p. 249.

This chapter first appeared in *Theory, Culture & Society*, Vol. 4 (1987), 339–61.

4

ON THE CIVILIZING OF APPETITE

Stephen Mennell

Although *The Civilizing Process* has a great deal to say about the civilizing of table manners — how people ate — it says relatively little about what people ate and how much. Elias mentions in passing the well-known carnivorous bent of the medieval upper classes, in marked contrast to the largely leguminous and farinaceous diet of the peasants, and he discusses the gradual growth of feelings of repugnance towards the carving at table of large and recognizable carcasses (Elias, 1978: 117–22). Of appetite he says nothing. Yet the general thesis of *The Civilizing Process* is of course a powerful one, capable of wide application, and it gives general grounds for looking for evidence of a long-term process of the civilizing of appetite. Elias has demonstrated, not only in *The Civilizing Process* but in *The Court Society* and in many essays and lectures, how civilizing processes were manifested in changing taste in literature and the arts. The culinary arts are no exception, as I have tried to show in my book *All Manners of Food* (1985). In this particular chapter, however, I am concerned less with changes in qualitative tastes in food than with the more difficult question of changes in the regulation of appetite in the quantitative sense. Is it not likely that the same long-term changes in the structure of societies which brought about changes in manners, in the expression of affect, and in the tension-balance of personalities would also be reflected in the patterning and expression of so basic a drive as appetite?

One aspect of the problem of control over appetite has been raised by Bryan Turner (1982a, 1982b, 1984) in his discussions of medical discourse about diet. Turner mentions Elias in passing, but his own theoretical orientation is derived from Foucault (especially *The Birth of the Clinic* and *Discipline and Punish*) and from Max Weber's views on rationalization in European culture and its roots in religion. In Foucault, however, as Turner pointed out, 'the discourse appears to be almost sociologically disembodied' and 'there is a pronounced reluctance to reduce systematic thought to interests, especially the economic interests of social groups, so that the growth of formal knowledge appears to be one which is immanent in discourse itself' (1982b: 257). Weber certainly is not vulnerable to that criticism, but in his case it is well to recall Goudsblom's (1977: 188–9) warning that although *The Protestant Ethic* will always stand as 'a masterpiece of well-documented "interpretative understanding"', it is hopelessly inconclusive when it comes to explaining the actual part played by Calvinism in the sociogenesis of capitalism. Attempts to extend notions of elective affinity into realms like medical writings on diet are likely to be even more inconclusive. Besides, medical opinion — and even the increasing power of the medical profession — are only small parts of the complex history of appetite and its control in European society. I therefore want to explore whether ideas derived from Elias and figurational sociology can help to make sense of that history, and to ask whether we can speak of the 'civilizing of appetite'.

Hunger and Appetite

Appetite, it must be remembered, is not the same thing as hunger. Hunger is a body drive which recurs in all human beings in a reasonably regular cycle. Appetite for food, on the other hand, in the words of Daniel Cappon, a psychotherapist specializing in eating disorders is:

> basically a state of mind, an inner mental awareness of desire that is the setting for hunger.... An individual's appetite is his desire and inclination to eat, his interest in consuming food. Eating is what a person *does*. Appetite is what he *feels* like doing, mostly a psychological state. (1973: 21)

We tend to think of hunger and appetite as directly linked, but in fact, as Cappon argues, there is no simple relationship. The link between hunger and appetite is provided by what is sometimes referred to as the 'appestat', by which is meant a *psychological*, not simply physiological, control mechanism regulating food intake. Just as a thermostat can be set too high or too low, so a person's 'appestat' can be set too high or too low in relation to the physiological optimum range. Too high a setting, too much food intake, is a condition of 'bulimia', likely to lead to excessive body weight; too low a setting represents the condition of 'anorexia', leading to problems of underweight.

A person's 'appestat' setting is determined not only by the underlying hunger drive, but also by often rather complex psychological processes in which social pressures can play a considerable part. Body image is a particularly notable element: how a person perceives his or her own body and its relation to what he or she perceives to be the socially approved body image. Today psychologists understand much more about the psychological problems which can lead individual people to have pathological 'eating disorders' and body weights deviating from what is healthy.

But what about the regulation of appetite in the 'normal' majority? Can that be studied according to the model provided by Elias in a long-term developmental perspective? Cappon (1973: 45) provides a clue that perhaps it can, when he argues that his patients with eating disorders are in some sense 'immature' personalities, and that the normal mature individual today 'is able to change his eating habits at will — when he eats, how long he lingers over a meal, what he eats, and the amount'. In other words, Cappon is arguing that normal eating behaviour involves a capacity for considerable self-control. Has this capacity developed over the long term in European society in the same way that Elias argues other facets of self-control have done?

The Appetite of Gargantua
The celebrated banquets of the Middle Ages and Renaissance, known to us from literary sources like Rabelais and from numerous documents throughout Europe, give a misleading image of typical eating in that period. Not only did they involve just a small minority of society — even if we allow that servants and retainers received their share — but from the spectacular bills of fare it is difficult to work out how much each individual actually ate. For example, the menu for a feast given by the City of Paris for Cathérine de Medici in 1549 (Franklin, 1887–1902: III, 93) lists twenty-four sorts of animals (mainly birds and other game, because butcher's meat was disdained for such grand occasions), many kinds of cakes and pastry, and a mere four vegetable dishes — but we do not know how many shared the food. At the feast for the enthronement of Archbishop Nevill at York in 1465 (Warner, 1791: 93ff.), a thousand sheep, two thousand pigs, two thousand geese, four thousand rabbits, fish and game by the hundred, numerous kinds of bird, and twelve porpoises and seals were eaten; but though we know the order of courses and even the seating plan for the most

important guests, it is uncertain how many others took part, or indeed how long the feast lasted — it may have been several days. There is little doubt that guests could if they wished eat as much as they could take. The number of dishes set before the diners on such great occasions was very large — for example, *Sir Gawain and the Green Knight* (c. 1400: 25) mentions twelve dishes between each pair of diners — but they did not necessarily finish them, for it is known that surplus from the high table generally found its way to lower tables and eventually to the poor. Whatever the uncertainties, however, there seems little doubt that prodigious feats of appetite were witnessed at these great feasts, which were at least symptomatic of great inequalities in the social distribution of nourishment. The great people who had the power to do so sometimes indulged in such banquets in times of widespread dearth,[1] which itself, as a sign of a relatively low level of identification with the sufferings of fellow men, marks in Elias's terms a relatively low point on the curve of civilizing processes.

In other ways, the great banquets are highly misleading as a guide to medieval patterns of appetite. Their social function can be understood more by analogy with the Kwakiutl potlatch than in relation to culinary taste and appetite (Mennell, 1985, chapter 3; Codere, 1950). Moreover they were untypical even of upper-class eating. They were high-points of an oscillating dietary regime even for the courtiers and nobility. Even this élite did not eat like that all the time. Perhaps, unlike most people, they rarely went hungry, but they did not always enjoy the wide choice which (rather than the sophistication of the cooking) was the hallmark of the feast. The rhythm of the seasons and the hazards of the harvest impinged even on their diet; even they knew periods of frugality.[2] Breakfasts even in a royal household 'would not now be regarded as extravagant in a day labourer's family', and on ordinary days dinners consisted of no more than two joints of meat, roast or boiled, or fish (Weber, 1973: 198). Robert Mandrou recognizes the significance of these fluctuations in the pattern of eating:

> ... without any doubt it was normal for all social classes to alternate between frugality and feasting. A consequence of the general insecurity where food was concerned, this oscillation imposed itself as a rite, some signs of which can still be found today. The festivals of the fraternities ... in the towns and those of the harvest, vintage or St Martin's Day in the country were always occasions for fine living for a few hours at least — and with innumerable variations in the form it took, of course.[3] But these huge feasts, after which a man had to live on bread and

water for months on end provided compensation, however meagre, for ill-fortune, and were appreciated for that reason; the very precariousness of existence explained them. The virtue of thrift, of making one's resources spread evenly over a given period, cannot be conceived of without a certain margin of supply.... One other factor to be taken into account in explaining these 'orgies' is the ever-present dangers threatening the granary; what was the good of laying up large stocks if brigands or soldiers might come along the next day and carry them off? (Mandrou, 1975: 24)

This oscillation between fasting and feasting runs parallel to the extreme emotional volatility of medieval people noted by Elias, their ability to express emotion with greater freedom than today, and to fluctuate quickly between extremes. And their sources are the same.

Mandrou, like Elias, Bloch (1961: I, 73 and II, 411) and Huizinga (1924: chapter 1) before him, notes this general psychological volatility but, curiously, relates it only indirectly to the insecurity of life in medieval and early modern Europe; he attributes it in large part to the physiological effects of inadequate and irregular feeding. 'The effect of this chronic malnutrition was to produce in man the mentality of the hunted, with its superstitions, its sudden outbursts of anger and its hypersensitivity' (1975: 26). Such direct physiological effects of nutrition on psychology should perhaps not be entirely discounted, but they should equally not be overstressed; the suggestion merely adds one more complication to an already complex causal nexus. More important — as Mandrou himself seemed to see clearly when specifically discussing the fluctuation between feasting and fasting — is the link between the general precariousness and unpredictability of existence and its reflection in personality, beliefs and social behaviour. Keith Thomas (1971) has emphasized the connection between the hazards of life in the sixteenth and seventeenth centuries and the prevalence of superstition and magical beliefs, which declined noticeably with the growing security of the late seventeenth and eighteenth centuries. But it is Norbert Elias who has traced most fully the general connection between the changing emotional economy of the personality and the gradually growing calculability of social existence brought about by long-term processes of change in the structure of societies.

The Civilizing Process presents a theory of state-formation and of the internal pacification of larger and larger territories which the growth of states involved. But Elias has also made it clear that state-formation is only one of several intertwining and interdependent long-term processes of social development which gradually increased the security and calculability of life in society. Internal pacification permitted the division of labour and growth of trade — eventually increasing the security of food supplies among many other things — which in turn provided the economic basis for further expansion of the territory and the internal regulative power of states. *The Civilizing Process* is also a study of the changing codes of manners and standards of social behaviour which broadly accompanied these processes. Elias (1982: 233–4) gives a characteristically vivid illustration of the connection between these two aspects of his study. Travelling by road, he observes, was dangerous in medieval times, and it remains so today — but the nature of the danger has changed. The medieval traveller had to have the ability — temperamental as well as physical — to defend himself violently against violent attack. Today, the chief danger is from road accidents, and avoiding them depends to a great extent on high capacity for self-control in the expression of (and skill in warding off) aggression, whether in overt or in disguised form. And aggression is only one of the manifestations of affect over which people came gradually to be subject to increased pressures to exercise greater self-control. Not that the expression of feeling by people in the Middle Ages lacked all social patterning and control. There is no zero-point. But in the long-term the controls grew not just stronger but also more even.

Against this background, the oscillation between extremes of gluttonous gorging and enforced fasting seems all of a piece with other aspects of the medieval and early modern personality. I would therefore argue that it is connected not simply with the insecurity and unpredictability of food supplies alone, but also with the more general insecurity of conditions of life.

Famines and Other Hazards
Life in medieval and early modern Europe certainly was by today's standards very insecure. Goubert (1960) speaks vividly of 'steeples' of mortality, from the appearance of the suddenly soaring graphs of death-rates in the Beauvaisis in the seventeenth and early eighteenth centuries. Mortality among élites, whom one might expect to have been better fed, seems to have been just as high as among the mass of the population in Western Europe. This is especially well-documented for Britain. T.H. Hollingsworth's calculations (1977) of mortality in British peerage families since 1600 differ scarcely at all from those of Wrigley and Schofield (1981). As late as the third

quarter of the seventeenth century, the life-expectancy of males at birth was only about thirty years. Mortality among ruling groups elsewhere in Europe was also high, 'which makes it unlikely that they enjoyed appreciable advantages over the rest of the population' (Livi-Bacci, 1985: 98).

There were many causes other than dearth for the steeples of mortality which from time to time towered over localities, regions, or even whole countries. In towns, there were frequent disastrous fires, made worse in their consequences by organization inadequate to control them (Thomas, 1971: 15). Epidemic diseases including smallpox and plague periodically cut swathes through all ranks of society; poor sanitation and hygiene — reflecting deficiencies in medical knowledge and technology as well as once more in social organization — played their part in this. And then there were wars and vagrancy. All these were in addition to crop failures, and they could interact in complex ways — war, for instance, not only killed people directly, but disrupted food supplies, led to increased vagrancy, and helped to spread disease.

Not even in the worst times of famine is it thought that a great proportion of people actually starved to death. The general view is that hunger made many more people susceptible to disease, and that others who survived the immediate famine had their lifespans curtailed by the effects of hunger and malnutrition. Even this is in some dispute: Livi-Bacci (1985: 96) has pointed out 'that the majority of cases of extraordinary and catastrophic mortality are independent of famine, hunger and starvation, and Watkins and Van de Walle (1985: 21) have contended that 'the evidence linking malnutrition and mortality is surprisingly sparse and inadequate'. Most historians would accept, however, at least that 'even if many of the deaths in a famine period were due rather to disease than to outright starvation, nevertheless the sudden rise in death rates was sometimes associated with an abrupt fall in the availability of food, whatever the causes of this scarcity' (Watkins and Van de Walle, 1985: 17).

Famines, in any case, are not a simple function of crop failure. Sen's study of modern famines (1981) has already influenced historians' thinking about famines in the past. Sen shows that even in times of famine, food is available. People starve because of their inability to command food through 'entitlement' relationships such as ownership, exchange, employment, and social security rights. In other words, the effects of crop failures have to be understood in terms of patterns of social interdependence. The breaking of the chain which linked crop failure to famines and famines to steeples of mortality is the story more of developing social organization's contribution to an increasing security of life than simply of increasingly reliable food production.

In medieval and early modern Europe, bad harvests and food shortages sometimes affected whole countries, even the whole continent at the same time. An example is the great European famine of 1315–17. Often, however, only a limited region was affected by harvest failure; though before authorities were able to organize the holding of sufficient stocks of grain, and before trade and transport were adequate to remedy local shortage, they could be serious enough.[4] Inadequate transport meant that food could not be moved, or could be moved only with difficulty, from surplus to deficit areas. Shortages led to panic buying, hoarding, and speculation, prices soaring and putting what food was available for sale quite beyond the means of the poor. Holding stocks could have helped to remedy this, but administrative difficulties defeated most governments before the late seventeenth or eighteenth century. The direct relationship between harvest failures and soaring rates of mortality only gradually disappeared from Western Europe from the late seventeenth century onwards. By then, large grain stocks held for example at Amsterdam were helping to alleviate the effects of dearth not only in the Low Countries but in coastal and other areas of neighbouring countries accessible to trade. In the eighteenth century, food production increased markedly, but so did population. There was more food, though not necessarily greater consumption per capita. Food supplies, however, became gradually more reliable and shortages less frequent. After 1750, according to Braudel and Spooner (in Rich and Wilson, 1977: 396), only 'suppressed' famines ('almost bearable ones') continued to occur in Western Europe, very largely because of improvements in trade and transport, the effects of which can be seen in the levelling out of food prices plotted (as on a weather map) across the continent. In England scarcity following crop failures no longer reached famine proportions by the first decade of the eighteenth century, though food prices rose very high and death rates were still noticeably up in years of bad harvests in the 1720s and 1740s. In France, the last full nation-wide famine was that of 1709–10, but regional dearths accompanied by rising mortality still happened as late as 1795–6 and 1810–12 (Cobb, 1970: 220–2).

Improved trade and transport were not altogether straightforward in their effects:

> the growth of trade, if it enabled the surplus of one region rather more often than
> before to relieve the dearth of another, also left a larger number of people at the
> mercy of market fluctuation, tended to depress or hold down real wages, and
> increase the gap between the rich and the poor. (Wernham, 1968: 5)

Furthermore, what Pelto and Pelto call the 'delocalization' of food-
use over the last few centuries — meaning 'processes in which food
varieties, production methods, and consumption patterns are disseminated throughout the world in an ever-increasing and intensify-
ing network of socio-economic and political interdependency'
(1985: 309) — had a differential impact between centres and
peripheries. In the industrialized countries it was eventually to
bring about increased diversity of available foods and improved
diets for lower as well as upper social ranks; in the less industrialized
world, in contrast, the same process has led through commercialization to concentration in many regions on only a few cash crops with
a concomitant reduction of food diversity. In a shorter-term period
of transition, the same sort of contrast could be seen *within* the
countries of Europe. This conflict between national markets and
local needs was one reason why food riots were still common in
eighteenth-century England and France (Tilly, 1975: 380–455;
Rudé 1964; Thompson, 1971; Cobb, 1970).

Another reason was more important: what could not immediately disappear with general famines was the fear of going hungry
engendered by centuries of experience. Mandrou observes that one
of the most characteristic features of early modern Europe was

> the obsession with starving to death, an obsession which varied in intensity
> according to locality and class, being stronger in the country than in the town,
> rare among the upper-classes and well-fed fighting men, and constant among the
> lower classes. (1961: 26–7)

The themes of starvation, child abandonment and outright cannibalism so common in European folklore are further evidence of the
pervasive fear of food scarcity.[5] So equally, as Jacques Le Goff
(1964) has argued, were the countering themes of the *mythes de
ripaille* ('myths about having a good blow-out') found in early
peasant folklore, becoming by the thirteenth century a literary
theme in the French fable *Cocaigne* and the English poem *The Land*

of Cockaygne, and the food miracles which multiplied around many saints. Both sets of themes, though superficially opposites, are signs of deep-rooted fears which could not disappear overnight. As late as 1828, notes Cobb (1970: 215), dearth was still being written about as a major threat to public order in France, because 'the fear of dearth was permanent, especially at the lower levels of society, and it took very little at any time for this fear to become hysterical and to develop into the proportions of panic'.

External Constraints on Appetite: Church, State and Doctors
In these circumstances, self-control over appetite was scarcely a pressing problem for the vast majority of Europeans from medieval until relatively recent times. At first glance, in medieval and early modern Europe there might appear to be at least three sources of pressures towards self-control over appetite: first, the large number of fasts expected of the fervent Catholic; second, the sumptuary laws which apparently demonstrated the interest of states in suppressing gluttony; and, thirdly, medical opinion. I shall, however, argue that each of these represented a form only of external constraint (*Fremdzwang* was Elias's original word), and only very gradually did this come to be accompanied by a considerable measure of self-restraint (*Selbstzwang*).

Fasting
Fasting was in theory required on three days a week (Wednesday, Friday and Saturday), on the vigils for major saints days, for three days at each of the Quarter Days, and for the whole of Lent except Sundays. Strict fasting consisted essentially of eating only once in twenty-four hours, after Vespers, and as far as possible then eating only bread and water. But, of course, for all but the most ascetic, fish was permitted, as were vegetables, but wine as well as meat and any other animal product were excluded (Franklin, 1887–1902: VIII, 124ff.; Henisch, 1976: 28–50). As time passed, the Church made more and more exceptions, such as permitting eggs to be eaten on fast days — and made the requirements less stringent, but the rules were still in principle in force in Catholic countries in the late eighteenth century. After the Reformation, the Protestant churches generally disapproved of fasting on specific days as an integral part of Catholic ritual. In a characteristic compromise, the Elizabethan Church of England frowned on fasting as a form of display, though it allowed that at the discretion of individuals it

could be a useful adjunct to prayer; and it adjured Christians to observe fasts decreed by law, not for religious but for political reasons:

> as when any realm in consideration of the maintenance of fisher-towns bordering upon the seas, and for the increase of fishermen, of whom do spring mariners to go upon the sea, to the furnishing of the Navy of the Realm, whereby not only commodities of other countries may be transported, but also may be a necessary defence to resist the invasion of the adversary. (Homilies, 1562: 300; cf. O'Hara-May, 1977: 122ff.)

Yet even when and where the Church's authority fully upheld the ritual of fasting, how much difference did it effectively make to how much people actually ate? The majority of people would have considered themselves fortunate if there was meat to eat as often as four days a week. Nor did the rules of fasting do anything to impede their enjoyment of the great binges which at times of plenty relieved the monotony and sparsity of their usual diet. As for the minority for whom plenty was not exceptional, they could eat sumptuously even on *jours maigres*, breaking not the letter but merely the spirit of the fasting rules. How little abstinence a dinner on a fish day might represent is suggested by the vigil dinner set before Sir Gawain on Christmas Eve:

> Several fine soups, seasoned lavishly
> Twice-fold, as is fitting, and fish of all kinds —
> Some baked in bread, some browned on coals,
> Some seethed, some stewed and savoured with spices,
> But always subtly sauced, and so the man liked it.
> The gentle knight generously judged it a feast,
> And often said so, while the servers spurred
> him on thus
>   As he ate
>   'This present penance do;
>   It soon shall be offset'. (Anon., 1974: 54–5)

Much later, French courtly recipe books of the seventeenth and eighteenth centuries also show what could be achieved within the rules on *jours maigres*. In fact, the observance of fasting in the medieval and early modern period has all the hallmarks of *Fremdzwang* rather than *Selbstzwang*. That is to say, there is very little evidence of people having internalized the controls the rules embodied; few evidently felt any personal guilt or repugnance at breaking the rules. In any case, the prescribed fasts in their full severity were probably only ever observed in some religious orders.[6] And such exceptional instances of extreme abstinence are indeed a symptom of the unevenness of controls over eating. This general unevenness of controls is, according to Elias, typical of socially highly unequal societies, and Jack Goody has specifically pointed to fasting as characteristic of hierarchical societies:

> The other side of hierarchical cuisine was the extended notion of the fast, a rejection of food for religious, medical or moral reasons. . . . Abstinence and prohibition are widely recognized as ways of attaining grace in hierarchical societies such as China and India. . . . Such a philosophy of rejection could develop only within the context of hierarchical cuisine since abstention only exists in the wider context of indulgence. (1982: 116–17)

Very gradually there was to take place a process of development towards controls over appetite which, to use a phrase of Elias's, were both 'more even and all-round' — meaning that individuals acquired the capacity typically to be able to exercise more consistent self-control, and that the controls came to apply more uniformly to people in all strata of society. But in this process, the teachings of the Church seem not to have played any very significant part.[7]

Sumptuary Laws
Perhaps more significant than the Church's teaching is that from the late Middle Ages onwards the secular authorities in England, France and other countries showed their concern to discourage over-elaborate banqueting by enacting sumptuary laws. That the problem was seen as one of social display, not of sheer physical appetite, can be seen from the fact that such laws often sought to control the clothes people wore as well as the food they ate (see Baldwin, 1926; Boucher d'Argis, 1765). The enactment of these laws is possibly a consequence of European society becoming somewhat more open. Enormous banquets were perhaps acceptable when given by feudal lords sharing their viands by custom and obligation with their followers and distributing remains to the poor, but were seen as excess and mere social display when copied by rising strata whose social obligations were ill-defined and dependants few. Not that sumptuary laws were ever effective. Like many other laws before the seventeenth century, the same law was often re-enacted at frequent intervals without ever being effectively enforced; the states simply did not have the power to enforce them. In France, a law of 1563 forbade even private families to have meals of

more than three courses, and the number and type of dishes to constitute each course was also specified in detail. But very much the same law had to be re-enacted in 1565, 1567, 1572, 1577, 1590, 1591, and finally in 1629 (Franklin, 1887–1902: I, 102). In England, Archbishop Cranmer and his bishops agreed in 1541 on very detailed rules carefully grading the number of courses and number of dishes which the archbishops, bishops, deans, archdeacons and junior clergy might eat; but Cranmer appends a sad little memorandum 'that this order was kept for two or three months, till, by the disusing of certain wilful persons, it came again to the old excess' (Combe, 1846: 491).

Medical Opinion
It would be equally incautious to overemphasize the influence of medical opinion, or of the rationalization of medical knowledge, in pressurizing people to exercise self-control over appetite. One of the major thrusts of *The Civilizing Process* is to demonstrate that ' "Rational understanding" is not the motor of the "civilizing" of eating or of other behaviour' (Elias, 1978: I, 116; see also Goudsblom, 1979). Throughout the Middle Ages medical opinion, dominated by the views of the Salerno School, had favoured moderation in eating in the treatment of numerous illnesses. Doctors were certainly aware of the medical dangers of obesity, although they tended to interpret it as a result of inactivity and laziness rather than of overeating per se (O'Hara-May, 1977: 127). But medical opinion is and was brought to bear most effectively on the ill, and there is little evidence to suggest that their opinions had much effect on the daily eating habits of the normally healthy.

Although the social power of the medical profession was growing during the eighteenth century, it is too easy to follow Foucault in looking too hard for dramatic *ruptures*, and thus to exaggerate both the profession's power and the novelty of its opinions at this period. Certainly, as Jean-Paul Aron has shown (1961: 971–7), the notion of *régime alimentaire* began to be prominent in medical circles during the eighteenth century, and was reflected in the writings of Rousseau, who favoured moderation and pure foods. Early in the century both in England and France a number of doctors advocated strict diets as a way to health: Bryan Turner has focused particularly on the writings of George Cheyne (1724, 1733), and a little earlier in France Philippe Hecquet (1709) propounded similar ideas in a famous controversy. Jones and Sonenscher (1983) describe how, later in the century, the diet of hospital inmates was the subject of conflict between doctors and nurses at the Hôtel-Dieu in Nîmes. The nursing sisters had traditionally seen their role as a charitable one and, aware that many illnesses had resulted from repeated subsistence crises, saw it as their duty to feed up the poor and needy ill. One of the doctors at Nîmes complained bitterly against the overplentifulness of the patients' diet, which often impeded their recovery. 'They are always afraid in this hospital that people will die of hunger . . . they always feed the sick too much.' A colleague in neighbouring Montpellier in the 1760s documented how over-feeding by the sisters had led to patients' premature deaths, and 'gave the impression that over-eating was one of the major causes of hospital mortality!' Significantly, the doctors in eighteenth-century Montpellier also launched an onslaught on the tradition of marking the hospital's patron saint's day with feasting.

All the same, it is unsound to pursue an explanation in terms of a few artificially isolated causal 'factors'. A figurational investigation looks first for the sorts of problems people encounter within the webs of social interdependence in which they are caught up. In this case, it is well to remember that the problem of appetite in relation to over-abundant food had still scarcely arisen in the eighteenth century for the great majority of the people of Western Europe; for them the most pressing external constraints on appetite were still the shortage or irregularity of food supplies. As for the minority for whom the problem had already arisen they had begun to show signs of adapting to it before any dramatic shift in medical opinion. (There is of course no reason why medical opinion, as one thread in a complex process of development, should not be both cause and effect in various ways and at different stages of the process.)

Quantity and Quality

When food was scarce for most and supplies insecure and irregular for nearly all, the powerful distinguished themselves from their inferiors by the sheer quantities they ate: 'those who could, gorged themselves; those who couldn't, aimed to' (Weber, 1973: 202). Evidence for this is found in one of the most detailed studies of diet in the late Middle Ages, Stouff's study of Provence. Stouff shows that in various ecclesiastical communities, not only did those in the higher echelons eat proportionately more meat, fish and other proteins in relation to bread and wine than did their inferiors, they also ate a great deal more overall. In one case study typical of the general pattern,

> One conclusion must be drawn: in 1429 (and it appears to be equally true throughout the fifteenth century), the food intake of the Archbishop of Arles and the senior members of his household was too large, but relatively well balanced. (Stouff, 1970: 238)

In the sixteenth and seventeenth centuries, there were many who seem to have been noted more for their capacity than for their refinement of taste. Cathérine de Medici was celebrated for her appetite and frequent indigestion. Diarists at the court of Louis XIV have left graphic accounts of the great king's prodigious consumption. Nor does he appear to have been untypical of his court.[8]

Faint traces of the beginnings of pressures towards self-restraint in appetite can be seen a century earlier. In appetite as in so many other facets of the civilizing process, Montaigne is a good witness (Mennell, 1981a). He reports that he himself has little self-restraint in eating, but bemoans the fact:

> if they preach abstinence once a dish is in front of me, they are wasting their time.... To eat greedily as I do, is not only harmful to health, and even to one's pleasure, but it is unmannerly into the bargain. So hurried am I that I often bite my tongue, and sometimes my fingers... My greed leaves me no time for talk. (Montaigne, 1967: 445)

By the mid-eighteenth century extreme gluttony appears to have become the exception. Louis XVI, who saw off chicken, lamb cutlets, eggs, ham and a bottle and a half of wine before setting out to hunt, without it diminishing his appetite at dinner, appears to have been considered something of a throwback:

> By his appetite, and by his appetite alone did the unfortunate Louis XVI revive memories of Louis XIV. Like him, he did not bother himself with cookery, nor with any refinements; to him, always afraid of not having enough to eat, sheer quantity was more important than anything else; he did not eat, he stuffed himself, going as far as to incapacitate himself at his wedding dinner, scandalizing his grandfather [Louis XV]. (Gottschalk, 1939: 232)

Even in England, another famous trencherman of that time, Dr Johnson, though of less exalted social rank, was also considered a coarse eater. Not only did he show so little sense of what was proper as to call for the boat containing the lobster sauce left over from the previous course and pour it over his plum-pudding (Piozzi, 1785), but he wolfed his food down in a shameful manner:

> When at table, Johnson was totally absorbed in the business of the moment; his looks seemed rivetted to his plate; nor would he, unless when in very high company, say one word, or even pay the least attention to what was said by others, till he had satisfied his appetite, which was so fierce and indulged with such intenseness that while in the act of eating, the veins of his forehead swelled and generally a strong perspiration was evident. To those whose sensations were delicate, this could not but be disgusting; and it was doubtless not very suitable to the character of a philosopher, who should be distinguished by self-command. (Boswell, 1791: I, 323)

Significantly, Boswell comments that everything about Johnson's character and manners was forcible and violent, and adds

> Johnson, though he could be rigidly *abstemious*, was not a *temperate* man either in eating or drinking. He could refrain, but he could not use moderately.

That sounds very much like a throwback to the mode of behaviour typical of medieval and early modern Europe. But by the mid-eighteenth century it was no longer considered quite the right thing in the better circles. What changes were taking place?

The civilizing of appetite, if we may call it that, appears to have been partly related to the increasing security, regularity, reliability and variety of food supplies. But just as the civilizing of appetite was entangled with several other strands of the civilizing process including the transformation of table manners, so the improvement in food supplies was only one strand in a complex of developments within the social figuration which together exerted a compelling force over the way people behaved. The increased security of food supplies was made possible by the extension of trade, the progressive division of labour in a growing commercial economy, and also by the process of state-formation and internal pacification. Even a small improvement was enough to enable a small powerful minority to distinguish themselves from the lower ranks of society by the sheer quantities they ate and the regularity with which they ate them. As the improvement continued, somewhat wider segments of the better-off groups in society came to be able to copy the élite. The same structural processes, however, served not only to permit social emulation but positively to promote it. The longer chains of social interdependence produced by state-formation and the division of labour tended to tilt the balance of power little by little towards lower social groups, leading to increased pressure 'from below' and to intensified social competition. The sumptuary laws, with their vain attempt to relate quantities eaten to social rank, seem symptomatic of that.

By the sixteenth or seventeenth centuries, for the nobility to eat quantitatively more would have been physically impossible.[9] That was one reason for increasing demands made upon the skill of the cook in making food more palatable; as a modern expert explains,

> A variety of studies demonstrates that hunger and palatability are substitutive for each other and algebraically additive in their effects. Equal amounts are eaten of a highly palatable food in a minimal state of hunger and even without hunger, and of a minimally palatable food in a state of hunger. Thus it is equally true to assume that hunger potentiates palatability and that palatability potentiates hunger in their common effect of eliciting eating. The consequences of this relationship is that the differential palatability of two foods decreases with increased hunger. (Le Magnen, 1972: 76)

Or, as Andrew Combe wrote in a nineteenth-century classic of dietetics,

> Appetite . . . may . . . be educated or trained to considerable deviations from the ordinary standard of quantity and quality . . . The most common source . . . of the errors into which we are apt to fall in taking appetite as our only guide, is unquestionably the *confounding of appetite with taste*, and continuing to eat for the gratification of the latter long after the former is satisfied. In fact, the whole science of a skilful cook is expended in producing this *willing* mistake on our part. (Combe, 1846: 29–30)

Here, then, is the psychological basis for the elaboration of cooking in an age of plenty. And the skills of cooks had another advantage: they could be applied not simply to stimulating the sated appetites of the glutton, but also to the invention and elaboration of an endless variety of ever more refined and delicate dishes; when the possibilities of quantitative consumption for the expression of social superiority had been exhausted, the qualitative possibilities were inexhaustible.

The links between the changing social figuration, changing patterns of social contest, the changing arts of the cook, and the civilizing of appetite are most clearly discernible, like so many facets of civilizing processes, in France. The development there of 'court society' was particularly significant (Elias, 1982; Mennell, 1985, Ch. 5). The revenues, political power and social functions of the old *noblesse d'épée* were gradually declining, while those of the bourgeoisie and of the essentially bourgeois *noblesse de robe* were increasing. Parts of the old nobility acquired positions at court and became highly dependent on royal favour. They became in effect specialists in the arts of consumption, entrapped in a system of fine distinctions, status battles and competitive expenditure from which they could not escape because their whole social identity depended upon it. They were under constant pressure to differentiate themselves from the *robins*, the despised *noblesse campagnarde*, and the bourgeoisie. How was this reflected in eating?

The break with medieval cookery seems to have begun in the city courts of Renaissance Italy, but the leadership in matters of culinary innovation seems to have passed to France in the late sixteenth or early seventeenth centuries (see Mennell, 1985, Ch. 4). By early in the reign of Louis XIV, the beginnings of modern French cuisine are visible in the more refined techniques, the less exuberant use of ingredients, and the greater variety of dishes given in a book like La Varenne's *Le Cuisinier François* of 1651. Another period of rapid development followed in the next reign. The gluttony of Louis XIV and many of his courtiers was replaced by the delicate *soupers* for which the Regent was noted. Indeed the Regent himself, like several others among the high nobility, seems himself to have been an expert cook, and his mother the Princess Palatine implies that this was a part of *bon ton* which could be ranked with skills in other arts like music:

> My son knows how to cook; it is something he learned in Spain. He is a good musician, as all musicians recognize; he has composed two operas, which he had produced in his chambers and which had some merit, but he did not want them to be shown in public. (Orléans, 1855: I, 349–50)

The change of fashion during the eighteenth century away from quantitative display towards more varied and delicate ragouts is noted by Louis-Sebastien Mercier in 1783:

> In the last century, they used to serve huge pieces of meat, and pile them up in pyramids. These little dishes, costing ten times as much as one of those big ones, were not yet known. Delicate eating has been known for only half a century. The delicious cuisine of the reign of Louis XV was unknown even to Louis XIV. (1783: V, 597–8)

The sense of delicacy and pressures towards self-control are, as Elias has shown, closely interwoven. In eating it is the developing sense of delicacy which first becomes apparent, but that eventually becomes entangled with restraint. In the late sixteenth century Montaigne, who as we have already seen claimed to have little self-restraint over his own eating, also poked fun in his *essai* on 'La vanité des paroles' at Cardinal Caraffa's Italian'chef for the gravity with which he held forth on the propriety of courses and sauces, sequences of dishes and balances of flavours (Montaigne, 1967: 134–5). By the time of La Varenne, French cooks were at least as much concerned with such matters as their Italian forerunners. And only a couple of decades later, the next generation of French cookery writers spoke of La Varenne's meals and dishes as coarse and rustic. Molière mocks the seriousness with which these growing conventions were taken, and their social significance (see *Le Bourgeois Gentilhomme*, Act 4; *L'Avare*, Act 3). By the middle of the eighteenth century the first truly gastronomic controversies were taking place, in which defenders of old styles of cooking and eating railed against the preciousness, pretentiousness and over-developed sense of culinary propriety of the proponents of the *nouvelle cuisine*.

By then too, larger segments of the bourgeoisie were seeking to copy the courtly models of refined and delicate eating, and this probably gave increased impetus to the movement towards greater delicacy and self-restraint. The connections are complex. We have noted that courtly fashion moved towards the proliferation of small, delicate and costly dishes, and that knowledgeability and a sense of delicacy in matters of food became something of a mark of the courtier. Now a sense of delicacy implies a degree of restraint too, in so far as it involves discrimination and selection, the rejection as well as the acceptance of certain foods or combinations of foods, guided at least as much by social proprieties as by individual fancies. No courtly gourmet would pour the lobster sauce over his plum pudding. But while the development of systems of fashionable preferences involves a degree of rationalization, what Elias calls 'court-rationality' was antithetical to that of bourgeois economic rationality; lavish consumption was too closely part of the courtier's social identity for him to economize like a good bourgeois. While there is plenty of evidence that, in France at least, the bourgeoisie wanted in the eighteenth century to follow courtly models of eating, it is also clear that most did not have the resources to eat on such a lavish scale; they were therefore both under more pressure than the nobility to choose and select, and also more easily able to do so. The bourgeoisie was in many ways a more appropriate *couche* for the emergence of a body of gastronomic theorizing. Moreover, given that a fairly high degree of internal pacification and a measure of economic surplus are prerequisites for the development of the cultural syndrome of bourgeois rationality as a whole, it seems no coincidence that gastronomic theorizing as a genre first appeared during the period when the insecurity of food supplies ceased to be of catastrophic proportions, and burgeoned fully during the nineteenth century.[10] At any rate, when it did emerge, the theorists were indeed mainly members of the high bourgeoisie, and the themes of delicacy and self-restraint were prominent in their writings, the latter increasingly so as time went on.

Gastronomy and Moderation
Neither Grimod de la Reynière (1803–12) nor Brillat-Savarin (1826), the two most noted pioneers of gastronomy, entirely dismissed a large capacity as an epicurean virtue. But their writings emphasize the need for a discriminating palate and scorn as vulgar any merely quantitative display. They set the pattern for gastronomic writing in both France and England for the rest of the century An Englishman strongly influenced by Grimod writes in 1822:

> Gluttony is, in fact, a mere effort of the appetite, of which the coarsest bolter of bacon in all Hampshire may equally boast with the most distinguished consumer of turtle in a Corporation: while Epicurism is the result of 'that choicest gift of Heaven', a refined and discriminating taste: this is the peculiar attribute of the palate, that of the stomach. It is the happy combination of both these enviable qualities that constitutes that truly estimable character, the real epicure. He is not only endowed with a capacious stomach and an insatiable appetite, but with a delicate susceptibility in the organs of degustation, which enables him to appreciate the true relish of each ingredient in the most compound ragout, and to detect the slightest aberration of the cook; added to which advantages, he possesses a profound acquaintance with the rules of art in all the most approved schools of cookery, and an enlightened judgment on their several merits, matured by long and sedulous experience. (Sturgeon, 1822: 3–4)

A few decades later, in 1868, another writer bemoans England's lagging behind France in gastronomic *savoir-faire*, and now directly disparages the lack of discrimination masked by plenty:

> Not only our merchant princes, but our gentry and nobility, have merely a superficial knowledge of the science of cookery and the art of giving good dinners. Consider the barbarism implied in the popular phrase for ample hospitality! The table is described as groaning under the plenty of the host. (Jerrold, 1868: 5)

By the twentieth century, the theme of moderation was still more explicit. G.F. Scotson-Clark, in a book entitled *Eating without Fears* published in 1924, writes that

> Consuming large quantities of food is only a habit. What is often called a 'healthy appetite' is nothing of the sort. The only people who should eat really large quantities of food are those whose regular daily life involves a vast amount of physical exercise — like the road-mender. (1924: 65)

And André L. Simon reiterates an argument prominent in his extensive writings between the 1930s and 1960s.

> There cannot be any intelligent choice nor real appreciation where there is excess. Gastronomy stands or falls by moderation. No gourmand and no glutton can be a gastronome. (1969: 94)

Gradually moderation became more clearly linked to questions of health as well as discrimination. Scotson-Clark says:

> Cookery plays such a large part in our life, it is really the fundamental basis of our life, our very existence, that it is foolish to belittle its importance. To take no interest in it is as bad for one's health as to take no interest in one's ablutions. An individual should cultivate his palate just as much as he should cultivate his brain. Good taste in food and wine is as necessary as good taste in art, literature and music, and the very fact of looking upon gastronomy as one of the arts will keep a man from becoming that most disgusting of creatures, a glutton . . .
>   I am sure that moderation is the keynote of good health, and I contend that anyone can eat anything I mention in this book, without increasing his girth, and if taken in moderation he can reduce to normal weight. It is not necessary for one to deprive oneself of all the things one loves, for fear of getting too fat, but it is necessary to take an intelligent interest in the provender with which one intends to stoke the human furnace. (1924: 8–9)

At about the same time in France, Edouard de Pomiane, the medical doctor turned cookery writer, was developing similar themes in books (1922) and in the popular press. Although dieting for health and slimness became a prominent concern in mass circulation publications like women's magazines (see Mennell, 1985, Ch. 9) only after the Second World War, the slim body-image had begun to appeal in higher social circles considerably earlier.

The Fear of Fatness
It would be interesting to know whether fatness was common and whether it carried any stigma in medieval and early modern Europe. The evidence is not entirely unambiguous. Kunzle (1982:

65) traces the ideal of the slender female figure as far back as courtly circles in the later Middle Ages, but it is easy to find literary evidence of plumpness being considered attractive. As for visual evidence, Jane O'Hara-May (1977: 127) argues that paintings show relatively few very fat people, and suggests that the frequent use of purges and the large amount of exercise which in this period even the wealthy could scarcely avoid tended to balance excessive intake. In contrast, Kristoff Glamann draws precisely opposite conclusions from portraits, and states that corporeal bulk was in all ranks of society a source not of shame but of prestige.

> Eating made one handsome. A thin wife brought disgrace to a peasant. But of a plump wife it was said that 'a man will love her and not begrudge the food she eats'. Men too ought to be stout. That this ideal was not confined to the rustic world is plain from a glance at the magnificent amplitude of the human frame so abundantly depicted by the Renaissance painters. (Rich and Wilson, 1977: 195)

The contradictory conclusions about average girth in paintings point to the need for more systematic studies. But on the more general question of the prestige or otherwise of bodily bulk, the most likely conclusion is that while obesity which impeded health and activity was deplored (particularly by the doctors whom O'Hara-May is studying), a healthy stoutness was widely considered prestigious.

The problem and the fear of being overweight seems, not surprisingly, to have started towards the top of the social scale and progressed steadily downwards. The 'magnificent amplitude of the human frame' which once constituted the cultural model in Europe — and still does in many societies where poverty is rife — was gradually replaced by the ideal of the slim figure. The changing standard of beauty among the upper strata can be seen around the time of the Romantic movement, when 'for both women and men paleness, frailness, slenderness became the vogue' (Young, 1970: 16). Burnett (1966: 80) quotes some fairly abstemious diets recommended for well-to-do ladies at that period. Up to the end of the Edwardian era, as Dally and Gomez (1979: 25) point out, many successful men tended to be rather stout, but today there tend to be lower rates of obesity among the upper socio-economic groups.

Exactly when the ideal began to be reflected in an actual decline in typical body weights, and how the decline progressed down the social scale, is very difficult to demonstrate. Quite a lot of historical evidence is available about people's *heights* (Fogel et al., 1985) but,

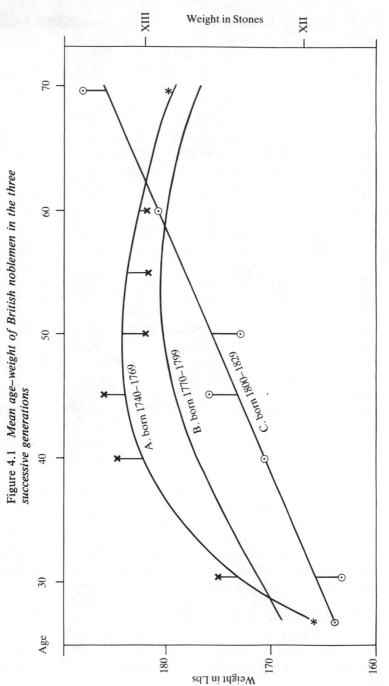

Figure 4.1 *Mean age–weight of British noblemen in the three successive generations*

given the complexities of relating body weights to height, age and sex, let alone to social class, little in the way of time-series data over the long period required is available or likely to become available. An interesting clue is an article by Sir Francis Galton in *Nature*, 1884, comparing the weights of three generations of British noblemen among the customers of Berry Brothers, grocers and winemerchants in St James's, London, from the mid-eighteenth century to the late nineteenth (see Figure 4.1). This evidence is far from conclusive, but it does suggest that by the late nineteenth century men in the highest stratum of English society were no longer putting on weight so rapidly as young men as their fathers and grandfathers had done. They reached the same weight in the end, but possibly this is consistent with them having over-eaten slightly but persistently rather than indulging in dramatically excessive overeating.

Whatever happened to actual body weights, however, there is plenty of evidence of the worry the subject caused in the upper reaches of society. Gastronomic writers from Brillat-Savarin to Ali-Bab (1907) discussed obesity as a worry and affliction among gourmets. In the latter part of the nineteenth century, great innovating chefs such as Escoffier, Philéas Gilbert and Prosper Montagné, cooking for a fashionable clientele, were beginning a trend towards simpler, lighter food and fewer courses. Yet at the same time, books were still being written on how to put on weight (for example, T.C. Duncan, *How to Become Plump*, 1878), and the cookery columns addressed to the lower middle classes (especially in England) emphasized the need to eat fat and heavy food for body-building (Mennell, 1985, Ch. 9). The upper and upper-middle classes often commented on the greed of servants:

> In towns we often observe the bad effects of overfeeding in young female servants recently arrived from the country. From being accustomed to constant exercise in the open air, and to the comparatively innutritious diet on which the labouring classes subsist, they pass all at once, with appetite, digestion and health in their fullest vigour, to the confinement of a house, to the impure atmosphere of a crowded city, and to a rich and stimulating diet. Appetite, still keen, is freely indulged; but waste being diminished, fulness is speedily induced . . . (Combe, 1846: 217)

And, at Buckingham Palace (no less), at the turn of the century:

> The plentiful meals of those days naturally enough encouraged greed, particularly among some of the servants. After a five-course breakfast those who visited the kitchens often slipped two or three hardboiled eggs into their pockets to help

them last out the next few hours until it was time for morning tea. (Tschumi, 1954:
63)

It is hardly surprising if people drawn from ranks of society where
the fear for centuries had been simply getting enough to eat did not
immediately develop self-control when suddenly confronted with
plentiful food.

Even at the present day, in the world's affluent societies the
incidence of obesity is highest in the lower and poorer strata, in
contrast to the countries of the Third World where it occurs only
among the privileged few (Bruch, 1974: 14). Obviously the plentiful
availability of food is a prerequisite for the development of obesity,
but clinical evidence suggests that psychological pressures to
overeat are often rooted in past hunger, perhaps in a previous
generation. For instance, among the mothers of obese children in
America,

> Many of these women had been poor immigrants who had suffered hunger during
> their early lives. They did not understand why anyone should object to a child's
> being big and fat, which to them indicated success and freedom from want.
> (Bruch, 1974: 15)

Conversely, cases of anorexia nervosa arise disproportionately
among the more well-to-do strata. There may have been instances
of this affliction, which is far more common among females than
males, in earlier centuries. Neither classical literature nor the Bible,
according to Dally and Gomez (1979: 1), contains any recognizable
picture of anorexia nervosa, nor does it seem to have been known in
the Middle Ages. A number of 'miraculously fasting' girls are known
to have excited attention from the sixteenth century onwards, and
though several were probably frauds, some were possibly cases
where psychological disturbance led to serious undereating
(Morgan, 1977). The first reliable description of cases seems to
have been by Morton in 1694, but the condition did not attract much
medical interest and was probably not at all common until the latter
half of the nineteenth century, when it was named by Sir William
Gull (1874). Gull in England and E.C. Lasègue (1873) in France
both gave clear accounts of it among their middle-class patients at
that period. Today, it is a very familiar illness in Europe and North
America. Again, there appears to be a clear connection with the
reliable and plentiful availability of food: apparently anorexia nervosa is not reported from countries where there is still danger of

widespread starvation or famine, nor among blacks and other underprivileged groups in the USA (Bruch, 1974: 13).

Anorexia nervosa and obesity can be regarded as similar if opposite disturbances of the normal patterns of self-control over appetite now normally expected and necessary in prosperous Western societies. Though the process may not yet be complete, in the course of the twentieth century the concern with weight-watching and slimming has gradually become more widespread in all ranks of society: its progress can be observed in cookery columns in popular magazines. For example, ever since the early 1950s, the French women's magazine *Elle* has had weekly columns giving menus and recipes with calorie counts, playing on and encouraging the reader's concern with her own weight and that of her family. A typical early instance is an article in *Elle*, 2 February 1953, entitled 'Unconscious Overeating can Threaten your Life', with a photograph of a slim girl in a swimsuit to illustrate the prevailing body image. The not-very-subliminal connection between self-control over the appetite, slimness, health, and sex-appeal is one of the most salient themes in British as well as French mass-circulation women's magazines since the Second World War. Which is not to deny that persistent slight but definite overeating remains a characteristic problem among the populations of England, France and other Western industrial states. But a general anxiety to avoid obesity is very widespread, and the fitful extreme over-eating of an earlier era seems less common.

Conclusion

The process of the civilizing of appetite is in detail more complex than it has been possible to depict here. Very broadly speaking, the argument is that the increasing interdependence and more equal balances of power between social classes has been reflected in more equal distribution of foodstuffs, which in turn has been associated with somewhat greater similarity of cuisine, and also with less extreme differences between festival or banquet food and everyday eating; and that these changes have been accompanied by the growth of pressures towards more even and 'all-round' self-controls over appetite. It has not, however, been a simple linear development; in fact there have been spurts and reversals, exceptions and sub-themes. For example, the seasonal rhythm and ritual of early modern eating, the observance of festivals and eating of festival fare, persisted longer in the countryside than in the towns,[11] where the special dishes of an earlier age have become the commonplace dishes of industrialized eating. At the opposite end of the social scale, a figure like King Edward VII might convince us that in the early twentieth century nothing had greatly changed since the carnivorous accomplishments of the medieval nobility. Yet within a couple of decades of his death, British royalty too was eating relatively abstemiously food which would not be very unfamiliar to most of their subjects (Magnus, 1964: 268–9; Tschumi, 1954). If it has not been possible here to pursue every detail and complexity of what I believe is one more example of a long-term civilizing process, I hope this chapter has served to suggest the fruitfulness of applying figurational sociology — and in particular ideas derived from *The Civilizing Process* — to the development of eating and appetite.

Notes

This chapter is one of the products of research undertaken mainly in 1980–1 with the aid of a grant from the Nuffield Foundation. One earlier version was presented at a conference on 'Civilization and Theories of Civilizing Processes' at the Zentrum für Interdisziplinäre Forschung, Bielefeld, 15–17 June 1984, and another forms part of my book *All Manners of Food* (1985). The argument has, however, been considerably clarified in the present chapter.

1. Henry IV was one culprit (Franklin, 1887–1902: III, 115), and in February 1558, the Pope gave a banquet while people were dying of hunger in Rome (Weber, 1973: 194).
2. Although this is true, it should also be noted that historians no longer believe that noble households had to exist throughout the winter on salt meat following the 'autumn slaughter' at Martinmas: some meat was salted, certainly, but some fresh meat was also generally available (see Dyer, 1983: 193). Again, however, the extent of autumn slaughter would probably be related to the success or failure of the harvest.
3. For more details of the cycle of feasts in medieval and early modern Europe, see Burke, 1978: 194–6; Coulton, 1926: 28–30; and Henisch, 1976: 50–1.
4. For a recent study of local famines in north-west England, see Appleby, 1978.
5. Nor should it be thought that fantasy was always necessarily very distant from reality: at least some incidents of cannibalism in time of famine seem reasonably well-authenticated — see Curschmann, 1900: 59–60.
6. And observed by no means in all. Accounts abound of monastic gluttony. See Alfred Gottschalk (1948: I, 343) who quotes St Bernard's denunciation of monks' gluttony.
7. For further discussion of religious views of gluttony in the medieval and early modern period, see Mennell, 1985: 29–30.
8. The Princess Palatine often describes the gorging of the French nobility, though the Duchesse de Berri's eating herself to death seems to have been even then

considered an instance of a pathologically abnormal appetite (Orléans, 1855: I, 348; II, 54, 85, 131, 145).

9. Cf. Eli Hecksher on the Swedish nobility, cited by Glamann, in Rich and Wilson (1977: 195).

10. For a more adequate discussion of the social context of the emergence of gastronomes, see Mennell, 1985; 142–3, 265ff.

11. For a general impression supporting this point, see Thomas Hardy, 1874; Oyler, 1950; Guillaumin, 1905; for more scholarly evidence regarding France, see Tardieu, 1964; Claudian et al., 1969; Weber, 1977.

References

Ali-Bab (Henri Babinski) (1907) *Gastronomie pratique: études culinaires suivies du traitement de l'obésité des gourmands.* Paris: Flammarion.

Anon. (c. 1400) *Sir Gawain and the Green Knight.* Harmondsworth: Penguin, 1974.

Appleby, A.B. (1978) *Famine in Tudor and Stuart England.* Liverpool: Liverpool University Press.

Aron, Jean-Paul (1961) 'Biologie et alimentation au XVIIIe siècle et au debut du XIXe siècle', *Annales E-S-C*, 16 (2): 971–7.

Aron, Jean-Paul (1973) *Le Mangeur du 19e siècle.* Paris: Laffont.

Baldwin, F.E. (1926) *Sumptuary Legislation and Personal Regulation in England.* Baltimore: Johns Hopkins University Press.

Bloch, Marc (1939–40) *Feudal Society.* 2 vols. London: Routledge & Kegan Paul, 1961.

Boswell, James (1791) *The Life of Samuel Johnson, LLD.* 2 vols. London: Odhams Press, n.d.

Boucher d'Argis, A.-G. (1765) 'Lois somptuaires', in D. Diderot (ed.), *Encyclopédie.* Neufchâtel: Samuel Faulche, 1751–80, IX: 672–5.

Brillat-Savarin, J.-A. (1826) *La Physiologie du Goût.* Paris: A. Sautelet.

Bruch, Hilde (1974) *Eating Disorders: Obesity, Anorexia Nervosa and the Person Within.* London: Routledge & Kegan Paul.

Burke, Peter (1978) *Popular Culture in Early Modern Europe.* London: Temple Smith.

Burnett, John (1966) *Plenty and Want.* London: Nelson.

Cappon, Daniel (1973) *Eating, Loving and Dying: A Psychology of Appetites.* Toronto: University of Toronto Press.

Cheyne, George (1724) *An Essay of Health and Long Life.* London: G. Strachan.

Cheyne, George (1733) *The English Malady.* London: G. Strachan.

Claudian, J., Serville, Y. and Tremolières, F. (1969) 'Enquête sur les facteurs de choix des aliments', *Bulletin de l'INSERM*, 24(5): 1277–1390.

Cobb, Richard (1970) *The Police and the People: French Popular Protest, 1789–1820.* Oxford: Clarendon Press.

Codere, Helen (1950) *Fighting with Property: A Study of Kwakiutl Potlatching and Warfare, 1792–1930.* Seattle: Washington University Press.

Combe, Andrew (1846) *The Physiology of Digestion, Considered with Relation to Dietetics.* Edinburgh: Maclachlan & Stewart.

Coulton, G.G. (1926) *The Medieval Village.* Cambridge: Cambridge University Press.

Curschmann, Fritz (1900) *Hungersnöte im Mittelalter*. Leipzig: B.G. Teubner.

Dally, P. and Gomez, J. (1979) *Anorexia Nervosa*. London: Heinemann.

Duncan, T.C. (1878) *How to Become Plump, or, Talks on Physiological Feeding*. London.

Dyer, Christopher (1983) 'English Diet in the Later Middle Ages', in T.H. Aston, P.R. Coss, C. Dyer and J. Thirsk (eds), *Social Relations and Ideas: Essays in Honour of R.H. Hilton*, pp. 191–216. Oxford: Past and Present Society.

Elias, Norbert (1939) *The Civilizing Process*, Vol. I: *The History of Manners*. Oxford: Basil Blackwell, 1978. Vol. II: *State Formation and Civilization*. Oxford: Basil Blackwell, 1982.

Fogel, R.W. et al. (1985) 'Secular Changes in American and British Stature and Nutrition', in R.I. Rotberg and T.K. Rabb (eds), *Hunger and History*, pp. 247–83. Cambridge: Cambridge University Press.

Foucault, Michel (1973) *The Birth of the Clinic*. London: Tavistock.

Foucault, Michel (1977) *Discipline and Punish*. London: Allen Lane.

Franklin, Alfred (1887–1902) *Vie privée d'autrefois, 12ᵉ à 18ᵉ siècles*. 27 vols. Paris: Plon.

Galton, Sir Francis (1884) 'The Weights of British Noblemen During the Last Three Generations', *Nature*, 29: 266–8.

Goody, Jack R. (1982) *Cooking, Cuisine and Class*. Cambridge: Cambridge University Press.

Gottschalk, Alfred (1939) 'L'appetit de Louis XVI au Temple', *Grandgousier*, 6(4).

Gottschalk, Alfred (1948) *Histoire de l'alimentation et de la gastronomie, depuis la préhistoire jusqu'à nos jours*. 2 vols. Paris: Editions Hippocrate.

Goudsblom, Johan (1977) *Sociology in the Balance*. Oxford: Basil Blackwell.

Goudsblom, Johan (1979) 'Zivilisation, Ansteckungsangst und Hygiene', in P.R. Gleichmann, J. Goudsblom and H. Korte (eds), *Materialien zu Norbert Elias's Zivilisationstheorie*, pp. 215–53. Frankfurt a.M.: Suhrkamp.

Grimod de la Reynière, A.-B.-L. (1803–12) *Almanach des Gourmands*. Paris.

Guillaumin, Emile (1905) *The Life of a Simple Man*. London: Selwyn & Blount, 1919.

Gull, W.W. (1874) 'Apepsia Hysterica: Anorexia Nervosa', *Transactions of the Clinical Society of London*, 7(2).

Hardy, Thomas (1874) *Far from the Madding Crowd*. London.

Hecquet, P. (1709) *Traité des dispenses du carême, dans lequel on découvre la fausseté des prétextes qu'on apporte pour les obtenir, les rapports naturels des alimens maigres avec la nature de l'homme et par l'histoire, par l'analyse et par l'observation leur convenance avec la santé*. Paris: F. Fournier.

Henisch, B.A. (1976) *Fast and Feast: Food in Medieval Society*. University Park and London: Pennsylvania State University Press.

Hollingsworth, T.H. (1977) 'Mortality in the British Peerage Families since 1600', *Population*, 32: 323–52.

Homilies (1562) *Certain Sermons or Homilies Appointed to be Read in Churches in the Time of Queen Elizabeth of Famous Memory*. London: George Wells, 1687.

Huizinga, Johan (1924) *The Waning of the Middle Ages*. Harmondsworth: Penguin, 1972.

Jerrold, William B. (1868) *The Epicure's Yearbook and Table Companion*. London: Bradbury, Evans & Co.

Jones, C.D.H. and Sonenscher, M. (1983) 'The Social Functions of the Hospital in

Eighteenth-Century France: The Case of the Hôtel-Dieu of Nîmes', *French Historical Studies*, 13(2): 172–214.

Kunzle, David (1982) *Fashion and Fetishism*. Totowa, N.J.: Rowman & Littlefield.

Lasègue, E.C. (1873) 'De l'anorexie hysterique', *Archives générales médicales*, 2: 367.

La Varenne, François Pierre de (1651) *Le Cuisinier François*. Paris: chez Pierre David.

Le Goff, Jacques (1964) *La Civilisation de l'Occident Médiéval*. Paris: Arthaud.

Le Magnen, J. (1972) 'Regulation of Food Intake', in F. Reichsmann (ed.), *Advances in Psychosomatic Medicine*, Vol. 7, *Hunger and Satiety in Health and Disease*. Basel: S. Karger: 73–90.

Livi-Bacci, Massimo (1985) 'The Nutrition-Mortality Link in Past Times: A Comment', in R.I. Rotberg and T.K. Rabb (eds), *Hunger and History*. Cambridge: Cambridge University Press: 95–100.

Magnus, Philip (1964) *King Edward VII*. London: John Murray.

Mandrou, R. (1961) *Introduction to Modern France, 1500–1600*. London: Arnold, 1975.

Mennell, Stephen (1981a) 'Montaigne, Civilization and Sixteenth-Century European Society', in K.C. Cameron (ed), *Montaigne and His Age*, pp. 69–85. Exeter: University of Exeter.

Mennell, Stephen (1981b) *Lettre d'un pâtissier anglais et autres contributions à une polémique gastronomique du XVIIIe siècle*. Exeter: University of Exeter.

Mennell, Stephen (1985) *All Manners of Food: Eating and Taste in England and France from the Middle Ages to the Present*. Oxford: Basil Blackwell.

Montaigne, Michel de (1967) *Oeuvres Complètes*. Paris: Le Seuil.

Morgan, H. Gethin (1977) 'Fasting Girls and Our Attitudes to Them', *British Medical Journal*, 2: 1652–5.

Morton, Richard (1694) *Phthisologia — or a Treatise of Consumptions*. London: Smith & Walford.

O'Hara-May, Jane (1977) *The Elizabethan Dyetary of Health*. Lawrence, Kansas: Coronado Press.

Orléans (1855) *Correspondance complète de Madame la Duchesse d'Orléans*. 2 vols. Paris: Charpentier.

Oyler, Philip (1950) *The Generous Earth*. Harmondsworth: Penguin, 1961.

Pelto, G.H. and Pelto, P.J. (1985) 'Diet and Delocalization: Dietary Changes since 1750', in R.I. Rotberg and T.K. Rabb (eds), *Hunger and History*, pp. 309–30. Cambridge: Cambridge University Press.

Piozzi, H.L. (1785) *Anecdotes of the Late Samuel Johnson*. London.

Pomiane, Edouard de (1922) *Bien manger pour bien vivre: essai de gastronomie théorique*. Paris: A. Michel.

Rich, E.E. and Wilson, C.H. (eds) (1977) *Cambridge Economic History of Europe*, Vol. V. Cambridge: Cambridge University Press.

Rudé, George (1964) *The Crowd in History*. London: Wiley.

Scotson-Clark, George F. (1924) *Eating Without Fears*. London: Jonathan Cape.

Sen, A.K. (1981) *Poverty and Famines*. Oxford: Oxford University Press.

Simon, André L. (1969) *In the Twilight*. London: Michael Joseph.

Stouff, Louis (1970) *Ravitaillement et alimentation en Provence aux 14e et 15e siècles*. Paris: Mouton.

Sturgeon, Launcelot (1822) *Essays, Moral, Philosophical and Stomachical on the Important Science of Good-Living*. London: G. and B. Whittaker.

Tardieu, Suzanne (1964) *La Vie domestique dans le Mâconnais rurale pré-industriel.* Paris: Université de Paris.

Thomas, Keith (1971) *Religion and the Decline of Magic.* London: Weidenfeld & Nicolson.

Thompson, E.P. (1971) 'The Moral Economy of the English Crowd in the Eighteenth Century', *Past and Present,* 50: 76–136.

Tilly, Charles (1975) 'Food Supply and Public Order in Modern Europe', in Tilly (ed.), *The Formation of National States in Western Europe,* pp. 380–455. Princeton N.J.: Princeton University Press.

Tschumi, Gabriel (1954) *Royal Chef: Recollections of Life in Royal Households from Queen Victoria to Queen Mary.* London: W. Kimber.

Turner, Bryan S. (1982a) 'The Discourse of Diet', *Theory, Culture & Society,* 1(1): 23–32.

Turner, Bryan S. (1982b) 'The Government of the Body: Medical Regimens and the Rationalization of Diet', *British Journal of Sociology,* 33(2): 254–69.

Turner, Bryan S. (1984) *The Body and Society.* Oxford: Basil Blackwell.

Warner, Richard (ed.) (1791) *Antiquitates Culinariae.* London: R. Blamire.

Watkins, S.C. and van de Walle, E. (1985) 'Nutrition, Mortality, and Population', in R.I. Rotberg and T.K. Rabb (eds), *Hunger and History,* pp. 7–28. Cambridge: Cambridge University Press.

Weber, Eugen (1973) *A Modern History of Europe.* London: Robert Hale.

Weber, Eugen (1977) *Peasants into Frenchmen.* London: Chatto & Windus.

Wernham, R.B. (ed.) (1968) *The Cambridge Modern History,* Vol. III. Cambridge: Cambridge University Press.

Wrigley, E.A. and Schofield, R. (1981) *The Population History of England, 1541–1871.* Cambridge: Cambridge University Press.

Young, James Harvey (1970) 'Historical Aspects of Food Cultism and Nutrition Quackery', in G. Blix (ed.), *Food Cultism and Nutrition Quackery,* pp. 9–21. Uppsala: Symposia of the Swedish Nutrition Foundation, 8.

This chapter first appeared in *Theory, Culture & Society,* Vol. 4 (1987), 373–403.

5

THE DISCOURSE OF DIET

Bryan S. Turner

Discipline and the Body
The recent work of Michel Foucault has brought the question of
the discipline of the body and the rise of scientific knowledge to
the centre of sociological theory. While it is difficult to
summarize Foucault's social philosophy, one central theme of his
treatment of knowledge is that the growth of systematic
knowledge coincides with the extension of power relations,
especially with the exercise of social control over bodies in social
space. This theme can be illustrated by his study of the development of penology and criminology which facilitated a more
precise, detailed and rigorous control of the criminal body within
the scientifically managed social space of the penitentiary
(Foucault, 1979a). Bentham's panopticon scheme provided a
systematic control and surveillance of the inmate world and
established a model of docility for schools, factories and
hospitals. Similarly, the rise of clinical medicine (Foucault, 1973)
and scientific psychiatry (Foucault, 1967) coincided with institutional developments in hospital architecture, workhouses and
asylums within which unruly bodies were exposed to detailed
control. It can also be argued that the emergence of the separate
disciplines of demography, geography, moral statistics and
sociology were manifestations of an increasing social control of
bodies within urban space. While conventional histories of
science regard such developments as rational and progressive,
Foucault, by contrast, claims that scientific advances do not
liberate the body from external control, but rather intensify the
means of social regulation. Blunt and primitive systems of
physical control and punishment – the mad-hut, the scaffold and
the torture chamber – give way to more precise, rigorous

disciplines of the penitentiary, lunatic asylum and classroom. In the treatment of madness, the reforms of Tuke and Pinel replaced chains by the inner discipline of private conscience operating within the regimented space of the modern asylum.

Although Foucault's application of discourse analysis to the relationships between knowledge, body and power has been widely regarded as original and creative, it is possible to see his contribution as an aspect of a more general interest in the rationalization of culture within the social sciences. While Foucault rarely acknowledges precursors, the influence of Nietzsche on his pessimistic and sceptical view of scientific rationality is well known (Sheridan, 1980; Foucault, 1980). Nietzsche condemned the optimism of evolutionary Darwinism and positivistic science which took social and moral progress for granted, subjecting such philosophical systems to the aphoristic critique of the 'gay science' (Kaufmann, 1974). Nietzsche's contrast between the creative energy of Dionysian forces and the formal discipline of Apollonianism subsequently became influential in Freudian psychoanalysis and Weberian sociology. Freud was reluctant to admit the influence of Nietzsche on his own view of the contradiction between instinctual gratification and the necessities of orderly social existence, but the intellectual debt was nevertheless real (Anderson, 1980). Freud's picture of *homo psychologicus* caught between libidinal drives and the demands of superego is clearly reminiscent of Foucault's analysis of the contradictions between irrational bodies and social order. The parallel between Weber's conception of instrumentally rational (*zweckrational*) systems and Foucault's analysis of scientific discourse is perhaps even more striking.

In *Discipline and Punish*, Foucault draws attention to the growth of organized knowledge in the form of timetables, taxonomies, typologies, registers, examinations and chrestomathies in the late eighteenth century. Such schema facilitated the control of large numbers of bodies within a regimented space. The drilling of armies, the schooling of children and the administration of hospitals required new forms of surveillance and control. The discipline of the school, the factory, the prison and the hospital was, however, anticipated by the discipline of the monastery in which bodies were subordinated to ascetic rules of practice. In this sense, factory discipline is a secularized asceticism which precludes unruly gratification and spontaneous enjoyment.

Foucault's account of the transposition of religious asceticism to secular space is, however indirectly and covertly, a return to the central theme of *The Protestant Ethic and the Spirit of Capitalism* where Weber explores the religious roots of the 'iron cage' of industrial civilization.

For Weber, the consequences of the Calvinistic calling were the rational organization of secular life, the creation of work disciplines and the subordination of 'natural man' to timetables and production requirements. The rationalization of industrial society meant the extension of instrumental rationality to every sphere of life, resulting in a disenchanted garden without prophets, passion and magic (Turner, 1981). In Weber's sociology, the concept of 'rationality' has many layers of meaning, but it does include the notion that knowledge is represented by formulae, schema and taxonomies. The systematization of knowledge is thus an important dimension to the general process of social rationalization. There is an interesting parallel between Foucault's concern with the timetable and Weber's commentary on budgetary management, capital accounting and double-entry book-keeping, and the growth of rational systems of musical notation. Although Weber did not formulate his views on capitalism around the theme of body/knowledge/society, he was clearly interested in the cultural implications of the ascetic control of the body, especially human sexuality.

It can be argued, therefore, that Foucault's account of the intimate relationship between scientific knowledge and the control of the body has to be located within a well-established tradition in social philosophy which recognized the problem of human passions as the critical factor in social order. While Weber explored this issue in terms of, for example, the contrast between orgy and chastity (Weber, 1978), it provides the central theme of Foucault's studies of sexuality (Foucault, 1979b) and medicine. With this theoretical context, the study of dietetics is especially pertinent to issues raised by both Weber and Foucault. Diet was a basic component of both traditional regimens in medical practice and of ascetic regulation in religion. Diet, asceticism and regimen are obviously forms of control exercised over bodies with the aim of establishing a discipline. The term 'asceticism' derives from *aketes* (monk) and *askeo* (exercise), having the general meaning of any disciplined practice on an object, such as metal. 'Regimen' comes from *regere* (rule) and is normally used in its medical sense of a system of therapeutic rules, especially an organized diet. 'Regimen', however, also has an archaic sense of 'a system of government'. Religious asceticism and medical diets are thus both governments of the body. Finally, the government of the body is couched in a series of instructions and commandments, namely the dietary table, the manual of exercise and the food chart. Dietary compendia thus represent an interesting illustration of discourse on the body and the rationalization of behaviour.

'Diaetetick Management'

Although medical advice on proper diet has a long history in western medicine, treatises on dietetic management, especially when combined with religious exhortation, became particularly popular in the seventeenth and eighteenth centuries. One of the most influential physicians in this connection was the Aberdonian medic and writer, George Cheyne (1671–1743), who practised in London and Bath amongst an aristocratic and professional clientele. Cheyne, who is best known for his *The English Malady* (1733) which recommends diet as the basic treatment of melancholy, counted amongst his friends and patients David Hume,[1] Samuel Richardson,[2] Samuel Johnson, John Wesley, Alexander Pope, the Earl of Huntingdon and the Duke of Roxburgh. Cheyne's publications on the general benefits of diet for mental health and longevity were the product of a personal crisis brought on by chronic obesity at the beginning of his medical career. Arriving in London at the peak of the popularity of coffee-houses and taverns as professional meeting places in the reign of Queen Anne, Cheyne fell into the company of 'free-livers' and 'bottle-companions' with the consequence that his weight rose to 448 pounds. Having been diagnosed as a sufferer from English melancholy, Cheyne, after some experimentation, hit upon a diet of milk and vegetables combined with regular exercise, regular sleep and temperance. As a result, he enjoyed a long life of personal tranquillity and mental stability.

The theoretical basis to Cheyne's medical regime was derived from Descartes' mechanistic model of the body, the medical rationalism of the Leyden school of medicine and the iatromathematical tradition of Herman Boerhaave (1668–1738). Descartes's position that 'the body' is nothing else than a statue or machine of clay (Descartes, 1927) and Harvey's work on the circulation of the blood provided Cheyne with the argument that the body is 'an Hydraulic Machine, fill'd with liquor' (Cheyne, 1740). The health of this system of pipes, pumps and passages could only be maintained by appropriate supplies of food and liquid as determined by clinical experience and scientific knowledge. The use of drugs and surgery was secondary to 'diaetetick management' in controlling disease and in promoting long life. These iatromathematical principles were combined with a Christian emphasis on health as a religious duty which regarded gluttony as tantamount to suicide. Cheyne's dietetics were thus part of a religio-moral tradition in which the control of the body was part of the religious calling.

There is some evidence (Cheyne and Richardson, 1943), that Cheyne's views on diet were influenced by the *Hygiasticon, or the right course of preserving life and health unto extreme old age* (1634) of Leonard Lessius (1554–1623) and by Luigi Cornaro's *Trattato della vita sobria* (1558), translated and published by George Herbert in 1634. Cornaro (1475–1566) was an Italian nobleman from Venice who, like Cheyne, had cured his own infirmities by diet and sobriety. The disorders of Cornaro's body were seen to be symptomatic of a general social malaise brought on by 'bad customs', namely: 'The first, flattery and ceremoniousness; the second, Lutheranism, which some have most preposterously embraced; the third, intemperance' (Cornaro, 1776: 14).

The solution to both social and physical disorders was a disciplined and sober life. In response to his own infirmities, Cornaro

gave over the use of such meats and wines, likewise of ice; chose wine suited to my stomach, drinking of it but the quantity I knew I could digest. I did the same by my meat, as well in regard to quantity as to quality, accustoming myself to contrive matters so as never to cloy my stomach with eating and drinking, but constantly to rise from table with a disposition to eat and drink still more. (Cornaro, 1776: 22–3)

Dieting produced a number of blessings: health, mental stability and aided reason to control the passions. Temperance and sobriety are our main defence against 'melancholy, hatred and other violent passions'. Indeed, the passions 'Have, in the main, no great influence over bodies governed by the two foregoing rules of eating and drinking' (Cornaro, 1776: 25). Cornaro thus conceives of diet within an exclusively religious framework as a defence against the temptations of the flesh, referring to 'that Divine Sobriety, agreeable to the Deity'. It is not surprising, therefore, that George Herbert found Cornaro and Lessius attractive writers on sobriety and that this religio-medical regimen found followers at Little Gidding. Herbert cured his own ague by refraining from meat and drink (Charles, 1977).

Just as Cornaro regarded disease as the product of unrestrained passions and social malaise, so Cheyne came to see human infirmities as the consequences of civilization. Expanding trade and economic progress had brought rich, exotic foods, drink and spices on to the British market with disastrous results for human digestion. He noted that 'Since our Wealth increas'd, and our Navigation has been extended, we have ransack'd all parts of the Globe to bring together its whole Stock of materials for Riot, Luxury, and to provoke Excess' (Cheyne, 1733: 49). Urbanization and overcrowding were also aspects of eighteenth-century social change producing mental and physical illness, especially in London where 'nervous Distempers are most frequent, outrageous, and unnatural' (Cheyne, 1733: 54). Lack of exercise, a surplus of food, intoxicating drinks and urban life-styles were particularly threatening to the health standards of the upper classes, especially among 'the Rich, the Lazy, the Luxurious, and the Unactive' (Cheyne, 1733: 28). The availability and abundance of strong drinks among the elite enraged their passions to 'Quarrels, Murder and Blasphemy' (Cheyne, 1724: 44). Changes in eating habits and fashions in cuisine stimulated the appetites of the upper classes in ways which were contrary to nature and which interfered with the natural processes of digestion. In various passages reminiscent of Rousseau, Cheyne (1733: 174) lamented that 'When Mankind was simple, plain, honest and frugal, there were few or no diseases. Temperance, Exercise, Hunting, Labour and Industry kept the Juices Sweet and the Solids brac'd.'

Cheyne's medical regimen was aimed at counteracting the ravages of civilization by returning men to a life of sobriety, exercise and regularity. Cheyne's prescriptions for a diet based on fruit, seeds, milk and vegetables were not necessarily original, since they embodied the classical Greek doctrine of 'contrary medicine' (Coulter, 1977). Because the ailments of civilized man were the products of abundance and inactivity, his regimen was based around abstinence, temperance and exercise. In order to guide his patients back to health, Cheyne produced detailed classifications of food and drink according to effects upon digestion. These classifications are particularly interesting in terms of the occupational, age and sexual characteristics of the clientele to which they were addressed. In general, he recommended a progressively reduced diet through the various stages of life, while recognizing variations in the level of exercise for various occupational groups. Thus, a man of 'ordinary Stature, following no laborious employment' should consume '8 Ounces of Fresh Meat, 12 of Bread, or Vegetable Food, and about a Pint of Wine, or other generous Liquor in 24 Hours' (Cheyne, 1724: 34). Cheyne was, however, principally concerned with the health problems of intellectuals, professional men and the aristocracy, whose sedentary and affluent life-style exposed their digestion to a diversity of dangers. For such groups, he recommended a light diet, a regular vomit, horse-riding and a regular pattern of sleep. This regimen would preserve their health, clear their minds and provide the blessing of long life and happiness.

Although Cheyne wrote for and was popular among an urban sedentary elite, his views on sobriety reached a wider audience through the mediation of John Wesley whose *Primitive Physick or an Easy and Natural Method of Curing Most Diseases* (1752) embraced Cheyne's prescriptions for a life of regularity and moderation. Wesley commended Cheyne's *An Essay on Health and Long Life* to his mother in 1724, noting that it 'is chiefly directed to studious and sedentary persons' (Telford, 1931).

In a letter to the Bishop of London, Wesley admitted that abstaining from wine and flesh was not a requirement of Christianity, but nonetheless was compatible with it. Since following Cheyne's advice, Wesley noted that: 'I have been free (blessed be God) from all bodily disorders. Would to God I knew any method of being equally free from all "follies and indescretions". But this I never expect to attain till my spirit returns to God.'

Cheyne's dietary management matched Wesley's religious asceticism and was incorporated with the Wesleyan 'method' of regular, disciplined and orderly life. While Cheyne wrote for the London elite, his model of regular exercise and dietary control reached a wider audience in the middle class through the norms of sobriety of the Wesleyan chapels.

Capitalism and the Spirit of Medicine

This relationship between medical regimens and religious asceticism in the eighteenth century suggests a rather obvious hypothesis that there may be an 'elective affinity' between dietary management and the rise of capitalism. It has become a commonplace of historical sociology to argue that the unintended consequence of Protestant sectarianism was to provide early capitalism with a sober, honest and hard-working labour force (Thompson, 1963; Hobsbawm, 1964; Pope, 1942). There is a *prima facie* case for believing that a dietary 'calling' to discipline the body by reference to a religio-medical regimen would have been compatible with a spirit of capitalism. A workforce which is not only sober but healthy is clearly desirable from the point of view of capitalist production. Religion and medicine could then both work in the direction of eliminating 'irrational' customs of consumption which were inefficient or dangerous. The docile, idle body of the criminal would provide a sharp contrast with the active, athletic body of the worker within the industrial panopticon. In fact, of course, Cheyne, Cornaro and Lessius had addressed their dietary management to an aristocratic and professional clientele and, although Wesley's *Primitive Physick* reached a wider audience, the notion of diet was irrelevant to a working class periodically subjected to starvation. Since the eighteenth-century worker depended on cereals, abstinence from meat was not a relevant issue (Cole and Postgate, 1964).

While individual capitalists may have an interest in the health of *their* workers, there was little economic incentive for them to be concerned with the health standards of the population as a whole. Within a Marxist framework, there would be strong reasons for expecting a fall in health standards in early capitalism. The competition between capitalists forces them to mechanize production, lower wages and reduce the labour force. Unemployment and hunger provided the general background to disease and sickness. However, each individual capitalist will want his workers to be healthy, clean and tidy in so far as these contribute to efficient production. Alternatively, it has been claimed that bourgeois interest in hygiene, diet and exercise for workers in the middle of the nineteenth century had important ideological functions (Temkin, 1949). The popularity of the organic metaphor of society meant that responsibility for disease could be squarely placed on the shoulders of intemperate individuals. Illness was thus the consequence of individual abuse of the body or the mismanagement of sanitation. Pietist reformers like Florence Nightingale, Edwin Chadwick and Dr Southwood Smith rejected the specificity of the germ theory of disease in favour of notions of moral responsibility for removing filth from the environment and encouraging personal cleanliness (Rosenberg, 1979). The diseases of civilization were to be countered by personal salvation and clean water. The dietary management of the body was thus parallel to the management of water and sanitation in the environment, since both were aimed at moral control of impurity.

The irony of moral sanitarianism was that, in an age of Spencerian evolutionism, it implied a large measure of state intervention which conflicted with the notion of personal moral responsibility and laissez-faire economics. While diet could remain an individual choice, clean water, adequate sanitation and urban ventilation required legislation and some measure of centralized supervision. The development of legislative control, however minimal, of the social environment implied a limitation of the freedom of individual capitalists to pursue their economic goals within the market. In this context, it would be wrong to assume that the ideology of personal hygiene and diet was especially attractive to capitalists, who had additional material interests in the health of the nation. While capitalists might patronize lecture programmes, through the mechanics institutes, on dietetics and physiology, there were three general factors which promoted a capitalist interest in general standards of health. First, the spread of contagious diseases in the nineteenth century from the insanitary conditions of the urbanized poor also threatened the health of the urban middle classes. An awareness of the hazard of urban squalor for all social classes stimulated a number of early enquiries into the correlation of class and disease in the nineteenth century. William Farr and T.H.C. Stevenson developed various sociomedical investigations into social conditions and disease, and found a clear association between poverty and the incidence of infectious diseases, tuberculosis, bronchitis and pneumonia (Susser, 1962). The interest in environmental improvement and the importance of quantification of disease was as much protective as philanthropic. The problem of infectious diseases cannot be separated from the second general condition which interested the middle class in the health of the working force, namely the problem of the tax burden of illness on the rich. In general, early capitalist society was caught between promoting political security or economic growth. As Foucault's study of the asylums of Paris suggests, incarceration of the urban poor achieved some measure of political stability, but this was at the cost of economic accumulation, because docile bodies were also idle bodies. Unless the unemployed sick are to die upon the streets, there must be some provision for the poor out of general revenue, which represents a drain on national wealth.

The third and most significant general factor in the emergence of the science of the body and for state intervention in general standards of health is modern, mass warfare. From the Crimean War to the Second World War, investigations into the health of recruits for military service revealed an appalling depth of general disability and disease in the male working-class population. Medical evidence from military sources suggested that Britain, as a leading imperial power, was in fact incapable of defending herself unless there was a dramatic improvement in health standards. General anxiety about military defence found its expression in the 'national efficiency movement' which sought to promote health and discipline through temperance, military service and physical education (Gilbert, 1966). The new emphasis on training the body coincided with an interest in the health of schoolchildren, school meals and regular medical inspections. Dr Arnold's public school reforms had already provided the model, not only of teamwork and fitness on the sports field, but of regularity in sleep, eating and work. In Foucault's terminology, the school, the factory and the hospital became social locations for the discipline of the body, under the control of the scientific discourses of pedagogy, dietetics, demography, criminology and Taylorism, within an urban space. Anxiety about urban space was reflected in uncertainty about appropriate policies – survival of the fittest versus state control.

The Labouring Body
Whereas seventeenth- and eighteenth-century writing on diet had its origin in a religious language about self-control among the aristocratic and professional classes, the science of dietetics in the nineteenth century still had moral connotations, but arose

out of the debate about urban management, industrial efficiency and the fiscal burden of incarceration. Thermodynamics replaced the traditional discourse of humours, digestion and quality. In Britain, scientific interest in measuring the effects of calorie intake on human energy output was associated with research into the nutritional requirements of prisoners and soldiers, namely the combination of a minimum diet with maximum energy production. The question of a scientific diet was also associated with poverty and family budgets in the social surveys of Charles Booth and Seebohm Rowntree. The conclusion of Rowntree's York surveys was that the working class, which provided the muscle power for industrial growth, was seriously underfed in terms of scientific nutritional standards and that the artisan class had a satisfactory food supply provided there was no 'wasteful expenditure on drink' (Rowntree, 1902: 28). While poverty and the efficiency of labour led to the early social survey, it was the impact of war conditions on production that generated the need for industrial research into health and economic production. Fatigue among munitions workers in the First World War led the government in 1915 to set up the Health of Munition Workers Committee to examine the relationship between hours of work, industrial output and health. These investigations gave rise to the creation of the Industrial Fatigue Research Board and the Medical Research Committee. Behind the empirical social survey and psychological investigations of fatigue, we can detect the metaphor of the body as a machine subject to the laws of thermodynamics, but the new discourse of the body is shorn of its religious terminology. The body is no longer informed by 'divine Sobriety', but by calories and proteins, so that discipline and efficiency can be measured with precision and certainty.

The discipline of the labouring body thus represents a powerful illustration of both Foucault's analysis of power/knowledge and Weber's comparative study of the origins of modern processes of rationalization. The development of the statistical survey is to be located within the growth of populations and the formation of classes within an urban space, perceived as chaotic and dangerous. The extension of knowledge – eugenics, dietetics, thermodynamics – corresponded with the exercise of political power over labouring men. These theoretical developments also signified a rationalization of culture in the trivia of dietary sheets and energy conversion tables. Dietary control of the passions within the monastic milieu found its way through the dietetic management of Cornaro and Cheyne into popular, secular works on physiology and health for working-class educational institutes. There is, of course, a major shift in the social parameters within which this dietary discourse is set, namely the problem of ageing populations. While Cornaro and Cheyne adhered to an ideal of aristocratic longevity, the problem of a society composed largely of retired geriatrics was not an issue they had to confront. The changing structure of populations in late capitalism suggests a new discourse of demography, centred on a regimen of diet, jogging and cosmetics to control the alienated and disaffected citizens of retirement compounds.

Notes

1. David Hume 'To Dr George Cheyne', (Greig, 1932: 12–18). E.C. Mossner (1944), however, claims that this letter was addressed to Dr Arbuthnot.
2. See correspondence between Cheyne and Richardson (1943). For an example of 'English madness' in continental literature, cf. Peter Horwath (1978).

References

Anderson, Lorin (1980) 'Freud and Nietzsche', *Salmagundi*, 47–8: 3–29.
Branscombe, Peter (ed.) (1978) *Austrian Life and Literature 1780–1938*. Edinburgh.
Charles, Amy M. (1977) *A Life of George Herbert*. Ithaca and London.
Cheyne, George (1724) *An Essay on Health and Long Life*. London.
Cheyne, George (1733) *The English Malady*. London.
Cheyne, George (1740) *An Essay on Regimen*. London.
Cheyne, George and Richardson, S. (1943) Correspondence, *Missouri University Studies*, 18: 31–137.
Cole, G.D.H. and Postgate, R. (1964) *The Common People 1746–1946*. London: Methuen.
Cornaro, Luigi (1776) *Discourses on a Sober and Temperate Life*. London.
Coulter, Harris L. (1977) *The Divided Legacy: a History of the Schism in Medical Thought*, 3 vols. Washington.
Cragg, Gerald R. (ed.) (1975) *The Works of John Wesley*. Oxford: Oxford University Press.
Descartes, R. (1927) 'Treatise on Man', in R.M. Eaton (ed.), *Descartes Selections*. New York.
Foucault, Michel (1967) *Madness and Civilisation. A History of Insanity in the Age of Reason*. London: Tavistock.
Foucault, Michel (1973) *The Birth of the Clinic. An Archaeology of Medical Perception*. London: Tavistock.
Foucault, Michel (1979a) *Discipline and Punish. The Birth of the Prison*. Harmondsworth: Penguin.
Foucault, Michel (1979b) *The History of Sexuality, Volume 1: an Introduction*. London: Allen Lane.

Foucault, Michel (1980) *Power/Knowledge. Selected Interviews and Other Writings 1972–1977.* C. Gordon (ed.). Brighton: Harvester Press.

Gilbert, Bentley B. (1966) *The Evolution of National Insurance in Great Britain: the Origins of the Welfare State.* London: Michael Joseph.

Greig, J.Y.T. (ed.) (1932) *The Letters of David Hume Volume 1.* Oxford: Oxford University Press.

Hobsbawm, E.J. (1964) *Labouring Men: Studies in the History of Labour.* London: Weidenfeld and Nicolson.

Horwath, Peter (1978) 'Richardsonian Characters and Motifs in Johann Friedel's Eleonore', in P. Branscombe (ed.), *Austrian Life & Literature 1780–1938.* Edinburgh.

Kaufmann, W. (1974) *Nietzsche: Philosopher, Psychologist, Anti-Christ.* Princeton, NJ.

Mossner, E.C. (1944) 'Hume's Epistle to Dr Arbuthnot, 1744', *Huntingdon Library Quarterly,* 7: 135–52.

Pope, Liston (1942) *Millhand and Preachers.* New Haven and London: Yale University Press.

Rosenberg, Charles E. (ed.) (1979) *Healing and History: Essays for George Rosen.* New York: Neale Watson Academic Publications.

Rowntree, B. Seebohm (1902) *Poverty, a Study of Town Life.* London: Macmillan.

Sheridan, Alan (1980) *Michel Foucault, the Will to Truth.* London: Tavistock.

Susser, M.W. (1962) 'Social Medicine in Britain: Studies in Social Class', in A.T. Welford et al. (eds), *Society: Problems and Methods of Study.* London. Routledge and Kegan Paul.

Telford, John (1931) *The Letters of John Wesley (Vol. 1).* London.

Temkin, Owsei (1949) 'Metaphors of Human Biology', in R.C. Stauffer (ed.), *Science and Civilisation.* Madison.

Thompson, E.P. (1963) *The Making of the English Working Class.* London: Victor Gollancz.

Turner, Bryan S. (1981) *For Weber: Essays in the Sociology of Fate.* London: Routledge & Kegan Paul.

Weber, Max (1978) *Economy and Society, Vol I.* Berkeley: University of California Press.

This chapter first appeared in *Theory, Culture & Society*, Vol. 1 (1982), 23–32.

6

THE BODY IN CONSUMER CULTURE

Mike Featherstone

In his paper 'The Discourse of Diet', Bryan Turner (1982) drew attention to the role of dietary management in the production of docile, disciplined bodies. Concluding in a speculative vein, Turner (1982, p. 14) remarked that the emerging problem of ageing populations within late capitalist society has pushed a new discourse, demography, to the fore 'centred on a regime of diet, jogging and cosmetics to control the alienated and disaffected citizens of retirement compounds.' This statement, which we will take as our point of departure, curiously draws together diet, cosmetics and jogging under the rubric of demography – yet these activities have already had the meaning pre-defined within the context of a consumer culture. The vast range of dietary, slimming, exercise and cosmetic body-maintenance products which are currently produced, marketed and sold point to the significance of appearance and bodily preservation within late capitalist society. Consumer culture latches onto the prevalent self-preservationist conception of the body, which encourages the individual to adopt instrumental strategies to combat deterioration and decay (applauded too by state bureaucracies who seek to reduce health costs by educating the public against bodily neglect) and combines it with the notion that the body is a vehicle of pleasure and self-expression. Images of the body beautiful, openly sexual and associated with hedonism, leisure and display, emphasises the importance of appearance and the 'look'.

Within consumer culture, advertisements, the popular press, television and motion pictures, provide a proliferation of stylised images of the body. In addition, the popular media constantly emphasise the cosmetic benefits of body maintenance. The reward for ascetic body work ceases to be spiritual salvation or even improved health, but becomes an enhanced appearance and more marketable self. Referring to Luigi Cornaro (1475–1566), an Italian nobleman who wrote a treatise entitled *A Sober and Temperate Life*, Turner (1982, p. 6) remarks that 'Cornaro thus conceives of diet within an exclusively religious framework as a defence against the temptations of the flesh.' Today, it can be ventured, diet and body maintenance are increasingly regarded as vehicles to release the temptations of the flesh. Discipline and hedonism are no longer seen as incompatible, indeed the subjugation of the body through body maintenance routines is presented within consumer culture as a precondition for the achievement of an acceptable appearance and the release of the body's expressive capacity. Consumer culture does not involve the complete replacement of ascetism by hedonism, this shift occurs primarily on the level of the cultural imagery; in reality, it demands a good deal of 'calculating hedonism' from the individual (Jacoby 1980, p. 63).

The emphasis upon body maintenance and appearance within consumer culture suggests two basic categories: the inner and the outer body. The inner body refers to the concern with the health and optimum functioning of the body which demands maintenance and repair in the face of disease, abuse and the deterioration accompanying the ageing process. The outer body refers to appearance as well as the movement and control of the body within social space. The study of the outer body can thus range from demographic and human ecological aspects (Park et al. 1925; Park 1952) down to face-to-face interactions in which appearance, preservation of self and management of impressions (Goffman 1972) become the focus of attention. It can also encompass the organisation and surveillance of docile disciplined bodies within social space (Foucault 1977; Giddens 1981) as well as the aesthetic dimensions of the body. For our purposes, it is the appearance and management of impressions of the outer body that are of particular interest. Within consumer culture, the inner and the outer body become conjoined: the prime purpose of the maintenance of the inner body becomes the enhancement of the appearance of the outer body.

Consumer Culture

Today's popular heroes are no longer the mighty, the builders of empires, the inventors and achievers. Our celebrities are movie stars and singers, 'beautiful' people of leisure who profess a philosophy of enjoyment rather than discipline and toil. (Pachter 1975, p. 330)

Mass consumption has been referred to as the necessary 'other' of mass production (Alt 1976, p. 71). While mass-produced consumer durables (cheap manufactured clothes, household goods etc.) had been displayed in the newly-created department stores (Miller 1981) of the second half of the nineteenth century, the development of scientific management, with its new techniques of work organisation and assembly line production, in the early decades of the twentieth century, dramatically increased productive capacity. Improvements in real wages, and not least the creation of consumer credit and instalment buying, stimulated demand. Workers who had become used to the rhetoric of thrift, hard work and sobriety, had to become 'educated' to appreciate a new discourse centred around the hedonistic lifestyle entailing new needs and desires. In the 1920s the foundations of a consumer culture became established with the new media of motion pictures, tabloid press, mass circulation magazines and radio extolling the leisure lifestyle, and publicising new norms and standards of behaviour. Advertising became the guardian of the new morality enticing individuals to participate in the consumption of commodities and experiences once restricted to the upper classes – albeit in scaled down versions in which the images of plenty soon outpaced the real properties of consumer goods. Images of youth, beauty, luxury and opulence became loosely associated with goods awakening long-suppressed desires, as well as reminding the individual that he/she has room for self-improvement in all aspects of his/her life.

Traditional values and mores gradually gave way as more and more aspects of life were brought under the influence of the expanding market with its propaganda for commodities. As free time and leisure activities also became drawn into the orbit of the market, hobbies, pastimes and experiences come to increasingly depend upon the purchase of commodities. Hence, free time demands systematic planning and the time spent in maintenance activities does not necessarily diminish. It has been suggested that women spend as much time occupied in housework in the post-Second World War era as they did in the early decades of the twentieth century. The decisive change has been in the nature of the tasks performed with the creation of an ever-expanding range of new 'essential' tasks and appliances for home maintenance by the domestic science experts and manufacturers of household goods (Ehrenreich and English 1979, p. 163). Consumer goods themselves need maintenance, as commodities voraciously demand other commodities, and looking after a house, car and an expanding array of consumer goods makes inroads into free time. Body maintenance, too, provides an expanding market for the sale of commodities as we shall see below.

The purchase of commodities also takes time and organisation. Shopping, with the increasingly sophisticated display of goods in department stores and supermarkets, encourages voyeuristic consumption. The organisation of space within department stores, supermarkets and the new shopping centres is very different from that found in the corner shop in the traditional working-class community. Shopping ceases to be a quick visit down the streets amidst neighbours and becomes a more organised expedition into more anonymous public spaces where certain standards of dress and appearance are deemed appropriate. The individual is increasingly on display as he/she moves through the field of commodities on display. Long term changes in the rationalisation of capital which have brought this about have also influenced leisure-time entertainment and social habits. To take drinking as an example: the traditional intimate 'local' pub has been gradually replaced by the large through-lounge pub, which incorporates a different organisation of social space with much greater opportunities for surveillance and display (Clarke et al. 1979, p. 245).

A further effect of the progressive expansion of the market is to discredit traditional norms and unhinge long-held meanings which were firmly grounded in social relationships and cultural objects. Advertising plays a crucial role in this process and has become one of the central purveyors of the new consumer culture values. The working of the 'magic system' (Williams 1960) can be illuminated by referring to Marx's theory of the commodity. An effect of the extension of the commodity form to more and more aspects of social life (Lukács 1971) has been the reification of social relationships and cultural artifacts, which leads to the primacy of a secondary exchange (monetary) value which rests uneasily alongside, and even conceals the original use-value or meaning. Theodor Adorno has taken this analysis a stage further by suggesting that increasing dominance of exchange-value means that the last vestiges of the original use-value of goods have been obliterated and forgotten (Rose 1978, p. 25). Hence goods are free to take on the mantle of a secondary, ersatz use-value, which now becomes perceived as their real use, which will vary with whatever illusions are saleable.

The detachment of use leads to a detachment of meaning, the converse of the apparent fixity of meaning in traditional cultures. Advertising in particular takes advantage of and promotes the 'floating signifier' effect (Williamson 1978; Lefebvre 1971; Baudrillard 1975) by transvaluing the notion of use so that any particular quality or meaning can become attached to any culture product. In this sense, advertising is inherently modernist promoting a pastiche or collage effect in which the breadth and depth of cultural values can be ransacked to achieve a desired effect. Advertising provides a poetics of everyday life, a consumer culture version of the high culture modernist transvaluation of values. In this sense, consumer culture has sometimes been conceived as an anti-culture which admits no settled convictions, favouring flexibility, mobility and the new. The dominance of the visual media since the inter-war years has enabled advertising to draw upon a wide pool of imagery and create more diffuse and ambiguous lifestyle images which can become associated with goods (Kline and Leiss 1978). Certain themes, infinitely revisable, infinitely combinable, recur within advertising and consumer culture imagery: youth, beauty, energy, fitness, movement, freedom, romance, exotica, luxury, enjoyment, fun. Yet whatever the promise in the imagery, consumer culture demands from its recipients a wide-awake, energetic, calculating, maximising approach to life – it has no placed for the settled, the habitual or the humdrum.

Writing about the role of advertising in the creation of consumer culture, Stuart Ewen (1976, p. 33) charts the process whereby business leaders in the United States in the 1920s, aware of the need for new markets to absorb the increased capacity for mass production, aggressively rose to the task by stimulating new needs, desires and buying habits: 'Advertising offered itself as a means of efficiently creating consumers', he remarks.[1] It helped to break down traditional values by discrediting puritan notions of thrift, patience, steadfastness, abstinence and moderation. Individuals had to be persuaded to adopt a critical attitude towards their body, self and lifestyle. Robert and Helen Lynd

(1929, p. 82; Ewen 1976, p. 37) in their study of *Middletown* suggest that modern advertising differed from that of the pre-First World War era by:

> concentrating increasingly on a type of copy aiming to make the reader emotionally uneasy, to bludgeon him with the fact that decent people don't live the way he does ... This copy points an accusing finger at the stenographer as she read her motion picture magazine and makes her acutely conscious of her unpolished finger nails ... and sends the housewife peering anxiously into the mirror to see if her wrinkles look like those that made Mrs X in the advertisement 'old at thirty-five' because she did not have a Leisure Hour electric washer.

Advertising thus helped to create a world in which individuals are made to become emotionally vulnerable, constantly monitoring themselves for bodily imperfections which could no longer be regarded as natural.

Consumerism, according to Ewen (1976, p. 54) did not emerge in the 1920s as a smooth progression from earlier patterns of consumption but rather represents 'an aggressive device of corporate survival'. Ewen quotes many sources from amongst the business community to illustrate the conscious effort to 'educate' and manipulate the masses to accept the new 'fanciful needs' and consumer values. Yet, however much business leaders like Edward Filene emphasised the need to teach 'the masses not what to think but *how to think*' (Ewen 1976, p. 55), this should not be taken as evidence that the masses were so easily duped. Elements of the new value complex were welcomed by individuals as genuinely progressive. The traditional values challenged by advertising and consumer culture did not surrender to false needs merely through a process of mass deception. Rather, however much advertising persuaded individuals to adopt instrumental strategies through a welter of scientific and pseudoscientific justifications for new products, it also involved a genuinely critical element. The discrediting of traditional values should not, therefore, be seen negatively as resulting in the loss of community and brotherhood – the romantic side of *Gemeinschaft* – but as involving a reasonable critique of dogmatic authority, arbitrary structures of prejudice and patriarchal domination. For individual family members to earn an independent income and be accorded the equality of independent consumers in the marketplace offered tangible freedoms, however limited and restricted they might turn out to be. Once established, advertising need not imply the total integration of the individual; rather, as Ellen Willis (1970, p. 78) notes 'advertising works (that is, stimulates sales) *because* buying is the only game in town and not vice-versa'.

Consumer culture latched onto certain strands within high culture, in particular modernism with its antinomial demands for self-realisation, self-conscious cultivation of style and distaste for ascetism. Writing in the early 1930s Malcolm Cowley (1951) noted that the new consumption ethic had first been promulgated by the Bohemians of Greenwich Village in their revolt against the business–Christian ethic – only to be taken over by the advertising industry by the end of the 1920s. Cowley (1951, pp. 62–3; Stein 1960, pp. 147–8) remarks:

> It happened that many of the Greenwich Village ideas proved useful in an altered situation. Thus self-expression and paganism encouraged a demand for all sorts of products – modern furniture, beach pajamas, cosmetics, coloured bathrooms with toilet paper to match. Living for the moment meant buying an automobile, radio or house, using it now and paying tomorrow. Female equality was capable of doubling the consumption of products – cigarettes for example – that had formerly been used by men alone!

In contrast to the pre-First World War production ethic which taught the virtues of industry, foresight, thrift and personal initiative the new consumption ethic celebrated living for the moment, self-expression, paganism, movement and the exotic of far-away places (Susman 1973, p. 4).

The imagery of consumer culture presents a world of ease and comfort, once the privilege of an elite, now apparently within the reach of all. An ideology of personal consumption presents individuals as free to do their own thing, to construct their own little worlds in the private sphere 'however Lilliputian' (Berger and Kellner 1964). Individuals are also encouraged to enjoy freedom of association, not to be constrained by family obligations, religious ethics or *civitas*. The basic freedom within the culture is the freedom to consume, yet the hedonistic lifestyle and ever-expanding needs ultimately depend upon permanent economic expansion. The ideology of progress and the ability of late capitalist society to deliver the goods has been jolted by the economic and ecological crisis of the late twentieth century. Not that this progress and the concomitant freedom to consume has ever reached down to all sectors of society. From the start of consumer culture large sections were excluded: advertisements were first directed at the middle class and only gradually were parts of the working class initiated into the consumer lifestyle. Consumer culture has its dark side, the realities of poverty and unemployment amidst images of affluence and the good life. Whatever the shortcomings in capitalism's ability to deliver consumer goods and the consumer lifestyle to all sectors of the population, it has never been short of images – and for those who inhabit the dark side of consumer culture, consumption is limited to the consumption of images.

Images of the Body

Ours is an age obsessed with youth, health and physical beauty. Television and motion pictures, the dominant visual media, churn out persistent reminders that the lithe and graceful body, the dimpled smile set in an attractive face, are the keys to happiness, perhaps even its essence. (Kern 1975, p. ix)

Within consumer culture the body is proclaimed as a vehicle of pleasure: its desirable and desiring and the closer the actual body approximates to the idealised images of youth, health, fitness and beauty the higher its exchange-value. Consumer culture permits the unashamed display of the human body. Clothing is designed to celebrate the 'natural' human form, a marked contrast to the nineteenth century in which clothes were designed to conceal the body. Victorian male attire reflected the concern for respectability with the male body regarded as a clothes-horse for loose fitting conservative clothes in subdued colours. The female form had to be crammed into corsets to achieve the hourglass figure despite the vigorous propaganda against tight-lacing and the resulting disablement of internal organs (Colmer 1979). In the bedroom the naked body was not regarded as a thing of beauty and joy, sex should take place in the dark. Even in the 'gay', 'naughty' 1890s sexual manuals like S. Stall's *What a Young Man Ought to Know* (1897) cautioned that sex should only take place once a week and partners should never undress in front of each other (Kern 1975, p. 111). Within consumer culture the body ceases to be a vessel of sin and the secularised body is found more and more contexts for display both inside and outside the bedroom. The popularity of the outdoor Californian lifestyle and centrally-heated living areas have helped to make more acceptable leisure clothing which makes visible the form of the human body.

While the body incorporates fixed capacities such as height

and bone structure, the tendency within consumer culture is for ascribed bodily qualities to become regarded as plastic – with effort and 'body work' individuals are persuaded that they can achieve a certain desired appearance. Advertising, feature articles and advice columns in magazines and newspapers ask individuals to assume self-responsibility for the way they look. This becomes important not just in the first flush of adolescence and early adulthood, for notions of 'natural' bodily deterioration and the bodily betrayals that accompany ageing become interpreted as signs of moral laxitude (Hepworth and Featherstone 1982). The wrinkles, sagging flesh, tendency towards middle-age spread, hair loss, etc., which accompany ageing should be combated by energetic body maintenance on the part of the individual – with help from the cosmetic, beauty, fitness and leisure industries.

The perception of the body within consumer culture is dominated by the existence of a vast array of visual images. Indeed the inner logic of consumer culture depends upon the cultivation of an insatiable appetite to consume images. The production of images to stimulate sales on a societal level is echoed by the individual production of images through photography (Sontag 1978). Christopher Lasch (1979a, p. 47) has noted the profound effect of photography on the perception of social life:

> Cameras and recording machines not only transcribe experience but alter its quality, giving to much of modern life the character of an enormous echo chamber, a hall of mirrors. Life presents itself as a succession of images, of electronic signals, of impressions recorded and reproduced by means of photography, motion pictures, television and sophisticated recording devices. Modern life is so thoroughly mediated by electronic images that we cannot help responding to others as if their actions – and our own – were being recorded and simultaneously transmitted to an unseen audience or stored up for close scrutiny at some later time.

Day-to-day awareness of the current state of one's appearance is sharpened by comparison, with one's own past photographic images as well as with the idealised images of the human body which proliferate in advertising and the visual media. Images invite comparisons: they are constant reminders of what we are and might with effort yet become. The desire for one's own body also becomes catered for, with one of the effects of the new camera technology (instant photographs, videotapes) being to further private narcisstic uses.[2] Women are of course most clearly trapped in the narcissistic, self-surveillance world of images, for apart from being accorded the major responsibility in organising the purchase and consumption of commodities their bodies are used symbolically in advertisements (Winship 1980; Pollock 1977). The cosmetic and fashion industries are eager to redress this imbalance and promote men alongside women to enjoy the dubious equality of consumers in the market place (Winter and Robert 1980).

Images make individuals more conscious of external appearance, bodily presentation and 'the look'. The motion picture industry has since the early days of consumer culture been one of the major creators and purveyors of images. In this context it is interesting to note that Bela Balázs speculated in the early 1920s that film was transforming the emotional life of twentieth-century man by directing him away from words towards movement and gesture. A culture dominated by words tends to be intangible and abstract, and reduces the human body to a basic biological organism, whereas the new emphasis upon visual images drew attention to the appearance of the body, the clothing, demeanour and gesture (Kern 1975).

The Hollywood cinema helped to create new standards of appearance and bodily presentation, bringing home to a mass audience the importance of 'looking good'. Hollywood publicised the new consumer culture values and projected images of the glamorous celebrity lifestyle to a worldwide audience. The major studios carefully disciplined and packaged film stars for audience consumption.[3] To ensure that the stars conformed with the ideals of physical perfection new kinds of make-up, hair care, and techniques such as electrolysis, cosmetic surgery and toupees were created to remove imperfections. Mary Pickford who subjected herself to a rigorous daily cosmetic, exercise and dietary regime in the early 1920s, later branched out into the cosmetic industry.

Helena Rubinstein, who amassed a fortune of over 500 million dollars, capitalised on these trends by enthusiastically advocating beauty for the masses. She reassured women that there was nothing wrong with wanting to hold onto youth and formulated the consumer culture equation of youth = beauty = health. 'To preserve one's beauty is to preserve health and prolong life' (Rubinstein 1930). The new female ideal (epitomised by the flapper) was not without its critics; Cynthia White (1970) remarks that editorials in British women's magazines in the late 1920s were firmly against the use of make-up and lipstick but by the late 1920s they had capitulated and were for cosmetics – a decision not unrelated to the increasing amount of cosmetic advertising they carried. The 1920s was a crucial decade in the formulation of the new bodily ideal. By the end of the decade women, under the combined impact of the cosmetic, fashion and advertising industries, and Hollywood, had for the first time in large numbers put on rouge and lipstick, taken to short skirts, rayon stockings and had abandoned the corset for rubber 'weight-reducing' girdles (Allen 1931). The new Hollywood styles threatened to carry all before them and iron out regional and local differences. J.B. Priestley (1977) on his *English Journey* of 1933, while taking tea in a rural cafe in Lincolnshire, noted that the girls of the nearby tables had carefully modelled their appearance on their favourite film stars:

> Even twenty years ago girls of this kind would have looked quite different even from girls in the nearest large town; they would have had an unmistakable small town rustic air; but now they are almost indistinguishable from girls in a dozen different capitals, for they all have the same models, from Hollywood.

The major impact of the cosmetic, fashion and advertising industries in the inter-war years was on women; only slow inroads were made in the field of male fashions and cosmetics (one of the most difficult taboos to break down), until the 1960s and 1970s. Yet Hollywood did help to bring about changes in the male ideal in the 1920s: Douglas Fairbanks, the first international cinema superstar, famous for the feats of athleticism he performed in costume spectaculars, was marketed as a virility symbol and fitness fanatic. Like his wife, Mary Pickford, disciplined body maintenance and routines played a prominent role in his private life with his daily training schedule of wrestling, boxing, running and swimming as strenuously publicised as his screen career (Walker 1970).

Fairbanks, who celebrated the athletic adventurous outdoor life in his films, also helped to popularise the suntan. Going against the established wisdom which held that the fashionable body must avoid the effects of the sun, lest it be associated with the tanned labouring body, he allowed his darkened face to appear in films and the popular press. Other celebrities followed suit and sunbathing, which had emerged in the 1890s in Germany as a form of treatment of the tubercular, now gained a wider cosmetic appeal alongside its claims for health: 'The skin of the average overclothed man is white, spotty and inelastic, the skin of a healthy man is brown, smooth and sleek', proclaimed an American article of 1929. The inter-war years also saw the transformation of the beach into a place where one gained a suntan – the hallmark of a successful holiday. For the first time sunbathing on the beach brought together large numbers of people in varying degrees of undress, legitimating the public display of the body.

From its early days the publicity machine of Hollywood has catered for and generated a great deal of interest in the 'backstage' areas, the private lives of the stars, their beauty tips, exercise and diet regimes.[4] The Hollywood fan magazines of the 1920s and 1930s 'indoctrinated their true believers with the notions that women were beautiful, men were manly, crime didn't pay, lovers lived happily ever after time after time, and Lana Turner was discovered eating a sundae at Schwab's Drug Store' (Levin 1976, p. 7). Magazines such as *Photoplay*, *Silver Screen*, *Screen Book*, *Modern Screen* and *Motion Picture* as well as publicising the 'secrets of the stars' also offered readers the chance of self-improvement with advertisements claiming to provide remedies for acne, over-sized busts, under-sized busts, fatness etc. In the early days publicity stills of the stars were re-touched to eliminate blemishes in the actor's or actress's appearance, increasingly this work became unnecessary through the effort stars put into maintaining and enhancing their appearance: in effect they were able to become what they seemed. Hollywood stars began to rely less on aids and supports to effect a given appearance, rather they carefully achieved the appearance of the 'body natural'. Body supports such as the corset (later to reemerge as the naughty basque – a titillating body packaging aid for sexual fun and games) found fewer advocates in a culture which endorsed the exposure of the body on the beach and the wearing of casual leisure clothing. Increasingly exercise was presented as a healthy means of strengthening the body's natural support system (Hornibrook 1924), a technique which would enable the body to pass muster under the close gaze of the camera.

Body Maintenance

> Stay young, stay beautiful, live longer. These are the catch phrases of today's
> hard living society. . . . While the secret of longer life is still a long way off,
> many people are searching for a short cut – through health foods, yoga,
> gardening. Grab your survival kit and live longer. (The *Sun*)

Body maintenance cannot of course be claimed as a novel creation
of consumer culture. In traditional societies, religious communities
such as monasteries demanded ascetic routines with an emphasis
upon exercise and dietary control (Turner 1982). the adoption of
ascetic regimes usually meant, however, that the body was subordinated to 'higher' spiritual ends. The dominant ethos of Christianity was to denigrate and repress the human body. Jesuits were
taught on entering the order to accept Ignatius Loyola's maxim
Perinde ac cadavar (henceforth as a corpse) (Benthall 1976, p. 69).
The Christian tradition glorified an aesthetics of the soul not the
body. Ascetic regimes would release the spirit and subdue the
sexual side of the body. Within consumer culture on the other
hand sexual experts proclaim that dietary control and exercise will
enhance sexual prowess; exercise and sexuality are blurred together
through neologisms such as 'sexercise' and 'exersex'. The shame
in the naked body gradually gave way under the persistent critique
of sexual experts and commercial interests. To enjoy heightened
pleasure individuals have not only to consult the sexual manual
and resort to a growing range of pills, aids and devices, they must
look good too. Self-surveillance through taking instant pictures
and videotapes celebrated sexual aesthetics: the naked body or the
body packaged in erotic sexual leisure-wear could be recorded as
proof of the achievement of a desired effect (Hepworth and
Featherstone 1982).

The term 'body maintenance' indicates the popularity of the
machine metaphor for the body. Like cars and other consumer
goods, bodies require servicing, regular care and attention to
preserve maximum efficiency.[5] As the consumption of goods
increases, the time required for care and maintenance increases,
and the same instrumental rational orientation adopted towards
goods is turned inwards onto the body. The tendency to
transform free time into maintenance work imposes even greater
demands on the individual and makes the monitoring of the
current state of bodily performance essential if individuals are to
get the most out of life: the hectic life increases the need for
'human servicing' (Linder 1970, p. 40).

Preventative medicine offers a similar message and through its offshoot, health education, demands constant vigilance on the part of the individual who has to be persuaded to assume responsibility for his health, introducing the category 'self-inflicted illness', which results from body abuse (overeating, drinking, smoking, lack of exercise etc.), health educationalists assert that individuals who conserve their bodies through dietary care and exercise will enjoy greater health and live longer. The calculation of the potential saving to state health services provides further grounds for castigating those who do not heed the new message as self-indulgent 'slobs' (Featherstone and Hepworth 1980, 1981; Hepworth and Featherstone 1982). In effect, the health education movement is trying to bring about a change in the moral climate so that individuals assume increasing self-responsibility for their health, body shape and appearance. To some extent, this can be seen as building on and accentuating self-help tendencies which were present within the Victorian middle class whose preoccupation with health matters led them to diet, take pills, take up athletics etc. (Haly 1979). Yet however much health educationalists appeal to the rationality of self-preservation and offer the incentives of longevity and lowered risk of disease, their body maintenance messages are strongly influenced by the consumer culture idealisation of youth and the body beautiful. In the late 1970s, the British Health Education Council found that the most effective advertising message was to highlight the cosmetic rewards of fitness and dietary care. Health educationalists have little time for the health food crank or the fitness fanatic in their advertisements, these are discarded in favour of images of men and women who maximise, who get more out of life, who 'look good and feel good', who are more attractive and therefore socially acceptable. Within this logic, fitness and slimness become associated not only with energy, drive and vitality but worthiness as a person; likewise the body beautiful comes to be taken as a sign of prudence and prescience in health matters.

The popular media and commercial interests have found the 'looking good and feeling great' health education message to be a saleable commodity. Eager to endorse body maintenance as a part of the consumer lifestyle, popular newspapers like the *Sun* and *Mirror* in Britain pass on the message to a wider audience with frequent articles on slimming, exercise, health foods and appearance. Centre-page spreads enable readers to calculate their degree of success or failure in meeting age/height/weight targets and how to complete questionnaires to work out their 'survival power'. Feature articles on the calorific value of different types of food complement centre-page spreads on the calorie-burning power of different types of activity (running, sitting, walking, sleeping, kissing, sex etc.), enabling the enterprising reader to draw up a daily calorific balance sheet to see if he or she can meet their designated target. In the last decade, there has also been a noticeable growth in the number of specialist magazines on jogging, running, health foods, exercise, and especially slimming. Self-help books on body maintenance also sell well: in December 1981 four out of ten books on the US bestseller list were of the 'how to lose weight' variety. Common to the popular media treatment of body maintenance, be it from the popular press, specialist magazines of the 'Doctor's Answers' type, advertisements for vitamins, slimming products or government health education propaganda, is the encouragement of self-surveillance of bodily health and appearance as well as the incentive of lifestyle benefits. Body maintenance is firmly established as a virtuous leisure-time activity which will reap further lifestyle rewards resulting from an enhanced appearance: body maintenance in order to look good merges with the stylised images of looking good while maintaining the body. The images in the advertisements, popular press and health education pamphlets are of lithe, bright-eyed beautiful people, in varying states of nakedness, enjoying their body work. The fat are invariably portrayed as glum and downcast: joke figures, survivals from a bygone age.

One of the noticeable features of the twentieth century, according to Theodore Zeldin (1977, p. 440), has been the triumph of the thin woman over the fat woman. It can be added that in the second half of the twentieth century this ideal is becoming firmly established for men too, with the last bastions of corpulence amongst the working class now under siege. As the slim form becomes mandatory, almost every conceivable consumer product is discovered to have slimming properties. In 1931, the manufacturers of Lucky Strike cigarettes spent 19 million dollars on advertising and successfully convinced many women that smoking was a vital aid to dieting (Susman 1973, p.132). Today grapefruit juice, disco dancing, plankton and sex are marketed with similar conviction. The beauty industry now offers 'shapeovers' ('look 10 pounds slimmer without dieting')[6] to accompany 'makeovers' as an essential part of every woman's cosmetic repertoire.

Within consumer culture slimness has become associated with health and the health education message that being overweight is a health risk has become absorbed into the conventional wisdom. Yet a good deal of the 'advice' that abounds in the media and advertisements is clearly of a pseudo-scientific nature. Rubin Andres has recently conducted an extensive review of a number of slimming studies and concluded that the overweight actually live longer. The age/height/weight charts originally constructed by insurance companies, which hang in doctors' surgeries and are publicised in the popular media, are inaccurate – in some cases as much as a stone out. Andres' conclusion that slimness has little to do with health merely confirms those reached by earlier researchers such as Bruch (1957) and Beller (1977) and may be destined to have a similar lack of impact.

Women of course are well aware that the major reason for dieting is cosmetic and that 'looking good' not only becomes necessary to achieve social acceptability but can become the key to a more exciting lifestyle. As one woman remarked in a slimming magazine article: 'Being overweight was, for me, like living with the brakes on. And I *hated* being held back.' The lifestyle benefits are played up in slimming magazines and the popular press: not only do successful slimmers get more admiring glances, they feel more attractive and are confident to go out more, take up new exciting hobbies and live out their version of the Martini people lifestyle (Hepworth and Featherstone 1982).

Like slimming, jogging provides further insight into the transvaluation of use within consumer culture: everything has to be good for something else and the range of alleged benefits multiplies endlessly. Apart from reducing the chance of coronary heart disease, it is claimed jogging helps to cure impotency, increase confidence, psychological well-being, and puts 'you in control of your body'. Jogging has also been claimed to result in prolonged cosmetic benefits – improving posture, reducing stomach sag, helping to burn off excessive fat (Hepworth and Featherstone 1982, p. 107). The notion of running for running's sake, purposiveness without a purpose, a sensuous experience in harmony with embodied and physical nature, is completely submerged amidst the welter of benefits called up by the market and health experts (Featherstone and Hepworth 1982).

The instrumental strategies which body maintenance demands of the individual resonate with deep-seated features of consumer culture which encourage individuals to negotiate their social relationships and approach their free-time activities with a calculating frame of mind. Self preservation depends upon the preservation of the body within a culture in which the body is the passport to all that is good in life. Health, youth, beauty, sex, fitness are the positive attributes which body care can achieve and preserve. With appearance being taken as a reflex of the self the penalties of bodily neglect are a lowering of one's acceptability as a person, as well as an indication of laziness, low self-esteem and even moral failure. Within consumer culture it is hardly surprising that ageing and death are viewed so negatively – they are unwelcome reminders of the inevitable decay and defeat that are in store, even for the most vigilant of individuals. The secularisation of the body has resulted in the eclipse of the traditional religious purpose of the body in which it was regarded as a transitory vehicle, a means to higher spiritual ends. Today, pain, suffering and death are seen as unwelcome intrusions in the midst of a happy life (Ariès 1974) and the consumer culture imagery has decreed that life can and should be everlastingly happy. Amidst images of comfort, fulfilment and cleanliness the unpleasant odours and sights surrounding death become intolerable: 'the dirty death' (Ariès 1981, p. 568) has to be hidden away.

Within the limitations of its logic consumer culture is incapable of providing other than flawed solutions to the problems of ageing and death. On the one hand it hides them away, suppresses them in the midst of illusions of endless hedonism, while flattering our vanity that we are enjoying the good life here and now. Yet it also needs to simulate the fear of the decay and incapacities accompanying old age and death to jolt individuals out of complacency and persuade them to consume body maintenance strategies. In a feature article entitled 'Have You the Looks that Last?' (day six of the *Sun*'s 'Staying Alive Week' in June 1978) readers were warned:

> You may look sexy and beautiful now, but will you still be attractive when you're 50? Or 60? Or even 70? To get the most out of life it makes sense to keep in tip-top shape in middle-age and beyond. Beauties like Joan Collins

and Cyd Charisse believe that lasting good looks takes lots of hard work.

The illusion of technical mastery and even transcendence of the lifespan fits in well with the 'calculating hedonism' (Jacoby 1980, p. 63) demanded by consumer culture. Within the 'live for yourself' calculus, children are seen as bad investments in terms of time, money and affection and even resented as possible rivals. Cars, jogging, tourism, self-actualisation and the new therapies offer more predictable pleasures and a better return on the investment of time and money (Jacoby 1980, p. 64). This suggests that within consumer culture a new relationship between the body and self has developed.

The Performing Self

Today's modern society puts a premium on youth and good looks, in fact *to look better, to look younger, to look more attractive* has become a basic need for most of us because *people who look good, are made to feel good*'. (The Lasertone Beauty Therapy Treatment leaflet 1982)

A number of commentators have suggested that a new personality type has emerged in the course of the twentieth century. David Reisman (1950), for example, refers to the replacement of the 'inner-directed' by the other-directed type and Daniel Bell (1976) mentions the eclipse of the puritan by a more hedonistic type. Interest in this new personality type has been sharpened recently by discussions of narcissism (Lasch 1976, 1977b, 1979a). This new narcissistic type of individual, which it is argued has recently come into prominence, is described as: 'excessively self-conscious', 'chronically uneasy about his health, afraid of ageing and death', 'constantly searching for flaws and signs of decay', 'eager to get along with others yet unable to make real friendships', 'attempts to sell his self as if his personality was a commodity', 'hungry for emotional experiences', 'haunted by fantasies of omnipotence and eternal youth'. Lasch (1979b, p. 201) argues that the culture of narcissism first took shape in the 1920s, matured in the post-war era and is now rapidly disintegrating.[7] For our purposes the interesting feature of the narcissistic type and the culture of narcissim which spawned it, is that it points to a new relationship between body and self. Within consumer culture, which approximately coincides with the culture of narcissism, the new conception of self which has emerged, which we shall refer to as the 'performing self' places greater emphasis upon appearance, display and the management of impressions.

One indication of the movement towards the performing self can be gleaned from the shift in the self ideal proclaimed in self-help manuals from the nineteenth century to the early twentieth century. In the nineteenth century, self-help books emphasised the Protestant virtues – industry, thrift, temperance, not just as means but as valid ends in their own right (Lasch 1979a, p. 57). Achievement was measured not against others but against abstract ideals of discipline and self-denial. With the bureaucratisation of the corporate career these virtues gave way to an emphasis upon competition with one's peers, salesmanship, 'boosterism' and the development of 'personal magnetism'.

Warren Susman (1979) has characterised this shift as entailing the replacement of the nineteenth-century concern with character by a new focus upon personality in the early twentieth century. The words most frequently associated with *character* were: citizenship, democracy, duty, work, honour, reputation, morals, integrity and manhood. Locating this transition in the middle of the first decade of the twentieth century, Susman argues that subsequent advice manuals emphasised *personality* and a new set of associated adjectives came into prominence: fascinating, stunning, attractive, magnetic, glowing, masterful, creative, dominant, forceful. In his book *Personality How to Build It* (1915) H. Laurent remarked: 'character is either good or bad, personality famous or infamous' (Susman 1979, p. 217). A comparison of two books written by O.S. Marden, separated by twenty years at the turn of the century, further illustrates the transition. His *Character: the Greatest Thing in the World* (1899), stressed the ideals of the Christian gentleman: integrity, courage, duty as well as the virtues of hard work and thrift. In 1921 he published *Masterful Personality* which emphasised a set of different virtues: now attention should be given to 'the need to attract and hold friends', 'to compel people to like you', 'personal charm' and women should develop 'fascination'. Good conversation, energy, manners, proper clothes and poise were also deemed necessary (Susman 1979, p. 220).

The new personality handbooks stressed voice control, public speaking, exercise, sound catering habits, a good complexion and grooming and beauty aids – they showed little interest in morals. Susman (1979, p. 221) remarks

The social role demanded of all in the new culture of personality was that of performer. Every American was to become a performing self . . . the new stress on enjoyment of life implied that true pleasure could be obtained by making oneself pleasant to others.

Individuals should attempt to develop the skills of actors, a message not just emphasised by self-help manuals, but by advertising and the popular press in the 1920s. Hollywood provided many of the models for the new ideal with stars marketed as 'personalities'. Douglas Fairbanks, the archetypal 'personality star', even wrote his own kind of self-help book *Make Life Worthwhile: Laugh and Live* (Susman 1979, p. 233).

Richard Sennett's book *The Fall of Public Man* is interesting in this context because he examines the historical origins of the new belief that appearance and bodily presentation express the self. In the eighteenth century, he suggests, appearance was not regarded as a reflection of the inner-self but more playfully distanced from an individual's character which was regarded as fixed at birth. The replacement of this traditional holistic world view by a more 'existentialist' view in which each individual was responsible for the development of his/her own personality, occurred in the nineteenth century. Following Marx's fetishism of commodities argument Sennett sees the development of the department store in the second half of the nineteenth century as crucial to the process. The department store sold the newly available cheap mass-produced clothing by using increasingly sophisticated techniques of advertising and display. Clothing which indicated a fixed social status came to be avoided and an individual's dress and demeanour came more and more to be taken as an expression of his personality: clothes in the words of Thomas Carlyle became 'emblems of the soul'. Individuals had now to decode both the appearance of others and take pains to manage the impressions they might give off, while moving through the world of strangers. This encouraged greater bodily self-consciousness and self-scrutiny in public life.[8]

The 'performing self' became more widely accepted in the inter-war years with advertising, Hollywood and the popular press legitimating the new ideal for a wider audience. Within consumer culture individuals are asked to become role players and self-consciously monitor their own performance. Appearance, gesture and bodily demeanour become taken as expressions of self, with bodily imperfections and lack of attention carrying penalties in everyday interactions. Individuals therefore become

encouraged to search themselves for flaws and signs of decay: as
Lasch (1979a, p. 92) remarks:

> All of us, actors and spectators alike, live surrounded by mirrors. In them,
> we seek reassurance of our capacity to captivate or impress others, anxiously
> searching out blemishes that might detract from the appearance we intend to
> project. The advertising industry deliberately encourages the pre-occupation
> with appearances.

If individuals are required to be 'on stage' all the time, it can
lead to what Goffman (1969) has termed as 'bureaucratisation of
the spirit', for the performing self must produce an even performance every time. The demand here are no less stringent for
professional actors: White (1981) recounts the story of a promis-
ing theatre actor from New York who was interviewed for a film
part in Hollywood, but was declared a non-starter by the studio
after his first interview, without being given a screen test, because
he lacked the stylised, off-stage actors' presentation of self which
had become mandatory in Hollywood. It is not enough to have
the capacity to perform within specific contexts, it becomes essential to be able to project constantly a 'winning image'.

Behind the emphasis upon performance, it can be argued, lies
a deeper interest in manipulating the feelings of others.
Anthropologists and ethnologists have long been interested in
developing theories of non-verbal bodily communication. One
offshoot in the post-war era has been the positivist study of body
behaviour: kinesics (Kristeva 1978) which seeks to reconstruct the
grammar of body language. Paul Ekman, a researcher in this
field, has recently catalogued 7,000 facial expressions, which
according to his experiments can be used to tell exactly what
individuals are feeling. There has also been some interest in the
practice of kinesics from the popular press and self-help
literature: 'keep a controlling hand in arguments and negotia-
tions', 'decide when the other person is lying', 'interpret gestures
of friendliness and flirtation', 'detect boredom' runs the advertising blurb for a popular paperback entitled *How to Read a
Person Like a Book*. Another, entitled *Kinesics: The Power of
Silent Command*, tells the reader how to learn to 'project
unspoken orders that must be obeyed', 'how Silent Command
brings you the love and admiration of others'. Arguing that we
should try to break through this type of body manipulation by
attempting to produce a widespread competence in body
language, Benthall (1976, p. 92) writes:

The body as a whole is still a repressed element in our culture, we tend to *believe* (or find it hard to disbelieve) the sincerity of the politician when he looks us straight in the eye over the TV screen, or that of the actress whose flashing teeth urge us to buy her brand of toothpaste. In both cases a verbal message is lent considerable persuasiveness by the controlled use of certain tricks of bodily deportment, which work largely at an unconscious rather than a conscious level. Until we become more aware of the body's power and resourcefulness, we will not feel a sufficiently educated outrage against its manipulation and exploitation. Rather than campaigns for literacy or numeracy, we may need a campaign for corporacy.

The performing self has also gained impetus from the institutional changes which have brought about the rise of the professional–managerial middle class. One effect of the bureaucratisation of industry and the growth of bureaucratic administrative organisations has been to undermine the bourgeois achievement ideology so that there are more and more areas of work in which the precise evaluation of an individual's achievement on universalistic criteria becomes impossible. Hence 'extra-functional elements of professional roles became more and more important for conferring occupational status' (Habermas 1976, p. 81). The difficulty of evaluating an individual's competence on strictly rational criteria opens up the space for the performing self, schooled in public relations techniques, who is aware that the secret of success lies in the projection of a successful image. In the dense interpersonal environment of modern bureaucracy, individuals depend upon their ability to negotiate interactions on the basis of 'personality'. Impression management, style, panache and careful bodily presentation therefore become important.

It has also been argued that this type of individual has been furthered by the growth of the 'helping professions' which have expanded by discrediting traditional mores and family-centred remedies in favour of a new ideology of health, based upon therapy, human growth and scientism (Lasch 1977a). In education, social work, health education, marriage guidance, probation, the helping professionals have not only been able to develop careers based upon interpersonal skills but have also transferred and imposed the new modes of emotional and relational management onto their clients (de Swaan 1981, p. 375). Social relations take on a veneer of informality and equality, but actually demand greater discipline and self-control as management through command gives way to management by negotiation. The 'negotiating self' is also granted legitimation outside the work sphere as the new styles of social interaction spread into family life not only through the direct intervention of experts but also through the feature articles, advice pages and problem programmes of the popular media (Hepworth and Featherstone 1982; Ehrenreich and English 1979). In effect the professional–managerial middle class, which expanded in the course of the twentieth century are in the process of becoming 'the arbiter of contemporary lifestyles and opinions' (de Swaan 1981, p. 375).

The tendency towards narcissism, the negotiating, performing self is therefore most noticeable in the professional–managerial middle class who have both the time and money to engage in lifestyle activities and the cultivation of the persona. It is arguably spreading to sectors of the working class (Dreitzel 1977) and up to the age scale to the middle aged (Hepworth and Featherstone 1982, Featherstone and Hepworth 1982). This is not to suggest that the implications of the consumer-culture imagery of the body and the performing self do not encounter resistance: groups like the Grey Panthers and the Women's Movement have mounted a strong (if as yet ineffectual) critique of 'ageism' and 'sexism'. While pockets of working-class culture clearly remain, it has been suggested that the working class increasingly draw upon the media as a source of identity models (Davis 1979). Consumer culture imagery and advertising cannot be dismissed as merely 'entertainment', something which individuals do not take seriously. In rejecting this position and its obverse, that individuals are somehow programmed to accept essentially false wants and needs, we can indicate two broad levels on which consumer culture operates: (a) it provides a multiplicity of images designed to stimulate needs and desires, (b) it is based on and helps to change the material arrangements of social space and hence the nature of social interactions. Taking the interactional level first, it can be argued that changes in the material fabric of everyday life have involved a re-structuring of social space (e.g. new shopping centres, the beach, the modern pub) which provides an environment facilitating the display of the body. Individuals may of course choose to ignore or neglect their appearance and refuse to cultivate a performing self, yet if they do so they must be prepared to face the implications of this choice within social encounters.

Finally, with regard to the proliferation of images which daily assault the individual within consumer culture, it should be emphasised again that these images do not merely serve to stimulate false needs fostered onto the individual. Part of the strength of consumer culture comes from its ability to harness and channel genuine bodily needs and desires, albeit that it presents them within a form which makes their realisation dubious. The desire for health, longevity, sexual fulfilment, youth and beauty represent a reified entrapment of trans-historical human longing within distorted forms. Yet in a time of diminished economic growth, permanent inflation and shortages of raw materials the contradictions within the consumer-culture values become more blatant, not only for those who are excluded – the old, unemployed, low paid – but also for those who participate most actively and experience more directly the gap between the promise of the imagery and the exigencies of every-day life.

Notes

I would like to thank John Alt, Josef Bleicher and Mike Hepworth for comments on the earlier draft of this chapter. Many of the ideas in this chapter draw on my joint work with Mike Hepworth.

1. Here we follow Ewen's assumption that consumer culture arose in the inter-war years, first in the United States in the 1920s (in Britain later, not until the 1930s). Advertising and other elements of consumer culture were of course present before this time. E. Peterson (1964, p. 19) for example notes a surge in the amount of money spent on advertising, an increasing dependence of magazines on advertising revenue and the creation of new advertising agencies, around the turn of the century. Nevertheless Ewen argues for the distinctiveness of the 'break' at the start of the inter-war era.

2. One British daily newspaper in 1981 referred to a firm which specialised in a home videotape service for couples. They would devise a plot and photograph the couple engaged in sex. The tape could then be played back at their leisure and would serve as a memento in old age of how they once performed.

3. The star system was not the invention of Hollywood. Hess and Nochlin (1973) remark that it originated in the 1890s with the theatrical publicity picture (e.g. Toulouse-Lautrec). The image of the star was reduced to a salient gesture on property (e.g. Sarah Berhardt's tresses). The more these attributes became fixed in the public's mind, the more the star's actual appearance tended to become stylised and rigid.

4. Today it is not only the secrets of the stars but those of politicians too which cause interest. Public relations experts take the media on tours of politi-cians, backstage areas to divulge the body-maintenance routines which produce the energy, vitality, health and zest-for-life of politician-celebrities such as Ford, Carter, Reagan and Thatcher.

5. See for example O. Gillie (1978) *The Sunday Times Book of Body Maintenance*, Diagram Group (1977) *Man's Body: an Owner's Manual*.

6. The headline of a double-page spread in the *News of the World* magazine, *Sunday*, in January 1982. The text, surrounding a picture of a young woman in a leotard smiling as she exercised, referred to exercises devised by Adrian Arpel, 'America's queen of self-improvement', the 'boss of her own international cosmetics business' who claimed 'anyone can shed ten pounds and ten years without a diet or facelift'.

7. A number of commentators have criticised Lasch's periodisation. Oestereicher (1979) sees the narcissistic as merely a continuation of the inner-directed individualist self. Wrong (1979, p. 310) and Narr (1980, p. 68) criticise the vagueness of Lasch's periodisation. Lasch (1979b) has since replied to his critics and attempted to clarify this issue. It is worth adding that Lasch (1977b, 1979a) has referred to the writings of Stuart Ewen (1976) linking together the rise of consumer culture in the 1920s with the growth of narcissim.

8. While Sennett traces the origins of the new personality structure back to the 1860s he argues that it became more noticeable in the 1890s revolt against Victorian sobriety and prudery. This brought into prominence tighter fitting more colourful clothes for women with a more widespread use of makeup – discreetly advertised in women's magazines (Sennett 1976, p. 190). Lasch and Susman both locate the transition from character to personality as occurring around the turn of the century.

References

Allen, P.L. (1931) *Only Yesterday*, Vol. 1. Harmondsworth: Penguin.

Alt, J. (1976) 'Beyond Class: the Decline of Labor and Leisure', *Telos*, 28.

Ariès, P. (1974) *Western Attitudes Towards Death*. Baltimore: Johns Hopkins University Press.

Ariès, P. (1981) *The Hour of Our Death*. New York: Knopf.

Baudrillard, J. (1975) *The Mirror of Production*. St Louis: Telos.

Bell, D. (1976) *Cultural Contradictions of Capitalism*. London: Heinemann.

Beller, A.S. (1977) *Fat and Thin: A Natural History of Obesity*. New York: Farrar, Strauss and Giroux.

Benthall, J. (1976) *The Body Electric: Patterns of Western Industrial Culture*. London: Thames and Hudson.

Berger, P. and Kellner, D. (1964) 'Marriage and the Construction of Reality', *Diogenes*, 46.

Bruch, H. (1957) *The Importance of Overweight*. New York: W. Norton.

Clarke, J., Critcher, C. and Johnson, R. (eds) (1979) *Working Class Culture*. London: Heinemann.

Colmer, M. (1979) *Whalebone to See-Through: A History of Body Packaging*. London: Johnson & Bacon.

Cowley, M. (1951) *Exiles Return*. New York: Viking.

Davis, H. (1979) *Beyond Class Images*. London: Croom Helm.

Diagram Group (1977) *Man's Body: An Owner's Manual*. London: Corgi.

Dreitzel, P. (1977) 'The Politics of Culture', in N. Birnbaum (ed.), *Beyond the Crisis*. New York: OUP.

Ehrenreich, B. and English, D. (1979) *For Her Own Good: 150 Years of Experts'*

Advice to Women. London: Pluto Press.

Ewen, S. (1976) *Captains of Consciousness: Advertising and the Social Roots of the Consumer Culture.* New York: McGraw-Hill.

Featherstone, M. and Hepworth, M. (1980) 'Changing Images of Middle Age', in M. Johnson (ed.), *Transitions in Middle and Later Life.* London: British Society of Gerontology.

Featherstone, M. and Hepworth, M. (1981) 'Images de la maturité', *Gerontologie*, Dec.

Featherstone, M. and Hepworth, M. (1982) 'Ageing and Inequality: Consumer Culture and the New Middle Age', in D. Robbins et al. (eds), *Rethinking Social Inequality.* Aldershot: Gower.

Foucault, M. (1977) *Discipline and Punish.* Harmondsworth: Penguin.

Giddens, A. (1981) *A Contemporary Critique of Historical Materialism.* London: Macmillan.

Gillie, O. (1978) *The Sunday Times Book of Body Maintenance.* London: Joseph.

Goffman, E. (1969) *The Presentation of Self in Everyday Life.* London: Allen Lane.

Goffman, E. (1972) *Relations in Public.* Harmondsworth: Penguin.

Habermas, J. (1976) *Legitimation Crisis.* London: Heinemann.

Haly, B. (1979) *The Healthy Body and Victorian Culture.* Cambridge, MA: Harvard University Press.

Hepworth, M. and Featherstone, M. (1982) *Surviving Middle Age.* Oxford: Blackwell.

Hess, T.B. and Nochlin, N. (1973) *Woman as Sex Object.* London: Allen Lane.

Hornibrook, F.A. (1924) *The Cult of the Abdomen: the Cure of Obesity and Constipation.* London: Heinemann.

Jacoby, R. (1980) 'Narcissim and the Crisis of Capitalism', *Telos*, 44.

Kern, S. (1975) *Anatomy and Destiny: A Cultural History of the Human Body.* New York: Bobbs-Merrill.

Kline, S. and Leiss, W. (1978) 'Advertising, Needs and Commodity Fetishism', *Canadian Journal of Political and Social Theory*, 2(1).

Kristeva, J. (1978) 'Gesture: Practice or Communication', in T. Polhemus (ed.), *Social Aspects of the Human Body.* Harmondsworth: Penguin.

Lasch, C. (1976) 'The Narcissistic Society', *New York Review of Books*.

Lasch, C. (1977a) *Haven in a Heartless World: the Family Besieged.* New York: Basic Books.

Lasch, C. (1977b) 'The Narcissistic Personality of Our Time', *Partisan Review*.

Lasch, C. (1979a) *The Culture of Narcissism.* New York: Norton.

Lasch, C. (1979b) 'Politics and Social Theory: A Reply to the Critics', *Salmagundi*, 46.

Lefebvre, H. (1971) *Everyday Life in the Modern World.* London: Allen Lane.

Levin, M. (1976) *Hollywood and the Great Fan Magazines.* London: Ian Allen.

Linder, S.B. (1970) *The Harried Leisure Class.* New York: Columbia University Press.

Lukács, G. (1971) *History and Class Consciousness.* Trans R. Livingstone. London: Merlin.

Lynd, R. and Lynd H. (1929) *Middletown: A Study in Contemporary American Culture.* New York.

Mandel, E. (1970) *Late Capitalism.* London: New Left Books.

Miller, M.B. (1981) *The Bon Marché: Bourgeois Culture and the Department Store.* London: Allen and Unwin.

Narr, W.D. (1980) 'The Selling of Narcissim', *Dialectical Anthropology*, 5(1).

Oestereicher, E. (1979) 'The Privatisation of the Self in Modern Society', *Social Research*, 46(3).

Park, R. (1952) *Human Communities.* New York: Free Press.

Park, R., Burgess, E.W. and McKenzie, R. (1925) *The City.* Chicago: Chicago University Press.

Peterson, E. (1964) *Magazines in the Twentieth Century.* Urbana: Illinois University Press.

Pollock, G. (1977) 'What's Wrong With Images of Women?' *Screen Education*, 24(1).

Priestley, J.B. (1977) *English Journey* (orig. 1934). Harmondsworth: Penguin.

Reisman, D. (1950) *The Lonely Crowd: A Study of the Changing American Character.* New Haven, CT: Yale University Press.

Rubinstein, H. (1930) *The Art of Feminine Beauty.* New York: Liveright.

Rose, G. (1978) *The Melancholy Science: An Introduction to Adorno.* London: Macmillan.

Sennett, P. (1976) *The Fall of Public Man.* Cambridge: Cambridge University Press.

Sontag, S. (1978) *On Photography.* London: Allen Lane.

Stein, M. (1960) *The Eclipse of Community.* New York: Harper.

Susman, W. (1973) *Culture and Commitment 1929–1945.* New York: Braziller.

Susman, W. (1979) 'Personality and the Making of Twentieth-Century Culture', in J. Higham and P.K. Conkin (eds), *New Directions in American Intellectual History.* Baltimore: Johns Hopkins University Press.

Swaan, A. de (1981) 'The Politics of Agoraphobia', *Theory and Society*, 10(3).

Turner, B.S. (1982) 'The Discourse of Diet', *Theory, Culture & Society*, 1(1): 23–32 (reprinted in this volume).

Walker, A. (1970) *Stardom: The Hollywood Phenomenon.* New York: Stein and Day.

White, C.L. (1970) *Women's Magazines 1693–1968.* London: Joseph.

White, E. (1981) *States of Desire.* New York: Bantam.

Williams, R. (1960) 'The Magic System', *New Left Review*, 41.

Williamson, J. (1978) *Decoding Advertisements.* London: Boyars.

Willis, E. (1970) 'Consumerism and Women', *Socialist Revolution*, 1(3).

Winship, J. (1980) 'Sexuality for Sale', in S. Hall, D. Hobson, A. Lowe and P. Willis (eds), *Culture, Media, Language*, London: Hutchinson.

Winter, M.F. and Robert, E.R. (1980) 'Male Domination, Late Capitalism and the Growth of Instrumental Reason', *Berkeley Journal of Sociology*.

Wrong, D. (1979) 'Bourgeois Values, No Bourgeoisie: The Cultural Criticism of Christopher Lasch', *Dissent*.

Zeldin, T. (1977) *France 1848–1945, Volume 2: Intellect, Taste and Anxiety.* Oxford: Oxford University Press.

This chapter first appeared in *Theory, Culture & Society*, Vol. 1 (1982), 18–33.

7

THE MIDLIFESTYLE OF 'GEORGE AND LYNNE': NOTES ON A POPULAR STRIP

Mike Featherstone and Mike Hepworth

'George and Lynne' is a comic strip which appears each day in one of Britain's most popular newspapers, the *Sun*. The central characters are an affluent married couple living in a spacious house on the banks of a river. George has an executive (though unspecified) position with a commercial organisation and Lynne, who has no children to look after, stays at home. They have a large number of friends, plenty of clothes and other material possessions, and enjoy a happy marriage and active social life. As portrayed in the strip their lifestyle, as we shall see below, is an expression of contemporary consumer culture and in particular a celebration of the naked (or almost naked) human body (Featherstone 1982).

© Conrad Frost & Associates **1982**

In the history of the comic strip (Inge 1982; Becker 1959; Perry and Aldridge 1971) the representation of the lives of married or courting couples is not new. During the 1920s 'Tillie the Toller' and 'Betty' were popular strips in the United States featuring fashionable glamour-girls whose respective boyfriends Mac and Lester De Pester were gawky and inept (Becker 1959, p. 79). The realistic style of representation of the characters in these strips was taken up in Britain in the shape of 'Jane', the most legendary of all British newspaper cartoon characters which ran from 1932 until 1959. During the 1950s and 1960s the titillatory style of 'Jane' found a number of imitators: 'Romeo Brown', 'Jane . . . Daughter of Jane', 'Patti', and 'Tiffany Jones' (Perry and Aldridge 1971, pp. 219–27). In contrast, two post-war husband and wife strips, 'The Gambols' and 'Andy Capp', both of which featured middle-aged couples, present a markedly different approach in style and in content to that of 'Jane' and more recently, 'George and Lynne'. Drawn as over-simplified cartoon characters, 'The Gambols' are a middle-class couple in their thirties and the husband who is decidedly henpecked is beginning to succumb to middle-age spread and is at his happiest reading the paper or snoozing (Perry and Aldridge 1971, p. 228). In even sharper contrast, though represented in a similar style, is the immensely successful 'Andy Capp', a boorish, drunken, lazy working-class slob who is constantly waited upon by his down-trodden, shapeless, middle-aged wife, Florrie.

Andy and Florrie who appear in the *Sun*'s arch-rival the *Daily Mirror* are, unlike George and Lynne, working class and live in a terraced house in a North of England town where the women still wear pinnies all day and have their hair in permanent curlers whilst their menfolk are perpetually clad in cloth caps and mufflers. In addition, Andy and Florrie look their age, indeed with his beer belly and her corpulence this couple represent the traditional image of middle age (Hepworth and Featherstone 1982). Whereas Andy and Florrie are always presented fully clothed in the block cartoon style, George and Lynne are frequently presented naked or semi-naked and their bodies, drawn in a detailed realist style, are firm, attractive and youthful. Andy's favourite home pastime is to stretch out on the settee, and relax with a bottle of beer, cigarette and the racing paper while watching television. In contrast, George is constantly maintaining the house, garden and car, though relieved by regular rewards of television and sex. Andy and Florrie have reached the routinised stage of a companionship marriage, sex is a thing of the past, they are stuck with each other and too old to learn new tricks. But George and Lynne who are somewhere in their middle years are active, energetic: they work at their relationship and sex life and endeavour to keep their bodies in an attractive, healthy and youthful state. The humour of the Andy Capp strip is survivalist, emphasising that we're all in the same boat together, but can have a laugh and accept our fate (Nuttall and Carmichael 1977). In the George and Lynne strip, which also sets out to be humorous, the laughs are more sophisticated and individualistic, concerned with displaying wit and scoring points.

The casual nakedness of the main characters in the George and Lynne strip is a major innovation. The strip has democratised the body beautiful with George like his partner presented as attractive, glamorous and sexy – a marked contrast to the over-simplified caricatures of men which appeared in earlier strips of couples. The fact that women readers find George attractive was recently confirmed by Conrad Frost, George and Lynne's creator, who commented that in the 1950s the reader response to strips such as 'The Heart of Juliet Jones' was predominantly from men. In the case of the George and Lynne strip the majority of letters come from women, and it is they, not the men, who write the 'unpublished' letters. Many of the letters come from groups of three or four young women working in offices or shops who ask for full frontal nudes of George. Frost rarely receives similar letters from men about Lynne. Here is a typical example:

> My colleagues and I buy your *Sun* daily and the highlight of the day is to do the *Sun* crossword in our tea break. We also get excited to know how many clothes Lynne will be wearing if any. Isn't it about time we saw less of Lynne and a *lot more* of George. Is he the man we all think he is? Please can we have a full frontal of George? Seeing as you have put the price up to 14p we think we ought to see more for our money.

Another letter runs:

> We are five working girls from Bristol
> and we feel we must write and complain
> for we all read the *Sun* in our lunch-break
> and it seems that we all feel the same.
>
> It's George and Lynne in the Cartoons,
> we really feel something is wrong,

whilst Lynne walks around without any clothes
it seems George is putting more on.

She always seems to be naked
which we're sure is great for the men
so we'd like to ask if George could be,
without any clothes now and then?

After all we've got equality
and no one would feel it was wrong,
but we do have another conclusion
maybe Lynne isn't turning him on!

It has been suggested by Perry and Aldridge (1971, p. 16) that strips can be taken as an accurate mirror of the times we live in. Whilst the George and Lynne strip is a long way from the realities of unemployment and diminished expectations which many individuals are faced with in our society, their way of life does illustrate a consumer-culture ideal, an affluent and upper-middle-class world with its promise of style, display and individuality. 'George and Lynne' celebrates the contemporary consumer culture notion that individuals should not just let life happen in their free time, but should plan and construct a lifestyle which expresses their identity and which can be taken by others as a statement of their social worth and individuality.

Midlifestyle

Although George and Lynne have clearly passed their twenties, it is not easy to determine their exact age. One strip which provides a clue has George reminding Lynne that a 'milestone birthday' is coming up and reassuring her that she has no need to worry because 'a woman's as old as she looks'.

© Conrad Frost & Associates 1982

Lynne then is well into midlife, probably in her mid-30s, on the verge of what used to be termed middle age. Not that there is much in the lifestyle and presentation of self of George and Lynne which would allow us to categorise them as middle aged. The more traditional images of resignation and bodily decline associated with middle age are captured by their friends, Alice

© Conrad Frost & Associates 1982

and her husband; she is fat and dowdy, he is balding and portly. Both look out of date and set in their ways. Alice cannot accept the maxim that life begins at forty, instead the forties are the decade in which everything starts 'to wear out, fall out or spread out'.

In marked contrast George and Lynne epitomise the new attitude towards middle age (Featherstone and Hepworth 1981, 1982; Hepworth and Featherstone 1982) which is celebrated in the popular media. It holds that individuals who look after their bodies and adopt a positive attitude towards life will be able to avoid the decline and negative effects of the ageing process and thereby prolong their capacity to enjoy to the full the benefits of consumer-culture lifestyles. This new orientation towards the middle years represents the endorsement of a new style of life, a 'midlifestyle' which suggests the middle years (30–60) are replete with opportunities to achieve new goals, fulfilment and personal growth. In contrast to the negative connotations of the term 'middle age', midlifestyle does not suggest the closed horizons, decline and fixed roles and capacities of the over-routinised life but points instead to the over-optioned life in which individuals can prolong vitality, energy and optimism and enjoy the benefits of an endless 'middle youth'. Self-renewal therefore is accorded a central place within this lifestyle and individuals are encouraged to defeat the negative effects of the ageing process by constantly revitalising their bodies, sex lives and relationships.

Within consumer culture we are surrounded by images of slim, attractive, youthful bodies and are constantly reminded that individuals who look after their bodies will stay healthier, live longer and preserve their figures and good looks (Featherstone 1982). In the media imagery fitness routines, dieting and body maintenance are presented both as means to an end – key resources to enable men and women to get more out of life – and as enjoyable and worthy lifestyle activities in their own right. George and Lynne spend a good deal of time engaged in body maintenance: they slim, exercise, jog, and massage, bathe and groom each other. Lynne manages to keep up her tan by sunbathing in the garden in summer – occasionally in the nude. The riverside location with its passing traffic of pleasure craft provides ample opportunities for exhibitionism and voyeurism. In winter the centrally-heated living spaces offer further opportunities for narcissistic bodily display; Lynne spends hours naked under the sun lamp, she exercises, weighs herself and relaxes in the nude. Both George and Lynne are at home with their bodies, they generally like the way they look

© Conrad Frost & Associates 1982

and Lynne especially. In spite of her constant desire to lose a few more pounds, is aware of her attractiveness and desirability. In one recent strip a semi-naked Lynne is unpacking a weekend case and pauses outside the dark-room door to ask 'Well – *wasn't* it unforgettable?' Inside George, crouched over an enlarger gazing at a naked image of Lynne replies: 'I'll answer that when I've printed the pictures.' Another strip which continues this theme of narcissistic display and self-surveillance presents a close-up of George and Lynne's bedside table which has a framed photograph of the naked couple, with arms and legs wrapped around each other, clearly enjoying another 'magic moment'.

© Conrad Frost & Associates **1982**

Not only sex, but watching television, George and Lynne's other major leisure-time pursuit, both afford considerable opportunities for bodily display. Whether they are depicted naked in front of the television in the bedroom, or relaxing semi-clothed in the lounge (Lynne invariably in a short dressing gown which is always gaping open), we are given the impression that sex has just taken place or is about to occur. Indeed sex is presented

© Conrad Frost & Associates **1982**

as permanently in the offing a treat that they can always hold in store for each other, both in sickness and in health. Sex can be the prize in a card game, which inevitably turns out to be strip poker. It is the reward for decorating the bathroom, where the sight of Lynne's undulating naked posterior soon has an exhausted George revived and whistling in anticipation of the delights in prospect. Lynne has only to appear at the bedroom

window scantily dressed and George is up the ladder in a shot
cleaning the window. In contrast to those middle-aged men and
women in previous times who may have accepted with resignation, or even looked forward to release from the 'tyranny of
sex', George and Lynne present a vision of sex forever. Yet
despite their obvious sexual attractiveness to others, they are
never tempted by the prospect of extramarital sex, for they
always seem able to fight routinisation and boredom and to
make their sex life infinitely exciting, infinitely varied. In one
strip we have the following exchange between the couple:

> *Lynne*: (sitting up in bed and reading a sex manual): It says here that one
> must be adventurous and imaginative to make love last.
>
> *George*: That's right, but when one has exhausted the *Karma Sutra* what's
> left?
>
> *Lynne*: Change the background it suggests. How do you fancy a black ceiling,
> a white carpet, four-poster bed, zebra rugs, a chaise-longue?

Lynne's purchase of a daring new dress or erotic leisure-wear,
the get-away weekend in the country or in 'town' (where on an
overnight stay in a top hotel they miss dinner and the cabaret
because George can't wait to bed Lynne) hold out the promise
of sexual excitement and fulfilment. In one strip George 'phones
Lynne to ask her to get dressed up and make a special dinner
because he is bringing home an important client, only to confess
bashfully his deception: all he wanted was to get Lynne dressed
up and 'looking good' for a romantic sexual scenario.

A further important element in the midlifestyle of George and
Lynne is that they constantly work at their relationship and build
up each other's ego. They are of course deeply in love: in one
strip George is sitting at home with Lynne in one of their
frequent intimate candlelit dinners, looking very wistful. When
they are undressed and in bed he manages to confess why he has
been so quiet all evening: 'I can't hide it from you. It niggles my
mind all day. I'm crazy about you, woman!' Both George and
Lynne manage to maintain the high of a permanent honeymoon
by consideration, humour and taking advantage of every opportunity to re-romanticise their relationship. They have friends,
but in this variant of the new intimacy, they really don't need
the company of others. New Year's Eve has, of course, George
and Lynne engaged in their favourite activities, watching

television and having sex in bed: 'Lovely, lovely way to see in
the New Year', Lynne remarks. George and Lynne don't really
need children, they have each other. They also have little time
for relatives apart from the occasional 'phone call or visit

by Lynne to her mother.

Their relationship is untouched by either the new therapies or Women's Liberation. Unlike their Marin County counterparts in *The Serial* (McFadden 1978), George and Lynne do not run the risks attendant upon identity exploration through the Awareness Movement which could result in demands for independence and self-actualisation which might threaten the basis of their marriage. In any case, Lynne is already a perfect combination of wife/mistress/best friend and George, as Lynne tells him in one strip, is a perfect husband, lover, close friend, companion, protector and man-about-the-house. Lynne is happy with the traditional feminine role and lives in a suburban area where the wives don't work, yet use their feminine wiles and women's ways to keep their boyish husbands firmly under control. In a confrontation with a representative of the younger generation of independent working women, Lynne triumphantly comes out on top in the following exchange:

> *Young Woman*: Of course things are different in offices now from when all of you left to get married.
>
> *Lynne*: My goodness is that so? For instance?
>
> *Young Woman*: Well, for instance we girls get a man's wages.
>
> *Lynne*: Honeychild all *us* girls get a man's wages too!

The message is clear: the sophisticated woman doesn't need feminism, she effectively controls her man, the home and consumption.

George's executive job provides the financial basis for the lifestyle and he stoically writes out the cheques and pays the bills in the wake of Lynne's shopping expeditions. Together George

© Conrad Frost & Associates 1982

and Lynne cultivate a lifestyle which expresses their individuality through the consumption and deployment of goods: furniture, household equipment, decoration, car, garden, clothing all function to display their status and wealth – yet also, and more subtly, they act as signs of their unique sense of style, good taste and personal worth. The lifestyle does not only involve consumption and display, consumer goods require maintenance, the moments of satisfaction and relaxation are purchased by cutting the lawn, re-decorating the bathroom, repairing the car. There is always something more to be done, and more often than not it is the ever-cheerful George who pitches in, consoled by the fact that Lynne is working at her tan. For George and Lynne the

© Conrad Frost & Associates **1982**

good life is here and now. They have created their 'own little world', a midlifestyle in which they have permission to indulge themselves and which with a little care and effort they can go on enjoying deep into the middle years.

Note

We wish to thank Conrad Frost for providing us with much helpful information about the creation of the strip and for permission to reproduce examples of the strip and readers' letters.

References

Becker, S. (1959) *Comic Art in America*. New York: Simon and Schuster.
Featherstone, M. (1982) 'The Body in Consumer Culture', *Theory, Culture & Society*, 1(2): 18–33 (reprinted in this volume).
Featherstone, M. and Hepworth, M. (1981, 1982) 'Images de la maturité', *Gerontologie*, Dec, Jan.
Featherstone, M. and Hepworth, M. (1982) 'Ageing and Inequality: Consumer

Culture and the New Middle Age', in D. Robbins et al. (eds), *Rethinking Social Inequality*. London: Gower.

Hepworth, M. and Featherstone, M. (1982) *Surviving Middle Age*. Oxford: Blackwell.

Inge, M.T. (1982) 'Comic Art', in M.T. Inge (ed.), *Concise Histories of American Popular Culture*. Westport: Greenwood.

McFadden, C. (1978) *The Serial*. London: Picador.

Nuttall, G. and Carmichael, R. (1977) *Common Factors/Vulgar Factions*. London: Routledge & Kegan Paul.

Perry, G. and Aldridge, A. (1971) *The Penguin Book of Comics*, rev. ed. Harmondsworth: Penguin.

This chapter first appeared in *Theory, Culture & Society*, Vol. 1 (1983), 85–92.

8

MARTIAL ARTS AS A RESOURCE FOR LIBERAL EDUCATION: THE CASE OF AIKIDO

Donald N. Levine

In the autumn 1984 issue of *Liberal Education* I published 'The Liberal Arts and the Martial Arts', an essay which explored how efforts to rethink the rationales of liberal education might benefit from comparing the liberal arts as developed in the West to certain educational programmes, commonly known as the martial arts, developed in the cultures of East Asia. The paper made three main points.

To begin with, I suggested that the distinction embodied in the Japanese contrast between *bujutsu* and *budo* parallels an age-old western distinction between strictly utilitarian arts and arts that possess a liberal character. The Japanese distinction contrasts techniques used for practical, combative purposes (*bujutsu*) with disciplines that employ training in combative forms as a means to cultivate the students' physical, mental and spiritual powers (*budo*). The western distinction derives from Aristotle's discrimination of knowledge in his *Politics* which is tied to necessities and so of a servile sort from the kind of knowledge that is worthy of free men (*eleutheron*) – a notion embodied in later formulations about the liberal arts (Greek: *eleutheriai technai*; Latin: *artes liberales*), arts whose study was intended to cultivate a person's 'humanity'. In both cases, techniques learned for mundane instrumental purposes stand in contrast with arts which are studied in order to enhance their learner's capacities as a free and virtuous human being. Sino-Japanese *jutsu* corresponds exactly to Greek *techne*.

Second, I suggested that affinities between the traditions from which both *budo* and western liberal arts emerged could be found by noticing parallels in their patterns of historical evolution. In the West, we find in ancient Greece the ideal of *paedeia*, the notion of using culture as a means to create a higher type of human being. Classic Greek thought celebrated the way to *arete*, or virtue, through cultivating powers of the body, like strength and vigour, as well as powers of the mind, like sharpness and insight. In later centuries cultivation of the body disappeared as a component of liberal training, so that only the intellectual arts, organized eventually as the trivium and quadrivium in the Middle Ages, emerged as suitable subjects for liberal learning. Transmitted by monastics for centuries, this curriculum entered secular universities during the Renaissance. American educators of the late nineteenth century harkened back to this Renaissance tradition while devising a programme of liberal education oriented to the 'formation of character' and the goal of self-realization. This formed the intellectual background for the experiments in the liberal curriculum which flourished in the United States after the First World War.

I traced a comparable development in East Asia, beginning with the movement in China during the Chou dynasty to form an educational programme aimed at producing a broadly cultivated person. This curriculum, often referred to as the 'liberal arts' of classical Chinese education, included training both in literary and martial subjects. Confucius articulated the conception of the ideal person to be produced by this Chinese version of *paedeia*. Max Weber noted 'For the Confucian . . . the decisive factor was that . . . in his self-perfection [the 'cultured man'] was an end unto himself, not a means for any functional end' (1951: 246). The eventual decline of that curriculum was followed by the institution of new kinds of martial arts training in Chinese monasteries, which cultivated Shaolin Temple boxing, derived from exercises introduced by the Indian Buddhist monk Bodhidharma and, subsequently, the Taoist-inspired forms of *tai chi chuan*. In Japan during the Tokugawa Shogunate, a number of samurai adapted the martial techniques into vehicles of spiritual training and, beginning with the efforts of Jigoro Kano in the 1880s, a number of Japanese arts evolved to constitute the resources of modern *budo*.

The main part of my paper, finally, drew on the experience of martial arts training programmes to suggest ideas relevant to a number of central issues in the modern philosophy of liberal education. These issues included the question of what is 'liberal' about liberal education; the kinds of cultural form most suitable for a liberal curriculum; the capacities liberal training should foster; the characteristics of training programmes designed to cultivate those capacities; the relationship between liberal and utilitarian learning; and the ethical justification of liberal learning.

In that earlier paper, then, I used training programmes in the martial arts as a source of ideas to enrich our thinking about the liberal curriculum. I did not explore the possible role which actual training in the martial arts might play in contemporary programmes of liberal education, nor did I explore the ways in which the philosophy of the liberal arts might provide ideas for enriching instructional programmes in the martial arts. These two questions form the agenda of the present chapter. In addressing them I shall first discuss some general issues raised by the aspiration to incorporate *budo* training into programmes of liberal education. I shall then report on an experiment in which I have incorporated martial arts training in an academic course and conclude by reflecting on the implications of that experiment for those who might like to attempt similar efforts in other institutions.

Is There a Role for *Budo* in the Liberal Curriculum?

In my earlier paper I proceeded on the assumption that there are no inherent differences between the educational approaches of *budo* and the liberal intellectual arts. At this point I wish to question that assumption and suggest that in certain respects *budo* training appears incompatible with the objectives of the kind of liberal education suited to modern democratic societies.

Although there are clear lines of continuity between the ideals of *paedeia* and *humanitas* which informed the liberal curricula of ancient Greece and Rome and subsequent developments in the history of western civilization, what constituted liberation and the development of humanity underwent changes. In each epoch new curricula and rationales had to be devised to accommodate changes in the state of knowledge, in the circumstances of life, and in the meaning of a free and fully realized human being. In the course of the twentieth century, a number of western educators have worked to articulate the aims and rationales of a liberal education appropriate to life in advanced industrial world society. If, now, we wish to find a place for *budo* within this emerging educational culture, we must consider whether or not the properties of *budo* as it emerged from Japanese feudal martial traditions are in all respects consistent with the ethos of a modern liberal education.

Suppose we identify the central features of the state of knowledge in our times as those of *accelerated rationalization* and *fragmentation*; and the central features of our historical situation as those of *one small world* and *cultural diversity*. Then what notions should guide the construction of educational programmes which cultivate the arts of freedom appropriate to the conditions of life in the late twentieth century? Two notions would command a great deal of consensus among modern exponents of liberal education, I believe: *autonomy* and *generality*. We want students to become autonomous as persons, able to critically understand rationalized courses of thought and action, to formulate rational grounds in support of their positions and present their thoughts clearly and persuasively, and to recover relevant traditions and adopt them creatively to changing circumstances. We want students to attain general breadth, in the sense of processing ideas and skills which can apply to broad domains of experience, of being able to find connections among dispersed branches of knowledge, and having the capacity to understand and communicate with persons oriented by radically diverse cultures. In a powerful elaboration of many of these points which Richard McKeon (1964: 171–2) set forth a quarter of a century ago, the liberating arts were described as 'general' in four senses.

> They are general in the sense of applying to all subject matters and therefore in the sense of providing an approach to any particular subject matter placed in a context of other parts of information or knowledge. They are general in the sense of embracing all fundamental skills that can be acquired in education and therefore in the sense of providing a basis for any particular skill. . . . They are general in the sense of bearing on the formation of the whole man and therefore in the sense of providing a model or ruling principle for any particular excellence fitted into achievements of a good life. . . . [T]hey are general in the sense of being the arts of all men and therefore in the sense of providing guidance for each particular man and each particular association of men responsive to the cultures and objectives of other men and of mankind.

If we take some formulation such as this as a standard for the kind of liberal curriculum that is suited for our times, then we may question whether contemporary forms of *budo* training are in fact conducive to the educational goals of autonomy amidst complexity and rapid change, and generality amidst fragmentation and diversity. A good deal of contemporary *budo* practice exhibits characteristics one could describe as authoritarianism, anti-intellectualism, particularism, doctrinaire rigidity, narrowness of focus, and excessive competitiveness.

Authoritarianism

It is common to attribute absolute authority to the instructor in a *dojo*. The *sensei* must not only be accorded complete respect, but no aspect of his teaching is to be questioned. In describing the pedagogy of the *dojo*, Richard Schmidt among others has observed: 'The sensei serves as the model for the trainee to emulate. Long and difficult hours of intense, repetitive training and prescribed movements punctuated at times by physical and verbal abuse by the sensei is the mode of instruction' (Schmidt, 1983: 47).

Anti-intellectualism

Budo teaching places a great premium on nonverbal training and often exhibits a studied hostility toward discursive presentations of any sort. As Richard Schmidt referring to H. Befu's study of Japan (1971) further observes: 'Reflective of the Zen method of training, the emphasis is on a nonverbalized, intuitive approach rather than rational intellection. The trainee is encouraged to "think with his body" and not with his mind' (Schmidt, 1983: 48). It is generally considered poor form to discuss issues regarding principles or techniques while training.

Particularism

Many martial arts *senseis* expect absolute loyalty to their persons and their organizations. Some *senseis* even forbid their students to train with any other instructor while they are under his tutelage. This trait accounts for the pronounced sectarianism which afflicts a number of *budo* organizations.

Doctrinaire rigidity

The combination of authoritarianism, anti-intellectualism, and particularism supports the belief that the teachings of a particular *sensei* represent the one right way of doing things. His approach is presented as one which all students must reproduce faithfully in every detail.

Narrowness of focus
Virtually all the training in most *dojos* is confined to the mastery
of a circumscribed set of techniques. Although these may be
taught on the assumption that this kind of training develops the
student in accord with certain more general principles, those
principles are rarely articulated. It is even more rare to find
explicit consideration given to ways in which those principles
might be applied in other domains.

Excessive competitiveness
Some schools of *budo* place considerable emphasis on competition, both within the *dojo* and with other, rival, *dojos*. It
becomes a primary goal to defeat the 'enemy', which can be
another student, members of another school, or another martial
art.

In so far as these characteristics are inherent in *budo*, it would
seem that they operate in an illiberal direction. However
appropriate they may have been in earlier times, they seem
inconsistent with the objectives of a liberalizing and humanizing
approach to education suitable for the late twentieth century.
Authoritarianism and anti-intellectualism run counter to efforts
to cultivate personal autonomy; particularism, rigidity and
narrowness of focus run counter to the spirit of generality; and
an exclusively competitive ethic runs counter to the capacities for
mutual understanding and synergistic collaboration which
arguably are essential to the advancement of the life of the
human species at this point in history.

   This raises the question whether one can modify these features
of traditional martial arts pedagogy in a liberalizing direction
without losing the heart and soul of authentic *budo*. I believe it
is possible. My belief is inspired by the fact that a number of
exemplary aikido teachers have shown ways of doing so.

   On the matter of authoritarianism I have witnessed a number
of prominent aikido teachers question this as an absolute value,
by example as well as by precept. Although they naturally expect
proper respect, they do not appreciate slavish compliance or
obsequious attention. While following the *sensei*'s directives
remains an important condition for proper training, if only for
reasons of safety, this is fully compatible with an active and
questioning spirit on the part of students. Some of the most

highly ranked aikido instructors with whom I have trained often conclude their demonstration of a certain technique with the remark: 'Try this out and see if it works for you.' In my own course, to be described presently, I give students an opportunity to raise questions from time to time on the mat, and encourage them to reflect on our practices critically when they are off the mat.

Again, one can affirm the importance of nondiscursive teaching and nonverbal learning in the *dojo* without supposing that committed training in a martial art entails the sacrifice of the intellect. Nonverbal learning is good for the mind as well as the body, but one can also benefit from reflection and discourse about what one has learned thereby.

Although it is natural and helpful to develop sentiments of attachment to one's *sensei*, this need not take the form of fanatic or highly partisan loyalty. As Mitsugi Saotome Shihan (1989b: 24) has written wisely on this point, 'Blind loyalty is most dangerous for it is all too easy to twist the ideas of loyalty and righteousness with the lever of human greed and selfish ego.' Similarly, Mitsugi Saotome (1989a: 198) comments:

> If you accept the idea that *budo* is a study that can encompass all respects of your life, there is another fallacy which you must avoid. This is the temptation to turn the teachings of your art into doctrines, or your teacher into an idol. . . . Your teacher is a guide, not a guru. There is a great difference between respect and idolization.

Some aikido *senseis* make a point of encouraging their students to visit other *dojos* and to train with different kinds of instructor. The founder of aikido, Morihei Ueshiba, encouraged aikido students to learn from as many teachers as possible.

On the issue of doctrinaire rigidity, two points can be made which draw on the most reputable of *budo* authorities. At the highest level of practice, one can cite the ideal which many *budo* masters subscribe to, that of the 'technique of no-technique' or the 'form of no-form'. Indeed, one interpretation of that formula could serve as a standard for the highest ideal of liberal education, in which particular forms are viewed merely as resources to be employed variably as the occasion indicates. A magnificent formulation of this appears in the dictum of Matsuo Basho, 'Only by entering into the principles and then taking leave of them can one attain autonomy' (Uzawa Yoshiuki, 1989). In addition, one can cite the importance that great *budo* masters

have accorded to continuous growth and change. Recall the
dictum attributed to the seventeenth-century master, Miyamoto
Musashi – 'the purpose of today's training is to defeat yesterday's understanding' – not to mention the experience of Founder
Morihei Ueshiba, who continuously changed ideas as his practice
evolved.

A certain amount of rote training is indispensable to any art.
One must drill basic movements in any martial art just as one
must practise scales and arpeggios in learning to play musical
instruments. Yet to master techniques without learning the principles which underlie them is patently illiberal, and it is also
illiberal to learn principles but to confine their application to a
narrow domain. *Budo* faces the challenge of finding ways to
apply its principles to domains outside the martial art in question. A number of aikido masters have met this challenge with
enormous creativity. Koichi Tohei Shihan has written books on
the application of aikido principles in daily life. Robert Nadeau
Sensei has devised a repertoire of ways to show the applicability
of aikido moves to interpersonal situations off the mat. Frank
Doran Sensei regularly articulates the more general human meanings of various aikido principles and gestures. On the connection
between *budo* applications and general knowledge, Mitsugi
Saotome (1987) notes:

> Budo means organizing society. It is management. . . . Unfortunately, many
> managers come from very narrow, categorizing educations. How many
> business schools are teaching universal knowledge? They give specialized
> knowledge but never make a 'general mind'. Modern universities seem to
> pursue the opposite of the original meaning [a place to study universal
> knowledge]. Some professors do not study biology or the ecology of systems,
> not even human psychology. They don't understand what it means to be
> human. Many of the problems are caused by very narrow professional people
> controlling the world. . . . Top executives must study philosophy, religion,
> nature, art, science; otherwise they do not have the knowledge to create a
> vision for themselves and their workers.

Finally, one must question the extent to which a competitive
spirit is needed to achieve the developmental goals of *budo* training. This question is complicated by the surface similarity of
competitive and combative ethics. While too much competitiveness is degrading, most forms of *budo* which are entirely 'liberal'
in orientation focus mainly on combat. At issue here is a distinction between becoming proficient at combat as a way to advance
at the expense of others and becoming proficient for the sake of

defending oneself and others, and improving one's own character.

Master Morihei Ueshiba understood this distinction and how easy it is to confuse the two notions. He wanted to guard against the competitive spirit in aikido, so he removed the aspect of competitive combat from the art. He proclaimed that the only victory worth going for was the victory over one's self, and that the only kind of character worth cultivating in our time is one devoted to the task of bringing peace to mankind around the world. His words eloquently depict the transformed *budo* this entails:

> In Ueshiba's *budo* there are no enemies. This mistake is to begin to think that *budo* means to have an opponent or enemy; someone you want to be stronger than, someone you want to throw down. In true *budo* there is no enemy or opponent. . . . True *budo* is the loving protection of all beings with a spirit of reconciliation. Reconciliation means to allow the completion of everyone's mission. (Morihei Ueshiba, 1974: 179–80)

Employing Martial Arts Training in a Liberal Arts Programme

I turn now to report on an experiment in which I have incorporated martial arts training in an academic course and to present some reflections on what that experience suggests for colleagues who might like to attempt similar efforts in other institutions.

Over the past few years I have twice taught a course at the University of Chicago which includes martial arts training as an integral component. Offered as a regular credit course under my Department of Sociology, it is called 'Conflict Theory and Aikido'. Half of the time this course proceeds like any other academic offering. Twice a week I meet with the students to discuss a series of texts, chiefly writings by sociologists and philosophers which deal with the sources, dynamics and consequences of different forms of human conflict.

In addition, twice a week the class meets at the mat, for a systematic introduction to the art of aikido. (I also ask the students to participate in at least half a dozen of the regular training sessions of the campus Aikido Club.) I define the mat training sessions as 'lab' sessions and ask the students to keep a lab notebook in which they write down after each session some lessons learned and questions raised by the mat training. The grade for the course is based on six components: frequency of training, performance in a modified 6th-kyu test taken during exam week, quality of the lab notebook, participation in class discussions, short assigned papers, and a final paper in which the students are asked to integrate the major things they have learned in the course as a whole.

In organizing the sequence of sessions on the mat, I attempt not only to provide a graduated introduction to the art of aikido, but also to time certain mat experiences so that they will be relevant to issues raised by the reading. For example, I introduce the notion of *ma-ai*, the proper distance between training partners, in connection with the sociologist Georg Simmel's (1971) discussion of the proper distance between individuals in social interaction; or I focus on the alternation of attack and defence in aikido training with the notion of 'reciprocal priority' discussed by the philosopher Walter Watson.

In presenting this course, I have four chief educational objectives.

First, by having the students experience regular physical activity as an integral part of the class work, I attempt to overcome the mind–body split which so pervades western education. Besides reading about issues involving human conflict, on the mat we have an opportunity to experience actual feelings that accompany the expression of physical aggression and the different responses, conflictual and non-conflictual, that one can make to that aggression. As a sociologist, I find this particularly valuable since my academic discipline tends to operate at a high level of abstraction and often represents human relations as though they took place outside human bodies.

Secondly, by acquainting students with traditional *dojo* etiquette and basic aikido ideas, I provide an experimental basis for some cross-cultural learning. Aikido is particularly suitable for affording an entrée into a number of Asian traditions, including Hinduism, Buddhism, Confucianism, Taoism, Shinto and Bushido, as well as elements of the Japanese language.

Thirdly, the major theoretical point of the course is to refine the student's abilities to think critically about human conflict, both descriptively and normatively. I try not to sell a particular point of view on the subject but require that students articulate and reflect on the assumptions about conflict which they bring to the class. At the first session I ask them to write a short paper indicating what they understand by conflict, whether they think that conflict is good or bad, and what questions about conflict they would most like to have answered. At the end of the course I ask them to return to their initial formulations and write a long essay which incorporates ideas and insights provided by the texts and the training experience.

Fourthly, throughout the course, I attempt to cultivate their ability to follow the *aiki* way in everything they do related to the course and not just on the mat. The central concept of aikido, *aiki*, refers to the process by which energies from different sources are brought into harmonious integration rather than opposition. In *reading*, I encourage them to respect the *ki* of the author and to blend with it in a centred way. In *learning*, I encourage them to treat mistakes as useful features of the learning process. When they communicate with one other in class discussion, I encourage them to use *aiki* principles of *communication*, instead of ignoring or combating responses from their fellow students. I encourage them to think of ways to adapt *aiki* principles to their life outside the classroom. In my own *teaching*, I attempt to model the *aiki* approach, respecting the *ki* of the students and blending with it to make the points I wish to get across. More generally, I encourage them to think of ways to extend *aiki* modes of response into all aspects of their *living*.

Outcomes of the course
In discussing the outcomes of the course, I shall incorporate statements made by the students in their lab notebooks and their final papers.

One outcome of the course related to the goal of integrating experiences of the body with experiences of the mind. Many students appreciated the challenge presented by an opportunity to experience nonverbal learning. Some expressed appreciation of the special kind of learning that only bodily practice provides:

> I am sore in a real and profound way that only a good night's sleep will cure. I had one worthwhile thought during the club session this evening. Conflict is only one possible outcome of one person's violence. The point of aikido is to prevent this violence from resulting in conflict. On paper, this hardly seems a profound comment, but my body is beginning to understand the concept.

or the access physical practice provides to truths which are not accessible through verbal means:

If, in fact, thinking and speaking and reasoning are all mere imitations or descriptions of some greater truth, it seems hopeless indeed that we could ever know such a truth. . . . Aikido is one way of learning the nameless truth – while I cannot explain what *ki* is, I can certainly experience it as it flows through me or when it throws me to the ground.

For some students the challenge of experiencing pain in a protected space provided a stimulus to reflection:

One thing that impressed me during our first meeting today was the obvious fact of physical stress. I am accustomed to exertion, but not self-imposed, arbitrary pain, i.e. the self-torture of sitting seiza. It is very interesting to experience, but only endurable if one assumes the view that it is good. One must adopt the ethos of nobility in self-denial, the importance of the ritual, and grim, unhesitating determination with the immediate task, in order to persist. I did so, though it is really contrary to my normal way.

Some students were able, after a relatively short period, to experience a different state of consciousness attendant on the bodily relaxation:

I have discovered a state in myself which I call the simple mind. I discovered the simple mind by accident when I actually joined with *uke's ki* [In aikido practice, *uke* signifies the person who initiates the attack and takes the fall.] and successfully defended myself against *katate-dori*. When *uke* attacked, I was daydreaming and relaxed; I was not thinking of the impending attack. When *uke* attacked, I simply reacted without thinking. My response was hardly fluid or graceful but it was more powerful than anything I have ever done. The simple mind, I deduce, is a state of readiness that can only be reached, permanently, through reasoning, but of knowing. The simple mind reflects an understanding that is so deep and innate that it operates without conscious thought or effort. I doubt that I have the discipline to achieve what I term the simple mind but I feel privileged to know that it exists. In other words, I feel as if I was afforded a rare glimpse of what I can possibly achieve.

Many students came to understand the importance of patience in learning worthwhile skills. Thus:

Frustration again wins the day. I can never seem to do anything in the way it is supposed to be done. I am beginning to think that I will have to conquer tremendous obstacles just to become coordinated. I wish that there was some short-cut to grace, but I know that effort is the only answer. . . . The first rule of aikido should really be patience!

Finally, many students came to an awareness of the possibility of new forms of body–mind integration. Thus one student wrote:

Strangely, I have always been cognizant of a *ki* force but I located its center in my skull, not my body. However, I like aikido's *hara* location better because it could forge a link between my mind and body that I have always lacked. In the past, I tended to view my body as nothing more than a vehicle for my brain. I am hoping to forge real mind–body connections so that I can break out of this mold.

Secondly, the course did appear to provide a relatively efficient way to give students entrée into exotic features of a different culture. This was particularly visible with regard to respect rituals, which are emphasized in the aikido *dojo*. Following the first day of training, one student wrote:

> Today, I overcame a taboo; I accepted bowing. In addition to the foreignness of the custom, bowing to another human is considered unacceptable to Judaism. However, I tried to think like a visitor in another culture. I know that bowing in Japan is a sign of respect, not worship and thus I should view it only as a courtesy. If I were in Japan I would bow and thus I should accept it here. If nothing else, today I accepted bowing.

Following the second day of training, this student wrote: 'Today I felt a little less intimidated with the rituals that accompany the training. I accepted bowing as a foreign but valid method expressing courtesy and respect.'

For other students, the course provided experiences which facilitated their understanding of notions from East Asian traditions which previously they had only grasped intellectually. So, one student wrote that although he had some understanding of the concept of *ki* from a Japanese civilization course, previously it was hard for him not to intellectualize the idea and just feel it. Others made similar comments regarding the concept of *hara*. Finally, some students responded to my invitation to regard the whole practice of aikido as a text and to consider it critically in comparison with other kinds of text. One student, for example, wrote an extended comment on the question of whether philosophical conceptions embodied in Asian notions of *ki* and *chi* are compatible with concepts generated by western positive science.

Thirdly, the practice of aikido facilitated the students' enquiry into the nature of human conflict in a number of ways. It not only gave them a concrete physical anchoring of some of the phenomena we were talking about; it gave them resources for raising new kinds of question about the meaning of conflict. This was true with respect to the status of conflict in aikido itself. As one student wrote:

It appears that on the mat that we are turning another's aggression toward ourselves to work for our benefit, but why all this talk of 'avoiding conflict?' The phrase, 'getting off the line' sounds like 'avoiding the conflict'. In the same movement we will use the force an opponent applies to us in order to engage in contact/conflict to overpower him or make him weak. Is that not engaging in conflict? Is that not using our forces to surmount another? So is the significance of aikido to avoid conflict – to reduce conflict – to resolve conflict – *or* to stimulate conflict?

It is precisely that kind of probing, that encounter with the ambiguities of conflict within and outside of aikido, that enables the students to reach a much more sophisticated level of thought when considering the subject of conflict.

Fourthly, in learning the *aiki* way, a number of students felt that they had acquired a resource that would be helpful in many other learning contexts. The students who habitually rebelled against authors found that they could learn to respect the *ki* of the authors without sacrificing their own individuality, their ability to remain centred. Students learned how to integrate mistakes as part of the learning process, rather than waste energy blaming themselves and expressing remorse for making mistakes. They learned to listen to and communicate with one other in a more empathic and constructive way. Thus, about half-way through the course, one student wrote in her lab notebook:

> I sense a different feeling among the numbers of our class in and out of the *dojo*. We all appear to communicate better and more freely among ourselves. Smiling and praising are so much more present than they were are the beginning of the quarter.

More generally, most of the students found some ways in which the training experiences on the mat carried over into benefits for their everyday living. One student summed up his experience:

> The most important thing I learned from the mat sessions is the concept of relaxing, 'joining with the surrounding *ki*'. . . . When relaxed, one feels more confident about working or studying; there exists no mental resistance or tension in writing or thinking or just talking with people. When stress or conflict arises, I relax and accept the *ki* of the offender or attacker, which in return calms him/her also. On one occasion, someone pointed out that I 'radiate an aura of calm', which caught me off guard, seeing I feel no different from when I began this course.
>   Not only did I learn to 'relax', I also learned the concept of being 'centered'. When one is centered, one is in control. In Coleman's diagram of the stages of conflict, conflict escalates because there does not exist a controlling element in its progression. Coleman presents barriers to control the

progress of the escalating conflict but provides no control for conflict itself. In the way of dealing with conflict, there exists a center, a calm, relaxed center, containing the range of conflict.

The notion of being centered also transcends aikido and the dojo; [it can] establish a sense of control or stability in your environment. Being centered allows one to be in control of the effect of external forces rather than being controlled by these same forces. These external forces will generally create unnecessary confusion and anxiety, causing one's *ki* to be 'off'.

Concluding Reflections

Courses on the dynamics of conflict or on conflict resolution provide logical contexts in which to introduce aikido practice. Yet I could imagine other kinds of thematic foci with which aikido practice might be coupled beneficially. One could readily organize a course around any of the other themes I mentioned at the beginning, such as an introduction to East Asian civilization or a course on body–mind connections.

Topics like the body–mind nexus, the East Asian connection, and the dynamics of conflict represent academic themes which could be linked with a wide range of martial arts, not just aikido. Other kinds of thematic foci might be specific to aikido. For example, I could imagine a course dealing with the *aiki* process – synergy – as it manifests itself in a wide range of human activities, from the domains of business enterprise or international diplomacy to those of family counselling and the organization of research projects. Training in other martial arts might imaginably be coupled with other, specific kinds of themes. But my sense is that there is a great range of possibilities relevant to both aikido and other arts which I have not yet begun to contemplate. One thinks of courses on religion; on anatomy and physiology; on approaches to healing; on the aesthetics of movement; and so on.

In concluding, I wish to reaffirm my sense that the search for linkages between martial arts training and the liberal arts holds promise for educators. The flow of influence can and should go in both directions. At a time when the pressures of a technicalized society, accelerated now on a worldwide scale, have weakened the traditional case of liberal education, the arts of *budo*, taught as they were originally intended – as vehicles for personal growth and spiritual enlightenment – provide a formidable exemplar of education for human excellence at its purest. Incorporated judiciously into high school and college curricula, they can add new dimensions to education by focusing on the richness of mind–body learning, new roads for intercultural understanding, new kinds of experience to illustrate general principles, and new ways of being centred in a decentring universe. On the other hand, martial arts pedagogy stands to be reinvigorated as a force pertinent to the needs of a truly liberating and humanizing culture in our time if it abandons older features of authoritarianism and provincialism in favour of a more open, inclusive and harmonizing ethos.

Note

This chapter is the text of a paper originally presented at the US–Japan Conference on Japanese Martial Arts and American Sports: Cross-Cultural Perspectives on Means to Personal Growth, University of Wisconsin, 7–10 August 1989. I am grateful to David Waterhouse and Clifford Winnig for suggestions which helped me improve the final version.

References

Befu, H. (1971) *Japan, an Anthropological Introduction*. San Francisco: Chandler.

McKeon, R. (1964) 'The liberating arts and the humanizing arts in education', in A.H. Cohen (ed.), *Humanistic Education and Western Civilization*. New York: Holt, Rinehart & Winston.

Mitsugi, Saotome (1987) 'Budo and management', *Aikidoka*, 1(3): 7–11.

Mitsugi, Saotome (1989a) *The Principles of Aikido*. Boston and Shaftesbury: Shambhala.

Mitsugi, Saotome Shihan (1989b) 'Selected teachings', in *University of Chicago Aikido Club Handbook*.

Morihei, Ueshiba (1974) 'Memoir of the master', in Kisshomaru Ueshiba, *Aikido*. Tokyo: Hozansha.

Schmidt, R.J. (1983) 'Japanese martial arts as spiritual education', *Somatics*, Autumn/Winter.

Simmel, G. (1971) *On Individuality and Social Forms: Selected Writings*. Chicago: University of Chicago Press.

Weber, M. (1951) *The Religion of China, Confucianism and Taoism*. New York: Free Press.

Uzawa, Yoshiuki (1989) 'The relation of ethics to *budo* and *bushido* in Japan'. Paper presented to US–Japan Conference on Japanese Martial Arts and American Sports, University of Wisconsin: Madison, 7–10 August.

9
BIO-POLITICS AND SOCIAL POLICY: FOUCAULT'S ACCOUNT OF WELFARE

Martin Hewitt

Introduction

At the close of *Discipline and Punish* Michel Foucault concludes that his book 'must serve as a historical background to various studies of the power of normalisation and the formation of knowledge in modern society'. This statement proposes a programme for further studies into the formation of power and knowledge governing society. Already this programme is underway in histories of punishment and sexuality (Foucault 1979a, 1979b, 1980), in studies by co-workers on family policy (Donzelot 1980) and psychiatry (Castel and Castel 1982) and in further studies on, among other things, clinical psychology (Rose 1979), childcare (Burchell 1981), education (Jones and Williamson 1979), social security (Squires, no date) and dietetics (Turner 1982). This body of work demonstrates the role of such practices in the emergence of present society – a history of the present. In these studies, social policy figures as a key domain wherein such practices are effected. Social policy plays a co-ordinating role in forming 'the social'. It promotes and organises knowledge, norms and social practices to regulate the quality of life of the population – its health, security and stability. For such statecraft Foucault and others employ the terms 'the politics of life' and 'bio-politics'; i.e. 'the proliferation of political technologies that invested the body, health, modes of subsistence and lodging – the entire space of existence in European countries from the eighteenth century onwards' (Donzelot 1980). By means of social policy the state manages the politics of life to shape the social to accord with the tasks and exigencies faced by the state. It is Foucault's contention that the body, individual and collective, becomes the raw material for this undertaking.

Foucault's work contributes to the mainstream of studies on agencies and modes of intervention, e.g. doctors, social workers, teachers, magistrates, hospitals, families, communities, schools, courts and prisons, and places them within structures of power and discourse. It also challenges aspects of Marxist political economy of welfare. This chapter attends specifically to Foucault and his co-workers' accounts of welfare so as to demonstrate their relevance to the study of social policy.

Foucault's Method

It is perhaps helpful to say something, serving as both a warning and exposition, about Foucault's approach to the study of history. He discards many of its accepted precepts, including for example, an insistence on tracing chronological developments and on establishing clear expositions of cause and effect. Instead he examines particular ways whereby the conception of a subject and its domain, such as sexuality, punishment or pathology, is constituted within knowledge as a concern central to a specific age, society or social stratum.[1] Subjects are not examined as factual givens or as the results of processes of causation. Their facticity and causality are constituted at a deeper but no less material level. The subjects of social policy, e.g. dependency and social needs, are not caused merely by social forces and do not exist as pure facts. They are constructed within the discourse of social policy as categories, classification systems and forms of knowledge by individuals and groups within the political, administrative and economic spheres. These constructs establish within any one instance of discourse (e.g. a report, an academic text, a social work case-file) a relation between the conception of a subject (e.g. a social problem, a system of welfare, a client) and the forces which reputedly determine it. Through this process the subject is endowed with particular forms of facticity and causality. These conceptions of the subject, the way they are constituted as knowledge within discourse, are available, Foucault (1972, pp. 31–9) argues, through the methods of 'archaeology' and 'genealogy'. Such methods reveal an ordering of facts, concepts, norms and theories that he terms a 'discursive formation'.

To English readers the terminology jars in the mind. The idea of the 'archaeology', 'genealogy' or 'constitutivity' of discourse demands a juxtaposition of borrowed notions uncomfortably conjoined in our thought. By archaeology Foucault is referring to a method of analysis that sites knowledge and its subjects by excavating the rules that form a particular discourse and exclude others (rules that have more to do with power strategies than scientific validity). Such rules establish both the boundaries dividing discourses and the continuities traversing these boundaries, which together make up a discursive formation. It is broadly this approach, for example, that enables him to argue that 'the (eighteenth century) theory of money and prices occupies the same position in the analysis of wealth as a theory of character does in natural history . . .' (1970, p. 203). During the 1970s archaeology with its structuralist leanings gave way to the genealogical method of tracing the movement and play of power and knowledge. By genealogy, the process of discursive formation is traced to produce a fuller understanding of presently constituted knowledge, a history of the present, and of its deployment as an instrument of power to promote authoritative pronouncements and mask criticism. This form of analysis is applied to seemingly diverse topics such as punishment, psychiatry, sexuality and the family.

For example, sexuality is presented as a 'scientifico-legal discourse' and practice, in medicine, religion, law and social policy, which affects the workings of the entire social body including, so to speak, even the parts that other forms of power cannot reach. Its genealogy is traced in operations of the state, the Church and other more dispersed centres of power which pronounce authoritatively on sexual knowledge and practice and which silence or reform departures from their codes. Discourses on sexuality have been conducted in a 'multiplicity of force relations' where 'man has been drawn for three centuries to the task of telling everything concerning his sex' in confessionals, novels, law, education and therapy (Foucault 1979b, p. 92 and p. 23). In each instance a dialogic form of power is established between the 'penitent' and his listener that penetrates to the utmost point of intimacy in a manner that is nonetheless carefully modulated (1979b p. 62). Yet the government of sexuality gives rise also to public controls that monitor the birth rate, the age of marriage, the legitimacy of births, the frequency of sexual relations, contraception, etc. Sex is a 'thing one administered'. Its effectiveness resides in the fact that it is both an intimately private and anonymously public form of regulation (1979b, p. 24; 1980, p. 125). Through Foucault's methods of analysis, we encounter the subject of sexuality as central to the formation of policies which form the basis of bio-power and are aimed at both the individual and social body.

The Formation of Bio-politics

Foucault and his co-workers explore several aspects of the rise and establishment of capitalism. These aspects are seen as constituting a new domain of political life – the politics of the body or bio-politics. They are, with reference to Foucault's work: the investment of the body with properties making it pliable to new technologies of control; the emergence of normalisation; the divestment of power from an absolute sovereign to a magnitude of regulative agencies located throughout the social body; and, the advent of the empirical human sciences, making possible these new technologies of control.

First, by the nineteenth century the body was no longer subject to the sovereign's absolute and unmitigated power, but endowed by various experts with a range of properties indicating types of crime, sexual aberrations and states of grace, health and mind. Each property was accorded a specific technology of control and form of corporeality. Correctional training, for example, was directed at 'the body, time, everyday gestures and articulation' of inmates to counter their economic and spiritual sloth with 'exercises, timetables, compulsory movements, regular activities, solitary medications', and so forth (1979a, p. 128). Medicine tended to individualise bodies, diseases, symptoms, lives and deaths within a disciplinary regime of architectural, administrative and therapeutic space; 'out of discipline, a medically useful space was born' (1979a, p. 144). Within hospitals, schools, prison workshops and military bases the practice of discipline was founded – a form of domination that extracts economic utility from the human body, whilst rendering it politically docile. In short, it dissociates power from the body (1979a, p. 138; cf. Bauman 1983).

Secondly, the application of discipline to correct deviations of the body, its behaviour, timing, speech, sexuality and even thought, required attending to the norm. A 'swarm' of technicians, 'normative judges', such as teachers, psychologists, psychiatrists and social workers, would differentiate, quantify and rank an individual according to his or her ability to conform to the normative prerequisites of disciplinary technology. Such interventions reach beyond the judicial domain into one governed by norms affecting aspects of the body that cannot be inscribed with the exactness of law (1979a, pp. 183–4, 304). Normalisation becomes one of the great instruments of power.

Thirdly, this shift to the effectivity of the norm is seen as the distinguishing mark that separates disciplinary power and bio-politics from sovereign power. A society that increasingly takes 'charge of life needs continuously regulatory and corrective mechanisms . . . it does not have to draw the line that separates the enemies of the sovereign from his obedient subjects; it effects distributions around the norm' (1979b, p. 144). However, rather than fade into the background, the law operates more and more as a norm, so that the judiciary is gradually incorporated into a continuum of apparatuses (medical, administrative, etc.) whose functions arc regulatory. 'A normalising society is the historical outcome of a technology of power centred on life' (1979b, p. 144).

Amidst these normalising activities, a new notion of rights arose – 'which the classical juridical system was utterly incapable of comprehending . . . The "right" of life, to one's body, to health, to happiness, to the satisfaction of needs' (1979b, p. 145). Bio-politics gave girth to the twin concerns central to modern welfare, to the notions of 'needs' and 'rights'.

Fourthly, these transformations involved new forms of knowledge and power, both reinforcing one another within what Foucault terms the power/knowledge complex (pouvoir/savoir). Clinical medicine, psychiatry, educational psychology and criminology arose to provide discourses that promulgated new technologies of intervention, new targets and new policies (Foucault 1979a, p. 224). Within these human sciences the individual was enthroned as through by humanitarian fiat (Foucault 1979a, pp. 189–91). In fact this centring of the human subject was instrumental to the economic deployment of the disciplines. Humanity is the respectable name given to this economy and its meticulous calculations. 'Where punishment is concerned, the minimum is ordered by humanity and counselled by policy.' In such endeavours the notion of policy enters history (Foucault 1979a, p. 92, n.6).

Throughout these themes Foucault develops an analysis of the form of power that actualised disciplinary practices, norms and knowledges. Bio-power was defined by its corporeal nature; it was power over bodies and by bodies. The body stood as both the raw material and the means of production. The health, welfare and productivity of bodies became the aim of bio-power. The social body itself became the engine of power, to produce and accumulate (cf. Bauman 1983). In an industrialising society power had to maximise human potential and not merely to threaten, punish or eliminate. Social policy in particular became one of the main apparatuses of the state for harnessing and circulating power. Welfare provision would improve labour power, regulate the unproductive indisciplinary institutions, sanitise the living conditions of the general population and order its living space in planned environments and partitioned dwellings. Yet the notions of order – the norms of medicine, education, public health, architecture, etc. – did not emerge as logically apparent solutions to the problems of capitalism, but had to be produced, their logic made clear, and applied as discourses and normalisation practices.

In principle the optimisation of this process of normalisation is the fully internalised, self-regulation of mind and body. Donzelot describes the psychic space opened up for family life by psycho-analysis and counselling whereby old and new norms, prohibitions and ambitions, public and private, are allowed to float together to achieve an equilibrium that enhances the family's autonomy and preserves state tutelage (1980, pp. 199–217). Similarly, Bauman (1983; cf. Featherstone 1982) comments on how the present consumerism of the body facilitates 'the joy of controlling the body of one's own will, with the help of sophisticated products of technology . . .' These effects of normalisation are part of the deeper process of the detachment of meaning and values produced by commodification in all its forms and the floating of signifiers, norms and currency to find their 'own' level – a process proclaimed by two instigators of modernism, Freud and Keynes (Donzelot 1980, ch. 5).

Power and the Politics of the Body
Each of Foucault's studies marks a further step in his quest into the nature of power, to which his subject and its ostensible domain – sexuality, punishment or madness – become ancilliary.[2] This does not imply that, in the development of his

work, each subject is replaced by power, but that power is seen to constitute the subject. Power is exercised upon, through and by the subject and its domain. For example, social policy constructs targets upon which power is inscribed (e.g. deprived individuals and neighbourhoods); it provides a capillary through which state power is circulated throughout the social body (e.g. administrative apparatuses affecting family life); moreover, by its own power social policy preserves and establishes its interests (e.g. by the self-legitimation of professional, academic and research practices). This chapter now turns to the analysis of power, which underlies the conception of bio-power, prior to examining its implications for social policy.

Foucault contrasts his 'analytics of power' with other approaches that see it as produced by particular institutions and laws, modes of repression or systems of domination. Instead it inheres in all relations from one moment to the next: 'power is everywhere; not because it embraces everything, but because it comes from everywhere' (1979b, p. 93 ff). Rather than conceive of it as extending downwards from some central point, head-quarters, ruling caste, economic elite, or sovereignty, Foucault sees it immanently as originating from below in each instance of the machinery of production, in families, groups and institutions. It is this conception that informs Foucault's account of the development of bio-power, its embodiment (in 'force relations', 'the body' and 'the social body') and its instruments of application (the disciplines and technologies of regulation, the 'Panopticon', the 'carceral' and the 'tutelary complex'). Each of these figures is examined in turn. While power is studied in ascending order from its local to its global formations, whether state, law or ideology, the analytic focus at each level remains the *force relation*. This relation is neither one of unchanging domination nor of total submission of one party to another. It is dialogic, exhibiting the never equal and yet ever mobile play of dialogue (1979b, p. 94). The force relation represents the energy of power by and upon the body. The *body* stands as a metaphor for the anatomical focus and embodiment of power; a materiality that acts as a source and target of power, whether expressed politically, sexually, juridically or in discourse. It is not assigned a binary value as either active or passive, as the perpetrator or recipient of power. Rather the body operates within the confines of force relations – whether between men and women, prisoner and warder, boss and worker, or client and social worker, whether individually or collectively – which frame strategies of power ranging from constructive complicity to repression (1979a, p. 136; 1979b, pp. 95–6; 1980, p. 104). This guiding metaphor enables one to analyse the play and effects of power. At one moment in history the body asserts itself; at another it is subject to regulation. At one level in a social formation it is assertive; at another subject by a process of relays to a different level of power. For example Donzelot recounts how during the second half of the nineteenth century in France the state gained access to working-class households, and in particular to the mother and child, by means of assistance schemes in housing, medicine and child-rearing. The mother was invested with new skills and powers and, in turn, exercised a moral influence over the husband and child. Neither the home nor its male head were dominated by the state. But the state via its agencies' links with the mother exercised moral influence in the patriarchal family at one remove – i.e. 'government through the family' – with the effect that relations between husband and wife were tactically reformed (1980, pp. 35–47).

The *social body* is a metaphor for the collective embodiment of the targets of power, the body as 'species', whether in the form of an entire population or a specific group of prisoners, school children, the insane and so forth, who are subject to specific types of administration and regulation. From the seventeenth century onwards, and especially during the eighteenth century, numerous technologies of control were developed to preserve and regulate the life of the body, its health, sexuality, subsistence, accommodation, education, etc. (Foucault 1979b, pp. 24–5; Donzelot 1980, pp. 6–7). Both Foucault and Donzelot describe the administrative, judicial, penal and educational methods of discipline employed. The body was invested with a significance concerning social well-being and required constant and detailed policing and regulation. Power began to exercise a relative control over life and avert some of the imminent risks of death. It replaced the sovereign's absolute power over life and death, epitomised by the public execution and the just war. From this point onwards life entered history and bio-politics was born; 'for the first time . . . biological existence was reflected in political existence' (Foucault 1979b, p. 142). Foucault places the methods establishing bio-power into two categories. The *disciplines*, an anatomo-politics of the individual body 'centred on the body as a machine: its disciplining, the optimisation of its capabilities, the exertion of its forces, the parallel increase of its usefulness and its docility, its integration into systems of efficient and economic controls . . .' The *regulatory controls*, a bio-politics of the population, 'serving as the basis of the biological processes: propagation, births and mortalities, the level of health, life expectancy and longevity, with all the conditions which cause these to vary' (original emphasis) (1979b, p. 139). The economic and political functions of these disciplinary controls were to increase the forces of the body, its productive utility, and to harness these same forces in terms of political obedience (1979a, p. 138). By means of these two types of discipline the government was enabled to intervene both publicly and privately. Detailed examples of disciplinary practices are given by Foucault et al., which include school time-tables, class room organisation, clinical examinations, scholastic examinations, hygienic and sexual prohibitions, clinical symptomatologies, courtroom practices, prison organisation and army camps – each marked by hierarchical supervision, individual scrutiny, and the normative adjustment of behaviour.

However, the texts under review furnish more than a catalogue of examples of bio-power. Foucault and Donzelot construct particular representations of these formations, i.e. the Panopticon, the 'carceral archipelego' and the 'tutelary complex'. The Panopticon (Bentham's plan for a circular prison from the centre of which the warder has all-round visibility of the cells) is portrayed as an ideal type that unites the social organisational, architectural and administrative features of various punitive and corrective establishments into a perfect disciplinary institution for regulating the body. Its idea at the close of the eighteenth century provided a basis for an instrument to inform the operation of different institutions, social and medical as well as penal. Several stages were involved. First, the Panopticon's idealised perfection stood as Bentham's blue-print for increasing the utility of individual bodies. Secondly, compact disciplines were extracted from their institutional sites and distilled into the Panopticon. This led further to the disciplines being broken down into flexible methods of control and then regrouped and disseminated throughout the social body. Philanthropic organisations, for example, were as disciplinary in securing their religious, economic, and social policies as many others. Finally, the state gained control over the methods of discipline (Foucault 1979a, pp. 297–8).

The development of the disciplines reaches its present position in what Foucault terms the 'carceral', i.e. the disciplinary regime that typifies prison incarceration. The prison reproduces within one apparatus the mechanisms found extensively within the social body, in barracks, schools, hospitals, workshops and so forth. However, unlike earlier prisons, the carceral domain no longer exercises its power in isolation from the wider society. The re-alignment of disciplinary measures involves the reorientation of numerous penal and non-penal organisations towards a prison-like state, the 'carceral archipelago'. The prison spreads outwards to include agricultural prisons, almshouses, penal colonies, orphanages, apprentice workshops; and non-prison bodies using carceral methods, such as charity societies, moral improvement associations, worker estates, hostels and so forth. In those areas of social life that remain relatively free of carceral discipline, e.g. the family and the community, there developed a corresponding formation of normalising discipline which Donzelot terms the 'tutelary complex'. This comprises the growing 'swarm' of social workers, benefits officers, psychiatrists, educators, etc., who home in on the deprived child and his family to ply their 'caring' skills. 'There are no longer two authorities facing one another: the family and the (state) apparatus, but a series of concentric circles around the child: the family circle, the circle of technicians (e.g. social workers), and the circle of social guardians (e.g. magistrates) . . . the more (social) rights are proclaimed, the more the stranglehold of a tutelary authority tightens around the poor family' (1980, p. 103). In this way judicial institutions are drawn into a continuum of apparatuses, alongside the 'judges of normality', to constitute the tutelary complex.

In each formation of discipline a central problem is posed: what is the nature of bio-power? Contrary to the view that describes the effects of power in negative terms which exclude, repress, abstract, conceal (labour, sexuality, knowledge, etc.), Foucault sees power as *production*: 'it produces reality – it produces domains of objects and rituals of truth' (1979a, p. 194). Bio-power constitutes the problems that call forth medical and administrative interventions. It engenders the forms of knowledge that structure these problems and interventions. Bio-power is also essentially regulative. It extends the body's abilities and the population's capacities by manipulating and harnessing them for its own ends. Sex, for example, is seen as 'a thing not simply condemned or tolerated but managed, inserted into systems of utility, regulated for the greater good of all, made to function according to an optimum . . . it is a thing one administered' (1979b, p. 24). To illustrate this in greater detail, the 'deployment of sexuality' through disciplinary intervention highlighted four areas of social life – the woman's body, the child's sexuality, forms of intervention, policy and scientific discourse (1979b, pp. 104–5). First the woman was analysed, positioned within medical practice, and imbued with a demeaning pathology (the 'hysterical woman') that subjected her, in the name of her responsibilities, to the service of the social body – as an instrument of regulated fecundity – and the family. Secondly, the child's sexuality was ambiguously cast as both a natural and unnatural activity (the 'masturbating child'), posing physical, moral and social dangers which led to its control by a pedagogy involving parents, educators, doctors and psychologists. Thirdly, procreative activity became the target of economic inducements and restrictions, political concern for the growth or limitation of the population, and medical concern with health and unhealthy methods of contraception. Fourthly, a sexual instinct was isolated, its perversions identified and categorised (the 'homosexual man'), its normal practices encouraged, and its pathologies therapeutically regulated. The positive forces of power, generated by these 'strategic unities', have advanced professional agents of intervention (social workers, doctors, teachers, etc.) with privileged bodies of knowledge that decide which behaviour is problematic and by what norms. It is the distinctive feature of bio-power and social policy that it generates positive and productive forces for the compliance and regulation of the body.

Bio-power and the Advent of Social Policy
Broadly, two histories are written about social policy which share a common sense of origins. First, in some accounts the origins of modern welfare are set in the central government reforms of the 1830s and 1840s in particular, in the Poor Law amendment, the Factory Acts and the public health reforms (Bruce 1968; Fraser

1973; Roberts 1960). Secondly, in others the significance of these reforms is said to lie less in their welfare impact – seen as relatively ineffective and endowed with non-welfare objectives – and more in the part they played in the genesis of the modern state, in providing economic regulation and central governance (Clark and Kitson 1967; Gilbert 1966; Richards 1980). Whatever the significance and effectiveness of these measures, the two histories share in common a notion of the conjunction between state and welfare which was conceived in the 1830s and determined developments thereafter. The roots of public welfare lie in those formative acts where the state intervenes with varying effects in the issues associated with destitution, sickness and squalor. Though its tentative beginnings go back to Elizabeth I and beyond, social policy's firm beginnings are fixed at around the 1830s when, for the first time, centrally administered, professionally staffed and informed health and welfare systems were introduced by the state. By locating the advent of social policy at this juncture these historical narratives presuppose a break between welfare's pre-history and its substantive history. The subject of social policy is conceived as coterminous with the modern industrial state, presupposing a functional relationship between welfare and the state. Prior to the emergence of the modern state, welfare had no clearly identifiable existence.

This functionalist presupposition (whereby the state provides welfare with an institutional and governmental site; and the state achieves its identity, in part, through intervening in problems of destitution, sickness and squalor) figures generally in accounts of social policy history and is articulated in the following ways.[3] First, because this conjunction occurs at the height of industrial capitalism, the characterisation of the state – as an institution relying on centralised government and operating in the public domain – gives welfare its particular institutional form. In Fabian accounts especially welfare comes into its own when it acquires a centralised and public apparatus (Webb and Webb 1963, pp. 3–5 and pp. 404–5). Early forms of welfare are relegated to a residual status 'enclosing little besides poor relief, sanitation and public nuisance' (Titmuss 1963, p. 40). Secondly, the presupposition governing the conjunction between state and welfare is articulated in political as well as institutional terms. The state is vouched increasing jurisdiction from the 1830s onwards in determining the objectives and forms of welfare.

During welfare's pre-history social provisions are largely independent of the state; thereafter they are drawn increasingly under its tutelage. Thirdly, in mainly Marxist accounts that attempt to address more closely the state's role in the management of capitalism, the tasks of reproducing labour and maintaining unproductive dependants are conferred on welfare – a more specific role in supporting the state's general functions in the accumulation of capital. Fourthly, the functionalist presupposition further predisposes descriptions of welfare's functions towards characterisations that rely heavily on binary terminology. Social policies are cast in a mould of either care or control, public or private, universal or selective, etc. Such characterisations of welfare inscribe its objectives with uniformity, overlook its modulatory functions in maintaining social cohesion, and obscure the multitude of alliances, each with varying purposes, amongst welfare's components and between welfare and the state. Though these four formulations offer important insights in understanding the social, political and economic functions of social policy within the capitalist state, their value is limited to comparatively recent developments in social policy's history and to rather sweeping characterisations of its functions informed by a global conception of the state.

Foucault's contribution to this history lies in his account of the role of bio-power in the advent of social policy. By examining its role in the transition from feudalism to the industrial capitalist state, Foucault et al. reveal: i) a substantive history of early welfare free from the pre-historic oblivion evident in the above accounts; ii) the multiple alliances between welfare practices and the state during the seventeenth and eighteenth centuries; iii) a range of functions that replace the simplistic binary attributes, of care and control, etc.; iv) the forms of knowledge and discourse that underwrite technologies of bio-power. Through these forms of knowledge and technology the politics of the body constitutes the subject of social policy and its objects of intervention.

Foucault and others locate the origins of bio-power in the local administration of 'policing', together with other technologies of discipline, that began in the fifteenth century and became fully-fledged by the eighteenth. 'Policing' was understood as more than a specific form of repression. It represented a range of interventions in the governance of the body during the advent of capitalism and the state. Foucault defines policing as 'the ensemble of mechanisms serving to ensure order, the properly channelled growth of wealth and the conditions of preservation of health "in general"' (1980, p. 170). The problems which policing addressed concerned the administration of the body and the population – new objects of analysis and intervention that occupied the energies of governments during the transition to capitalism and subsequently.

These characteristically bio-political objectives were evident in the extensive discourse that engaged writers throughout Europe in the seventeenth and eighteenth centuries. In one proposal, dating from 1608 and quoted by Pasquino, three tasks were identified: information, conceived as a statistical table bearing on all the capacities and resources of the population and territory; a set of measures serving to augment the wealth of the population and enrich the coffers of the state; and lastly 'public happiness', the business of maintaining the general well-being of the population. The targets of policing included, *inter alia*, religion, customs, highways, public order, commerce, health, subsistence and the poor (1978, pp. 44–5). Bentham also recommended eight police departments, including police for the prevention of offences, calamities and endemic diseases, police for charity and police for collecting statistical information of all kinds (Henriques 1979, p. 269, n.8; cf. Corrigan and Corrigan 1979). Moreover, to Adam Smith it meant 'the regulation of the inferior parts of government, viz. cleanliness, security and cheapness or plenty', though he considered such matters too demeaning to examine in his *Wealth of Nations* (quoted in Henriques 1979, p. 269, n.9). The 'science of policing' subsumed aspects of economics, health and welfare, religion and law and order within a body of discourses which, by means of various institutions and regulations, affected diverse areas of life. By 1834 the Poor Law Commissioners saw their task as organising 'a measure of social police' which would encourage the development of a free market for labour (Briggs 1959, p. 280).

Yet both policing and welfare remained largely hidden discourses over-shadowed by the key intellectual themes of the eighteenth and nineteenth centuries, concerning the accumulation of wealth and the limits to state intervention (Pasquino 1978). For example, the target of welfare, i.e. poverty, appears as the dark side of wealth, 'in as much as it is the territory of unfulfilled needs, or of those not yet invented' (Procacci 1978, p. 58). The ever present threat of poverty to labour is posed in nineteenth-century thought in one sense negatively, in diverting resources from the accumulation of capital and in breaching the limits of state action, and yet in another sense positively, in acting as an incentive to produce wealth. Policing and welfare played a necessary role in effecting this fine balance without which capital and state could not exist – a balance that involved not a choice between welfare and capital, care and control, life and death, etc., but a modulation of these exigencies via the technologies of bio-power. With the advent of welfare, new normalising agents from doctors to social workers emerged with these technologies to modulate degrees of compliance between the state and its dependants. This development obviated the necessity for absolute choices and permitted adjustments around the norm.

The emergence of the human sciences at the end of the eighteenth century made problematic norms of conduct and promoted new technologies for adjusting both behaviour and its norms. The human sciences and the disciplines are two facets of the wider transformation in western thought which Foucault refers to as 'an epistemological thaw' in the bedrock of certainty surrounding earlier sciences that took for granted the order of (physical and human) nature and its representation in discourse and thought (Foucault 1970; 1979a, p. 191 and p. 224).

The Domain of Social Policy
Social policy is conventionally concerned with the mainly governmental institutions and arrangements for promoting social welfare through the amelioration of individual and collective needs as socially defined. The institutional and normative specificity, however problematic, ascribed by British writers to welfare has contributed towards regularising and demarcating the subject matter. The welfare domain is distinguished from others such as the economic and judicial. By contrast, French studies of welfare are less clearly defined and partitioned. 'The social' stands as both the title for the welfare domain and its components (*aide sociale, assurances sociales, action sanitaire et sociale, assistantes sociales,* etc.) and as an epithet describing wider formations of society. Such lack of specificity, far from eliding welfare and society, forms and interesting analytic for

Foucault et al. which is largely absent from British policy analysis. Rather than presuppose an identity between the provision of public welfare and a particular view of society (e.g. the welfare state) these writers examine *how* social problems and provisions are constructed to accord with this view of society and the state. The social becomes a constituted phenomenon binding together particular institutional arrangements and normative objectives to pronounce that society is, or can be, secure and consensual in the face of inequalities, dissensions and insecurity (Donzelot 1980, xxvi). Welfare is placed firmly within the bio-political sphere with its accompanying regulatory and normalising mechanisms for preserving the social whole. One of the important features of modern society is the role played by welfare as a mode of power and knowledge in forming the social.

There are several respects, therefore, in which this view of welfare contrasts with that of mainstream social policy. First, because social policy's concerns are seen as the pursuit of social objectives, mainstream studies tend to overlook social policy's role in constructing these objectives as an aspect of the social. It is often unclear what is meant by 'social ends' other than forms of consolidation gained through promoting preferred social institutions, groups and norms, i.e. social policy as an area of study limited by its normative orientation. By contrast, Foucault and Donzelot, in particular, have drawn attention to the workings of a 'social economy' surrounding the practices of punishment, sexuality, family life and the government of the body. The late-nineteenth-century interest in *Socialpolitik* in Germany and *economie sociale* in France, through to Keynesian economics in the present century, suggests an intermediary discourse in the genealogy of policy between the social and the economic. Within such discourse the formation of society-as-welfare can be traced (cf. Procacci 1978, p. 55; Cahman and Schmitt 1979).

Secondly, Titmuss advocated that social policy study 'takes its stand on aims and not on the administrative methods and institutional devices employed to achieve them' (1963, p. 42). This emphasis has contributed towards a subsequent breach between the traditional study of social administration, drawing largely on the juridical and governmental concepts of public administration, and social policy (cf. Walker 1981). However, the identification of the disciplinary processes operating within administrative, therapeutic and architectural practices, referred to earlier – which in their very operations contribute to our normative view of modern society – transcends this division. In studies of the bio-political we see more clearly the circular and emerging relations between administrative methods and normative aims that are articulated through the processes of normalisation.

Thirdly, perhaps the most widely accepted assumption of social policy is that it is the study of the *intended actions* promoting welfare. It is grammar relying heavily on the active mode. Walker's recent critical discussion of mainstream social policy quotes well-known definitions of the subject area, where activities 'bring about . . .', 'contribute to the making of . . .', or use 'political power to supersede, supplement or modify . . .' and so forth (Walker 1981, pp. 227–9). Moreover, the notion of 'policy' as 'action directed towards given ends' reinforces this active disposition (Titmuss 1974, p. 23). Individuals and groups, official and unofficial, are actively engaged in conducting strategies of intervention. As a corollary to this mode, such actions and decisions involve the policy-maker in exercising choices which are by definition inescapably normative (Carrier and Kendall 1977, p. 31; Rein 1970, pp. 9–10; Warham 1973, pp. 193–4). The study of social policy accords a centrality to the actor (benefactor *and* beneficiary) as a moral agent and attributes an importance to the normative evaluation of policy. Yet it is increasingly clear to analysts that this orientation can grasp only part of the welfare domain – that which is ideal-typically rational. Writers now, as a matter of course, refer to the intended and unintended consequences of welfare and to the consequences of actions in other spheres upon welfare. But such formulaic corrections leave standing several problems. The grounds whereby analysts demarcate territory into segments of intended and unintended action, explicit and implicit rationales, planned and unplanned, manifest and latent, etc. are unclear. Moreover, such divisions promote a theoretical divide between accounts privileging intentional and conscious action and those promoting a system (Functionalist and Marxist) that makes some sense of the unintended rationales of policy.

The development of Marxist social policy has helped to displace social policy's central concern away from the recipient and welfare service and onto systemic notions of the relations between economic, social and ideological formations that engender needs and welfare services. The policy apparatus is no longer a domain where just, informed, or otherwise disposed, choices are made. It is determined by interests that reflect the positions of policy-makers, practitioners and recipients within a wider class-structure. It is the relations between productive and non-productive activity which condition policy, and the functions policy performs in connection with these wider structures which are the subject of study. Foucault's work extends this process of decentring further, though in a manner that is challenging to the programmes of Marxist and Fabian social policy alike. The constitution of needs and interventions is not addressed via structures such as social class, ideological hegemony, social formation and the state. The constitution itself of these structures is questioned. The starting point is taken as the formation of the subject as conventionally conceived. From this point Foucault then examines the misconceptions governing these conventions, the surrounding power relations preserving such misconceptions in forms of practice and knowledge, and the elaboration of the regulatory and normalising apparatuses governing social life. Thereby the centrality of the actor is displaced onto an interweave of power relations; the illusion of normative choice is transformed into normalising procedures for gaining the beneficiary's 'voluntary' compliance; the wooden notion of active practitioner and passive recipient (e.g. 'the unilateral transfer') is transposed into one of active complicity based on a dialogic model of power relation akin to the confessional; the over-arching assumption of state governance (central to both Fabian and Marxist traditions) is diffused into a complex and immanent network of disciplinary technologies, supported by discourses concerning the management of numerous aspects of the body, and forming an updated and diversified version of the Panopticon.

Knowledge, Resistance and Intervention

Mainstream social policy might respond that this challenge to its sacred tenets appears to shift the focus away from the fundamentally practical task of tackling ever-pressing social problems and onto an area more the concern of sociology, history and other less practical studies. This challenge has little to do with social policy as praxis and intervention. Conventionally, the topic of social policy demands that to advance welfare, the position of individuals and groups must remain central and the relationship between knowledge and practice close. However, Foucault's analyses of these imperatives show them as the ploy of prevailing forms of power and knowledge, and suggest how dispersed forms of critical knowledge partake in the formulation of new political interventions (1980, pp. 79–83; cf. Minson 1980). The entrance of the human sciences into administration was not guided by humanitarianism, but by the advent of disciplinary technologies which sought to apply normalising judgements, to differentiate bodies according to types of observable behaviour and to compare and rank them against quantifiable norms, such as average household size, housing types, health profiles, income bands, behavioural and psychological functioning. Placed at the centre of each categorial system is the individual body, unit or personality. However, this centrality is functional to the operations of the numerous 'normalising judges' who standardise aspects of human life. It is precisely the process of individualising the body that makes scientific and rational administration possible, by enabling human qualities to be measured, ascribed to a level, affixed with a quantitative value, accorded a specialist function or aptitude, and so on (Foucault 1979a, pp. 182–3). The central importance invested in the individual in all the social services and in the ethic of social policy is a constituted event. Yet such an observation neither makes a fiction of the individual's centrality nor denigrates the sincerity of the practitioner. It merely displaces such factors and shows them as a reality functional to the disciplinary apparatus.

Despite the evaporation of social policy's central concerns, Foucault distils a new set of subjects that were previously unseen, in particular those associated with discipline and bio-power. It is here that the work contributes to the new forms of political intervention. Through the construction of new subjects and the dispelling of old ones, social policy can re-appraise existing methods and promote new forms of intervention and resistance. If existing methods are shown to support particular conceptions of social problems and interventions, both governed by a dominant problematic of welfare and need, then a critical advance must be mounted on an understanding of how this problematic is constituted and of the alliances and dependencies of power comprising it. Foucault suggests that new forms of intervention are initiated in each locality where power is activated in the unearthing of 'subjugated knowledges' buried or disguised beneath the 'global' strata of functionalist and other systematising theories. By unearthing such knowledge, e.g. the hidden histories of struggle or the disqualified accounts of low-ranking personnel, local criticism emerges as part of a wider and more dispersed offensive waged against various centres of power – the hospital, the asylum, the prison, the welfare organisation. These provide a basis for histories that throw light on present systems of discipline and knowledge; genealogies that promote tactical interventions (1980, p. 85). The unified though elusive functioning of Power/Knowledge, the theme that binds Foucault's studies and underwrites the disciplines, demands that intervention and resistance should strive to forge connections between such knowledge and practice.

Bio-politics and the Political Economy of Welfare

Foucault's work provides an account of welfare and its function-ing in society that is especially challenging to the political economy of welfare. It is Foucault's somewhat sweeping conten-tion that functionalist and economistic features are endemic in the 'sovereign' theory of power in Marxism. In attempting to assess this contention (which has not been applied specifically to Marxist studies of welfare) it is necessary to develop an elabora-tion of Marxist studies to show where his critique applies and where not.

Political economy sees the capitalist state, its nature, structure and role, including its welfare functions, in Gough's words, as 'constrained by the mode of production and nature of exploita-tion in that society'. The welfare state is seen as a 'constituent feature of modern *capitalist* societies, situated within the economy and its attendant relations' (1979, p. 19 and p. 3). This characterisation forms a radically different conception of welfare from earlier ones. However, the characterisation of welfare as constrained by the mode of production and as a constituent feature of capitalism posits a relations of domination-subordination between welfare and the economy of a func-tionalist and economistic kind. The welfare state is born of surplus value and is functional to capital accumulation. Writers emphasise different aspects of these two major functions: welfare produces use-values that capital cannot or will not provide (Ginsburg 1979); it socialises some expenses of capitalist production (O'Connor 1973); it reproduces labour power (O'Connor 1973; Gough 1979); it maintains the surplus or non-working population (O'Connor 1973; Gough 1979).

The first three functions contribute indirectly towards surplus value and further accumulation; whilst the last controls those outside the production process under the guise of meeting their dependent needs. This 'caring' function contributes towards the legitimacy of the state which has the interests of all at heart. These different functions specify complementary aspects of welfare's role in capital accumulation and legitimation. However, the political economy of welfare recognises a growing crisis between these two processes. Increasingly the state's preference for capital over labour becomes blatant, its impartiality and legitimation threatened, and its welfare provisions reduced as the surplus population, especially the unemployed, increases. The functional relations between welfare and capital grow shaky.

Yet the functional propositions that characterise the political economy of welfare are less problematic than the explanations that underpin them. As Marxist accounts they are concerned with the structural relations that arise between both economic and social relations. Yet these structural connections – e.g. between, on the one hand, welfare's production of use-value and, indirectly, surplus value; and, on the other, the management of the non-working population and the historical emergence of class-struggle over the provisions of welfare – are insufficiently demonstrated. The explanations of the functions of welfare are provided more *within* one of these two domains than the other, and not, in the main, *between* the two. These accounts are functionalist because what is stated as the functions of one domain remains no more than an assertion of what is explained in the other. There are exceptions. Ginsburg's (1979, pp. 126–37) account of the role of building societies, for example, within British capitalism and the welfare state demonstrates the manifold processes that function, among other things, to increase profits, promote the wider interests of the bourgeois class and attract state support. Such an account largely succeeds in integrating analyses of capital accumulation, its distribution and consumption, the formation of social class struggle, and the development of state intervention, as they determine social policy. A structural account is provided of the economic, social and political relations that inform social policy (cf. Taylor-Gooby and Dale 1981, ch. 4).

The failure of writers generally to determine more precisely the nature and extent of the relations between welfare and capital leads to accounts that see welfare as functioning in a subordinate and economistic manner. According to Gough the functions of the welfare state are twofold: to produce labour power and maintain the non-working population. Following O'Connor, he allocates these activities under two state expenditures: social capital and social expense. But the irreconcilable conflict between the expenditures that contribute indirectly to production and the expenditures that do not, leads to a fiscal crisis for the state and welfare services. Both O'Connor and Gough suggest skilfully how 'the long-term imperatives of capital accumulation' shape expenditure programmes and associated social and political activities. But the approach whereby state expenditures are matched with welfare and other programmes assumes that the content of these programmes reflects the capitalistic functions attributed to state expenditures. Consequently the parts of welfare concerned with maintaining the dependent population are 'a necessary but unproductive expense' (Gough 1979, p. 51), whilst other parts that increase the productivity of labour, e.g. education and public transport, or lower its reproduction costs, e.g. housing subsidies and provisions, are indirectly productive. This produces the hair-splitting problem of designating instances of welfare provision to either category of expenditure. But more importantly, we are not led to study more closely the forms of labour and production that comprise the 'social expense' activities of welfare. To say that social work, the police, etc. produce legitimacy for the state, that they perform a function, only begins to address the problem.

Without a positive conception, welfare stands as a *tabula rasa*, a neutral entity, upon which the state inscribes the functions it requires of it in support of accumulation and legitimation. The approach cannot state what is inherently specific to welfare and what was appropriated by the state for the advancement of capital during the nineteenth and twentieth centuries. It is not surprising that for O'Connor welfare is indistinguishable from war in so far as it plays the same role in the 'warfare-welfare state' where 'the structural determinants of both military spending and welfare outlets are broadly the same and the two kinds of spending can be interpreted as different aspects of the same general phenomena' (1973, p. 150). These functionalist accounts rely on attributing to welfare (and to other activities) an absence of intrinsic attributes that only the over-riding state can ascribe. The welfare state is dependent for its defining qualities on the state's investing it with functions.

At the root of this economistic account of welfare lies an assumption that betrays the ideological constructions of capitalist thought. We are told that '*all* societies contain groups that are unable to work for their living . . . children, the elderly, the sick . . .'. Therefore, 'it follows that *all* societies must develop mechanisms for transferring part of the social product from the direct producers to these groups' (Gough 1979, p. 47 my emphasis); hence the twofold division of functions mentioned above. But whilst Gough, and others, acknowledge that the boundaries are not fixed and will be predominantly determined by the prevailing mode of production, which under capitalism sharply differentiates production from other activities, the universal distinction between work and non-work remains, and consequently between worker and non-worker and production and non-production. However, these oppositions are the construction of capitalist society and not merely its characterisation. What capitalism achieves is the privileging of production and the banishing of all other activities to a domain where 'production' is absent. To accept the *distinction* between capitalist production and its absence as a fundamental and universal *opposition* between production and non-production is to partake in this ideological construction. All societies engage in labour as a universal lifeform but they conceive of labour's constituent activities in widely differing ways and attribute different values to them. Physical effort, tending, nurturing, the display of wisdom, authority and artistic creativity are all different forms of labour with their own specific outcomes and productions. Each constituent can be combined with others to constitute organic forms of labour that differ from one society to another.

Yet once the opposition between work and non-work has taken hold, the ideological connotations abound. Welfare is but one victim of this process. It plays a circulatory role within capital accumulation – it diverts, transfers, distributes, allocates, but doesn't produce.[4] At best it is on occasions indirectly productive. An account of welfare and state functions that began as a critique and characterisation of capitalism now has the making of a universal characterisation that affects even the language and presuppositions of its critique.

In summary, the Marxist political economy of welfare approach is led by its functionalist presuppositions to characterise welfare economistically as lacking any intrinsically productive potential apart from its indirect contribution to accumulation. By contrast, Foucault accredits bio-power, a domain that today takes the welfare state as one of its principal apparatuses, with a positive and productive role in disciplining the body and forming the social. It is not just a 'constituent feature of modern capitalist societies', but is constitutive of important features of modern society and the state. Moreover, the social and the economic are not understood simply as different though related systems (each with its own institutions, modes of intervention, problem-conceptions and discourses), but as different modes of functioning that affect all sectors of society. Not only is the advent of welfare concerned with the rise of the social, but it produces a new configuration of social, economic and juridical practices that takes on a distinctly social form under the imprint of bio-power.

However, not all Marxist analyses of social policy and the state are economistic, in the sense formulated above, and therefore conform to Foucault's critique. For example, an approach that credits social and other areas of state policy with productive attributes is given by Offe (1975) in his account of the transformation of the state during a period of advanced capitalism. Policy emerges as a distinctive feature of the capitalist state when capitalists are no longer able to coordinate production and to further accumulation. At this moment the traditional mode of state activity, the *allocation* of taxes and repression by political authority, is insufficient for capital accumulation and must be augmented by *productive* activities undertaken by the state. This mode of state activity requires a new form of decision-making because what must be produced does not lie at the disposal of the state in the way that it can allocate taxes and repression. So policy formations takes over from the political authority that cannot produce health, education, R&D, etc. from scratch.

However, in the long-run the state has merely taken on the crisis of accumulation itself. For its internal structure – highly bureaucratic, instilled with purpose rationality and desperately feigning consensus – cannot be reconciled with the functions it performs for accumulation. Though coming from distinctly different traditions, there are interesting similarities between Offe's and Foucault's account. Specifically, they both credit state policy, including welfare, with productive capacities. On a more general level, Offe's two modes of state allocation and production – with their respective concerns with the political and judicial allocation of 'resources, taxation, state demands, tariffs, repression, subsidies, etc.', and the policy-led production of 'education, skills, technological change, control over raw materials, transportation, housing, a structure of cities, physical environment, energy and communication services' (1975, p. 129 and p. 134) – bear a limited similarity to Foucault's sovereign and bio-political systems of power, though the time scales in both cases do not overlap.

Foucault's underlying challenge to Marxist thought is waged at its 'sovereign' notion of power – which he claims it shares with Liberalism (1980, pp. 88–9). Under the sovereign, prior to the formation of the disciplines, power was exercised negatively according to rules and laws that prohibit and by sanctions that repress. Both the discursive and practical expressions of sovereignty came in the form of a binary system of norms, in terms of permitted or prohibited behaviour, the breakdown of which was repaired by imposing a 'levy' on the transgressor. Repression was exerted by taking the body, property or money of a transgressor to restore the social order, to right the wrong done to the sovereign or the social body. This view still holds in Marxist and Liberal thought where power is conceived of economically. Under Liberalism it is a right which one possesses as a commodity. Its possession is maintained by contractural obligations, of a legal or political kind, which are universally binding and, if broken, remedied by the judiciary or the sovereign (parliament or monarch). Similarly in Marxism power is a possession. Though in this case it is a form of property which one class holds over another in maintaining the relations of production for its own benefit, and which one must wrest from the other in transforming these relations. Economism is fundamental both to the Liberal and Marxist 'sovereign' suppositions of power, with their notions of levying and repression. Power is exercised through the medium of things (commodities, wealth, subjects, etc.) that are extracted, deducted, exchanged or expropriated. Moreover, the maintenance or transformation of power relations involves the use of repressive force in allocating possessions, whether by a judicial apparatus sanctioned by the state or by a revolutionary overthrow of the state.

The sovereign presuppositions in the political economy of welfare are revealed in its functionalism (in the role welfare plays in fulfilling the needs for capital accumulation); in its absolutism (in the ascription of a binary mode of functioning to welfare, e.g. as care *or* control, public *or* private, and so forth); and in assuming an intrinsically neutral character for welfare as a *tabula rasa* on which the state inscribes functions in support of accumulation and powers to support or repress the non-working population. Whilst Marxists see these presuppositions as contradictions inherent in the nature of the capitalist state (Gough 1979, p. 11), Foucault might respond that they are inherent in a discourse bedecked in the remnants of a past era of sovereign thought. To use his oft-quoted metaphor, there are aspects of Marxist as well as Liberal thought where the King's head has yet to topple.

The Ubiquity of Power
In contrast to the above conception of power, Foucauldian studies provide one that is more diffuse and ubiquitous. 'Power is neither given, nor exchanged, nor recovered, but exercised . . . it exists only in action' (Foucault 1980, p. 89). Power in the welfare state is seen in the practices of the agents of bio-power. In the context of various force relations, these agents strive to enhance the body's utility through the deployment of regulatory technologies that increase its manipulability. The body is made pliable and amenable to disciplinary norms that operate no longer according to binary injunctions, but to an increasing register of dexterities, aptitudes, desires and needs geared to the requirements of economic productivity, family life, sexual conduct and so forth. The shift from sovereign power to bio-power involved, for example, the deployment of sexuality for enhancement rather than repression. In the development of the sexual disciplines, the ascending bourgeoisie applied sexual strictures, whether as health-inducing practices of abstinence or

problematising pathologies of sex, to themselves and to their women and children especially, to secure their wider economic and political advancement. The extension of these sexual norms to the poorer classes came later (Foucault 1979b, p. 123).

At this juncture two problems concerning Foucault's work are briefly noted. First, his conception of the ubiquity of power can be construed as a form of vitalism whereby power becomes the all-pervasive and essential driving force of social life. It is not economic production but power which brings social organisation into being with its specific class forms and ideologies. Such absolutism, as in economism, can also lead to the dangers of functionalism and reductionalism. (But see Foucault's rebuttal, 1980, pp. 141-2.)

Secondly, whatever subject Foucault pursues, the reader encounters a void on the question of causation, e.g. on why bio-power emerges with the decline of medieval sovereignty and gains dominance throughout the nineteenth and twentieth centuries. Yet underlying his account of the development of discipline, power and knowledge are structure notions of change, of expanding, shifting and segmenting populations and transformed methods of production (1979a, p. 218). But Foucault never elevates these material factors to an unequivo-cably determinant status. Any hint of a base-superstructure compact between productive forces, on the one hand, and power relations or forms of knowledge, on the other, is avoided. Indeed he nullifies such causal connections. The two processes – the accumulation of men and the accumulation of capital – are inseparable; 'it would not have been possible to solve the problem of the accumulation of men without the growth of an apparatus of production capable of both sustaining them and using them; conversely, the techniques that made the cumulative multiplicity of men useful accelerated the accumulation of capital' (1979a, p. 221). For example, without an effective accumulation of persons, the monarchical methods of control were ineffective, creating numerous instances of 'bad political-economy': ineffective or over-repressive punishments, sexual promiscuity, unregulated populations of the sick, vagrant, over-crowded, insane, etc. (1979a, p. 219; cf. Donzelot 1980, pp. 40-5). The difficulty in discerning a clear process of causation in these accounts lies in the vitalistic conception of power underlying them.[5] This force is never defined in itself, though it is everywhere 'made manifest' in all things. The indiscernibility of power in itself leads Foucault to attend to its manifestation in the way that his various subjects are constituted, rather than caused, and embodied in social practice and discourse.

Conclusion

Foucault accepts that his approach in conceptualising and describing the workings of power requires closer scrutiny and development. In view of this, his conception of bio-politics and its role in the formation of social policy awaits further development. The study of bio-power is set in the context of economic functioning, but avoids the various forms of global thinking. First, power and its economic correlates are set in terms that are local and immanent to provide for a political economy of specific practices and knowledges rather than global structures. Through this conception, formations such as the state and ideology are produced from the nexus of numerous force relations, struggles and resistances rather than from the imposition of macro-forms of power. The state, though nonetheless a powerful formation, is less important to the analysis of power than the local practices of bio-politics and the inter-connections and alliances built up between them that underwrite the state and ideology. Secondly, there is no determinant status accorded the economy 'in the last instance'. Instead the economy and the social are constitutive of each other and likewise manifest the workings of power (though in a manner that suggests power as a vitalistic force and prime-mover). Lastly, the conception of bio-power overcomes the 'either-or' dilemma of sovereign theories.

This chapter has counterposed Foucault's work on bio-politics with Marxist studies of social policy. In the space of this chapter it is not possible to suggest the positive contribution of Foucault's analyses to the understanding of several of the problems with which Marxist scholarship grapples; the conception of the state, the functions and nature of welfare, the social and economic divisions of welfare, the reproduction of labour and the ideological role of welfare. The work of Foucault et al. touches on all, and indeed illuminates many, of these issues. Nonetheless, these works suggest that a critique of political reason is overdue. They therefore contribute 'to such a critique by showing concretely how *sieve-like concepts* such as "crisis" and "contradiction" are inadequate'. Other concepts could be added, which together 'make it possible to neglect crucial transformations by referring them to the terms of a simple but out-moded debate; they blur the positivity of these transformations and obscure their efficacy' (Donzelot 1980, p. 8). The notions of discipline and bio-politics and their role in constructing welfare as practice and discourse, help to bring into clearer focus the conception, subjects and efficacy of social policy.

Notes

I am grateful to Peter Squires for his comments on an earlier draft of this chapter and to Peter Dews for elucidating aspects of Foucault's work that I would otherwise have overlooked.

1. The use of the term 'subject' normally denotes specific meanings accorded to context, for example: an area of academic study; a particular object or topic examined within a study; and, the behaviour, experiences and meanings held by a person examined in a study. The reconstruction of the subject as s/he/it passes through each system of knowledge – e.g. the subject of the schizophrenic as a patient, a client, an object of diagnosis and treatment, a textbook case, a diarist and so forth – raises fundamental questions about the production and structure of knowledge for Foucault and other post-structuralist writers and poses difficulties in understanding the relationship between knowledge and practice in social policy and other applied studies.

2. Foucault (1982, p. 777) has reformulated the goal of his work: 'It has not been to analyse the phenomenon of power, nor to elaborate the foundations of such an analysis. My objective, instead, has been to create a history of the different modes by which, in our culture, human beings are made subjects.' This appears to differ from his accounts of his own work in the late 1970s (e.g. cf. 1980, pp. 92–102).

He has not, however, departed from his view concerning the centrality of power in constituting the subject.

3. For studies that depart from this approach, see Corrigan and Corrigan (1979), Henriques (1979).

4. Gough (1979, ch. 6) seems to acknowledge this problem in his analysis of the gains and losses to capital and labour caused by state expenditure.

He comments that there has been a tendency to assess the state in terms of its role in the realisation of existing output rather than contributing towards the production of output. However, the question of the nature of the labour process within social welfare remains an area for further conceptual and empirical work.

5. Donnelly (1982) has recently elaborated on the troubles attending Foucault's eschewal of causality and his conception of an extensive, undifferentiated domain of power.

References

Bauman, Z. (1983) 'Industrialism, Consumerism and Power', *Theory, Culture & Society*, 1, 3.

Briggs, A. (1959) *The Age of Improvement*, London: Longman.

Bruce, M. (1968) *The Coming of the Welfare State*, London: Batsford.

Burchell (1981) *Putting the Child in its Place, Ideology and Consciousness*, 8.

Cahman, W.J. and Schmitt, C.M. (1979) 'The Concept of Social Policy (Sozial Politik)', *Journal of Social Policy*, 8, 1.

Carrier, J. and Kendall, I. (1977) 'Social Administration as Social Science', in H. Heisler (ed.), *Foundations of Social Administration*, London: Macmillan.

Castel, F. and Castel, R. (1982) *The Psychiatric Society*, New York: Columbia University Press.

Clark, G.S.R. and Kitson (1967) *An Expanding Society*, Cambridge: Cambridge University Press.

Corrigan, P. and Corrigan, V. (1979) 'State Formation and Social Policy until 1871', in N. Parry et al. (eds), *Social Work Welfare and the State*, London: Edward Arnold.

Donnelly, M. (1982) 'Foucault's Genealogy of the Human Sciences', *Economy & Society*, 11, 4.

Donzelot, J. (1980) *The Policing of Families*, London: Hutchinson.

Featherstone, M. (1982) 'The Body in Consumer Culture', *Theory, Culture & Society*, 1, 2: 18–33 (reprinted in this volume).

Foucault, M. (1970) *The Order of Things*, London: Tavistock.

Foucault, M. (1972) *The Archaeology of Knowledge*, London: Tavistock.

Foucault, M. (1979a) *Discipline and Punish, the Birth of the Prison*, Harmondsworth: Penguin.

Foucault, M. (1979b) *The History of Sexuality, Volume I, an Introduction*, London: Allen Lane.

Foucault, M. (1980) *Power/Knowledge, Selected Interviews and Other Writings 1972–1977*, Brighton: The Harvester Press.

Foucault, M. (1982) 'The Subject and Power', *Critical Inquiry*, 8, 1.

Fraser, D. (1973) *The Evolution of the British Welfare State*, London: Macmillan.

Gilbert, B. Bentley (1966) *The Evolution of National Insurance in Great Britain*, London: Michael Joseph.

Ginsburg, N. (1979) *Class Capital and Social Policy*, London: Macmillan.

Gough, I. (1979) *The Political Economy of the Welfare State*, London: Macmillan.

Henriques, U.R.A. (1979) *Before the Welfare State*, London: Longman.

Jones, K. and Williamson, K. (1979) 'The Birth of the Schoolroom', *Ideology and Consciousness*, 6.

Minson, J. (1980) 'Strategies for Socialists? Foucault's Conception of Power', *Economy and Society*, 9, 1.

O'Connor, J. (1973) *The Fiscal Crisis of the State*, New York: St Martin's Press.

Offe, C. (1975) 'The Theory of the Capitalist State and the Problem of Policy Formation', in L. Lindberg et al. (eds), *Stress and Contradiction in Modern Capitalism*, Massachusetts: Lexington Books.

Pasquino, P. (1978) 'Theatrum Politicum, the Genealogy of Capital-Police and the State of Prosperity', *Ideology and Consciousness*, 4.

Procacci, G. (1978) 'Social Economy and the Government of Poverty', *Ideology and Consciousness*, 4.

Rein, M. (1970) *Social Policy: Issues of Choice and Change*, New York: Random House.

Richards, P. (1980) 'State Formation and Class Struggle 1832–48', in P. Corrigan (ed.), *Capitalism, State Formation and Marxist Theory*, London: Quartet.

Roberts, D. (1960) *The Victorian Origins of the British Welfare State*, Yale University Press.

Rose, N. (1979) 'The Psychological Complex: Mental Measurement and Social Administration', *Ideology and Consciousness*, 5.

Squires, P. (n.d.) 'Internal Security and Social Insecurity', Mimeo, Department of Social Administration, Bristol University.

Taylor-Gooby, P. and Dale, J. (1981) *Social Theory and Social Welfare*, London: Edward Arnold.

Thorpe, D.H. et al. (1980) *Out of Care: The Community Support of Juvenile Offenders*.

Titmuss, R.M. (1963) *Essays on the Welfare State*, London: Allen and Unwin.

Titmuss, R.M. (1974) *Social Policy*, London: Allen and Unwin.

Turner, B.S. (1982) 'The Discourse of Diet', *Theory, Culture & Society*, 1, 1. (Reprinted in this volume.)

Walker, A. (1981) 'Social Policy, Social Administration and the Social Construction of Welfare', *Sociology*, 15, 2.

Webb, S. and Webb, B. (1963) *English Poor Law History, Part I: The Old Poor Law*, London: Frank Cass.

This chapter first appeared in *Theory, Culture & Society*, Vol. 2 (1983), 67–84.

10
GENEALOGY AND THE BODY: FOUCAULT/DELEUZE/NIETZSCHE

Scott Lash

Introduction

Anglo-American commentators in the human sciences have for some time now taken Michel Foucault at his word, that he has been, as archaeologist and as genealogist, most fundamentally a Nietzschean. It is as a genealogist, in *Madness and Civilization*, *Discipline and Punish* and *The History of Sexuality*, that Foucault has had the greatest impact. But what *is* genealogy? The problem is of the utmost import. Genealogy can not only potentially serve for sociology, taken in its very broadest sense, as a method. It has not only, as Habermas (1981) has noted with some vexation, provided a theoretical counterpart to 'postmodernist' developments in the arts. It has, moreover and most of all, been understood by its main proponents to be a possible successor to Marxism as a doctrinal basis for the multiplicity of 'micro-struggles' in today's fragmented capitalism.

Genealogy patently, all are agreed, concerns knowledge; it concerns power; it concerns probably above all the body. But there are two central shortcomings in the otherwise very useful work of the growing legions of Foucault commentators and exegetes (e.g. Sheridan 1980; Dreyfus and Rabinow 1982; Racevskis 1983). We are given first and foremost to understand that only Foucault among contemporary French analysts in the human sciences is a genealogist. Gilles Deleuze, we shall see below, can justifiably claim equal status as a genealogist with Foucault; the works of the one are inextricable from, indeed inconceivable without, the works of the other. Yet the standard and highest-quality commentary on Foucault (Dreyfus and Rabinow 1982) mentions the name of Deleuze only once, and at that only *en passant*. Moreover, the *oeuvre* of Nietzsche is, in most of the secondary literature, given insufficient consideration for questions of genealogical method.

The task of this chapter is to develop a notion of the body in a broadly (not just Foucauldian) genealogical framework. The means towards this end, and subsidiary aims of the chapter, are several. They are: to provide a more critical understanding of Foucault though a consideration of Deleuze's influence. To begin to flesh out a broader concept of 'agency' in genealogy, through the systematic scrutiny of the notions of 'desire' and the body in Deleuze and Guattari's *Anti-Oedipus*. To present a consistent and in-depth account of Nietzsche's considerations of the body, which I shall argue below are at the same time functionalist and heavily privilege action over structure.

Foucault: the Body as Passive

Pessimism, classical and modern

Foucault's chronology of history, which puts at centre stage the transition from the 'Classical' to the Modern, revolves mainly around two different modes through which discourse acts upon the body. In the Classical period, heralded by Descartes and absolutism, when souls and discourse are separate from bodies, knowledge relates to bodies from the outside, through representation and direct repression. The point of entry to the Modern was provided by the French Revolution, the usher was Sade. We Moderns have witnessed the cementing of souls back onto bodies; the breaking of discourse with representation to enter bodies themselves; its constitution, individuation and normalisation of bodies; its recruiting and drilling of bodies, acting through incarnate souls, in the interests of the reproduction of society.

In *Madness and Civilisation*, whose original Plon edition was entitled *Folie et déraison* (1961), reason and unreason were separated during absolutism; that is, at a point in time when words were disengaging from the sensuous, the bodies of madmen were enclosed and separated from the light of reason. Modernity, in contrast saw the dawn of the psychiatric hospital, whereby discourse, operating via families and 'bad conscience', began to normalise and mobilise the bodies of the mad. In *Birth of the Clinic* (1973a), Classical medical texts were entrenched in the philosophy of representation, and inferences about organisms were deductive; the study of anatomy was king, as words referred to parts of the body; the light of the medical gaze itself ended at the surface of bodies, whose shadowy interior remained unknown and unknowable. Modernity witnessed the advent of the clinic, the disappearance of the signifier, as doctors came to know the body and its organs as 'in-themselves'. Corporeal penetration through physiology meant that experimentation replaced deduction and that bodies were to be regulated, their interior movements made calculable.

In *The Order of Things* (1970, whose French title literally translates as *Words and Things*) bodies disappeared altogether, but Foucault's Classical *episteme* circumscribed a two-world conception of words, ideas and the subject, on the one hand, and things, which were understood as real and material, on the other. In the 'sciences of man' in the Modern *episteme*, there is no longer a clear hegemony of words over things. Now what is broadly conceived along the lines of the body (or the material) is at the centre of discourse, quintessentially in Marx and Freud, while the *cognito* has retreated towards the periphery. *Discipline and Punish* (1977a), Foucault's first full-length text in a genealogical framework, has a quite pronounced focus on the body. While Foucault was writing the book, his series of lectures given at the Collège de France was entitled *La volonté de savoir*, the will to knowledge, which was also to be the title of the French edition of *The History of Sexuality*. Nietzsche often spoke of a will to knowledge, but, as we shall see below, one which is functional for the prosperity of individual bodies. Foucault in his genealogical texts on punishment and sex, speaks almost only of a will to knowledge which disintegrates bodies while reproducing the social. In *Discipline and Punish*, which drew most directly on *The Genealogy of Morals*, Foucault used to advantage Nietzsche's concept of 'memory'. Here punishment and discipline, through a sort of socialisation process, create a 'memory' for offenders and for society in general. This memory, which exists at the level of the unconscious, is at the same time an agent of social control, and functions in the interests of social reproduction. In Foucault's 'narrative', memories were engraved directly on bodies in the seventeenth and eighteenth centuries through the ghastliest and cruellest rituals; through a 'mnemonics of pain', which functioned as spectacle for the audience and towards the reproduction of absolutist rule. From the nineteenth century as the Word loses its dominance over things, power is no longer separated from the social field. Previously, penal practices affected the body directly and negatively in the reproduction of a power which was transcendent in relation to the social. Now penal discourse reproduces a power which is immanent in society; for this purpose it individuates, normalises and mobilises human bodies; it operates on bodies not through direct physical cruelty, but via a gaze that has its effects on the soul, via the 'bad conscience' which is attached to bodies.

If Classical punishment consisted of the physical engraving of a memory directly on bodies, in Modern punishment it is discourse which creates such a memory. Thus the applied science of Man (penology, psychiatry) and the 'pure' sciences of Man (psychoanalysis, economics), which characterise Modernity, function as structures in the engraving of memory. In opposition to 'memory' and to 'discourse' Foucault has proposed the construction of a 'counter memory', or a 'non-discursive language'. Most of Foucault's discussion in this context concerns how literature can serve as a non-discursive critique of the often oppressive rationalities of discourse in the human sciences. But there is evidence that Foucault has intended such non-discursive language (he seems to view his own work under this heading) to be part and parcel of everyday life. If the discourse of the social sciences has made possible the subjection of the body in a number of institutional settings, then non-discursive language can help create a counter-memory as a resource for resistance to such subjugation (cf. Bouchard 1977, pp. 8–9; Foucault 1964).

Nonetheless in the corpus of Foucault's work, in each case and in each period, bodies are acted *upon* in discursively-constituted institutional settings. Resistances are rarely constructed, struggles are not engaged. This bodily passivity, this pessimistic vision of agency, is perhaps even more pervasive than elsewhere in *The History of Sexuality*, volume one. In his demolition of the 'repressive hypothesis', Foucault shows that sexuality has never been more the object of discourse than in Modernity, and that the function of discourse on sexuality, from the early nineteenth century through to Freud and Lacan, has been to normalise and recruit bodies and thus to facilitate social reproduction. Previously, we shall see below, Foucault worked closely with

Deleuze; now he attacks even him and views 'desire' as part and parcel of Modern discourse (Foucault 1980a, pp. 81–90). Barthes in *The Pleasure of the Text* (1975) celebrated '*jouissance*' which he defined in terms of the *absence* of 'desire'. Foucault likewise argues against *scientia sexualis*, and for an *ars erotica* based on an amorphous, unstructured body, from which desire is excluded. Deleuze's 'desire' is conceived along the lines of Nietzsche's 'will to power'. To argue as Foucault does that 'desire' is a servant of power, is effectively to break with Nietzsche. More important it is to endorse a cipher-like delibidinised vision of agency that would be incapable of constructing resistances, incapable of mobilising resources.

A genealogy of bodies

'Nietzsche, Genealogy, History', observe Bouchard (1977, p. 22) and Dreyfus and Rabinow (1982, pp. 106–14), is perhaps Foucault's key methodological essay after his break with archaeology. In it he underlines Nietzsche's opposition to any idea of 'origins', and instead emphasises that genealogy is a question of two processes – of 'descent' (*Herkunft*) and 'emergence' (*Entstehung*). It is under the category of descent that Foucault begins to introduce systematically a notion of the body. *Herkunft* is here the equivalent of 'stock'; 'it is the ancient affiliation to a group, sustained by the bonds of blood, tradition, or social class' (Foucault 1977c, p. 145). Equally, 'descent attaches itself to the body' (Foucault 1977c, p. 147). When Foucault thus mentions 'stock' and 'blood' he should be taken *à la lettre*. He writes, 'the analysis of *Herkunft* often involves a consideration of race or social type'; in developing the idea of a 'double soul', nineteenth-century 'Germans . . . were simply trying to master the racial disorder from which they had formed themselves' (Foucault 1977c, p. 145).

Violence is not done to our common-sense notion of genealogy, whether we conceive of 'descent' in terms of a genealogy of morals, of things, or of attributes. Descombes's (1980, p. 157) definition, as a search for antecedents, 'with an eye to establishing the baseness or nobility of lineage', could refer to any of these entities. Nietzsche (1956b, p. 210; 1966, p. 818) seems to lend credence to such an unfocused conceptualisation when he, for example, writes, 'Thus the whole history of a thing, an organ, a custom becomes a continuous chain of reinterpretations and rearrangements, which need not be causally connected among themselves, which may simply follow one another.' But Foucault's idea of 'descent' suggests not a genealogy of morals but a genealogy of *bodies*. This itself is a perfectly justifiable, indeed very insightful, conception. The problem is that it draws on only a selection of Nietzsche's writings which offer a very partial treatment of the body. Foucault is in particular overly dependent on *The Genealogy of Morals*. Here, for example, in speaking of the value distortion and resentment which the ascetic priest arouses in his suffering followers, Nietzsche explains, 'the wish to alleviate pain through strong emotional excitement is, to my mind, the true physiological motive behind all manifestations of resentment'. And further, 'sinfulness is not a basic human condition but merely the ethico-religious interpretation of physiological distemper'. For Nietzsche (1956b, pp. 263–5; 1966, pp. 867–70) such a physiological 'cause may lie in an affection of the sympathetic nerve, or an excessive secretion of bile, or a deficiency of alkaline sulphates and phosphates in the blood'. Morals and psychology may be explained then by an understanding of the body or physiology.

This is not the fully-formed, both functional and activist Nietzschean theory of the body which we will explain below. But the body here, if not a conscious actor, is at least a *causal* agent. Curiously enough, however, Foucault reads even this partial theory (which is the only theory of the body enunciated in *The Genealogy of Morals*, and the theory which is associated with 'descent') in a rather backwards manner, whereby cause largely becomes effect and the body becomes passive. For Foucault thus, (1977c, p. 148) 'the body is . . . a volume in perpetual disintegration. Genealogy, as an analysis of descent, is thus situated within the articulation of body and history. Its task is to expose a body totally imprinted by history and the process of history's destruction of the body.' And, 'The body is moulded by a great many distinct regimes; it is broken down by the rhythms of work, rest and holidays; it is poisoned by food or values, through eating habits or moral laws; it constructs resistances' (Foucault 1977c, p. 153). We are then provided by Foucault with a body largely deprived of causal powers.

Foucault and Deleuze

It is well known that May–June 1968 fuelled Foucault's adoption of genealogy in the place of archaeology. Three central 'methodological' essays prepared the way for the new approach which was first put into practice in *Discipline and Punish*. Two were written in 1970. One of these was *L'ordre du discours*, his inaugural lecture at the Collège de France. In this, after outlining a relatively archaeological definition of discourse, Foucault adumbrates the 'rules of exclusion' from discourse in a Nietzschean context (cf. e.g. Major-Poetzl 1983). He then continues almost literally to equate discourse and slave moralities observing that the birth of discourse took place as Socratic philosophers replace pre-Socratic poets (Foucault 1971, pp. 16–17). The other benchmark article of 1970 is 'Theatrum Philosophicum' and is a review of two of Deleuze's books, *Logique du sens* (1969b) and *Différence et répétition* (1969a). It is here that Foucault (1977d, p. 165) famously commented, 'perhaps one day this century will be known as Deleuzian' and spoke of Deleuze as proceeding 'with the patience of a Nietzschean genealogist' (Foucault 1977d, p. 181). The third essay was 'Nietzsche, Genealogy, History' published in 1977 and was, we shall see below, as much influenced by Deleuze's writings as by Nietzsche's concept of 'descent'. During the period between the publication of *L'archéologie du savoir* (1969) and *Surveillir et punir* (1975), Foucault's only other publications on any scale, that looked forward to his genealogical writings, were the 'Presentation' and 'Les meutres qu'on raconte' in *Moi, Pierre Rivière*, which were not methodological essays. The remainder of his output of this period – on Cuvier, Bachelard, a response to Derrida, the essay 'What is an Author?' – treated topics central to his books of the 1960s.

There is a good bit of further evidence of the centrality of Deleuze's influence. In *The Order of Things* (1970), Nietzsche and Mallarmé are treated as a sort of epiphany of postmodernity and counter-memory; this echoed resemblance noted by Deleuze in 1962 (cf. Deleuze 1983, pp. 32–4). Foucault and Deleuze collaboratively wrote the introduction to Pierre Klossowski's 1967 translation of Nietzsche's *Fröhliche Wissenschaft*; they were interviewed together in 1972 on the relationship of intellectuals to power; Foucault wrote the preface to the 1977 English translation of *L'Anti-Oedipe*. More generally, it was Deleuze who was by most accounts the prime mover in the French Nietzschean renaissance of the past two decades (cf. Leigh 1978); a recent book on Foucault rather matter-of-factly states that in France, Deleuze has stood to Nietzsche as Althusser has to Marx and Lacan to Freud (Major-Poetzl 1983). Probably most important is that *The Anti-Oedipus* was, as Turkle (1979, pp. 148–53) has argued, the intellectual culmination of 1968 in France. This is true in terms of its widespread popularity; its thoroughly Nietzschean, playfully eclectic and extremely influential reconciliation of Freud and Marx; and most of all in its spirit of irreverence that stood in counterposition to the sober back-to-Marx-and-Freud of Althusser and Lacan, and that captured the '*sous les pavés la plage*' ambience of the May–June events. It is likely then that Foucault's conversion to genealogy was catalysed by – indeed was effectuated through the prism of – Deleuze's infectious interpretations of the May–June days. Foucault's subsequent practical involvement with the prison information movement even seems to emulate Deleuze's involvement with anti-psychiatry militants. The 1970s, Descombes (1980, pp. 136–90) has suggested, were largely Deleuzian years in intellectual France. Late 1970s intellectual celebrities like Jean-François Lyotard have taken a number of cues from Deleuze. The parameters of Barthes's late period of *The Pleasure of the Text* and *A Lover's Discourse* were largely set, for better or for worse, by Deleuze, and *nouveaux philosophers* such as Bernard Henri-Levy continue to write extended anti-Deleuzian tracts.

Foucault in his commentary on *Différence et répétition* praises Deleuze – and the unnamed opponent could effectively be Derrida – for breaking with a tradition which has understood 'difference' as a difference within something; it ought, instead, he concurs, to be treated in terms of an irregularity of '*intensities*' (Foucault 1977a, p. 182). This quantitative difference of intensities is a figural distribution of points on bodies. It is, for Deleuze, given rise to by another quantitative difference; a difference between 'active' and 'reactive forces' which yield values, 'events', and bodies and their properties. The active and reactive forces are themselves constituted through the 'affirmative' and 'negative' qualities of the will to power (Deleuze 1983, p. 50). The unity of a body is then, Deleuze (1983, pp. 40–1) states, 'a plurality of irreducible forces' and 'what defines a body is this relation between dominating and dominated forces'. We should note here that for Deleuze the will to power is prior to the 'forces', which themselves are prior to the body. Nietzsche on the other hand, we shall see below, defined the will to power in terms of a drive of the organic to increase the 'quanta of power' under its disposition. He could not, as Deleuze does, conceive of the will to power as logically prior to, and distinct from, the body. Deleuze's systematic valuation of 'forces' at the expense of the body is also pervasive in the *Anti-Oedipus* where it is 'desire', a 'flux', which will assume centre stage and not the body. The important point for us here is that Foucault rather uncritically accepts Deleuze's very undynamic view of the body.

In 'Nietzsche, Genealogy, History' (Foucault 1977c, pp. 148, 154–5) and 'Theatrum Philosophicum' the concept of 'event' plays a central role. In the latter, Foucault endorses a concept of the body that Deleuze developed in terms of 'phantasms' and 'events'. Phantasms are 'figures' on the surface of human bodies. They arise between the surfaces of bodies and constitute a sort of 'incorporeal materiality'; they can only be characterised 'quantitatively', by a multiplicity of points of given intensities (Foucault 1977d, pp. 169–72). The term 'phantasm' comes from Freud's analyses of phantasy in, for example, his discussions of 'phantasmic castration' (Foucault 1977d, pp. 179–87). Yet phantasms are neither Freudian images nor Lacanian signifiers; they are on the contrary *real* and material (Foucault 1977d, p. 177).

'Events are produced by bodies colliding, mingling, separating' and also are created on the surface of bodies. They are also non-corporeal; events are not causes, not states of things and cannot verify or falsify. They do not take the adjectival form of qualities, but verb forms such as 'he is dying'. Events and meanings coincide; events take place simultaneously on the surface of bodies and the surface of words (Foucault 1977d, pp. 173–5). We can speak of the 'series' of phantasms and the series of events. The phantasm however is 'excessive' in regard to the singularity of the event. 'Thought' produces phantasms, which have 'primal appendages', in a theatrical vein. Phantasms are intoned by the body through the mouth, as the objects of thought; the corresponding event is 'I am thinking' (Foucault 1977d, pp. 176–9). Phantasms, unlike signifiers which are constituted through the identity of a language, are pure difference in the sense that 'intensities are pure difference'. Thought therefore is 'intensive irregularity'. The production of 'meaning-events' takes place through the repetition of a phantasm. The event then is 'displaced and repeated difference' (Foucault 1977d, pp. 182–3).

Deleuze and Foucault have rescued the notion of phantasm from its psychoanalytic usage in the understanding of illusion. Bodies (and not subjects) 'think' not through concepts, nor categories, nor even language, but through phantasms. Philosophy becomes schizophrenia, it becomes theatre. Deleuzian phantasms, we shall see below, are constituted at the interface where society meets human bodies. Inscribed on the human body by means of the social they govern not only our thought events, but our political practices, our sexuality. Under capitalism, for example, the marking of phantasms through oedipalisation organises our sexuality and use of language in forms conducive to the reproduction of capitalist social relations. In competition, for Deleuze, with the capitalist social formation for the creation of phantasms on the human body, is, of course, 'desire'. Deleuze's body is then an object of competition, for whose control the active forces of desire and reactive forces, mobilised by capital engage in struggle. The problem is that Foucault, unlike Deleuze, operates without a developed notion of desire or its equivalent; thus Foucault's body is only the prey of *reactive* forces – normalising and individuating forces, and Foucault's genealogy remains incomplete.

Foucault approvingly mentions that the concept of the body advanced in Deleuze's *Logique du sens* is a near-polar opposite to that of Merleau-Ponty's theory. For Merleau-Ponty wrote Foucault, 'the body-organism is linked to the world through a network of primal significations, which arise from the perception of things, while according to Deleuze, phantasms form the impenetrable and incorporeal surface of bodies', and give rise to 'something that falsely presents itself as a centred organism' (Foucault 1977d, p. 170). Foucault writes similarly in 'Nietzsche, Genealogy, History', 'the body is the inscribed surface of events (traced by language and dissolved by ideas). The locus of a dissociated Self (adopting the illusion of a substantive unity)' (Foucault 1977c, p. 148). There is here an extraordinary convergence between this definition of the body and the 'body without organs' in Deleuze and Guattari's *Anti-Oedipus* (see discussion below). The 'body without organs' as well is a surface on which figures of varying intensities are inscribed. It is the locus of a dissociated self, insofar as it is separated from desire. It gives rise to the illusion of a unified subject. It is moreover operated on by discourse. Deleuze and Foucault seem here to have less in common with Nietzsche than with Merleau-Ponty, whose 'lived body' was also a body without organs (Dreyfus and Rabinow 1982, pp. 111–12).

Deleuze: Between Desire and Society

There is rather broad agreement that Deleuze and Guattari's *Anti-Oedipus* dissimulates, under a reconciliation of Freud and Marx, a Nietzschean critique of both Freud and Marx (cf. Seem 1977; Turkle 1979, pp. 148–53; Descombes 1980, pp. 173–80).[1] The book is divided into two parts, the first develops the notion of 'desire', the main locus of agency, in a psychodynamics – but, we shall see, a very sociological psychodynamics – whose main components are desire, the body and the subject. The second part is an account of how desire is 'coded' in different historical periods. It is only the first part which we will deal with here. Perhaps I may be forgiven for the following rather detailed treatment, which can, hopefully, serve as an aid to the reader in coping with what is a very difficult text. My central goal in this discussion, however, is to show how Deleuze and Guattari's 'schizodynamics' are part of the project to provide us with a 'counter-memory', how their de-oedipalised notion of agency constructs resistances to institutional psychiatric practices; how their de-familised unconscious is at the same time an attack on phallocentricism. In short to underscore how the *Anti-Oedipus* is integral to the whole genealogical enterprise.

Schizodynamics contra Lacan and Freud

Deleuze and Guattari have two central objections to Lacan. The first concerns the notion of 'desire'; the second is the question of the mode of investment of desire. The *Shorter Oxford English Dictionary* defines 'desire' as 'the fact or condition of desiring; that emotion which is directed to the attainment or possession of some object from which pleasure or satisfaction is expected; longing, craving; a wish'. Lacan's notion of desire is rather close to this everyday usage of the term insofar as it entails the absence or lack of the object of desire. Lacan's concept diverges from our ordinary usage insofar as he specifies that desire must be unconscious. Here the category dovetails with Freud's concept of 'wish', which in *The Interpretation of Dreams* is *inter alia* seen as developing from a need that was satisfied in the past but not in the present; hence from a lack. Lacan distinguishes desire from 'need' and 'demand'. The infant at first cannot distinguish need from demand. With separation from the mother and identification with the father, demand and need become distinct and desire is born. Demand is conscious, desire is unconscious. Desire is, then from the outset a question of lack; it is desire to have the mother and desire to be the phallus (Wilden 1968, pp. 185, 189). 'Desire' for Deleuze and Guattari (1977, p. 26), in contrast to this, corresponds to Freudian 'libido'. It does not entail the absence (or presence) of objects. It consists of flows of energy created by the id.

Lacan, it can be argued, also works with some sort of notion of psychic or sexual energy. The point is that in contrast to Freud, on the one hand, and Deleuze and Guattari on the other, whose understandings of libido are more-or-less physical – Lacanian psychic energy is structured by language. And the manner in which the latter is structured by language is based on absence or lack. Lacan's tripartite over-arching schema consists of the Real, the Imaginary and the Symbolic orders. The Imaginary comes into existence at the same time as desire (Wilden 1968, pp. 295–6). Desire, though born in the unconscious with the advent of the Imaginary, is, in connection with the castration complex, reconstituted in the Symbolic. Classical psychoanalysis distinguishes between imagination on the one hand, which conceives representation of objects and events not actually present, and symbolism on the other, in which the unconscious substitutes one image for another, the latter being a representation of a repressed object (Rycroft 1972). In poetics, 'metonymy' is a figure in which an attribute of an entity is substituted for the entity. In this context Lacan speaks of the Symbolic as operating on the model of metonym. The entity which operates in such a fashion for Lacan is the 'signifier or signifiers', the phallus. The phallus 'represents . . . vital thrusting or growth . . . which cannot enter the domain of the signifier . . .' (Lacan 1958a, p. 252, cited in Wilden 1968, p. 187). This 'transcendental' phallus nonetheless appears as metonym in each of the signifiers which structure the unconscious and constitute desire.

If libido has its basis for Lacan in the Symbolic, for Deleuze and Guattari (and for Freud) its grounding is in the Real; its foundations are material, even biological. Freud's libido has its basis in the id and exists in various forms corresponding to biological – oral, anal and genital – 'part objects'. What Deleuze and Guattari call 'desiring-machines' closely resemble Freud's id. Desiring-machines produce desire. The 'parts' of desiring-machines are the 'part objects' of psychoanalysis (Deleuze and Guattari 1977, pp. 6–7). Deleuzian desire is also conceived as the equivalent of Nietzsche's will to power (Descombes 1980, p. 173), and it is significant as we shall see below that the will-to-power doctrine is pre-eminently biological.

The first point, then, on which Deleuze and Guattari are in disagreement with Lacan, concerns the constitution of desire. The second point concerns the way in which desire is invested. Here too the main bone of contention is a matter of Deleuze and Guattari's attribution of primacy to the Real in contrast to Lacan's focus on the Symbolic. On this matter Lacan is found in Freud's corner, inasmuch as classical psychoanalysis has stressed the investment of psychic energy in imaginary and symbolic objects. For example, in a feminist commune, classical psychoanalysis might view the cathexis of an older woman by a younger woman at least partly in terms of symbolic cathexis of the mother. Deleuze and Guattari (1977, pp. 84ff) would prefer to understand this simply as a real and material investment of libido in the older woman. They would thus reject the 'oedipalisation' of desire. Oedipalisation, the authors claim, is a product of capitalism. With the breakdown of tradition-bound relations of precapitalist societies – what the authors refer to as 'decodification' – a problem of social control arises. The only way in which capitalism can ensure its reproduction is for the family through oedipalisation to take on functions of social control (Deleuze and Guattari 1977, pp. 284–6). They maintain, as Foucault did in *Madness and Civilization* and *The History of Sexuality*, that psychoanalysis only continues and strengthens a process – social control through the familial codification of desire – which preceded it by a century.

The body without organs
The first element of schizodynamics is, as we noted, desiring-machines. The second element is the body. Deleuze has gone farther in thinking out a notion of the body than the other

French post-structuralist theorists. Let me briefly outline this concept of the body, drawing not just on *Anti-Oedipus*, but on Deleuze's work more generally. Although Deleuze's desiring-machines are modelled on biological lines, his view of the body, unlike Nietzsche's is not at all biological. Deleuze, following Artaud, speaks of a 'body without organs'. Here he and Guattari are also influenced by Freud's (1958) most considered account of schizophrenia in which the schizophrenic's body was experienced as ungendered. By 'body without organs' Deleuze means that we do not experience our bodies in terms of their biological organisation, or, more precisely, that we *should* not so perceive our bodies. Deleuze recognises the convergence between this non-organic view of the body and Merleau-Ponty's 'lived body', only he does not want to attribute the unity, coherence and intentionality to the body that Merleau-Ponty does (Deleuze and Guattari 1980, pp. 185–204; Deleuze 1981).

Deleuze's body is conceived as a sort of hollow sphere, whose surface is structured in four ways, through each of which it is marked by a pattern of intensities. First, 'figures' are recorded on the surface of bodies which correspond to the part objects (the anus, the breast, the penis) of desiring-machines themselves (Deleuze and Guattari 1977, pp. 60–1). Here Deleuze and Guattari agree with Melanie Klein (1932) about the importance of libidinal investment in such entities; they, however, reject Klein's understanding of such cathexis as symbolic and in terms of the Oedipus complex. They advocate instead a real investment in such objects, which would then promote a sexuality free of the phallocentricism and normalisation entailed by oedipalisation (Deleuze and Guattari 1977, pp. 70–5). Second, figures are recorded from the outside world on the body; an example of this would be the illustration in regard to the feminist commune which I gave above. This is the point at which the third element of schizodynamics, 'the subject', is introduced. Deleuze and Guattari (1977, p. 100) propose, in opposition to the unified subject constituted through the oedipus triangle, a 'decentred ego' which serially identifies with a number of real and historic subjects in whom psychic energy is invested. The third type of zone of intensity which circumscribes bodies is the 'phantasm', which was discussed above. The fourth is the sense organs themselves. Deleuze suggests in this context that we should confront art in a manner similar to that in which the hysteric perceives his or her body. This means that for example when we listen to music, the ears should be distorted to take the shape of a 'polyvalent organ' which not only hears, but sees and feels (Deleuze 1981, pp. 36–7, 79–80).

There are innumerable problems in the work of Deleuze and Guattari. They present insufficient argument for their thesis concerning capitalism and oedipalisation. They seriously underestimate the extent to which the family has already declined as an agent of libidinal coding and investment. At points they push their theory of desire and the body just a bit too far for belief. Finally, I would reject their (and Foucault's) anti-Marxism, both for its conservative political resonances and because their theoretical arguments against Marxism are at best sloppy. We should not, however, let these shortcomings lead us to underestimate Deleuze's contributions, which are not inconsistent with a neo-Marxist perspective. He has contributed importantly to the development of a non-organic concept of the body. He and Guattari have given us a set of prescriptions for the investment of libido which is condemnatory of hierarchy and sexism and enabling of healthy diversity. Most of all, their genealogy puts in the place of Foucault's passive body, the active forces of desire.

Nietzsche: Bodies and their Resources
For Nietzsche the 'body is not hypostatised as a concept, as it is in Foucault and Deleuze. It is spoken of in a rather more mundane manner as one of a set of biological terms, such as 'physiology', 'the organism', 'the senses', 'the sensuous'. The key point here is that – unlike Foucault, whose bodies were riddled and cross-cut by the power of knowledge, and by the use of knowledge by power – for Nietzsche knowledge is functional for the body; indeed the capacity to acquire knowledge is the most important 'organ' of the human body.[2]

Organic processes
Nietzsche saw his 'post-Darwinian epoch' as one in which philosophers have begun to speak of bodies rather than souls. He did not consider his focus on the body, then, to be particularly original. Where he differed from his contemporaries was in his rejection 1) or their Whiggish understanding of the body's ever-increasing perfection in favour of his theory of

eternal recurrence and 2) of the primacy they placed on feelings of pleasure and pain as fundamental causes; for Nietzsche (*The Will to Power* (*WP*), pp. 347, 353, 357–8) these were instead *effects* of the will to power.

Nietzsche understood the human body or 'organism' in the context of the bodies of all organic beings. The body in any species, is 'a multiplicity of forces, connected by a common mode of nutrition'. These forces include 'resistance to other forces'. To a mode of nutrition belongs 'feelings' and 'thoughts'. An organic species is 'an enduring form of processes of the establishment of force' and relations of force. 'Life' refers only to what is organic, and is the organic process through which the will to power of the dominant forces extend their boundaries (*WP*, pp. 341–3). To all organic beings, to all organisms or bodies – from amoebae to humans – the will to power is basic. This is more than a 'will to preservation', but a drive to absorb and dominate other organisms, other bodies, and thus add to the body's 'quanta of power' (p. 345). In other words the will to power is a drive towards 'expanded reproduction', with which bodies are possessed. In this supremely functional model the body is both agency and structure; agency insofar as it initiates reproduction, structure insofar as it is reproduced.

What are the functional elements then of organisms, of bodies? They are the organs themselves. The body, writes Nietzsche, is a 'political structure', in which 'cells and tissues' 'struggle'; in which lower organs are subdued by higher ones, and the former serve as 'functions' for the latter. A body's organs, as well as the whole 'multiplicity of events within an organism' are an effect of its will to power (*WP*, pp. 348, 355). Sense organs in animals and humans serve as means of 'interpretation' (p. 360). These organs can never reproduce 'truth' itself, but can only, in interpreting the environment, yield 'errors' which are more or less functional for bodies. Thus in general 'truth' is that species of error which is most functional (i.e. contributes most to its expanded reproduction) for a given body. And human sense organs are more highly developed than those of animals insofar as they can provide interpretations, whose errors are particularly functional.

The same theme informs his differentation of the Overman, as 'a higher body' from Man:

perhaps the entire evolution of spirit is a question of the body; it is the history
of development of a higher body . . . The organic is rising to yet higher levels.
Our lust for knowledge of nature is a means through which the body desires
to perfect itself. (*WP*, p. 358)

Organs, and especially sense organs, are then absolutely
fundamental to Nietzsche's notion of the body; this stands in
sharp relief to the body 'without organs' of both Deleuze and
Foucault.

Bodies and knowledge

Nietzsche's central theme here is that human bodies develop
'beliefs' as adjuncts of their sense organs. One subset of such
beliefs concerns knowledge, in which 'truth', the 'subject', and
the logical categories are far from *a priori* or unconditioned.
They are instead inscribed on a body's organs only insofar as
they serve as resources which contribute to its expanded
reproduction. Nietzsche attempts to demolish the whole conceptual apparatus of epistemology through his critique of the
subject. His case against the 'I' (treated as the equivalent of
'ego', 'subject' and 'will') is better and more clearly put than it
is by contemporary post-structuralists (cf. e.g. Derrida 1978,
pp. 45–51). Descartes, he notes, begins from the assumption that
'thinking' exists. This itself, Nietzsche remarks, is a 'strong
belief', at best 'questionable', hardly 'indubitable'. This shaky
assumption is followed by the non-sequitur that the 'I' exists.
Even if thinking was indubitable, the argument for the 'I', would
depend on another assumption – that there must be a 'substance'
which thinks, which itself, observes Nietzsche, is dependent on a
belief in 'substance' (*WP*, secs 483–4). Nietzsche may have, with
justification, added that there is no necessity that such a
substance be the 'I'.

The subject, for Nietzsche, must be understood in terms of
perspectivism and interpretations; it is an apparent unity on the
'surface' of a body characterised by multiplicity. The later Nietzsche is an anti-positivist; he will allow no facts, only interpretations. There is no subject, no interpreter behind the
interpretations; it is instead our 'drives and needs' that interpret
the world, 'each one (with) its perspective' (*WP*, p. 267). It is the
same with 'events'; we should be able to understand events as
activities without subjects; we should be able to think of
'flashing lightning' without thinking 'lightning flashes' (*WP*,

p. 288).[3] The 'ego' then is a 'perspective illusion', an 'apparent unity that encloses everything like a horizon'. The 'evidence of the body (however) reveals a tremendous multiplicity; (we are to study these) richer phenomena as evidence for the understanding of the poorer' (*WP*, p. 281). The reason that we believe in the subject stems from our perspective; that is, such belief is functional for the expanded reproduction of human bodies. The ego's stability lends to our interpretation of the world an unchanging, ordered nature, which (though it has no necessary relation to reality), 'has helped us control and dominate over our environment'. If the ego is not in a state of being, but in a 'state of becoming', then all logic falls apart (*WP*, pp. 280–1).

Negative doctrine
In the *Nachlass* that became *The Will to Power*, the body is discussed least of all in its negative doctrine, the critique of our highest values. These latter 'slave' values are promulgated by weak bodies, or by 'classes', 'races', 'ages', 'peoples' (pp. 226–8) or weak bodies. At the same time these belief-systems assign a low value to bodies in comparison with 'spiritual' entities; that is their ethos is spiritual rather than bodily. In spite of their overall life-destroying character such values serve as resources for the expanded reproduction of weak bodies.[4] If weak bodies can convince strong ones to accept such valuations, then their life-destroying power will enable the weak to dominate the strong. Nietzsche and Nietzsche-commentators sometimes rather misleadingly speak of such slave values as forms of the will to power, and thus maintain that the will to power can be a drive which fosters a 'diminished reproduction', so to speak, of bodies. There is a confusion in such formulations of the drive (the will to power) with the *resources* over which it disposes. The drive is always towards the expanded reproduction of bodies to further the latter; the strong and the weak will make use of antithetical sets of resources.

Life-destroying value-systems can be moral, cognitive or aesthetic. In terms of morality, for example, in the Christian 'type the excitability of a degenerate body predominates'. The Christian in turn disregards the 'demands of the body', 'reduces bodily functions to moral values', 'mistreats the body (a necessity for the Christian) and prepares the ground for the sequence of "feelings of guilt"'. For this 'one has to reduce the body to a morbid and nervous condition' (*WP*, pp. 131–3). As with morality, cognitive and aesthetic realms consist of valuations. We speak for example of judgements or propositions in terms of their 'truth-value'; we evaluate research programmes as more or less progressive, more or less degenerating. In art, Nietzsche contrasts bodily and non-bodily values. He criticises his early work (in *The Birth of Tragedy*) as inscribed in a 'two-world' conception, as an 'aesthetic justification' – or 'aesthetodicy' – in which a 'will to beauty' is counterposed to the ugliness of this world. Against such Romantic, or even Modernist notions, for the later Nietzsche 'the eternally-creative' appears as the 'compulsion to destroy . . . associated with pain, (where) things assume the form of the ugly' (*WP*, p. 224). Artistic creation should, for Nietzsche, enhance the quanta of power at the disposition of the artist's body. It must function towards the expanded reproduction of bodies of consumers of art (cf. Nietzsche 1982, p. 28). Its form and content should be consistent with the bodily ethos of the Dionysian.

Summary

We have isolated, in the previous discussion, the following characteristics of Nietzsche's conception of the body.

1. All organisms or bodies are driven by a basic instinct for their own expanded reproduction, a drive towards the increase of quanta of forces under their disposition. This drive is the will to power.
2. Whether such expanded reproduction ('life-enhancement') will take place depends on a body's struggle with other external bodies, and on relations of force between struggling entities (organs, structures, values) within the body.
3. Our beliefs in 'the subject', 'truth' and the categories of logic have no objective validity. We hold these beliefs insofar as they function towards the expanded reproduction of bodies.
4. Such beliefs lend a certain (false) stability to the external world. This yields interpretations of the world that are functional for the prospering of human bodies. The beliefs attach themselves so to speak to our sense organs, to the 'surfaces of bodies'. Thus the 'I' doesn't think, but bodies think through the 'I'.
5. The spiritual (in knowledge, art and morality) is born out of

the bodily. These two principles, the spiritual and the bodily, then co-exist in a state of irreconcilable tension within the body.

6. The balance of forces between these principles underpins cognitive, aesthetic and moral discourse. For example, a Nietzschean aesthetic would value artistic creation wherein the production of art will lead to the expanded reproduction of bodies of both producer and consumer. Such art would break with the predominance of the (Apollonian) signifier to carry a bodily message through bodily forms.

7. Slave moralities which are non-bodily in content, attach themselves to weak bodies or groupings of weak bodies, because they function in *their* expanded reproduction. The weak are able to impose such value-systems on stronger bodies who are enfeebled and thus come under the domination of the former. Such moralities are life-destroying, however, for the species. Given values can be life-destroying (for the species) at one point in time and life-enhancing at another.

Concluding Remarks

A theory of the body is important for social theory, and in particular for action, as distinct from structural, approaches to sociology (Lash and Urry 1984). In (at least) Continental philosophy, there has been a shift in the locus of agency from the mind to the body. Thus we can understand Merleau-Ponty's theory in which the body is an intentional agent. Sartre, as well, criticised his own earlier position as being overly Cartesian in nature, and in *The Critique of Dialectical Reason* and subsequent work on Flaubert adopted a number of Freudian precepts which in effect relocated the bases of action towards the body. Even theology was not untouched by this shift as Karl Rahner – whose work is of some influence in contemporary Catholicism – re-read Aquinas partly through Heideggarian spectacles, entailing an anti-dualism which involved a fundamental revaluation of the body. To stress the centrality of the body of the unconscious for *sociological* action theory is hardly novel. Parsons, crucially influenced by Freud, came to understand the unconscious as the interface of structure and agency. Goffman consistently maintained that the 'presentation of self' took place largely apart from our conscious strategies. The influential action theory of Pierre Bourdieu features the notion of the 'habitus' which is clearly below the level of discursive unconsciousness.

I think that the importance of 'genealogy' – of the work of Foucault, Deleuze and Nietzsche – is partly by way of its potential contribution to the development of such a sociology of action. To work out such a theory is beyond the scope of this chapter. But let me briefly draw on the three writers discussed here to delineate a few guidelines. Such a theory should first of all enable us to account for the effects of social structures on agency, and at the same time provide a critique of extant social structures. It is here that Foucault's special genius lies. On a number of counts Nietzsche and Foucault are engaged in the same enterprise. For both of them discourse (values) exert power over bodies. For both, discourse can exercise such power either directly on bodies, or through souls ('bad conscience'). For both, one important effect of such powers of discourse is to individuate, to 'invent subjects', which are attached, so to speak, to bodies. Nietzsche's indications of how power acts on bodies are, however, even on a generous reading, incomplete. He, first, mainly discusses the body *not* in the context of how discourse acts on it, but in terms of how it can use discourse. Moreover, even when values are dysfunctional for bodies, Nietzsche does not relate them to forms of society, but sees them restrictively as values of slave classes. Foucault provides remedies for both of these insufficiencies. It is by substituting power (power not in Weber's sense of the Same being an extension of the Other's will; but power as the Other itself, be it as absolutist monarch or 'the people') for the slave classes that Foucault can avoid the aristocratic ethos of Nietzsche's genealogy, as well as Nietzsche's brand of methodological individualism. It has been necessary, thus, for Foucault to 'twist Nietzsche out of shape' in order to provide bodies with practical and critical weapons; resources which he has most visibly supplied to those in penal institutions and their advocates, but also for bodies in psychiatric institutions, and those subject to medical discourse in general. It may be that Foucault's genealogy in the end will be of greatest use to feminists, especially in struggles around sexuality. Taken together, *Madness and Civilization* and *The History of Sexuality* can yield a portrait of the female body which has since the onset of Modernity, been structured – by discourse on mental health and sexuality – along familial lines. The effects of such structuration have been, arguably, to invent a female sexuality and subjectivity (and the inventors surely have been men) which in turn acts, as a bad conscience or 'soul', as a 'prison-house' on the bodies of women.

Secondly, in such a theory the body should possess some positive, libidinal driving force. That such a force is largely absent, as I argued above, in the work of Foucault, is confirmed by the latter during an interview (Foucault 1983). Here he described his *oeuvre* in terms of recounting the price man has had to pay for his pursuit of self-knowledge. Foucault put this characterisation in context by contrasting it with the life's work of Deleuze which he saw as working out a notion of more positive force in the concept of 'desire'. For Deleuze, the body is the surface of intersection between libidinal forces, on the one hand, and 'external', social forces on the other. It is the interplay of these forces which gives the body its shape and its specific qualities. For Deleuze and Guattari libido itself is socially structured by the global characteristics of the social, acting through the mediation of significant groups, like the family. The authors of *Anti-Oedipus* have added to genealogy's critical power by their alternative prescriptions for the investment of psychic energy. The central proposal here is that we should *not* understand libidinal investment in non-familial persons and objects as symbolic investment in the family. The uses of these notions are not confined to the criticism of orthodox psychoanalysis and psychiatry. The gay movement can find a resource in such a non-normalised understanding of identification and cathexes; feminists in the alternative provided to Lacanian phallocentrism; anti-racialists in its censure of the segregative subject and its alternative serial identification.

I think that Nietzsche's biological view of the body should be rejected, partly because we do not experience our bodies in such terms. A theory of the body should include, however, some set of mechanisms with which the body reproduces itself. This is the value of Nietzsche's contribution, which is at the same time a criticism of Merleau-Ponty's understanding of the body. Here we can conceive of the body's unity and intentionality as resources created by the body in the interests of its own reproduction. Moreover, Nietzsche's Dionysian aesthetics of the body look forward to postmodernism in the arts, in which –

from Dali and Bunuel to Sylvia Plath and Peter Brook –
the unconscious has come to be the dominant organising principle.

Notes

I would like to thank Roy Boyne, Brian Longhurst, an unnamed German Nietzsche scholar, and Mike Featherstone for their comments on a previous draft of this chapter.

1. This is made clear in Deleuze's contemporaneously delivered (1978) paper, 'Nomad thought', in which of the 'three moderns' Nietzsche is pitted as a 'dawning of the counter culture' against 'Marxian' and 'Freudian bureaucracies'.

2. I shall draw extensively on *The Will to Power* in the following discussion. *The Will to Power* consists of material from Nietzsche's notebooks which were edited and published posthumously. These notebooks which date from 1883 to 1889 contain the basis for most of Nietzsche's work after *Thus Spake Zarathustra*; for *Beyond Good and Evil, The Genealogy of Morals, The Antichrist* and *Twilight of the Idols*. Ideas which are presented in a literary form in these latter works, often only through rhetorical hints, are spelt out and argued for in the notebooks. Because it was not Nietzsche himself who edited and published the notebooks, there are some, though arguably not major, problems with their validity. Thus I shall make no claims as to Nietzsche's concept of the body which are inconsistent with the published work of 1883 to 1889; indeed all the points I shall make are at least touched upon in this published work.

3. Deleuze adopts this notion of 'event' in *Logique du sens*; see above.

4. Let me emphasise at this point that I am not maintaining that most of Nietzsche's discussion or moralities *is* phrased in such terms, however, and the rest of his treatment of moralities is consistent with such a conceptual framework. Equally, in this chapter I use the term 'body' much more frequently than Nietzsche, who as I mentioned above spoke in more general context, in which 'the organic', 'the organism' and 'physiology' play as great a role as 'the body'. My usage of the body is in this section, nonetheless, consistent with Nietzsche's usage, as well as with his more general notions of 'the organic' and 'physiology'.

References

Barthes, R. (1975) *The Pleasure of the Text*, NY: Hill and Wang.
Barthes, R. (1979) *A Lover's Discourse, Fragments*, London: Cape.
Bouchard, D. (ed.) (1977) *Michel Foucault: Language, Counter-Memory, Practice*, Oxford: Blackwell.
Deleuze, G. (1969a) *Différence et répétition*, Paris: PUF.
Deleuze, G. (1969b) *Logique du sens*, Paris: Editions de Minuit.
Deleuze, G. (1978) 'Nomad Thought', *Semiotexte*, 3(1): 12–20; trans of 'Pensée nomade', *Nietzsche aujourd'hui*, Paris: UGE 10/18 (1973).
Deleuze, G. (1981) *Francis Bacon, logique de la sensation*, Paris: Editions de la différence.

Deleuze, G. (1983) *Nietzsche and Philosophy*, London: Athlone Press; trans of *Nietzsche et la philosophie*, Paris: PUF (1962).

Deleuze, G. and Foucault, M. (1967) Foreword to F. Nietzsche, *Oeuvres philosophiques complètes: Le gai savoir*, trans Pierre Klossowski, Paris.

Deleuze, G. and Foucault, M. (1977) 'Intellectuals and Power', in D. Bouchard (ed.), *Language, Counter-Memory, Practice*, Oxford: Blackwell; trans of 1972 interview.

Deleuze, G. and Guattari, F. (1977) *Anti-Oedipus, Capitalism and Schizophrenia*, New York: Viking (trans by R. Hurley et al. from *L'Anti-Oedipe*, Paris, 1972).

Deleuze, G. and Guattari, F. (1980) *Mille plateaux, capitalisme et schizophrénie*, Paris: Edition de Minuit.

Derrida, J. (1978) '*Cognito* and the History of Madness', in *Writing and Difference*, London: Routledge.

Descombes, V. (1980) *Modern French Philosophy*, Cambridge University Press.

Dreyfus, H.L. and Rabinow, P. (1982) *Michel Foucault, Beyond Structuralism and Hermeneutics*, Brighton: Harvester.

Foucault, M. (1964) 'La Prose d'Actéon', *Nouvelle Revue Français*, 135: 444–59.

Foucault, M. (1965) *Madness and Civilization*, NY; trans of abridged version of *Folie et déraison. Histoire de la folie a l'age classique* (1961).

Foucault, M. (1967) 'Nietzsche, Freud, Marx', in Cahiers du Royaumont, *Nietzsche*, Paris: Editions de Minuit.

Foucault, M. (1970) *The Order of Things*, London: Tavistock; trans of *Les Mots et les choses*, Paris: Gallimard (1966).

Foucault, M. (1971) *L'ordre du discours*, Paris: Gallimard.

Foucault, M. (1972) *The Archaeology of Knowledge*, London: Tavistock; trans of *L'archéologie du savoir*, Paris: Gallimard (1969).

Foucault, M. (1973a) *Birth of the Clinic*, London: Tavistock; trans of *Naissance de la clinique. Une archéologie du regard medical* (1963).

Foucault, M. (1973b) 'Présentation', in *Moi, Pierre Rivière . . .*, Paris.

Foucault, M. (1977a) *Discipline and Punish*, Harmondsworth: Penguin; trans of *Surveillir et punir, Naissance de la prison*, Paris: Gallimard (1975).

Foucault, M. (1977b) Preface to G. Deleuze and F. Guattari, *Anti-Oedipus*, New York.

Foucault, M. (1977c) 'Nietzsche, Genealogy, History', in D. Bouchard (ed.), *Language, Counter-Memory and Practice*, Oxford: Blackwell (trans from an essay which appeared in *Hommage à Jean Hippolyte*, Paris, 1971).

Foucault, M. (1977d) 'Theatrum Philosophicum', in D. Bouchard (ed.), *Language Counter-Memory, Practice*, Oxford: Blackwell (trans from an essay which appeared in *Critique* 282, 1970).

Foucault, M. (1980a) *The History of Sexuality*, Vol. 1, NY: Vintage; trans of *La volonté de savoir, Histoire de la sexualité*, Paris: Gallimard (1976).

Foucault, M. (1980b) 'Truth and Power', interview published in C. Gordon (ed.), *Michel Foucault, Power/Knowledge*, Brighton: Harvester.

Foucault, M. (1983) 'Structuralism and Post-Structuralism: An Interview', *Telos*, 55 (Spring): 195–211.

Freud, S. (1958) *Psycho-Analytic Notes on an Autobiographical Account of a Case of Paranoia (Dementia Paranoides)*, Standard Edition, Vol. 12, London: Hogarth Press.

Habermas, J. (1981) 'Modernity versus Postmodernity', *New German Critique*, 22: 3–14.

Klein, M. (1932) *The Psycho-Analysis of Children*, London: Hogarth Press.

Lacan, J. (1958a) 'Les Formations de l'inconscient', *Bulletin de Psychologie*, 12(4): 250–6.

Lacan, J. (1958b) 'D'une question preliminaire à tout traitement possible de la psychose', *La Psychanalyse*, IV: 1–50.

Lash, S. and Urry, J. (1984) 'The New Marxism of Collective Action: A Critical Analysis', *Sociology*, 18(1).

Leigh, J. (1978) 'Free Nietzsche', *Semiotexte*, 3(1): 1–6.

Major-Poetzl, P. (1983) *Michel Foucault's Archaeology of Western Culture*, Brighton: Harvester.

Nietzsche, F. (1956a) *The Birth of Tragedy*, trans F. Golffing, NY: Anchor; orig. German edition 1872.

Nietzsche, F. (1956b) *The Genealogy of Morals*, trans F. Golffing, NY: Anchor.

Nietzsche, F. (1961) *Thus Spake Zarathustra*, trans R. Hollingdale, Harmondsworth: Penguin; orig. German edition 1883–92.

Nietzsche, F. (1966) *Werke in drei Bänden*, Munich: Carl Hauser Verlag.

Nietzsche, F. (1968a) *The Will to Power*, NY: Vintage.

Nietzsche, F. (1968b) *Twilight of the Idols, the Antichrist*, trans R. Hollingdale, Harmondsworth: Penguin; orig. German edition of *Twilight and Antichrist* 1888.

Nietzsche, F. (1973) *Beyond Good and Evil*, trans R. Hollingdale, Harmondsworth: Penguin; orig. German edition 1886.

Nietzsche, F. (1974) *The Gay Science*, trans W. Kaufmann, NY; orig. German edition 1882.

Nietzsche, F. (1982) *Daybreak*, trans R. Hollingdale, Cambridge: Cambridge University Press; orig. German edition 1881.

Racevskis, K. (1983) *Michel Foucault and the Subversion of the Intellect*, Ithaca: Cornell University Press.

Rycroft, C. (1972) *A Critical Dictionary of Psychoanalysis*, Harmondsworth: Penguin.

Seem, M. (1977) 'Introduction to Deleuze and Guattari', *Anti-Oedipus*, New York.

Sheridan, A. (1980) *Michel Foucault: The Will to Truth*, London: Tavistock.

Turkle, S. (1979) *Psychoanalytic Politics*, London: Burnett.

Wilden, A. (1968) Commentary in J. Lacan, *Speech and Language in Psychoanalysis*, Baltimore: Johns Hopkins University Press.

This chapter first appeared in *Theory, Culture & Society*, Vol. 2 (1984), 1–18.

11

THE ART OF THE BODY IN THE DISCOURSE OF POSTMODERNITY

Roy Boyne

Introduction

It has been suggested that postmodernism can be described as a culture of ontological doubt, and that therefore the key shift from modernism has been the replacement of the plurality of interpretation by the exploration of multiple realities, each one as inherently meaningless or meaningful as any other. We may also refer here to Lyotard's (1971) parallel distinction between discourse and figure. Even though such views may be too simple — for we are not yet beyond discourse, nor beyond the conflict of interpretations — the notion that the postmodern sensibility involves a shift of emphasis from epistemology to ontology, if it is understood as a *deprivileging* shift from knowledge to experience, from theory to practice, from mind to body, is one that is, as far as any such notion can be, broadly correct.

I do not wish to say that the art of the body is the art of post-modernism, nor do I wish to label Francis Bacon as *the* postmodern artist, nor, finally, am I centrally concerned with distinguishing the modernist and postmodernist moments in his work — although, inevitably, there will be something of the latter in what follows. What I want to argue is that the postmodern sensibility and the art of Francis Bacon have a certain affinity, and that the work of Francis Bacon can reveal certain facets of our contemporary culture *in a much more persuasive way than even the best sociological commentaries because his work encourages experience rather than 'mere' knowledge of the world he depicts.*

With its suspicion of any notion of a single objective world the postmodern sensibility will tend to be exercised on the past as well as the present (notions which the postmodern sensibility will place, as Derrida would say, *under erasure*), on Goya or Baselitz, Hegel or

Baudrillard, Silicon Valley or the Greek city state. In the space of a single chapter, I cannot hope to do anything but exemplify this thesis, and I do this in the realm of painting by presenting a practical exercise with a work by Mondrian.

The fact that the postmodern aesthetic sensibility is with us, however, means that it also has its effect on cultural production in the widest sense. Although I am concerned almost exclusively with art, in this chapter, some mention has to be made of the social condition that supports the postmodern aesthetic. The key sociological concept is that of *progress*. The key social event was World War II, which for millions of people was the ultimate illustration of the death of God. The postmodern condition derives from the desperate search for the meaning that will validate the effort and striving to progress, which still defines the Western socialization process from start to finish, combined with the knowledge or feeling that all findings are bogus, all results falsified, all products disposable.

I explore this, only at the edges, by fastening onto the work of Francis Bacon. Bacon is taken as an icon *only within this chapter*. Although his work is highly susceptible to the postmodern aesthetic sensibility, a definitive characterization of his work as postmodern is not possible: to attempt this would be a category mistake not least because the postmodern sensibility rejects epistemological certainty.

The Interpretation of Art
From a formal point of view, there are three principal ways in which a modern artwork may be understood. The first of these ways locates the work within the history of art. Reference here will be made to genres and predecessors. Such reference may be either positive or negative, affirming continuity or rejection. Postmodern architecture is exemplary in this respect. It rests upon an aesthetics which combines homage and historical disrespect. A comment from Charles Moore, on his Piazza d'Italia in New Orleans, illustrates the simultaneous working of both attitudes:

> I remembered that the architectural orders were Italian, with a little help from the Greeks, and so we thought we could put Tuscan, Doric, Ionic and Corinthian columns over the fountain, but they overshadowed it, obliterating the shape of Italy. So instead we added a 'Delicatessan Order' that we thought could resemble sausages hanging in a shop window. (Moore in Jencks, 1980: 20)

A focus on genres also opens the way to grammars of art, to a structuralist approach which would work toward an *explanation* of works of art, construing an individual work as a statement within a discursive system. Such an approach might be seen as having the potential to solve the question of what successful art is, in the same way that the grammar of a language, if fully specified, would unambiguously determine the systemic propriety of any statement. The disadvantage of the internally systemic approach, whether of the historicist or structuralist kind, is that questions of meaning and ideology become, at best, peripheral.

The second way in which the modern artwork may be understood looks to its place within the present conjuncture: what is the *function* of the work within the culture? The link between the artwork and the cultural totality brings both normative and referential questions to the fore. Questions of meaning and socio-political acceptability arise. The debate between Kandinsky and the Constructivists, which took place in Russia in the early 1920s, shows just how central the interconnected issues of function, meaning and artistic obligation may become. Kandinsky was the champion of the spiritual purity of the individual artist, against the Constructivist demand for social relevance, but he nevertheless spoke the language of meaning and duty:

> The artist has a triple responsibility to the non-artists: (1) he must repay the talent which he has; (2) his deeds, feelings and thoughts, as those of every man, create a spiritual atmosphere which is either pure or poisonous. (3) These deeds and thoughts are materials for his creations . . . (Kandinsky, 1977: 54–5)

Kandinsky's inner-directed asceticism, and the materialism of the Constructivists, are different variations on the same logical structure of duty, function and meaning. In both cases, the artistic imagination is stamped on the world in the terms of a particular ideology. It is the relation between art and politics that is at stake in apparently rational debates over function and meaning.

To be precise, it is only to the second way that the term 'understanding' can be properly applied, for it is here that the intellect strives to grasp the whole under the deceptive sign of objectivity and truth. The power of the first way rests on the reassurance of the familiar, the force of convention and the supremacy of the idealized standard.

The third form of understanding is, correctly speaking, not understanding at all. For it is not the intellect that is engaged, but the body, with its more or less repressed sensual faculties, and along its more or less compressed emotional range. The sculptor has fabulous potential here, producing work that would never be released: at the limit, the artist's experience of touching, holding, moulding would not be relinquished. We are speaking here, not of what the work means, nor about how it measures up to some Platonic ideal, but rather about what it does: the embodied reaction that it summons up for both artist and audience. Psychoanalysis has been of particular importance in understanding this dimension of art. But the theorization of the psychic and sensual aspects of art can effect a withdrawal, into discourse, from these aspects. For example, the psychoanalytically grounded explanations of Jackson Pollock's work engender an intellectual rather than an embodied reaction to it. They function as devices of distantiation, raising questions of meaning and making the work something to be understood as well as experienced. But the general western presumption of the superiority of mind over body may result in the eclipse of the embodied reaction by the intellect.

Kaiser and Mondrian

Can there be a discourse on art which is not obstructive of the embodied experience of art, which on the contrary, can help to elicit that form of involvement in the artwork? Or should we banish all but the children from the galleries of the West?

The argument of this chapter is that discourse can be deployed in such a way as to allow the embodied experience of art to take its place as one of the most valuable ways of 'understanding' art. This argument will not depend upon logically compelling demonstrations of this or that truth, but rather upon (and in the nature of the case there can be no guarantees here) the disclosure of existentially significant effects arising out of an interplay between art and text.

Much of what follows will be concerned with the work of Francis Bacon, and with the commentaries on that work by Bacon himself, and by Gilles Deleuze. But it may be thought that Bacon's work is so much of the body that to take it as the only example would be just a little too easy, So, first of all, I want to suggest the possibility of experiencing the work of Piet Mondrian — geometric artist and theorist of abstract art, whose work was seen by, for example, Pollock and de Kooning as uninvolving and cold — in a psychic-sensual kind of way. This will be done by placing some of his work in apposition to an extract from *Gas II*, a play, published in 1920, by Georg Kaiser.

It need not be a question of looking to see if the meaning behind the text can illuminate the meaning behind the paintings; it can be a question of *slipping inside* the one (in this case the text may be more accessible) and then across into the other. With what result? The situated experience of monotony and linearity within the factory facilitates a movement into the painting itself, makes possible travel along its lines. Once there, one experiences a sequence of elation and despair, promise and fear: the safety of the line versus the threat of the space, the exhilaration of turning a corner into a different colour; but soon the exhaustion, the insufficiency, and the first steps away from the line and into the void (steps which ineluctably led the body rather than the mind in the direction of colour field painting). How else, but from being enclosed within the paintings themselves, could Mondrian cry, 'Oh the work, it is so hard'? (Carmean, 1979: 38). Why else would Rothko end his life, if not from the realization that the field is empty? And how prejudicial and narrowly intellectual a statement is the following from van Doesburg seen to be: 'It is alright for [Mondrian] to use the diagonal. It means, however, he has not understood neo-plasticism' (Carmean, 1979: 35).

There are two particularly important differences between the embodied experience of an artwork and the other two forms of understanding. In the first place, the question of representation is absolutely central to any theory of art which is within the horizon of the first two forms of understanding. Where the emphasis is on genre, the quest is for the perfect representation of the generic ideal; where the emphasis is placed upon function and meaning, the quest is for representations of the world, whether in its surface detail or in its deep structures (in this respect the work of Goya and Rothko, for example, is strictly comparable, the difference between them being that the latter seeks to represent the ineffable depth of the world, while the former will lead us along its damaged surface). Secondly, and following from the centrality of representation, the first two forms of understanding are judgmental.

Paradigmatically, then, the art critic is a judge of representations for whom the embodied experience of art will be at best peripheral. Although it is not being claimed that the three different forms of understanding correspond strictly to three types of art, and, indeed, the point of the brief examination of Mondrian was partly to show that this claim is not being made, different artworks do incline themselves in one of the three directions rather than another. So far

Act One

Concrete hall. Light cascading from arc-lamps. From the hazy height of the dome a cluster of wires vertically down to the iron platform and thence distributed to small iron tables — three right, three left. The wires coloured red to the left — green to the right. At each table a BLUE FIGURE *– sitting stiffly in uniform staring at a glass panel in the table, which — red left, green right — colours the face as it lights up. Slantwise across the front of the stage a longish iron table with a chequered top, in which green and red plugs are being manipulated by the first* BLUE FIGURE. *Silence.*

SECOND BLUE FIGURE: (*Before red-glowing panel*) Report from third battle sector: enemy concentration growing.
(Panel-light fades. FIRST BLUE FIGURE crossplugs red contact)
FIFTH BLUE FIGURE: (*before green-glowing panel*) Report from third workshop: production one point below quota.
(Panel-light fades. FIRST BLUE FIGURE crossplugs green contact)
THIRD BLUE FIGURE: (before red-glowing panel) report from second battle sector: enemy concentration growing.
(Panel-light fades. FIRST BLUE FIGURE crossplugs red contact)
SIXTH BLUE FIGURE: (before green-glowing panel) Report from second workshop: production one point below quota.
(Panel-light fades. FIRST BLUE FIGURE crossplugs green contact)
FOURTH BLUE FIGURE. (before red-glowing panel) Report from first battle sector: enemy concentration growing. (Kaiser, 1985: 245–6)

*   *   *

Figure 11.1 *Piet Mondrian,* Composition with Red, Yellow, and Blue *(c. 1937–42)*

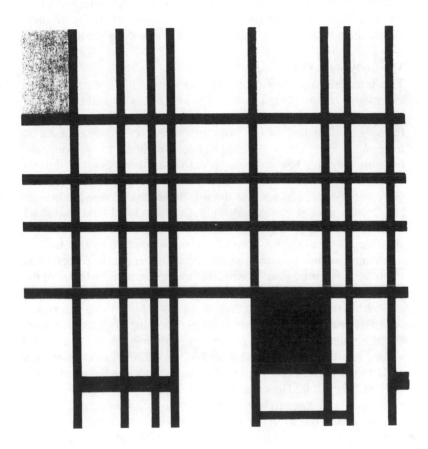

*   *   *

as painting is concerned, I wish to describe those works that tend toward the body and away from the intellect as postmodern. This is a usage that, in some ways, differs from the pronouncements of Jean-François Lyotard who seems to find the categories of judgment and representation (even though given a new twist by subordinating them to a reinterpreted notion of the sublime) unavoidable.

The Body of the Other
The term 'representation' is hard to avoid; the experience and knowledge of one thing standing for another is central to much of western culture. There are lacunae, however. Foucault (1967) found such a hiatus in his work on madness: the discourses on unreason fail to capture the experience of madness itself. Foucault, of course, argued that this was never their intent. Science did not subject madness to the bright light of reason; it denied madness as valid experience, and set free the minds which had passed through the Otherness of madness only when they also would live that same denial. It may have been possible to summon madness, without simultaneously denying it (and thereby repudiating the task of implicating in madness anyone who could not resist the journey), in the time of Hieronymous Bosch. But today such presentation of the thing itself is much harder, we do not think in such ways. We tend, as Baudrillard (1983) has explained, to look at one thing in terms of another; and this process never stops. Nothing is granted reality. All is simulation, with no ground or stopping place for ultimate value. There is no Other, and social process is infinite deferment and ubiquitous deference. In such circumstances, is not representation the heart of it? How can we avoid such a force, if it is *the* organ which must not cease to beat. The notion of representation, however, invites the question, 'If this is secondary, what is first?' Thus ordinal matters are invoked from the start. Because, in the present era, *all* is representation (a Sophistical position whose unassailability led Plato to repudiate art itself), the answer to the question, 'What is first?' can only be evasive. Thus, if we wish to avoid complicity with the culture of evasion which we inhabit, we have to stop asking the question. We must finish with representation and the political cowardice that it now connotes (which brings up the question of *real* democracy, which cannot be pursued here). So let us return to art and the body.

Consider Expressionism. It was, we may say, concerned with the Other. Its desire was to move aside the curtains of a seductively velvet but synthetic objectivity, and so to expose a view from which we are normally screened. In a world of deceptive appearance, however, such a view is hard to attain. It will not be a question of seeing it, but rather of being oneself through it, of abolishing the difference of quiddity in an expanded subjectivity. The entry in Kafka's (1972) diary, 4 May 1915, can be taken as an illustration:

> In a better state because I read Strindberg (*Separated*). I don't read him to read him, but rather to lie on his breast. He holds me on his left arm like a child. I sit there like a man on a statue. Ten times I almost slip off, but at the eleventh attempt I sit there firmly, feel secure, and have a wide view.

A representational understanding of that passage from Kafka would be similar to a naively objectivist interpretation of a Magritte canvas, echoing the child who asks, 'What's that train doing in the fireplace?' We are dealing, then, with experienced conditions of being, rather than statements of fact. So, contrary to what might first be thought, a certain naivete is necessary, in particular a certain prerational kind of co-existence with the world. A child reading Kafka's (1961) *Metamorphosis* becomes the beetle, feels the hard shell, and wakes in the night, shivering and frightened with the horror of it. A sophisticated intelligence has already developed the means of repressing this physical involvement; it is sufficient to ask what the text means, or to assign the text to some literary genre.

There are certain traditions in which one finds a determined refusal to name the Other. Judaism is one example; the tradition of Enlightenment rationalism is another, although in the latter case the motivation for the refusal is rather different. In an age of pluralization where suspicion of metanarratives has become an increasingly dominant cultural characteristic, prohibitions against the specification of the Other grow weak. This is understandable since the field of the Other unless dispersed through a process of multiple specification remains a site of totalizing potential and metanarrativistic desire. One of the current specifications of otherness today pertains to the body. In certain of Francis Bacon's paintings, otherness is meat.

The Architecture of Butchery
In 1966, Bacon wrote: 'We are meat, we are potential carcasses. If I go into a butcher's shop I always think it's surprising that I wasn't there instead of the animal' (Sylvester, 1980:46). What is the difference between animal meat and human flesh, between the twist of

the spine in a Degas painting and the bones on the plate at the end of a meal? For the rational mind this is an absurd and even disgusting question, the spectres of cannibalism and mass slaughter confirm the greatest possible moral divide. But beyond the rules of division between human and beast, and beyond the meaning of life, is there difference? Is there not a profound parallel between the regime of the abattoir and the ritual of the crucifixion? The similarity works both ways, as the suffering animals take on a human and moral identity. The idea that suffering is a basic form of Being is hardly a new one, but the innovation wrought by Francis Bacon is to communicate this directly through and to the body by focusing on the body as meat and bone. Deleuze puts it like this: 'Have pity for meat! . . . Meat is not dead flesh, it has preserved every torment and assumed the colours of living flesh . . . Bacon does not say, "Pity the beasts", but rather everyone who suffers is meat' (Deleuze, 1984, Vol.2: 20).

If poststructuralism turns on the principle of undecidability, as Derrida's critique of structuralism might indicate, then, for Deleuze, Bacon is *the* poststructuralist artist, for he paints in that area of indeterminacy between life and death, between flesh and meat, between human being and the beast. There is even something more profound about such a Deleuzian-Baconian delineation of poststructuralism than the Foucauldian emphasis on the body. Foucault will speak of the distribution and redistribution of bodies, of the refinement, development and focusing of their powers, and of their medical and neurological redefinition, which all amounts to a sociologization of the body. Bacon, on the other hand, through a pulpy deconstruction of language will direct us to the mouth, a side-to-side slash in a mass of suffering meat, bone, blood and nerve:

> What, personally, I would like to do would be, for instance, to make portraits which were portraits but came out of things which really had nothing to do with what is called the illustrational facts of the image; . . . if the thing seems to come off at all, it comes off because of a kind of darkness which the otherness of shape which isn't known, as it were, conveys to it . . . you could draw the mouth right across the face as though it was almost like the opening of the whole head, and yet it could be like the mouth. (Sylvester, 1980: 105–7)

Bacon himself does not fully understand how such effects are achieved. His image of the process is of a tightrope walk between

Figure 11.2 *Francis Bacon,* Triptych August 1972 *(left panel)*

Reproduced by kind permission of the artist. © Tate Gallery, London.

Figure 11.3   *Francis Bacon,* Triptych August 1972 *(centre panel)*

figuration and abstraction, and this poorly defined area is seen as a part of the territory of the nervous system. When we say that someone is 'on edge', or, more dramatically, that someone is 'on the edge', a particular range of bodily states is conjured up. Bacon will ask us to consider these, not as abstractions or theorizations, nor as images or symbolizations, but as specimens of embodied nervousness. On edge while he paints, Bacon will link his nerves to ours. As he said in a recent interview, 'each artist . . . works according to his own nervous system' (Gilder, 1983: 18).

Perhaps a view of reality as tunes on irritated nerves is defensible. It would certainly make sense for the victims of the dental disorders pictured in a medical text which was one of Bacon's formative influences. But, of course, he is not unaware of other visions of reality. The following is not uninstructive in this respect:

> I've lived through two world wars and I suppose those things have some influence on me. I also remember, very well, growing up in Ireland, the whole thing of the Sinn Fein movement. I remember when my father used to say — this is when people were being shot all around — 'If they come tonight, just keep your mouth shut and don't say anything.' And I had a grandmother who was married to the head of the police in County Kildare and used to live with windows sandbagged all the time, and we used to dig ditches across the road so the cars would go into them. (Gilder, 1983: 17–18)

The sociologist would normally seek to connect Bacon's painting to his politically spectacular upbringing (he even left Ireland to go and live in Weimar Berlin). But how can we connect such a personal history to the project of painting on our nerves, and to the aleatory painting technique which results in the communication of the feeling in the meat? There is no simple connection, such as the one found in the experience of Joseph Beuys who, saved from a frozen death by fat and felt, went on to work with these materials as an artist. We can, no doubt, attain a high degree of understanding of Bacon's work by documenting his homosexuality, the influences upon him, and his realization (in common with millions of others) that the world is a place of pain and butchery. Such understandings can help us to become a part of the work that Bacon creates, but they can also get in the way of sensation, obstructing the connection which makes for temporary coalescence of art and audience, of object and subject.

Bacon has often remarked that narration gets in the way of sensation. For this reason, the catalogue of his 1985 exhibition at the Tate Gallery contained no explanatory commentary upon the pictures which were reproduced there. For Bacon, that way lies boredom. His refusal of narration goes much further, extending to the subjects of all his work: faces, single figures, couples locked in a kind of presocial embrace. None of these pictures is meant to tell a story, for stories are evasions. So it is that Bacon claims that the violence of war is not represented in his work. Although he accepts that his work is about violence, and that it is produced in search of a certain truth, that truth and that violence lie within the image, within the paint, rather than in the events or characters which might be taken as forming the subject of the work. But there is little doubt that Bacon is the most illuminating commentator on his own work, and therein lies the paradox. At its simplest, it can be put like this, that those few paintings which are given informative titles (consider, for example, *Three Studies for Figures at the Base of a Crucifixion* or *Triptych Inspired by T. S. Eliot's Poem 'Sweeney Agonistes'*) owe part of their power to generate sensation in the viewer to the narrative effect of the title. The effect of that minimal narration is to deepen the physical response. It can be argued that the same is true for Bacon's portraits, that some of the profoundest physical response will be found in viewers who have listened to the pertinent elements of the story of Bacon's struggle with the head. The pictures themselves cannot constitute a self-sufficient language; that modernist dream was never realized. This is not to say that Bacon's words form the only mechanism for channelling and forming the physical response, but it is to say that some mechanism is necessary, some discursive complement to the pure figure, because the pure figure does not exist: Bacon's work as a whole attests to the realization of that fact.

If explicit narration will obstruct the process of sensual communcation, some less explicit mechanism is required: suggestions rather than didacticism, experience rather than logical plot. The personal world of a viewer of Bacon's paintings may be constructed in such a way that it may fulfil the supplementary discursive function; then the paintings, freed from titling, authorship, narrative accompaniment, will have their effect. Bacon's art may aspire to a universal communication (a residual modernism does have its place in his body of work), but such aspirations are no longer tenable. If the paintings are to provide a temporary completion of the partial and decentred subjectivity of the viewer, it is necessary that there be a junction. If such a locking device is not pregiven within the

Figure 11.4 *Francis Bacon,* Three Studies for Figures at the
Base of a Crucifixion 1944 *(right panel)*

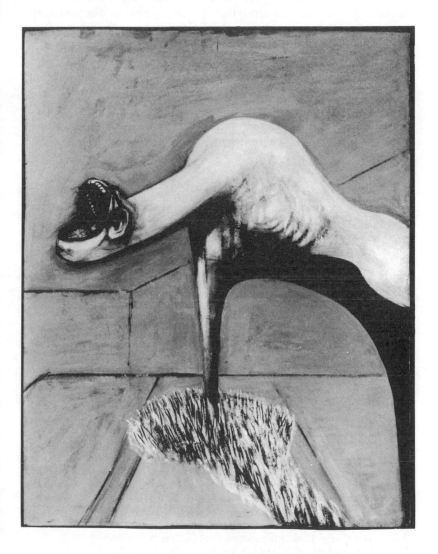

viewing subject, then it has to be created (the ambience of an exhibition space, the persuasive rhetoric of the artist, an unexpected juxtaposition between picture and text, these are just some of the ways of creating receptivity). This is the heart of the postmodern condition, that the subject needs to be processed to completion.

Another side of this rather more humble conception of the subject is our corporeality, our untranscendable condition of being edible. If the separation of subject and object was the achievement of the age of reason, and the desubjectification of the world was the secret of modernism, then postmodernism marks the return of the subject, but cut down to size, packaged in plastic, and offered for consumption complete with instructions for preparation and a sell-by date.

Note

The illustrations which appear here are reproduced by kind permission of The Tate Gallery.

In order of appearance, they are:

Figure 1. Piet Mondrian, *Composition with Red, Yellow, and Blue*
Figure 2. Francis Bacon, *Triptych August* 1972 (left panel)
Figure 3. Ibid., (centre panel)
Figure 4. Francis Bacon, *Three Studies for Figures at the Base of a Crucifixion 1944* (right panel)

References

Baudrillard, Jean (1983) *Simulations*. New York: Semiotext(e).

Carmean, E. A. Jr. (1979) *Mondrian: the Diamond Compositions*. Washington: National Gallery of Art.

Deleuze, Gilles (1984) *Logique de la sensation*. (two vols), Paris: Editions de la Différence.

Foucault, Michel (1967) *Madness and Civilization*. London: Tavistock.

Gilder, Joshua (1983) 'I Think about Death Every Day'. Interview with Francis Bacon, *Flash Art* 112 (May).

Jencks, Charles (1980) *Post-Modern Classicism*. London: Architectural Design and Academy Editions.

Kafka, Franz (1961) *Metamorphosis and Other Stories*. Harmondsworth: Penguin.

Kafka, Franz (1972) *The Diaries of Franz Kafka* (edited by Max Brod). Harmondsworth: Penguin.

Kaiser, Georg (1985) *Plays Volume One*. London: Calder.

Kandinsky, Wassily (1977) *Concerning the Spiritual in Art*. New York: Dover.

Lash, Scott (1985) 'Postmodernity and Desire', *Theory and Society* 14 (1).

Lyotard, Jean-François (1971) *Discours, figure*. Paris: Klincksieck.

McHale, Brian (1987) *Postmodernist Fiction*. London: Methuen.

Sylvester, David (1980) *Interviews with Francis Bacon, 1962–1979*. London: Thames and Hudson.

This chapter first appeared in *Theory, Culture & Society*, Vol. 5 (1988), 527–42.

12

LOVE'S LABOUR LOST?
A SOCIOLOGICAL VIEW

Margareta Bertilsson

Love is seldom regarded as a proper sociological topic, and traditionally it falls within the realm of the psychology of emotions. In this chapter I seek to illuminate the social aspects of love via a discussion of some of the major sociological theories.

If we review the status of love in social theory, it appears as (a) an *instrumental* agency making social development possible and (b) a *functional* device making social integration possible. The Marxist tradition, generally, has tended to view love as the ideological component of the reproduction of surplus labour. Max Weber viewed love and the modern culture of eroticism as *Ersatz* to the quest for religious salvation, and as accompanying the process of rationalization at large. The critical theory of the Frankfurt School has, since its very inception, attempted to rescue *Eros* from the imperatives of *Ananke*, the workhouse. The Frankfurt School seemed to end in the purity of aesthetic reflection, in which men and women preserve love's pleasures while freeing it from the suffering imposed by other dependence.

The functionalist tradition focuses on the differentiation and specialization of love in the modern nuclear family. It is argued that such love specialization, in channelling the bio-physical energies of individuals, increases the steering capacities of the social system as a whole. Our passionate love experience helps us to carve out an identity in a universe of impersonal and formal relations. A final question addressed in this chapter is whether these two major traditions in social theory adequately account for and exhaust the topic of love. Borrowing extensively from the conceptual framework suggested by Habermas in his theory of communicative action I finally suggest that there are aspects of love which are 'lost' in current theories. An account of reciprocal love allowing for the communality of perspectives and a joint life is needed to counterbalance the 'monological' maximization of pleasures which prevail in current conceptions. In emancipating women from slavery and oppression, modernity provides individuals with hitherto unknown opportunities for reciprocal love.

On Extraordinary Love – Plato

In *Symposion* and in *Phaedrus* Plato gives his views on love. Both of these essays have stimulated philosophers and writers in all times (e.g. Thomas Mann and Sigmund Freud) to view love as an extraordinary virtue – as a *diamonion* – from which great art and literatures spring. The further process of civilization has had to routinize love and to circumscribe it considerably in order to control its charisma.

It has often been remarked that the Greek concept of love, and that of Plato in particular, is exceedingly male-oriented (Saxonhouse 1984). The one woman present at the *Symposion*, the flute-player, is asked to leave the room when the discussion turns to love. At the end, however, Socrates speaks on love, and in so doing he relates the words of the wise Diotima.

In Plato's philosophy there is a hierarchy and a fixed ranked scale of values. Lowest on the scale is the desire for the human body, as there is nothing permanent to it, it soon decays. Highest on the scale is the desire to produce 'eternity', the ideals of truth, goodness and beauty. Accordingly, love for eternity is a higher and more signified form of love than the 'human' desire for the merely transient, the body of the Other. Plato's view of love is an *ode* to the artist.

Love's *diamonion* takes possession of an individual, and the one who is haunted is capable also of great acts and deeds. The lover can break with the present and start history anew. Love, in Plato's sense, is a most extraordinary quality, it borders on madness and is utterly solitary. Love, tragedy, and death are adjacent topics in the classic literature. While in love, life has a purpose, and it is sweeter to die for a purpose than without it. In Weber's account of charismatic personalities and of the great prophets one can in fact trace a remote impact (shared with Freud and Mann) of Plato's theory of (extraordinary) love.

Extraordinary love is related to eternal life and to Being itself. It occurs in stark opposition to the life of the here and now, to the reproduction of everyday life. Considered from its extraordinary side, the Platonic conception of love has been related to the acts and deeds of men rather than those of women. The *creative* individual gives birth to eternal forms, to truth, beauty, and goodness, while women give birth to life. But Sophocles let Antigone die because of the love that she felt for her brother, and Plato mentions Alcestis, Pelias' daughter, as the one who was carried away by the immensity of love and who died for it. Platonic love is both sexless and timeless, it reveals humanity in us. The Christian religion managed to control *extraordinary love* by spiritualizing its anima.

The Routinization of Charisma and Love's Spiritualization

Religion and love have been closely related topics in the history of western thought. In our own time the connection is no longer evident. One way to view religion is to see it as control of sex. Some feminist theologians have asked pertinent questions as to what happens in the course of religious development, when women are dispossessed and ranked second to men (Reuther 1975; Halkes 1979).

For Max Weber there is 'an irreconcilable' tension between religion and love, which is evident in his *Religionssoziologie* (Weber 1978, I, pp. 399–439). It is common in classical social theory to view primitive religion and its symbol-life on an ascending scale of spiritualization. In Weber's sociology this process also entails rationalization and a greater distancing between humankind and nature. Lowest on the scale is animist religion, hardly distinguishable from magic and sorcery, and highest on the scale are different forms of symbolism. With the development of human language, and thus of symbol-life, the interpreting process becomes a wedge between humans and nature. The symbol system controls humanity's interpretation of the outer and inner environments. An invisible world emerges, in stark contrast to the visible and animated life-form of primitive people. A new contingency is brought into human lives, as symbolic life requires constant interpretation and confirmation:

Magic is transformed from a direct manipulation of forces into symbolic activity . . . a new level of experience plays a part in human life. (Weber 1978, p. 403)

Prior to the rise of the monotheistic world religions, primitive religious life passes through its functionalist stage with each human task regulated by a corresponding spirit or god, so that the spiritual sphere closely reflects the human sphere and its division of labour. Female gods are not uncommon at this stage of religious evolution. In the course of religious rationalization a masculinization of the gods seems to take place and the divinity then loses all its human qualities – and comes to defy humankind in the end. This is in stark contrast to magical and animist religion, where human beings represent their gods and seek to appease them with gifts.

Religion, once developed, centralizes and monopolizes people's inner lives by removing the anima from the visual world of objects (the stone, the tree, the woman . . .) to the invisible world of pure symbol construction. The perpetuation of the religious faith, threatened by not yet completely repressed magic, requires occasional wonders so that people can see the holy spirits. The more abstract and the more rationalized religion becomes, the greater is the need for wonders. The rise of the religious symbol-system also give rise to a social sphere, distinct and different from nature. This differentiation process between the social and the natural has been a central theme in much of classical social theory. The understanding of individuals becomes spiritualized, it undergoes greater abstraction, and becomes manipulated by a central control agency from above.

The spiritualization of the inner life of human beings simultaneously requires the de-spiritualization of their outer life. Nature loses its human qualities, and becomes the object of human manoeuvres rather than the subject of a mutual dialogue. A centralized divinity allows for no other spirits other than those *he* himself controls from above. Monotheistic world religions move charisma away from the visible world of persons and objects, and centralize it in a high office:

> Here we find that peculiar transformation of charisma into an institution: as permanent structures and traditions replace the belief in the revelation and heroism of charismatic personalities, charisma becomes part of an established social structure. (Weber 1978, p. 139)

It has often been held that the rise of the major religions occurs simultaneously with the emergence of the imperial state formations. Religious monotheism would then correspond to state domination in the geo-political sphere (Habermas 1981). The religious symbol-system can confirm and consolidate earthly rulers and declare them divine deputies. In the language of both Michel Foucault and Norbert Elias, the rise of the religious sphere is a most effective tool to control people's inner lives. Most effective among God's commands is perhaps this one; 'Thou shalt have no other Gods but me'!

The routinization of charisma, and its incorporation into specific offices tends to exclude women from the 'charmed circles'. They cannot hold office in the church or in organizations controlled by the church. Women are largely excluded from the seminars of higher learning and thus from the cultivation of that distinct rationalism which had such an impact on the growth of the sciences in the West. Women become the enigmas of modern life and of its cultured world of thought and of action. In the terms of Horkheimer and Adorno, they become wandering megaeras in a spiritualized symbol-world from which their sex from the very beginning excluded them (on the megaera, see below).

To control sexual love and to make it subservient to religion has always been a central task for the Christian religion. According to Weber sex competes with religion: the more developed and the more rationalized the religion, the stronger is its agony of sex and of women. We shall look at the tension in more detail in the next section.

Weber on Erotic Love

In the *Zwischenbetrachtung* Weber (1946, p. 343) includes a section dealing with the irreconcilable tension between sex and religion. The tension comes about gradually, he says. In animist religion, the spasms of the body could be the sign that the spirits had taken domicile in the individual. The split between sex and religion is a component in the overall intellectualization of culture and thus of the rationalization of life. The development of theodicy which is necessary for salvation religions, requires the evolution of special 'discourses' on the question of evil. The spontaneous eruption of sexuality must be regarded as the work of evil, especially if it drains the soul. The full spiritualization of individuals requires their sexualization as well. As goodness and evil are dialectically linked, and both are necessary for thought, so are the soul to its body. The agony must be felt by the true Christian.

Eroticism means the cultivation of pleasures, and can develop quite independently of the sexual act. Once the eroticization of sex occurs, Weber says, 'cultured' humans lose for ever the simple and organic sexuality of the primitive peasantry. The development of eroticism enriches and enchants life as it reveals sensuality to people. Sensuality can become an end in itself and lose touch with the sexuality of its origin.

But when pleasure and sensuality develop, so does tragedy as well. The individual experiences suffering when separated from the beloved one; something which is well captured by the old eros-myth. The development of eroticism, tragedy and aesthetics are closely linked in classical Greece. Aesthetics is the cultivation of pleasures independent from the body of another; the sexual pleasure is invested in the object rather than in the subject of another (Freud 1962).

According to Weber (1946, p. 345) erotic love has not always been directed at the woman. On the contrary, and despite Sappho, the Hellenic ideal of passionate love is reserved for men, and directed at the boy or the comrade. The eroticization (and sexualization) of the woman is a rather late occurrence. It appears to begin in the age of chivalry with troubadour love by which the vassals paid 'erotic services' to their masters' ladies. 'Therewith began the "probation" of the man, not before his equals but in the face of the erotic interest of the "lady"' (Weber 1946, p. 345). However, love in this context is not meant to be consummated, it aims rather at eroticizing the lady and to provide her with a love-code through which she can 'bespeak' herself. The chivalric love reflects its social embeddedness as well; the love-code bears the imprint of warriorhood. Love conquers, besieges and honours.

The freeing of the love-code from its immediate sociocultural context occurs with the rise of the salon culture among the French literati. From then on, the culture of love develops its own codes. These codes form the bases of the gallantry of the epoch, and lay the ground for an emergent market of sensual literary words; the ladies' confession stories and the pornographic novels. With the rise of bohemian cultures among artists of all kinds, Weber sees a summit of erotic cultivation.

The eroticization of love is a component in the intellectualization of culture and the rationalization of life in general. It develops in a parallel process to the rise of the work ethic. The two cultures of work and pleasure only *appear* to negate one another; they are in fact the result of the same process of rationalization working itself out in two different spheres. They both seek salvation in this world, and reject other-worldly mysticism. 'When God is dead', the religion of erotic love will be the one and only means of salvation in the modern world. The tension between sex and religion puts a strait-jacket on the interpretation of marriage. Inner-worldly asceticism accepts only 'the rationally regulated marriage', whose aim is to 'procreate and rear children, and mutually to further one another in the state of grace' (Weber 1948, p. 349). Sexual pleasure is strictly forbidden, as it leads 'the hopelessly wretched' into *Kreatur-vergötterung*. Other-worldly asceticism forbids sexual contact altogether. Weber claims that Luther had a rather 'gross' interpretation of marriage for 'in order to prevent worse, God peeks at and is lenient with these elements of passion' (Weber 1948, p. 349). Weber's own ideal of a marriage is borrowed from the Quakers, it is possible for a man and a woman to develop a 'higher' and more 'responsible' life together. '. . . a mutual granting of oneself to another and the becoming indebted to each other' (Weber 1948, p. 350). The first volume of his *Religionssoziologie* is dedicated to his wife, Marianne, with the inscription: '. . . bis in Pianissimo zum höchsten Altens' (to live calmly into old age). However, such a fate among the sexes he believes to be rare: 'to whom it is given may speak of fate's fortunes and grace – not of his own merit' (Weber 1948, p. 350).

Fate's fortune and grace will become more and more accentuated, as the process of rationalization continues. When religion loses its hold on people the only means of salvation left to them is the religion of erotic love. But eroticism, Weber says, is intimately attached to brutality. The more sublimated the culture of eroticism, the more brutal is the act of love. The brutality is not grounded in jealousy primarily or in the will to possess, but 'is the most intimate coercion of the less brutal partner' (Weber 1948, p. 348). The woman – as the less brutal partner (?) – is then the one who has most to lose once God is dead.

It is possible to read a warning in Weber's text, directed at the increasing eroticization of life and of love. This is a correlate to the process of rationalization in general, and to the intellectualization of our cultural milieu in particular. Eros places salvation within the reach of everybody whereas religious salvation is

a selective process for the 'elect'. While Providence could be
helped a little by hard labour or faithfulness, it is essential to the
religious complex that only God himself knows what will happen
to humankind after death, and his judgements are incomprehen-
sible to humans. Instead, erotic love profits from being democratic and within the reach of all. Through it people can come
to believe that they have control of their own destiny – or be
lulled into accepting it.

Erotic love continually discovers new erogenous zones. Instead
of the de-eroticization that Freud had predicted would accompany the growth of productive forces, these forces can develop
through eroticization. The language of war, for instance, can veil
violence by recurrent use of erotic metaphors (Lakoff and
Johnson 1982). Eros can be just as totalizing as agape, the Christian love relation between the individual and God. Under the
auspices of its ideology, people confront one another, not as the
brethren of God in a primitive community, but rather as a means
to one another's lust and passion. There is a Kantian warning in
Weber's text, that when religion is dead we will become each
other's means rather than ends.

One can illustrate the two kinds of love, eros and agape, and
further bring out the tension between sex and religion in the
following way:

Love – salvation	Eros – inner-worldly	Agape – outer-worldly
Extraordinary	The erotic experience, orgasm, self-sensation	The religious experience, other-sensation
Ordinary	Routinization of love, marriage, prostitution	Asceticism world-escapism

The eroticization of life could lead to a war-game between
individuals in general and between the sexes in particular. 'To
live calmly into old age' is perhaps a gift given to us by
Providence rather than something which can be earned or
bought.

In Weber's discussion of love and eroticism his general
sociology seems to be condensed. The process of rationalization
in the end turns into its opposite, and the modern individuals'

escape from religious superstition results in them losing both a sense of meaning and freedom. In such a world only *Kreaturvergötterung* remains.

Differentiation as the Basis of Love – Georg Simmel

Among the classical writers in sociology only Georg Simmel (1984) addresses the topic of love directly. While Weber does it as a minor part of his *Religionssoziologie*, and Parsons in the context of his theory of the modern nuclear family, Simmel's essay on love is important as it takes up some classical themes, especially love's affinity with tragedy and its resultant paradoxes.

Erotic love, Simmel remarks, is found only among the species which are highest on the evolutionary scale, i.e. human beings. Human beings are a highly differentiated and individualized species, and love and flirtation among them serve as mechanisms of procreation. In the case of lower animals the needs of procreation are guaranteed by much simpler biological means (Simmel 1984, p. 161 ff).

Apart from its objective meaning, to guarantee the survival of the species, love among humans also has a subjective meaning. It means something to us individually and quite apart from its sexual undertones, it reveals to us the sweetness and sorrows of life. Simmel says that an antagonism often develops between the objective and the subjective meanings of love, and in this antagonistic relation lies the tragedy of love.

The more individuated life is, the more individual is love. When in love, we love one *particular* individual rather than a general one of the opposite sex (or the same sex). We harbour the impression that we have chosen our beloved one, e.g., that our will is still exercised. The more we descend on the evolutionary scale, Simmel notes, the less individuated (and less controlled by will) are the sexual contacts among species. Humans, Sartre has said, *are* bodies, but they also *have* bodies, they are capable of controlling their sexual acts.

Furthermore among humans we find general (and not only individuated) love (Simmel 1984, p. 171). Simmel illustrates different forms of human love with examples from Goethe's *Faust*. Gretchen falls in love with Faust because he is a man of high social standing and great virility; he belongs to 'them' among whom Gretchen otherwise would not find company. She does not understand Faust as an individual with highly specialized interests. She relates to him only as a member of a social class and of the other sex. Likewise, Faust falls in love with Gretchen hoping to find a Helen in her. The ancient saga of Helen of Troy contains everything which Faust considers feminine and pure. He cares little for actual existing women, including Gretchen and having made her pregnant, he deserts her. Both Gretchen and Faust relate to one another as *categories*; as individuals they do not understand one another. Love's fate is in this case destined to be tragic.

The antithesis of this general type of love is found in the highly individuated love-relation between Eduard and Ottilie. Neither one of them could possibly be replaced by another; they complement one another as individuals, and they relate to one another on a highly differentiated basis. This kind of love Simmel calls *absolute* in contrast to the general and relative one between Faust and Gretchen. An *absolute* love 'brackets' sexuality as but one aspect of a total union, a *general* love is founded on sexuality:

> Sexuality as a total coloration of the individual, but not as an autonomous entity abstracted from love itself, is a decision for such absolute love . . . Eduard and Ottilie love one another because it is written in the stars. Faust and Gretchen love one another because they have met. (Simmel 1984, p. 176)

The more individuated love becomes, the greater its fragility and possibly its tragic side. In absolute love, the tragedy of life comes to the forefront. Simmel notes how love, when highly individuated, soon develops a secret logic of its own, often in sharp tension with the surrounding world. Love's tragedy lies in the fact that the two different meanings, love's objective and subjective sides, must fuse, and the fusion is costly. The procreation of life cares little for the highly individuated demands of a secret love. Absolute love has no real place in the empirical world, it develops secretly and often in sharp tension to it:

> love has its source in the empirical world and because its real development must be implicated in the contingencies of this world, it is subject to a fatal contradiction from the outset. (Simmel 1984, pp. 170–1)

One of Simmel's more remarkable contributions to a social theory of love is to locate the philosophical – and often tragic – side of love within a theory of the development of social forms. Before turning in more detail to a discussion of the social (and institutionalized) forms of love presented by Parsons and by Luhmann, I shall end this section by giving some examples of love's paradoxes.

> I cannot say I loved, for who can say
> He was killed yesterday?
> He is stark mad, who ever says,
> That he hath been in love an hour,
> Yet not that love so much decays,
> But that it can ten in less space devour.
> (Donne, *The Paradox*, from Elster, p. 74)

> Who will believe me, if I swear
> That I have had the plague a year?
> Who would not laugh at me, if I should say
> I saw a flask of powder burn a day?
> (Donne, *The Broken Heart*, from Elster, p. 74)

Love transforms both the subject (the lover) and the object of desire (the beloved one) so that they both become different individuals. No longer identical with themselves, some descriptive models are no longer applicable . . . Who can say he was killed yesterday? (Elster 1978, pp. 74–5). Some verbs give rise to what Elster (after Hintikka) calls an 'existential inconsistency'. Love is such a verb, as Simmel has already noted:

> As one who loves, I am a different person than I was before, for it is not one or the other of my 'aspects' or energies that loves but rather the entire person. (Simmel 1984, p. 161)

Love is 'une passion inutile', Jean-Paul Sartre (1957) has said. Love puts the holder in an extraordinary Being-in-the-World; it seeks to 'possess a liberty'. Once in our possession, there is the risk, however, that love will vanish. Reciprocity is the death of love, yet it is also the object of our desires (Elster refers to Racine's *Andromaque*; 'Je t'aimais inconstant, qu'aurais – je fait fidèle?'). Love's inherent inconstancy throws us into oscillating between hope and despair.

'I need no longer feel Angst, I have already lost him' (Barthes). Because of its inconstancy, love consumes energy. For love to last, social institutions are required which can stabilize and routinize our emotions. To fall in love, Francesco Alberoni (1982) points out, is very different from being in love permanently. The former is identical with a religious conversion or a revolutionary experience, it changes our perspectives on reality completely. The latter experience is to have found permanency in a world of contingency. Love's routinization requires the embeddedness of social institutions. An institutionalized love no longer negates reality but accommodates to its demands.

Parsons and Love's Functionalization

In Parsons' social system theory, love is brought under guaranteed social control; it is functionalized and intensified at the same time. Its confinement within the modern nuclear family secures the steering capacities of the social system at large, and reduces social complexity. Eros serves Ananke, but experiences no unhappiness! We shall briefly review Parsons' theory of the emotional–affectional complex and love's restriction to the modern nuclear family.

As a result of the profound structural changes of modern society, the kinship unit has lost many of its previous functions (Parsons 1955). The occupational system takes over the economic tasks of the family. Normally, the modern family is a small unit, consisting of two generations only: parents and children. From the point of view of the labour-market, the modern nuclear family is also a highly flexible unit. At the same time as the family decreases in size, it also becomes more intensified: the task of child-rearing, for instance, which was previously in several hands is now in the hands of only the parents (mainly the mother). The modern father has an 'interpenetrating' role; he works for a wage/salary outside the home, and his family is dependent for its subsistence on his income. He is both worker and a father at the same time, and has to mediate between different system-imperatives (Parsons 1955, p. 12 ff).

The woman, however, fulfils her interpenetrating role in the home, she mediates between the social and psychological systems. Her role is carthartic-affectual (Parsons 1955, p. 20 ff). From psychoanalysis Parsons has taken over the insight that the adult person carries around his/her own childhood. When meeting our beloved one, the oedipal drama is again actualized. At the bottom of every love-relation are our own relations to our parents. In the husband–wife relation the woman catalyses her husband's mother-relation. Instead of the oedipal father, the man (and the woman) must take the children into account. In Parsons' view, children are necessary for the development of an adult personality. The woman–mother has a key role in handling this triangular drama, she mediates between her husband (to whom she is a lover) and her children (to whom she is a mother). her love-work is two-edged, it is both erotic and *caritas* at the same time, and is essential to the cathartic complex. The woman sets the boundaries for the socially permissible, and she partakes in the system-maintenance of the social order at large. Her constant shifting of roles requires a skilled and professional attitude. She is a central agent of the rationalized society where she occupies a specialized cathartic–emotional role. Her rational attitude to love is shown by the fact that the modern woman attends academic courses in how best to perform her erotic roles.

Parsons' vision of love and marriage is indeed a continuation of the 'inner-worldly asceticism' which accepts only 'the rationally regulated marriage' . . . 'to procreate and to rear children, and mutually to further one another in the state of grace' (Weber 1948, p. 349). Sex and religion are in the early 1950s happily fused in Parsons' social theory.

In the 1970s and sparked by the expressive revolts among youth, Parsons (1978, p. 233) took a new and fresh look at the religious complex, including the sexual–erotic component. He now acknowledges that the eroticization of modern marriage has a greater significance. In contrast to Weber, Parsons never really accepts that 'God is Dead' in the modern world. According to Parsons the Christian belief system has spread throughout society and infused previously secular concerns with religious values. This reversed process of secularization (which is commonly held to be a one-way process, moving society away from religious concerns) will typically end in what Bellah calls 'civil religion', e.g. the full institutionalization of denominationalism as in the United States. Individuals can choose the faith to which they wish to adhere. Parsons (1978, p. 233) equates this individualization of religious choice with the same evolution in the political sphere of parliamentary voting.

If in fact religion has spread throughout the social order and become fully institutionalized in the administration of previously secular concerns, one could agree with Parsons' view that in the course of its development religion is cognitivized while the secular society is valorized. From within such a view the new expressive revolts of the 1960s among youth and students are enigmatic; is the 'resurgence of the non-rational' a continuation or a break with the process of religious revolution at large? (Parsons 1978, p. 252). The new movements (hippies, students and women) share with early Christianity 'the immense concern with love' (Parsons 1978, p. 253). Yet, in some important respects they differ: they no longer adhere to the theism of early religion, and locate the love-complex in the midst of the here and now. Absorbed as they are in the present they shun the 'after-worldly' and the transcendent: 'make love, not war' was one of the typical phrases of the 1960s. Their acceptance of Christian love is qualified by the fact that the love they preach is hardly distinguishable from eroticism, e.g., their concern with body-love (Parsons 1978, p. 256). Early Christianity, Parsons says, managed to keep love separate from eroticism, and this separation he believes is functional for the generalization of love to humanity in general. Accordingly, he is troubled by the new resurgent movements and their fusion of love and eroticism. It is interesting to follow the reasons he gives in greater detail, as they link up with his earlier concern with the modern nuclear family as catalyst of the erotic complex.

The primordial solidarity and erotic relation, Parsons (1978, p. 256) says, occurs between a mother and her child, substantiating his views with evidence from psychoanalysis and social anthropology. This primordial relation can spread to the adult level in a sublimated form. The sexual intercourse between spouses in the modern nuclear family grounds the sentiments which today we are prone to call 'love'; love and eroticism are intimately linked in modern society. The love complex which religion once administered has spread throughout the social order, as inclusive values it informs our general concerns for human rights for everyone, as eroticization and intimization it satisfies the needs for the organism and stabilizes the modern marriage. Parsons carries the conviction that the two wings of the love complex are functionally related to one another and have become differentiated in the course of the evolution of societies. The restriction of eroticism and body-concerns to the conjugal family and the diadic relation between spouses enables the generalization of the love-concern to humanity as a whole.

The new expressive movements with their strong emphasis on eroticism and on body-concerns may lead to a 'dedifferentiation', and hence regression, of the evolutionary development, according to Parsons. The diffuse and general eroticization of social life (as suggested in the claim 'make love, not war') may in fact result in the de-eroticization of the affective complex. A deep erotic relation, Parsons believes, can only occur in one, or at least very few, relationships. Furthermore, if one is going to make love with all those one cares for, the numbers of such loves may in fact be quite small (Parsons 1978, p. 256). The early Christian separation between love and eroticism was probably quite functional; it enabled the Christian world community to arise. He is also troubled by the resurgent 'moral absolutism' that follows in the wake of the new expressiveness. The other side of love is hatred, he notes, and he fears the darker and inevitable side of the new 'religions'. The Christians managed to maintain the strong value of love, Parsons believed, only on the condition that they also circumscribed this love with a strong moralism; 'love thy neighbor' (Parsons 1978, p. 257). Christianity in his view fused at an early stage with cognitive values, and has therefore managed to survive a series of attacks.

The attack against rationality and the cognitive complex in general among youth in revolt obviously troubled Parsons. Love can spark creative moments, but it could equally well lead to hatred and war. In the larger affective complex of a general love for humanity, the channelling of eroticism to the modern nuclear family may in fact be quite functional.

Love and Body-presence as the Reduction of Social Complexity

Love, as we have seen, can be interpreted in a number of ways. Niklas Luhmann (1983) has advanced a theory in which love is an important medium of symbolic exchange, especially in the modern world. Through love we can come to know ourselves better.

One of the first and foremost axioms of modern sociology is that it is difficult to penetrate the modern world from the point of view of the individual. It has been argued that the modern world has lost its centre, and has become a merry-go-round of constant information flows. The self-understanding of individuals in the modern world must rely on information from the environment, and we need to identify the criteria individuals use when selecting among information stimuli from an amorphous system-environment.

While contemporary society extends the possibility of formal and impersonal relations for individuals, it simultaneously increases the need for intensified informal relations among them. In a world where we are apart from one another, we also need to be closely together. Romantic love, Luhmann suggests, is an important means of symbolic exchange in the modern world. Without it the world would lack an integrative force. Interestingly enough, while Habermas, as we will see, stresses the need for rational understanding as a medium of symbolic exchange, Luhmann stresses the need for love. Their two theories are different responses to the same felt malaise – to find a link between people in 'les temps modernes'.

In his analysis of romantic love, Luhmann offers an interesting sociological account of the social and historical origin of romantic love. This account resembles the one already offered by Weber, although the social functions of love are perceived differently. Love as passion – *passion d'amour* – gains social significance par excellence, when the society of stratified relations moves into a society of functional relations, in for example the transition from the feudal to the market society. In all previous societies, love has been strictly circumscribed as to who could love whom and when. As noted above, love in classical Greece is a matter for men mostly. It is with the age of chivalry that women first become eroticized. Their love, at the time, is more poetic than sexual. The social stratification systems does not allow sex between the lady and the vassal knight. Their love-exchange is socially important, however, as their songs and poetry ground a wholly new and sensate realm of experience – to be offered to the common people in the centuries to come. With the rise of industrial society passionate love became a regular means of symbolic exchange between men and women. The anonymous world needs new links of communication. The erotic pleasures, which previously were reserved for the privileged classes, now became the possession of the population as a whole.

In an increasingly complex and impersonal world, where individuals have broken away from local village customs, *passion d'amour* allows strangers to meet and to converse. Romantic love shares a structural resemblance to fashion, which is another symbolic means of communication in the modern world. They both arise as a response to anonymity, but love differs from fashion in one important aspect (Simmel 1950, p. 324 ff).

Fashion strikes the eye only, love strikes the heart. The love literature of the eighteenth and nineteenth centuries, whether in the forms of confessions or pornography, gains social significance as providing the 'codes' for exchanging information in a society of strangers. By the same token, erotic love is an urban rather than a rural phenomenon.

The function of love, we have suggested, is to mend communication among strangers, preferably between men and women. But the purpose of the communicative love-act is directed to ourselves rather than to the other. In our love-talk to one another, we mostly talk to ourselves, Luhmann says. While in love, we experience more of our inner self than we experience of the other. How little we know the other usually becomes apparent once love has gone away:

Was man als Liebe sucht, wird somit in erster Linie dies sein; Validierung der Selbstdarstellung. (Luhmann 1983, p. 208)

With the popularization of romantic love in the eighteenth century, love becomes linked with sexuality. Love among young people is sanctioned, and with the opposite sex preferably (Aubert 1965). Love, sex, and youth become the modern marriage-pillars. The economic market finds a correspondence in the market of free emotions. The social closures of class, race and religion – circumscribing love in the modern world – are of no concern to the new ideology of love. On the contrary, such closures spur the excitement of love even further. When in love, everything is possible, it can move mountains.

Wonders were necessary for religious salvation and wonders are possible in the love salvation of our times. Niklas Luhmann agrees with Weber that romantic love has become significant as a modern means of inner-worldly salvation. Love breaks the routine and the drudgery of ordinary life. In the words of Francesco Alberoni (1982; 1984) love is a *status nascendi* comparable in force and in momentum to a religious conversion. When we fall in love, something very profound happens to us. Life appears different, and our body goes through a physical shock. Love opens up 'the oceanic feelings' and we participate in a cosmos over which we have no control. Once religion did the same (Freud 1964).

Love and religion, thus, elicit the same extraordinary feelings, but their codes differ markedly. The language of after death was important as a means to regulate life here and now, and the language of love is more for the ego than the alter. The difference between love and religion, however, is that while religion is a communal experience, love is an individual one. The tension between love and religion that Weber foresees is the tension then between passion consummated individually and passion consummated collectively.

Critical Theory from Adorno to Habermas – on the Dialectics of Love

Within the tradition of critical theory, love (and womanhood) occupies an ambiguous position. As desire it plays the role of a repressed nature. At the same time once unleashed into social form it threatens individuals with subjugation and eventual annihilation.

In *Dialectic of Enlightenment* Horkheimer and Adorno draw on Nietzsche's genealogy of morals when describing the torments of Odysseus. If men were to give in to the sirens, or to the songs of Circe, and thus to their bodily desires, raw and untamed nature would threaten them with annihilation and awful death. The authors let the roving expeditions and the torments of the hero express the fate of mankind in general. Within the chambers of horrors of a *verwaltete Welt* (administered world) love, as calculated desire, plays an affirmative cultural role. The identical sexual (woman) types, generated by the beauty-machine of the capitalist world, threaten all individuality, whether female or male. From within the spirit of pessimism pervading the reading of *Dialectic of Enlightenment* it seems typical for the authors to evoke the image of the megaera as representing a not yet subjugated womanhood.[1] The ridiculed female represents a lost nature, she indicates the tragi-comical scene of a humanity struggling against the forces of homogeneity and control. The megaera is an outcast in this world. As the repressed truth of a lost humanity, her appearance is awkward. She is at odds with the streamlined fabrication of the modern world. She engages like a fury in the cultural and the scientific activities of her time (!) while belonging to neither. She is not yet domesticated and she never will be. Her revenge on male civilization is not planned or calculated, but confused and accidental. Her beauty lies in her mutilated figure, in her tragi-comical disabledness in a world of fabricated identicals:

The shrew, a fossilized survival of the bourgeois esteem of woman, is invading society today. With her endless nagging she takes revenge in her own home for the misery inflicted upon her sex from time immemorial . . .

Subjected woman in the guise of a Fury has survived and still wears the grimace of mutilated nature at a time when our rulers are already busy melding trained bodies of both sexes, in whose uniformity the grimace disappears. Against the background of this kind of mass production the scolding of the Fury, who at least retained her own distinctive features, will become a sign of humanity, and her ugliness a mark of the spirit. (Horkheimer and Adorno 1972, p. 250)

This passage on the Fury in *Dialectic of Enlightenment* seems significant both with regard to how the authors view womanhood and life in the modern world in general. The authors continue the themes of Nietzsche's aesthetic–expressive programme, to search for difference and the non-identical in a world of regularity and normality (Habermas 1985). One can already anticipate in *Dialectic of Enlightenment* the enquiries into the madnesses and the follies of western civilization of the now popular studies of Michel Foucault (Habermas 1985).

Herbert Marcuse differs from his Frankfurt colleagues with regard to his more optimistic perspective on the future. A yet-to-be realized eros-principle stands against the necessities and the work-life of Ananke. In the one-dimensional world of the present, love and life are unhappy and disabled (Marcuse 1962, 1964). Humans pay for their material well-being with a damaged life. The eros-principle, when catalysed in the spontaneous social movements emerging in the 1960s, promised a radical shift in social relations as well as in our relation to nature. Instead of treating nature as an object of exploitation it is to be a speech-partner in an unrestrained dialogue. The libidinal forces, once unleashed from their imprisonment, would in Marcuse's (1964, p. 166 ff) view provide for a qualitatively different society.

As is well known, Habermas has been sceptical about both the optimism of Marcuse and the darker perspective of his Frankfurt mentors (Habermas 1981: i). This study is in a sense stimulated by Habermas' own work, especially his rereading of classical social theory from within the theory of communicative action (Habermas 1981). The question does arise, however, whether or not love as a form of human sociation can be dealt with at all in Habermas' social theory with its alleged rationalist overtones? A common critique of Habermas' philosophy and social theory in general is that the sensual and musical aspects of life are simply buried. His rationalist theory suffers from that which O'Neill (1976, pp. 1–103), Heller (1982) and others have called 'atonality'. His search for a counterfactually and universally valid formal speech act theory, some would argue, threatens the multiplicity and idiosyncrasies of *particular* language games (Lyotard 1979). Habermas' (1981) momentous work leaves the reader with a sense of unease: is his theory of communicative action at all sensitive to the differences of speech, and thus to its expressive richness in creating and recreating the world of the present? Can the theory deal at all with the originality and the individuality of artistic expressions? Is the theory of communicative action sensitive to issues of human freedom and creativity rising above that which is merely postulated and given? Can it harbour a system of not yet cultivated feelings? Do the forms of universally valid speech conditions suppress that which cannot yet be spoken? What happens to desire? What happens to women and to their gendered forms of life and of social interaction in the wake of Habermas' communicative theory (Fraser 1985)?

I cannot elaborate here to any great extent on Habermas' (1981) theory as formulated in his magnum opus. Suffice to mention that in order to enlarge the steering capacities of the modern social order, Habermas suggests a complex and multifaceted theory of communicative action. He insists on a dual social perspective: contemporary society must be viewed from the viewpoint of the system *and* from that of the lifeworld. While the co-ordinating media of the system-level can be administered by the media of money and power (as suggested by Parsons), the co-ordination of the lifeworld requires a very different set of symbolic media; communicative understanding. Three sets of symbolic media of exchange are thus recognized, but the most precious of them all is the last one of communicatively mediated understanding. Between the system and the lifeworld there are necessary mediations; as wage-earners individuals receive money which in turn is used for consumption, and as clients to the welfare state individuals receive social services of various kinds. But in the extent to which the system media of money and power enter into the lifeworld perspective as steering devices, they 'colonize' the latter. As a result, different pathologies emerge, and the possibilities for reaching a valid (and not manufactured) consensus regarding, for example, political issues, may then be greatly hampered. With the dual but interconnected concepts of system and lifeworld Habermas seeks to reformulate the classical themes of alienation and reification in Marxian theory.

Borrowing from Weber, Durkheim, and Parsons, Habermas sees the modern social order as characterized by a very high degree of differentiation of previously unified realms of action. The cognitive/scientific, the legal/moral and the expressive/aesthetic action complexes have developed in accordance with their own inner and specialized dynamic. As a consequence of the forces of differentiation and rationalization, modern world understanding is decentred and posited in the realm of communicative action among individuals themselves. When individuals are themselves the genesis and providers of meaning in and through communicative interaction, there is a risk of overburdening the social system. This is the malaise already recognized by Durkheim in his theory of anomie in modern society. The communicative system of interaction occupies then a very special status in the modern world; it alone generates the legitimate meaning needed both for system maintenance and for identity formation.

On the level of everyday social interaction the communicative system harbours the different validity conditions of speech: truth, rightness and veracity. On the level of expert knowledge drawn upon by the system forces (economy, policy and administration) these validity conditions constitute the different action realms of science, law and art. The differentiation of these action realms and their internally generated rationalization dynamics have led to the emergence of expert cultures in each of these realms. The distinct problem of modernity, Habermas suggests, is to find links in mediations between the separated realms of these expert cultures *and* the everyday system of understanding among individuals. Lacking such mediation, common understanding risks either colonization by the system forces or its exposure to the loss of meaning (as anticipated by Max Weber's *Sinnverlust*). According to Habermas' view the problem of modernity lies less in the invention of *reenchantment* devices by which the differentiated understanding could again fuse. That a diffuse and omnipotent eros-principle in the manner visualized by Marcuse could bless the alienated and administered world of the present seems to Habermas but wishful thinking.

Accordingly, and like Parsons, he has shown a certain scepticism towards the contemporary attempts to 'aesthetize' understanding (Habermas 1985).

Because of his scepticism towards the reenchantment industries, whether in the form of fundamentalist social movements or contemporary French philosophy, Habermas has been criticized for a 'non-musical' and overly rationalist attitude. He has been quite insensitive to the joyous cultures of resistance (whether in music or in art) (Lash 1985). Yet, he himself admits to a certain 'nervousness' with regard to these and similar imputations (Habermas 1981, p. 235).

Perhaps as a response to these often repeated criticisms Habermas (1985) devotes his most recent publication to a large-scale enquiry into the emergence and the fascination of the artistic-expressive complex in the modern world. At the same time he joins company with Adorno, Benjamin and Marcuse, each of whom were concerned with the redeeming possibilities of art in a fully rationalized world. As Sherry Weber (1976) has argued in a seminal essay, the tradition of critical theory must be seen from the dual perspective of seeking redemption both in the cognitive sphere (the possibilities of self-reflection) and in the aesthetic–expressive sphere (art as emancipating the individual). Until now Habermas' work has fallen mainly in the cognitive realm. His latest book does however recognize as equally pervading themes in the critical tradition art and aesthetic expressions. The question is whether or not his present work can also deal with the issue of love?

Love continues to be as minor a theme in this book as it has been in his previous work. He does however address the topic explicitly in one essay, namely in his discussion of George Bataille's 'erotic economy' (Habermas 1985, p. 248 ff). What emerges here is the moot relation between the aesthetic attitude and the wonder of love. Common to both themes is the overt suspicion of the word and of the cognitive attitude, for example, in the wake of love's aestheticism, there is a risk of unleashing the irrational forces of raw nature! Habermas' (1985, pp. 34–64) enquiry into the wondering world of art and into its philosophies opens with Hegel and Schiller's still positive theories of art and beauty as providing the mediations between the modern separation of *Wissen* and *Glauben*. These classic theories are turned around by Nietzsche's philosophy of art which is no longer a glorification of the present but rather its condemnation. It is significant, Habermas (1985, p. 104) notes, that Nietzsche sees the grounds of science and morality in taste; the gay science uses as its model a singer from Provence who can delight the audience by the strength and beauty of his voice. Lyotard's (1979) philosophy of science borrows its main impetus from Nietzsche.

The pervading theme in Foucault's investigations of madness and sexuality is power; the power to will and the power to know are responsible for the homogenization of culture and the reduction of all differences. This theme as we have seen also informed Horkheimer and Ardono's account of the megaera. It is Habermas' (1985, p. 313) contention, however, that this reductive theme (of a diffuse power) is incapable of detecting the differentiation and the nuances of the present. The emphasis on power provides a critique of science and its method, but it does not seek an alternative mode of conducting (social) science. Instead it turns the social sciences into literary criticism: the aesthetic attitude replacing the cognitive one.

In the wake of this transformation of the social sciences into aesthetic modes of expression there is not only the risk of overlooking all the differences which modernity has achieved in the course of its development but of trivializing the routine and the ordinary while giving emphasis to the extraordinary and the charismatic. Bataille's erotic economy well expresses the surrealistic project turned into a science according to Habermas (1985, p. 248): to break away from the world of the present in order to gain entrance in sur-reality!

Perhaps Habermas' 'nervousness' with regard to these attempts at reenchantment should be seen in the context of German culture. As a child of its 'resurgent' past Habermas must be weary of the suspension of reason and of the primacy given over to the theatrical and the expressive as guiding principles of social life. When the love theme is exploited and manipulated by powerful artistic–expressive means, the sacrifices which men have to pay can be enormous and hideous. The innocence of love disguises its cruelty and its absolutism (see Parsons). In the critical tradition love's embeddedness in desire gives its appearance a distinct dialectic in the wake of which both humanity and inhumanity have arisen.

Conclusion

In this chapter I have looked at how several of the major social theories view love. There are clear differences, on the one hand, between the instrumentalist tradition of Max Weber, which is also reflected in critical theory, and the functionalist tradition of Georg Simmel, Talcott Parsons, and Niklas Luhmann, on the other. The instrumentalist tradition foresees a social development which is either void of love or which draws on love in order to further exploitative forces. In the functionalist tradition, however, romantic love becomes an important resource for the steering capacities of the system at large.

In both the instrumentalist and the functionalist tradition love in the modern world is an important means of securing salvation, and of experiencing something beyond the routine and the ordinary:

> Dazu ist Liebe nötig als Ausdifferenzierung einer Bezugsperson, im Hinblicke auf die die Welt anders gewarten werden kann als normal; in deren Augen auch der Liebende selbst ein ander sein kann als normal. (Luhmann 1983, p. 215)

Both love and religion secure the self-identity of the individual, religion on the collective level and love on the individual level. Both can function as symbolic media of exchange, and enrich the present by adding extraordinary dimensions. On the system level, love helps to coordinate action among individual strangers, and secure the biological reproduction of the species. On the individual level, love becomes an extraordinary means of salvation from the drudgery of routine. From one point of view, love's labour is not really lost in social theory. A few remarks, however, remain to be made.

In the course of historical development, love becomes both increasingly democratic and sexual–erotic. Earlier love was the creator of history and of being, today its role is much more modest. Once a life-giving force, love is reduced in its modern form to the passionate bonds between humans (as Luhmann's title *Liebe als Passion* reveals). But even if love has become more human and within reach of us all, it has retained – as reflected in social theory – some of its ancient features. Love is featured as a solitary and extraordinary venture, it breaks with the present and starts individual history anew. It is fresh and spontaneous and thus wholly unpredictable. Out of order it makes chaos, out of chaos it creates order. Under the spell of love, life is being shaped.

But as Simmel notes, the more extraordinary love becomes, the more tragic is its destiny. Love develops a logic of its own in stark opposition to the life of the here and now. When love dictates its own authority, it interrupts the powers that are, and the revenge is often harsh. In the classic love poems of the western tradition, the lovers can become united by death alone.

Even if it does not lead to (actual) death, Sartre's reflection on love as 'une passion inutile' captures the un-reality of love. Once in possession of the liberty it desires, love ceases to exist. Reciprocity is the death of love, while at the same time being the object of its desire. Ego seeks the Other for the sake of its own maximization of pleasure. Being demands the annihilation of the Other.

All the theories reviewed above have in common the fact that they are authored by men who are well situated within the hemisphere of western thought. The inclusion of non-western sources would probably have necessitated a change in the instrumental–functional perspectives which this chapter has utilized. Love need not of course be seen as identical with lust and sexual passion, but with the growth of wisdom and of judgements. Love can be thought of as a non-personalization. Love can thus be seen as the cessation of man and his gradual inclusion into a cosmic and mystical order. But instead of reflecting love's labour from a non-western and other-worldly perspective, this chapter limits its concern to the western path alone. Paraphrasing Weber, it seems possible to claim that it is in the West – and only here – that the culture of eroticism has developed without interference. Where else but in the West would pornography make sense? Seen from the perspective of a woman, one may – with Weber – ask whether or not women gained once God was proclaimed dead?

Women are remarkably silent in social theory at large, even when love is featured. If in fact women had been given time off from their practical love-labours in order to reflect on their lives, would they then reflect on love's labour differently than what we have seen above? In what sense is love sexless, and in what sense is it sex-bound? In what sense is it timeless and in what sense is it time-bound? A social theory of love needs to be developed, not the least one which is grounded in the experiences of the silent sex, up to the present the mere object and instrument of desire in the domain of action where they could have claimed a special competency.

How would a woman finding herself in the position to care for the ordinary and for the routine respond to the Platonic view on extraordinary love? Jesus Christ needed the love labours of both Martha and Mary: the one cared for his physical well-being while the other listened to his thoughts. Isn't the dual love of the two different women archetypical of women's love labour? What would Gretchen have told Faust – or perhaps Goethe – if somebody had cared to listen? What would Parsons' specialized role-mother do when the necessities of life demands that she can interpenetrate the fragmentation of the present? How does a woman take to reading Donne's *Paradox* knowing that her family's existence hangs on the stability of her love? What does Sartre's *passion inutile* mean to a woman who sacrifices her love to the beings of the other? How will women in fact read Luhmann on love as complexity-reduction, knowing that they are the chief means of symbolic exchange in the modern world?

One way to start to enquire into 'lost love' – and especially that of women – would be to ask what happened to the Christian agape in the course of secularization in social theory. What happened to the ideal of devoting oneself to a *cause*, to something which is outside the narcissistic self, to the care for the other or for the community as a whole, once eros was proclaimed the religion of the day?

In the course of increasing calculation of action and the predominance of wage-labour, the caring side of love may be difficult to detect and to estimate. The more ruthless erotic love becomes, and the further it interpenetrates the zones of experience, the more the altruism and reciprocity of love (as secularized agape) is needed. The significance of such love lies less in the erotic domains of action than in the union of perspectives and the commonality of projects such love can give rise to. Also this kind of love can become extraordinary, but it does not fear the ordinary and the routine.

Reciprocal love demands the maturation of moral principles to be applied equally to the community of mankind as a whole. Above all, it demands the emancipation of women to equal social worth to that of men. Only modernity – to use the terminology currently in use – provides the possibility of reciprocal action, and thus the possibility of new social forms of love between the sexes. These emergent forms of love's labour need to be sought by theory. In the social theories of love, its passionate (solitary and extraordinary) side needs the countervailing force of reciprocal love. In a real sense then, love's labour is still lost – at least in social theory!

Notes

An earlier version of this chapter was presented at the Symposium 'Wie männlich ist die Wissenschaft' in Bielefeld, December 1984. I am grateful to Helga Nowotny for critical comments and various suggestions for improvement. While working on this chapter I was supported by a grant from the Swedish Social Science Research Council.

1. The megaera (as one kind of the furies) once guarded the Kingdom of Hades, they were bewildering to look at and ready to attack oncomers. However, as a character type the megaera exists for us primarily because this is how Plato refers to Xantippa, Socrates' wife, whom Socrates willingly had chosen to marry in order to harden his own patience. In his *Geschlecht und Character* (1903) the Austrian psychologist, Otto Weininger, labels a special character type, the untamed and aggressive woman, a megaera. In *Dialectic of Enlightenment* Horkheimer and Adorno let the megaera play an important role in the shape of female awkwardness in modern civilization.

References

Agonito, Rosemary (ed.) (1977) *History of Ideas on Women, A Source Book*, New York: Paragon.

Alberoni, Francesco (1982) *Förälskelse* (Passion), Göteborg (translated from the Italian original).

Alberoni, Francesco (1984) *Vänskap* (Friendship), Göteborg (translated from the Italian original).

Aubert, Wilhelm (1965) 'Tankar om kärleken' (Thoughts on Love), translated into English in *The Hidden Society*, New York.

Berger, P. and Kellner, H. (1966) 'Marriage and the Construction of Reality', *Diogenes*.

Bernstein, Richard (1984) *Beyond Objectivism and Relativism*, Oxford: Blackwell.

Elster, John (1978) *Logic and Society*, New York: Wiley.

Fraser, Nancy (1985) 'What's Critical about Critical Theory – The Case of Habermas and Gender', *New German Critique*, Spring/Summer (35).

Freud, Sigmund (1962) *Civilization and its Discontents*, New York: Norton.

Freud, Sigmund (1964) *The Future of an Illusion*, New York: Anchor.

Habermas, Jürgen (1969) *Towards a Rational Society*, Boston: Beacon.

Habermas, Jürgen (1981) *Theorie des Kommunikativen Handelns*, (Vols I and II), Frankfurt: Suhrkamp.

Habermas, Jürgen (1985) *Der Philosophische Diskurs der Moderne*, Frankfurt: Suhrkamp.

Halkes, Catharina (1979) 'Feministisk Teologi – Ett nytt fenomen', in Westman-Berg (ed.), *Gråt Inte – Forska, Kvinnovetenskapliga Studier* (Feminist Theology – A New Phenomenon), Stockholm.

Heller, Agnes (1982) 'Habermas and Marxism', in John Thompson and David Held (eds), *Habermas, Critical Debates*, London: Macmillan.

Horkheimer, Max and Adorno, Theodor (1972) *Dialectic of Enlightenment*, New York: Herder and Herder.

Lakoff, George and Johnson, Mark (1982) *Metaphors We Live By*, Chicago: Chicago University Press.

Lasch, Christopher (1977) *Haven in a Heartless World*, New York: Basic Books.

Lash, Scott (1985) 'Postmodernity and Desires', *Theory and Society*, 14(1).

Luhmann, Niklas (1983) *Liebe als Passion, Zur codierung von Intimität*, Frankfurt: Suhrkamp.

Mann, Thomas (1913) *Döden i Venedig* (fr. German *Tot in Venezia*, 1912), Stockholm. *Death in Venice* (1955) Harmondsworth: Penguin.

Mann, Thomas (1947) *Doktor Faustus*, Stockholm. *Doctor Faustus* (1977) Harmondsworth: Penguin.

Marcuse, Herbert (1962) *Eros and Civilization*, Boston: Beacon Press.

Marcuse, Herbert (1964) *One-Dimensional Man*, Boston: Beacon Press.

Marx, Karl (1972) 'Economic-Philosophical Manuscripts', in Robert Tucker (ed.), *The Marx and Engels Reader*, New York: Norton.

O'Neill, John (ed.) (1976) *On Critical Theory*, London: Heinemann.

Parsons, Talcott (1955) 'The American Family: Its Relation to Personality and Social Structure', in T. Parsons and Robert F. Bales (eds), *Family, Socialisation and Interaction Process*. Glencoe, Illinois: Free Press.

Parsons, Talcott (1978) *Action Theory and the Human Condition*, New York: The Free Press.

Reuther, Rosemary (1975) *New Woman, New Earth*, New York.

Rorty, Richard (1979) *Philosophy and the Mirror of Nature*, Princeton: Princeton University Press.

Sartre, Jean Paul (1957) *Being and Nothingness*, trans Hazel Barnes, London: Methuen.

Saxonhouse, Arlene (1984) 'Eros and the Female in Greek Political Thought', *Political Theory*, 12(1): 5–28.

Schluchter, Wolfgang (1981) *The Rise of Western Rationalism*, Berkeley/Los Angeles: University of California Press.

Simmel, Georg (1950) *The Sociology of Georg Simmel*, translated and edited by Kurt Wolff, New York: Free Press.

Simmel, Georg (1984) *On Women, Sexuality and Love*, translated and edited by Guy Oakes, New Haven: Yale University Press.

Weber, Max (1948) *From Max Weber*, Hans Gerth and C.W. Mills (eds), New York: Oxford University Press.

Weber, Max (1978) *Economy and Society*, vol I, translated and edited by Guenther Roth and Klaus Wittich, Berkeley/Los Angeles: University of California Press.

Weber, Sherry (1976) 'Aesthetic Experience and Self-Reflection as Emancipatory Processes', in John O'Neill (ed.), *On Critical Theory*, London: Heinemann.

This chapter first appeared in *Theory, Culture & Society*, Vol. 3 (1986), 19–35.

13

BIOGRAPHICAL BOUNDARIES: SOCIOLOGY AND MARILYN MONROE

Graham McCann

> Those who know me better,
> Know better.
>
> Marilyn Monroe

This chapter was inspired by certain tensions I encountered while I was researching the myth of Marilyn Monroe. Research which has led me to write a book on Monroe (McCann, 1988) which is both a sociological and a biographical study. It generated tensions which have brushed against the grain of both genres, with both positive and negative effects. Why write another book on Marilyn Monroe? I was not unusually attracted to the image of Monroe, yet her recorded remarks affected me in ways which, at first, surprised me. Inevitably then, a measure of autobiography must intrude in my defence. W.J. Weatherby, author of a 'Marilyn' memoir, explains *his* motive by saying: 'I was disturbed by the way in which several pseudo-biographers had merely used her and so I felt I might help to set the record straight as she was someone I liked very much.'[1] The inspiration for my own, meta-biography of Monroe, resides in her own, quite distinctive, comments: she once said of potential biographers:

> I don't think I've ever met a writer I'd like as my judge. They observe people, but often they don't feel them . . . But I think you've got to love people, all kinds of people, to be able to have an opinion about them that's worth anything . . . We can try to be better, and part of trying is not to condemn other people. (quoted in Weatherby, 1976: 170)

I liked this comment, and I began to view a sociocultural study of Monroe as an exceptional opportunity to develop a critique of the cult of celebrity, the problem of men 'interpreting' women, and the problem of the living trying to 'know' the deceased. I then discovered a further problem, largely unexpected and unwanted: the prejudices of my academic discipline.

Stars encourage us to face our fantasies, to reflect on the separation of ourselves into producers and consumers, extroverts and introverts: this is a key reason for why stars matter to us. Movie stars, as an integral part of the machinery of Hollywood, provide an accessible way into an analysis of its political economy, the organization of the narratives it produces, and the relationship between the two. A more problematic, often troubling aspect of studying stars is our fascination with them, our fantasies about them, which can prove disturbing to apparently 'objective' academic analysis. We do not fully understand these pleasures. Indeed, we may consider them too embarrassingly banal for academic study. Equally, we may be reluctant to scrutinize them for fear they may dissolve or slip away or even reveal a darker side we had only dimly and uneasily perceived. Thus, what may initially have seemed an attractively straightforward topic turns out to be anything but.

Sociologists became increasingly uneasy as they learned more about my study of Monroe. Not only would it attempt to refer the figure to the institutions within which her biography was enacted, but it would also strive to include an awareness of my involvement in this study, my obligation to note my own inevitable prejudices. Furthermore, my aim was to retain some notion of identity, some awareness that my subject was not simply a 'social construction' but a real person, an individual, a woman, with hopes and fears and strengths and weaknesses. In other words, I felt an obligation to authenticity, to the presence of the person — whether she be in the library or between the lines. Some sociologists were sceptical: the sneaking feeling was that I must have a 'soft spot' for Monroe. My response was that no social study worthy of that name can give an adequate account of a biographical subject unless it respects the integrity of that subject, unless it refuses to reduce the person to a type. In order to achieve this aim one must, I believe, try in every conceivable way to empathize with the subject, to feel for her and to relate these feelings to the wider social context. This makes for a much more risk-laden, complicated analysis which is potentially vulnerable to accusations of obscurity. I take as my subtext the comments by Adorno (1978: 101) on 'Morality and Style':

Regard for the object, rather than for communication, is suspect in any expression: anything specific, not taken from pre-existent patterns, appears inconsiderate, a symptom of eccentricity, almost of confusion. The logic of the day, which makes so much of its clarity, has naively adopted this perverted notion of everyday speech.

This discussion is not a resignation: I believe that sociology and Marilyn Monroe can enjoy a 'special relationship'. I do not believe that a hermetically sealed sociology, a sociology which shrinks from problems of morality, has anything constructive to contribute to this project. In the following sections I intend to substantiate this thesis: first, by outlining the conventional contours of biography as a genre; second, by looking at some of the Monroe biographies; and third, by examining some possible sociological treatments of biography. I will conclude by stressing the need for interdisciplinarity, for an open-textured, reflexive method which acknowledges a commitment to some notion of authenticity.

I

Monroe once said: 'Those who know me better, know better'. In fact she was replying to reporters who had inquired if she 'wore falsies'. The comment, I feel, has some significance for our study of biography. How can a biographer re-present and remember a person? *Is* there a body lurking beneath the text, between the lines, somewhere in the library? Is the only body present my own? Do biographies wear falsies?

Walter Benjamin (1982: 45-6) wrote that 'The presence of the original is the prerequisite to the concept of authenticity'. A biographer, bounded by fact, still invents her form and, through language, directs the reader's impressions, images, and interpretation of the subject. How she achieves this could become the focus of a theoretical approach initiated by the recognition of figurative language and its function in a biography. Furthermore, discourse in a biography is narrative and in that role assumes properties other than that of recording events. No biographer merely records a life; every biographer, no matter how objective she declares herself, interprets a life. How the biographer expresses the life becomes, to some extent, the real subject of the biography.

Biography is an institution, a profession, and a genre. Since its establishment and its development by figures such as Leslie Stephen, the biography has contained the social function of supplying an overarching direction to the activities of an individual which constitutes an organizational 'career'. In this sense biography is a 'structuring' medium, used in various ways to regularize conduct across time and space. The individual, as Foucault says, is kept 'under the gaze of a permanent corpus of knowledge'. Biography is a profession: it carries certain obligations to conventional rules of conduct and it relates to certain standards. The biographer is expected to produce a study which formally pertains to a certain literary genre.

Sartre, in *Nausea,* has his character reflect on biography's nagging formalism:

> Nothing happens when you live. The scenery changes, people come in and go out, that's all. There are no beginnings . . . But everything changes when you tell about life; it's a change no one notices: the proof is that people talk about true stories . . .

Increasingly, the traditional and current practice of biographers — the chronological and comprehensive life — is incommensurate with what we know about the complexity of individual lives. Today, new demands are placed on biography from psychology, anthropology, sociology and history; as a literary enterprise, biography must respond by registering in its form and content new means of expressing human experience. Dissatisfaction with previous biographies of an individual seems endemic to readers and writers alike. Consequently, multiple lives of major figures are not uncommon. Marilyn Monroe has featured in well over forty studies. Why should we need so many?

As a genre, biography continually unsettles the past; versions of a life are necessary stages in the evolution of the genre as well as in the understanding of the subject. Writing biography is always a relative exercise, bounded by cultural and historical forces which alter, as do the personal conditions of the biographer. When a biographer recognizes that the life she writes is itself an aesthetic construct involving fictions, imagery, style, and narration, parallel to the inner life of her subject, itself a fiction, the result may be a biography that is at the same time literary and truthful. It will also reflect the ambiguous, subtle, self-contradictory, special individual that is its focus. Such reflections often rebel against the old *Dictionary of National Biography* motto, 'No flowers by request'. Accurate biography does not always mean methodical reiteration; as Lytton Strachey said, 'History is not the accumulation of facts, but the relation of them.'

The division between public and private self separates myth from fact — but one always unites the other. Biography is essentially a demythologizing form. Consistently, it functions to correct, restate, revise or reinterpret false or distorted accounts of the subject. Freud (1970: 127) remarked to a prospective biographer: 'Anyone who writes a biography is committed to lies, concealments, hypocrisy, flattery and even to hiding his own lack of understanding, for biographical truth does not exist, and if it did we could not use it.' Freud's own conceit was to persuade his subjects to research their own biography. Generally, through fact and revision, biography strives to demythologize the individual; inevitably, this becomes an ironic effect, since readers replace old myths with new if they read biography uncritically. The representational aspect of a life, a picturing of the experience of a single person, become elements of a universal type. In universalizing the narrative, drawing on archetypes and conventions, biography moves from the realm of history to that of myth. As Benjamin (1977: 45–6) writes: 'That which is original is never revealed in the naked and manifest existence of the factual; its rhythm is apparent only to a dual insight. It . . . is related to its history and subsequent development.'

Reading lives both destroys and creates our image of the subject; even though the historical figure dies, the biography continues her presence — in itself a mythic, phoenix-like activity, re-creating and perpetuating the self. The biography's task of reconstructing while deconstructing intensifies the difficulty of its factual and literary nature. The finest biographies re-invent rather than reconstruct. Virginia Woolf (1979: 150) wrote of 'creative fact': 'In order that the light of personality may shine through, facts must be manipulated; some must be brightened; others shaded; yet, in the process, they must never lose their integrity.' Biography is fundamentally a narrative which has as its primary task the enactment of character and place through language — a goal similar to that of fiction. 'We make sense', says Hayden White (1978: 99), 'of the real world by imposing on it the formal coherency that we customarily associate with the products of writers of fiction.' For a fact to exist in a biography it needs an imaginative as well as a referential dimension which the process of writing provides. For a biography to refer to other constituents of society, a turn to other disciplines must occur, a divining of generalities.

II

Marilyn Monroe, after reading a screenplay on the life of Jean Harlow, sighed and said, 'I hope they don't do that to me after I'm gone'. She has gone, and they *have* done it, many times. More has been written about Marilyn Monroe, both during her lifetime and since, than any other figure in film hagiography. Each study sees Monroe diffracted by a different textual prism. Successive writers in successive studies have drawn out the image and sketched in their ideal, told us all about 'Marilyn', that gentlemen prefer 'Marilyn', that 'Marilyn' was one of the misfits. Images are invoked: 'Marilyn' in and out of control, in and out of bed, in and out of love — Exhibit A and Exhibit B, you are the jury and the inquest has begun.

Of the biographies published, one finds a wide spectrum of treatments and tastes, ranging from Maurice Zolotow (1961) and Fred Lawrence Guiles (1986) — both containing material from Monroe's colleagues and critics — to the sober 'investigative' approach of Anthony Summers (1985) and the 'factoid' flourishes of Norman Mailer (1973, 1980). All of these texts, I believe, can be most rewardingly read as preconceived answers to a preconceived set of questions — questions thoroughly permeated by social, cultural and political presuppositions. Interpretation reveals more about the author as, suddenly, the lady vanishes. Mailer began his *Marilyn* study with a sense of financial necessity: he rapidly became obsessed with his subject. He told *Time* magazine (16 July 1973): 'When I read the other biographies of Marilyn, I said to myself, "I've found her; I know who I want to write about".' He confessed in 1980, after his second Monroe book: 'I always thought that if I had been a woman, then I would have been a little bit like Marilyn Monroe.' This may explain why his 'Marilyn' often sounds 'a little bit' like Norman Mailer.

Monroe was not separate from other women, but they were separated from her. 'Marilyn' was a male fantasy, fiercely protected by men from any threat — even from Monroe herself. Mailer says that 'Marilyn suggested sex might be difficult and dangerous with others, but ice-cream with her'. 'Norman's' 'White Marilyn' is his self-made escape from the threat posed him by real female sexuality: he wants wonderful sex uncomplicated by anxiety about satisfying the woman. This male fantasy 'Marilyn' is made for men's pleasure: she giggles, she shakes her shoulders, she moves to his rhythm, she attends to his needs, she lives only *where* and *when* he wants her, when he can *deal* with her. Monroe carried around with her Wilde's *The Ballad of Reading Gaol,* which contains the lines:

And all men kill the thing they love—
By all let this be heard.
Some do it with a bitter look,
Some with a flattering word.

At the same time as men write Monroe's womanhood, they also write their manhood. He wants to get things straight, to put things in order.

Mailer's imaginary affair with Monroe is by no means unusual among her biographers. In fact, one may read one of two possible morals into the panoply of plots: either, 'Dear Reader, I would have saved her', or 'Dear Reader, I would not have tried'. It is a common feature in Monroe biographies (nearly all of which were written by men) to find the 'Arthur Miller' figure (the Writer, the Intellectual) 'cut around' and replaced, in spirit, by the author. Such a movement is indicative of the more general historiographical process wherein certain facts are animated by their placement in a certain dramatic plot. Monroe's death, her 'ending', ascribes her a beginning and a middle, a moving coherency, turning her into a work of art with a message and a meaning.

Norma Jeane Baker was born on 1 June 1926, became world famous as 'Marilyn Monroe', and died in mysterious circumstances on 4 August 1962. These two dates form quotation marks around a life which many biographers have found, according to the cover of *Goddess,* 'as absorbing as any fiction'. Each writer has set out to strip the myth bare, to retrieve the body from the literary embodiment, to find the flesh and blood of Marilyn Monroe. Anthony Summers' book, *Goddess,* rests on his reputation as an 'investigative journalist' rather than on the uniqueness of his approach: he has, we are told, steadier hands and sharper eyesight. His publishers make the aim eminently clear: to remove the clothing from Clio. *Goddess,* the jacket notes claim, will decorticate the myth: such phrases as 'reveals', 'casts light on', 'lays bare', 'exposes' and 'uncovers', emphasize the presumptions at work. 'With *Goddess',* it is announced, 'all previous books on Marilyn Monroe become redundant.'

Is Summers the highly trained historical paint-stripper he sets out to be? He makes much of his reputation for not being swayed by sentiment or malice, and indeed his sobriety assumes a high profile throughout a discussion which often resembles a detective story. Summers cannot resist trying to 'find Marilyn' — even to the extent of entering the morgue. It is a particularly great misfortune that Summers should find it necessary for his narrative to include a photograph of Monroe's corpse. It is not so much what she looks like that appals, but rather the feeling that this is the ultimate intrusion, on our part as well as on the author's. It is a needless gesture from the author, a cynical sign, one which reflects very badly on the genre of 'investigative biography'. The sign is also a sign of screening out the recognition of one's own mortality. Even an image of a corpse is an image of *something,* it fills the absence staring back at one.

W.J. Weatherby's *Conversations with Marilyn,* according to the jacket notes, presents a 'revelation in [Monroe's] own words, of her own thoughts and feelings. It is probably the closest we shall ever come to knowing the real Marilyn, the persona behind the pin-up photograph, the tinsel glamour and the Hollywood publicity machine'. Weatherby intends to keep his comments to a minimum, in order to 'let her speak for herself'. In fact, there follows the most curious example of the 'author-as-actor' in the narrative. Monroe is cast opposite 'Weatherby', a character redolent of the sharp, shrewd features of Raymond Chandler's hard-boiled sleuth, Philip Marlowe. Indeed, 'Weatherby' reminds one of the Bogart parody in Woody Allen's *Play It Again, Sam,* moving the narrative on with *film noir* nous: 'I was determined not to become obsessed with Monroe, as so many journalists had' (Weatherby, 1976: 25). 'She stared at me as if she was about to speak, but I hurried on' (Weatherby, 1976: 42). '[N]ow she was trying to woo me, to win over yet another journalist, another interviewer. I had been through that experience before with movie stars and politicians, and she began to lose me' (Weatherby, 1976: 60). Allen's 'Bogart' is an outrageous misogynist who claims that there is 'nothing a little bourbon and soda won't fix'. Weatherby (1976: 66) appears to sympathize: 'I had been invited for a drink because I had seemed not to be interested. If you showed lady luck the back of your hand, sometimes she came crawling'. The text then begins to feature Monroe's conversations with Weatherby, and the material is frequently charming and sometimes touching, undermining the earlier self-indulgence. Weatherby's text represents a rare case of the 'subject' overcoming the vagaries of the form. There is a curve of cynicism moving from the sweaty, seedy prose of Mailer to the supposedly 'sensitive' study by Gloria Steinem (1986) — a curve which seems to chart a growing anxiety over whether Monroe (between you and me) was really, after all, something of a 'dumb blonde'. Mailer's maler-than-thou noisy posturings are obvious to the point of self-parody; his book is at least open in its obsession with 'Norman's' panting pursuit of his fantasy 'Marilyn'. Steinem, famously feminist, is a more surprising cynic. She dedicates the book to the 'real' Marilyn, and spends much of her discussion lamenting Monroe's inability to grow up to resemble Gloria Steinem. She arrives on the biographical scene like a caseworker, retrieving Monroe's life from a faded manila folder. By emphasizing so exclusively Monroe's vulnerability, Steinem has, no doubt without intending to, given the legend a decidedly *anti-feminist* slant. For although Monroe was undoubtedly exploited, she also actively participated in the creation of her legend and to play this down is to make her less powerful than she really was. Steinem draws out a 'lesson' from the story of Monroe: in this way Steinem *uses* Monroe in a disrespectful manner.

The 'raw material' is eminently worthy of biographical reflection: the childhood traumas, the nude calendar controversy, the celebrity marriages, the movies, the Mafia, the Kennedys, the mysterious death, the FBI file, the flurry of 'retrospectives'. The story, typically, would appear as a frown if charted point by point: beginning low (an 'orphan'), rising to a peak ('sex goddess'), and falling to its end (suicide or murder). The biography is a kind of 'pinball machine': the plot is planned; the supporting cast (Monroe's mother; Joe DiMaggio; Natasha Lytess; Arthur Miller; the Strasbergs; the Kennedys) are positioned beforehand, often static in terms of personality; finally, 'Marilyn' is fired into the network, made to bounce from figure to figure until the game is completed. She sometimes emerges as victim, sometimes as the 'dumb blonde', other times as a cynical star performer — but always as someone's 'Marilyn', the author's 'Marilyn'.

A survey of the biographical mediations of Monroe will show how polysemic is each 'finished' text, how manifold are the meanings as the writer works towards closure while the material breaks out from every boundary. A character in Julian Barnes' *Flaubert's Parrot* expresses this dialectic:

> The biography stands, fat and worthy-burgherish on the shelf, boastful and sedate: a shilling life will give you all the facts, a ten pound one all the hypotheses as well. But think of everything that got away, that fled with the last deathbed exhalation of the biographee. What chance would the craftiest biographer stand against the subject who saw him coming and decided to amuse himself? (Barnes, 1984: 38)

The books on Marilyn Monroe do not contain 'the real Marilyn', signed, sealed, delivered, and yours. The human being that was Marilyn Monroe cannot be reconstructed by piecing together the black and white marks in the text, but what *can* be reanimated is the cultural praxis at work in each interpretation, each word-picture. One may not find out 'all about Marilyn', but the meta-biography can provide (at least) a proper appreciation of her fictions.

III

Monroe once said:

> The truth is I've never fooled anyone. I've let men sometimes fool themselves. Men sometimes didn't bother to find out who and what I was. Instead they would invent a character for me. I wouldn't argue with them. They were obviously loving somebody I wasn't. When they found this out, they would blame me for disillusioning them — and fooling them. (Monroe, 1974: 105).

In Barthes' words:

> I am searching the other's body, as if I wanted to see what was inside it, as if the mechanical cause of my desire were in the adverse body (I am like those children who take a clock apart in order to find out what time is).

The sociologist who comes to the subject of Marilyn Monroe with great expectations of logical consistency and analytical clarity will soon be rather distressed. Monroe is not an easily understood figure, and any single approach will experience a problem akin to the 'sweet shop' in *Through the Looking Glass* where all shelves seemed full when viewed as a group but empty when seen in isolation. 'Things flow about so here!' Fascinated, the analyst will follow Alice: 'I'll follow it up to the very top shelf of all. It'll puzzle it to go through the ceiling, I expect!' (Carroll, 1979: 68–9). Right through, perhaps, to a meta-level, relating all the 'shelves' to each other and thereby locating their meaning.

In *The Sociological Imagination,* C. Wright Mills argues that to understand the biography of an individual we must 'understand the significance and meaning of the roles [she] has played and does play; to understand these roles we must understand the institutions of which they are a part'. This is inoffensive as sociological instruction, but it only acknowledges a programme which is of quite extraordinary ambition. To do full justice to all levels and structures would demand several volumes; to write a single study would involve considerable problems of social-biographical balance. Interpretation is thus often somewhat aloof. John Dunn (1985: 153) has alluded to such a problem on a general level:

> The claim to know better is flourished menacingly at identities, personal, cultural, and political, from the outside as much as it has ever been before in human history. But today . . . we know that it can be vindicated only within identities, that the only authority which it can possess is a human authority, an authority for human beings not an external domination over them.

Those who know Monroe better, know better: they respect the source of the image. It is the commitment to some conception of authenticity which makes a biography a redemptive reflection and avoids the irresponsibilities of Derridian deconstruction. It is the absence of such a commitment in so many sociological studies of individuals which is so disturbing (c.f. Lévi-Strauss, 1961; 362–4).

There are two sociological strategies in particular — let me call them the 'distant' and the 'dumb' — which are necessarily at odds with biographical integrity. The 'distant' sociologist views the figure from such an Olympian height that the person remains impenetrable; it is debatable whether this stance is simply indecisive or just insensitive. Certainly, all that is sorry melts into air when the distant sociologist prods the subject with a mass of generalities and secondary sources. This approach is particularly prevalent among sociologies of art, wherein the analyst appears afflicted with a form of anhedonia: it is hard to discover what they believe 'art' to be, and it is almost impossible to discern if they like or dislike the subject, even if they care. Turning to the 'dumb' sociologists, we find the figure surrounded by a surfeit of interpretations, from critics and colleagues, mostly borrowed and sometimes blue, wherein all that is sordid hangs in the air. This approach does not avoid interpretation, but it does avoid evaluation.

Neither the distant nor the dumb approach will illuminate the biography. The biographies of Marilyn Monroe are perforce phenomenological, with the works defining the life and serving as the experience of the life. Each fiction becomes a stage of fact, each fiction a factual experience, the interaction of the two establish a life (the biography) via aesthetics. The fact becomes the source of fiction; fiction for the biographer the substance of the subject's life. The sociologist must, crucially, avoid producing a 'macro' survey with a token mini-biography. One must engage with the subject, one must risk intuition; one may well find oneself expressing things one did not expect to express or perhaps not even wish to express. Out of that obscurity one reaches the wish for genuine intelligibility, as though poetry were lodged in every cave of memory and locked in every object of thought. The sceptical sociologist will do well to note the observation from Barthes (1984: 49):

> clarity is a purely rhetorical attribute, not a quality of language in general, which is possible at all times and in all places, but only the ideal appendage to a certain type of discourse, that which is given over to a permanent intention to persuade.

IV

Samuel Johnson declared that the principal value of biography is in 'giving us what comes near to ourselves, what we can turn to use'. For modern readers and writers of social biography this means a more sympathetic as well as more psychologically and more sociologically informed 'use' of biography — avoiding an emphasis on the mass of data at the expense of conveying the vital struggles that confront the subject and the student. I believe the approach to accord with George Steiner's description of the critic in 'Human Literacy': 'To read well is to take great risks. It is to make vulnerable our identity, our self-possession . . .' The critic, he says, should 'help us to read as total human beings, by example of precision, fear, and delight. Compared to the act of creation, that task is secondary. But it has never counted more' (Steiner, 1985: 29).

Monroe is a significant subject for sociological study, raising questions of gender and of celebrity, of the role of popular icons in the marketplace and in the memory. Yet she is also significant in herself, for the personality evident in the images and the interviews. It is important to retain a sense of the tragedy involved when anyone dies so young and so alone in such dubious circumstances. There seems a frightening continuity between many sociological studies and the one-dimensional biographies they are meant to supersede. A more sensitive approach is needed to overcome some fundamental contradictions: that between outside and inside, public and private, the sociological and the psychological, between my being-for-others and my being-for-myself, between the political and the poetic, objectivity and subjectivity — between society and the monad. In my own study of Monroe, I must situate the person within the time and space and social structures wherein she was seen, I must attempt some kind of judgement about her roles and her relations. Yet I must also accept the boundaries of my *own* biography: those parts of my own personality which remain an impenetrable mystery to me; my own all-too-human propensity for mistakes; and my distressing capacity, still, for sometimes hurting those people I most care about. No social study can truly be distant or afford to be dumb.

The sociological study of Monroe, I believe, must strive to recover intentions, to reconstruct connections and to restore contexts. It will neither be told naively as a simple narrative nor judged once and for all from a 'higher' sociological point of view. Instead, it should be reflected in the branching of sociological specialities, in the elaboration and exchanges of sociological centres and peripheries, in the formation of distinct cultural attitudes in and towards the subject, and, last but not least, in the migration of sociological thought into other fields of knowledge and into other academic disciplines, and its storage and transformation there. The biographer obtains a certain power over the subject through understanding the psychological and moral forces that shape her life. Such knowledge gives the writer a certain verbal and ethical authority as she recharts the life of the subject under her direction. If the sociologists remain uncomfortable with Monroe, perhaps this reflects more on the borders of sociology than the boundaries of biography. What I seek is not a figure, but a being; not the indispensable, but the irreplaceable. To finish by paraphrasing Forster: if I had to choose between betraying my discipline and betraying my subject, I hope I should have the guts to betray my discipline.

Note

1. Correspondence with the author: 15 April 1986.

References

Adorno, T.W. (1978) *Minima Moralia*. London: New Left Books.

Barnes, J. (1984) *Flaubert's Parrot*. London: Picador.

Barthes, R. (1984) *Writing Degree Zero*. London: Jonathan Cape.

Benjamin, W. (1977) *The Origin of German Tragic Drama*. London: New Left Books.

Benjamin, W. (1982) *Illuminations*. London: Fontana.

Carroll, Lewis (1979) *Through the Looking Glass*. London: J.M. Dent & Sons.

Dunn, J. (1985) *Rethinking Modern Political Theory*. Cambridge: Cambridge University Press.

Empson, W. (1984) *Using Biography*. London: Chatto & Windus.

Freud, S. (1970) Freud to Arnold Zweig, 31 May 1936 in E.L. Freud (ed.) *The Letters of Sigmund Freud to Arnold Zweig*. New York: Harcourt Brace World.

Giddens, A. (1987) *Modern Social Theory and Sociology*. Cambridge: Polity.

Guiles, F.L. (1986) *Norma Jean: The Life and Death of Marilyn Monroe*. London: Grafton Books.

Hembus, J. (1973) *Marilyn Monroe, die Frau des Jahrhunderts*. Munich: Wilhelm Heyne Verlag.

Kyrou, A. (1972) *Marilyn Monroe*. Paris: Denoel.

Lévi-Strauss, C. (1961) 'The Place of Anthropology in the Human Sciences', in *Structural Anthropology*. New York: Basic Books.

Lowenthal, D. (1985) *The Past is a Foreign Country*. Cambridge: Cambridge University Press.

McCann, G. (1988) *Marilyn Monroe: The Body in the Library*. Cambridge: Polity. Polity.

Mailer, N. (1973) *Marilyn*. New York: Grosset & Dunlap.

Mailer, N. (1980) *Of Women and their Elegance*. London: Hodder & Stoughton.

Mellen, J. (1973) *Marilyn Monroe*. New York: Pyramid Publications.

Mills, C. Wright (1970) *The Sociological Imagination*. Harmondsworth: Penguin.

Monroe, M. (1974) *My Story*. New York: Stein and Day.

Speriglio, M. (1986) *The Marilyn Conspiracy*. London: Corgi.

Steinem, G. (1986) *Marilyn*. New York: Henry Holt.

Steiner, G. (1985) *Language and Silence*. London: Faber & Faber.

Summers, A. (1985) *Goddess*. London: Gollancz.

Veyne, P. (1971) *Comment en ecrit l'histoire*. Paris: Seuil.

Wagenknecht, E.C. (ed.) (1969) *Marilyn: A Composite View*. London: Chilton.

Weatherby, W.J. (1976) *Conversations with Marilyn*. London: Robson Books.

White, H. (1978) *Tropics of Discourse*. Baltimore: Johns Hopkins.

Woolf, V. (1979) *Granite and Rainbow*. London: J.M. Dent & Sons Ltd.

Zolotow, M. (1961) *Marilyn Monroe*. London: Panther.

This chapter first appeared in *Theory, Culture & Society*, Vol. 4 (1987), 619–32.

14

CARMEN – OR THE INVENTION OF A NEW FEMININE MYTH

Dick Pels and Aya Crébas

Jamais Carmen ne cédera, Libre elle est née et libre elle moura.

1. *'Belle dame sans merci'*

Puccini's *La Bohème*, Verdi's *La Traviata* and Bizet's *Carmen* are the most famous operas of the nineteenth century — if not of all time. Remarkably, the dramatic climax of all three involves the death of a woman on stage. These women, moreover, are not average types, but citizens of the sociological fringe: a *grisette*, a courtesan and a gypsy. Of these marginal types, the gypsy Carmen is easily the strangest and most exotic; to the nineteenth-century bourgeois she must have seemed a being from an alien world. While Puccini's and Verdi's languishing and passive heroines are far closer to home, all three operas none the less seem to explore the same two inextricably intertwined themes: each suggests a symbolic masculine revenge on the world of femininity as well as an exorcism of the morally alien and illicit by a bourgeoisie which is at once both fascinated and horrified. As such, the three operas appear to be as many explorations into the fate of women in a world which is dominated by a masculine ideal of romantic love — an ideal propagated above all by male moralists. In *Carmen*, the final triumph of this bourgeois morality takes the fatal turn of a crime of passion in which the man, driven to desperation, murders the independent and egocentric woman who refuses to let him possess her.[1]

In the hitherto usual interpretation of the theme of Mérimée's novella and Bizet's opera, the figure of Carmen is indeed regarded as the typical *femme fatale*, the personification of the exotic-erotic, the sphinx who inevitably destroys those unfortunates who succumb to her irresistible charms. Mario Praz, (1970: 206-7) for example, includes her in his gallery of *belles dames sans merci*, the beautiful but cruel women who so bounteously populate the decadent literature of the nineteenth century. As the dark side or 'risk' of the ideal of romantic love, and as the antithesis of demure feminine propriety, the *femme fatale* is portrayed as the accessory to a deep moral ambiguity. The enthralled male, the hapless victim of the entice-ments of such 'carnivorous plants', is morally redefined as a helpless being no longer in full command of his faculties. Like the proverbial moth, he can only fly toward the flame that will consume him. Killing the *femme fatale* is therefore less a crime than a final act of despera-tion, an act of defiance against a cruel fate become flesh — that is, if it is not understood in the first place as the public execution of a witch whose diabolical effrontery has for once gone too far. The type of the fatal, sexually voracious woman therefore appears to provide men with a moral *carte blanche*, and to exonerate them *a priori* from the violence they may perpetrate against her. While the woman who refuses to submit to the prevailing code of modesty and dependence may therefore feel that she has escaped the constricting 'game' of conventional femininity and become free as a bird, she thereby runs the risk of becoming 'fair game' in quite another sense.

It is no doubt this tension-ridden balance between the mainte-nance of moral proscriptions and the illicit craving for the forbidden and the exotic that has given the Carmen theme its enduring popu-larity. *Carmen* has survived the double standards of both the nine-teenth century and our own with flying colours; it is still the most frequently performed opera world-wide. Moreover, there has been a marked resurgence of interest over the past ten years — a resur-gence which at first sight seems baffling when looked at in the light of the prevailing interpretation of the Carmen theme. None the less, it is hardly an exaggeration to conclude that Mérimée's gypsy has achieved the glamour of a true cult figure, and has been 'discovered' by the major producers of style and fashion as a heroine for our time. At the opera's premiere in 1875 the story was considered too obscene for public performance. By 1984, little more than a century later, it enjoyed such prestige that a performance of the opera was deemed serviceable as an official gift by President Mitterand on the occasion of his state visit to the Netherlands. The performance in question, moreover, was the highly controversial new interpretation by Peter Brook: *La Tragédie du Carmen*. To stage it, the entire cast was flown over from New York for a single performance in Amsterdam's *Carré* theatre. Later that evening, Brook's inter-pretation was also broadcast on television for the edification of the common public. Around that time, two films were circulating internationally, in which the familiar theme of fatal passion and crime were reinterpreted for modern filmgoers. Godard's film, *Prénom Carmen*, was a paraphrase in which the heroine robs a bank and takes a policeman as her lover. Carlos Saura's dance-film *Carmen*, which circulated for nearly two years, portrayed a relationship between the director of a *Carmen* production and his lead dancer, and contained innumerable double references to Mérimée's novella and Bizet's opera. In addition to these dramatic reinterpretations, Francesco Rosi's more recent and traditional movie version of the opera has enjoyed world-wide success.

The Carmen rage has touched not only the world of the cinema, but that of fashion as well, from Parisian *haute couture* to popular confection outlets. Carmen featured in April 1984, as cover-girl on the German magazine *Stern*, and in June of that year on the Dutch *Cosmopolitan* and *Avenue*, as if she were just another member of royalty or the international jet-set. The new fashions then beginning to be pushed by leading magazines were a refined conglomerate of the so-called 'gypsy' or 'pirate' look, the 'down and out' look, and an eclectic mixture of styles from the 1940s and 1950s. Particularly striking features of these fashions are their alluring sensuality, their humouristic citations and parodies and the vibrant and expressive use of colours, ranging from bright yellow to jade-green and vermillion, often in combinations which until very recently were regarded as unappetizingly discordant. Under the influence of the Carmen phenomenon, the American designer Norma Kamali, for example, has shown styles which combine the 'impossible'. Her fashions are simultaneously dignified and daring, vampish and comic, chic and vulgar (see for example *Vogue*, American edn, November 1984). This colourful, strong and simultaneously chaotic style was also disseminated world-wide in the allied field of pop-music by comediennes such as Bette Midler and new pop stars — Pat Benatar, Cyndi Lauper, and more recently, by Sapho.[2]

Although a wholesale surrender to the 'Carmen look' was already widely predicted for the summer of 1985, one had to wait until 1988 before it finally found its way into mail order catalogues and boutique windows, and before it appeared in numerous details in that ultimate battleground of social distinction: the streets. In the Netherlands, the summer of 1988 was universally announced to be 'Spanish' in temperament and 'flamenco' in style, although popular journals such as *Viva* had already quite successfully beaten the drum of the gypsy-Carmen-flamenco theme in previous years (*Viva* 1, January 1986; 6 and 19, February and May 1987; 17, April 1988). A provisional pinnacle was reached when no less than two Carmens were seen to contest the figure skating championship at the Calgary Olympic Games last February. There, East Germany's Katarina Witt, already dubbed the 'communist sex-bomb' by the American papers, convincingly defeated the American Debi Thomas, whose interpretation of Bizet's Carmen rather looked, as the Dutch *Volkskrant* icily wrote, like a 'nervous Barbie doll'.

In and of itself, the recent Carmen revival is nothing new. In the cinema, for example, two earlier Carmen revivals are worthy of note: one immediately following World War I and one in the 1950s. There was a silent(!) *Carmen* directed by Lubitsch in 1918, a Cecil B. De Mille *Carmen* and one by the Fox Studios (with Theda Bara as Carmen). In the same period Chaplin and Edna Purviance acted in a *Carmen* burlesque (1916). In the 1950s, a new series of films was released including, among others, Rita Hayworth as a white Carmen and Dorothy Dandridge as a black Carmen in, respectively, *Loves of Carmen*, with Glenn Ford (1948) and *Carmen Jones*, with Harry Belafonte (1954). Just like its contemporary counterpart, the cinematic Carmen revival of the 1950s influenced the fashion of the period. Part of the current revival may even be accounted to this connection, in the sense that the aesthetics of that period have been influencing decorative and fashion styles for several years now.

At the same time, however, it is clear that the recent wave has a much more comprehensive influence, and that it also implies a consequential moral re-evaluation of the Carmen type itself. In the older opera performances, as in the films of the 1920s and 1950s, Carmen is quite uniformly portrayed as a *femme fatale*, as a fickle, promiscuous, and therefore dangerous woman. Current fashion oracles and recent movie productions promulgate a Carmen-inspired female type which, while idealized, is much more common in our time, and with which a rather large group of contemporary young women can apparently identify. Carmen is no longer portrayed as a vamp, a hysteric or as forbidden fruit, but as an alluring young woman, joining independence and self-consciousness to an expressive femininity, and thus fusing characteristics considered incommensurable in the older morality.

In March 1984, for example, when the French *Vogue* devoted an article to Peter Brook, the accompanying fashion-spread was entirely cast in the style of his interpretation of the opera. The essence of Brooks' *mise-en-scène* is sobriety: the piece is acted on a bare stage with a sand floor. The cast of major characters is reduced to four: Carmen, Micaëla, Don José and Escamillo. The clothing ('costumes' would be a pretentious term here) betray none of the familiar operatic splendour: the garments are simple but effective; Carmen radiates sensuality in her loose dress, Micaëla is serious and decent, Don José is sober. Only Escamillo, clothed in the traditionally spectacular dress of the toreador, recalls the glamour we usually associate with opera. Brooks' vision thus accentuates the existential drama surrounding Carmen; in the accompanying fashion-spread *couturiers* such as Féraud, Laroche and Cardin correspondingly display a theatrical Carmen dressed simply in crimson or dramatic black.

Shortly thereafter, the Dutch oracle of stylish elegance, the monthly *Avenue*, also published an article on Peter Brook in combination with a fashion story on the Carmen style. As far as the article goes, it is enough to state that — aside from a large number of independently invented historical and literary errors — it is pilfered lock, stock and barrel from the French *Vogue* article. In contrast to this unusual sample of intellectual sloth and plagiarism, however, the accompanying fashion report is excellent and original. A young, aristocratic Carmen is portrayed in a series of exquisite photographs using Seville as a backdrop, wearing splendid outfits in startling colours — fuchsia, bluish-purple and a glossy yellow — all couched in a distinctly feminine style with, here and there, a contrapuntal masculine note represented by the toreador.

Just as *Avenue's* Carmen fashions are delightful and unconcerned, those portrayed in the April 1984 edition of the German *Stern* are aggressive and over-sexed. Fearsome looking and barely nubile damsels exhibit a brand-new version of the nineteenth century's double standard. The material is trendy red and black leather, cut so that the fragile bodily forms and the emphatic nakedness are ominously accentuated. This fashion-psychological style is interesting — not least because it deviates from the general trend, and as such proves the rule. The accompanying article, significantly, concludes with a warning against the return of the vamp: Carmen is in actuality a 'she-devil', a female role created by men which, alas, women are all too eager to play. In this sense too, *Stern* assumes an eccentric position in relation to the rest of the Carmen revival.[3] Thus, the June 1984 edition of the English *Cosmopolitan* again features Carmen-inspired fashions very much in tune with the earlier interpretation of *Vogue* and *Avenue*. *Cosmo* reaffirms this emphasis upon strength and individuality in its issues of May 1987 ('Come on strong with the sultriest look for seasons . . . a style that takes its cue from the fiery Carmen spirit') and March 1988 ('Hard-edged and thoroughly modern, this is definitely a look for brave individualists').

2. In Search of the 'Real' Carmen
It is telling that Brook, as well as the cineasts, Godard, Saura and Rosi, have all independently laid claim to having successfully

recovered the 'real' Carmen in their works — a Carmen held by them to have been hitherto thoroughly repressed by nineteenth-century interpretations. These claims refer to the actual performances of the opera, but above all to the personage of Carmen herself. The new interpreters are virtually unanimous in their rejection of the opera cliché of the *femme fatale* and aim at achieving psychological depth by drawing directly on Mérimée's and Bizet's original material. Brook, for example, refers directly to the importance of the 1845 novella in achieving a deeper understanding of Carmen's character. With respect to Bizet, moreover, he reiterates the modern cliché that the composer had to prostrate his authentic artistry before the commercializing and popularizing tendencies of his librettists Meilhac and Halévy. Be that as it may, the net result of these purification rituals is a virtual inversion of the traditional psychology of the Carmen tragedy; it is now the woman who embodies the ideals of individualism and will-power, while the man, assailed by jealousy and possessiveness, is portrayed as a childish, immature creature.

In part, this rupture with the operatic tradition is effected by a principled emphasis on sobriety as exemplified in Peter Brooks' production, from which all the usual tinsel of complex sets, flashy costumes and overcrowded scenes has been rigorously eliminated. Godard too, in *Prénom Carmen*, seems to want to avoid any and all associations with the opera, evident in, among other things, his choice of Beethoven instead of Bizet for the sound-track. Carlos Saura, for his part, weaves authentic Spanish guitar music into Bizet's theme and refers quite pointedly to Mérimée on several occasions. His lead actress, Laura del Sol, looks as though she has just walked out of the novella itself (she has 'almond-shaped eyes . . . full but exquisitely defined lips . . . raven hair'). This Carmen is portrayed as an independent young woman, with her own job and house, whose word — especially in matters of love — is law. And this law goes beyond mere sexual candour; Saura's Carmen is more nearly a female Don Juan than a *femme fatale*. None the less, the dancer–director, played by Antonio Gades, succumbs to this new Carmen as fatally as his predecessors did to the old. And, as in the old stories, he can in the end free himself only by killing her.[4]

Rosi's opera-film, shot in Spain, also deviates from the classic tradition, even if, of all recent interpretations, it is the most faithful to Bizet's original opera. The difference, such as it is, is partly attributable to the interpretation of her role by Julia Migenes-Johnson who, like Laura del Sol, has been universally praised for her expressive and sensual Carmen, and who has also explicitly and publicly rejected the traditional image of Carmen as whore and vamp (see, for example, *Gramophone* March 1984). With Julia Migenes, wrote the progressive French daily *Libération*, 'C'est le sexe qui chante'. Prior to this film Rosi had already established a solid reputation as a dedicated left-wing film maker, so that many were surprised at his infatuation with the quintessentially 'bourgeois' opera *Carmen*. But as he explained in interviews, the Carmen story in fact re-enacts at an individual level the same drama that he had previously been filming as social struggle: a conflict between the vested establishment and the will to freedom which here takes the form of a confrontation between the son of petit-bourgeois parents and an authentic 'daughter of the people' (cf. *Positif* and *Cinéma*, both April 1984).

In the operatic tradition itself the moral transvaluation of the figure of Carmen has meanwhile become an accomplished fact. Of course, the 'anti-bourgeois' interpretation has always served as a counterpoint to the mainstream tradition, but it remained ephemeral and strongly tied to the individual temperament of the singers themselves. The legendary Conchita Supervia, for example, amply endowed her Carmen role with those qualities she herself possessed in such abundance: guts, a striking femininity and a hearty laugh. Geraldine Farrar and Victoria de los Angeles also created a distinctively 'different' Carmen, as did Maria Callas — even if hers remained the closest to the fatalistic 'cruel' interpretation.

Not until the 1970s, however, was this latter conception finally swept offstage, and the new 'anti-bourgeois' interpretation came into its own. The major Carmen interpreter in those years was Teresa Berganza, who also studied Mérimée and Bizet as original sources in preparation for her role. She rejected as a 'false idea' the popular understanding of Carmen as a glamorous but unprincipled courtesan, and tended to interpret Carmen as the prototype of the 'truly emancipated' woman. Her Carmen was no floosy, superficial and dangerous, flighty and fickle, but an expressive personality of great character, 'fully aware of her femininity', 'free', 'sovereign', and 'mistress of all her decisions'.[5]

Thus, gradually, the workshops of modern morality are seen to give shape to a new feminine icon. The figure of Carmen seems eminently suited to serve as a focus for such new identifications, as a kind of strategic crossroads where a number of styles and tastes impinge on sociological and psychological changes in the moral economy, especially in so far as these affect relationships between men and women. The classic icon of the *femme fatale* is here stood on its head, in such a way that the characteristics imputed to her are in part stripped of their negative connotations and in part simply transvalued by being typologically reordered. Capriciousness and the hunger for power now become self-assurance and sovereign wilfulness; provocativeness becomes self-conscious femininity and expressiveness; whorishness becomes sexual frankness. In this way the *femme fatale* is transformed from a masculine fantasy (which is sometimes enacted by women) into a *women*'s fantasy, in which the woman can usurp all kinds of 'masculine' characteristics without losing her feminity, that is, without having to adopt the false and cynical femininity of the *belle dame sans merci*. Social stigmas still potent in the 1950s — evinced by epithets like tramp, vixen or hussy — seem to have become the compliments of the 1980s.[6]

An important precondition for the current popularity of the Carmen type, therefore, is that it contains sufficient ambiguity to accommodate two opposite idealizations. The stylistic pose of the recovery of the 'real' Carmen, the Carmen as 'originally intended' by Mérimée and Bizet, already betrays the fact that we are dealing with the construction of a myth, which is of course as deeply rooted in current emotional life as it is in the study of historical sources. The interesting point, in fact, is that both the new and the old myth can claim legitimate descent from the same historical material. Both the 'bourgeois' and the 'anti-bourgeois' interpretations appear to assume a textual coherence in the original which simply cannot be discerned there. In this way, the search for the authentic Carmen becomes a bit like a pilgrimage to a holy shrine; a search for a historical legitimation of a contemporary projection, of the symbolic stylization of a new idol. For this reason it makes sense to reconsider Mérimée's novella and Bizet's opera at somewhat greater length. We shall therefore attempt to relate the ambiguities of the Carmen story to certain elements of the socio-biographies of author and composer. More particularly, we shall focus on their relationship with the emerging urban Bohemia: the modern 'gypsydom' of marginal artists, intellectuals, politicians and their *amourettes* and mistresses, which has its origins in mid-nineteenth-century Paris.

3. Mérimée and Morality: *Arsène Guillot*

At the time of the publication of his novella *Carmen*, in October 1845 in the *Revue des deux mondes*, Prosper Mérimée had just become forty-three and was already a man of considerable standing in the France of Louis Philippe, the 'bourgeois-king'. After graduating as a lawyer, he had advanced rapidly in the footsteps of the comte d'Argout, who occupied various cabinet posts in the years after 1830. As early as 1831 (at the age of twenty-eight) Mérimée had been awarded the Légion d'honneur for services rendered, and three years later had been appointed Inspector of Historical Monuments by Thiers. Mérimée was a man of the world: well-travelled, erudite and a polyglot. His waxing literary and dramatic reputation was sensationally confirmed on 14 March, 1844 by his election to the Académie française.

A single day later and the tables would undoubtedly have turned against him. On 15 March, his story *Arsène Guillot* was published and caused an immediate scandal. While Mérimée had always been a libertine in his choice of and approach to his topics, this was too close for comfort. The story was not safely quarantined within a historical or exotic setting, but was set squarely within the Parisian milieu itself and dealt with the conflict between free and spontaneous love (as idealized by Mérimée) and the hypocrisy of bourgeois prudery and religious obligation. It is worth relating the story line briefly, both because of its similarities to *Carmen*, (which appeared in the following year) and because it offers us a glimpse of what might, with some exaggeration, be called Mérimée's 'double life'.

Arsène Guillot is a young cocotte, a *fille d'opéra*, who allows herself to be maintained by her lovers. When her mother dies and she is abandoned by her gentlemen, she attempts suicide. A rich and religiously devout bourgeois lady regards it as her Christian duty to take Arsène into her care. This Mme de Piennes aims to impress on the fallen woman (quite literally: Arsène had jumped out of a third-floor window) the error of her ways and to teach her to prefer 'sacred' to profane love. With the aid of a clergyman and a generous supply of morally uplifting literature, she appears to succeed in her aims — until Arsène threatens to recover her former self with the arrival of Max de Salligny on the scene. De Salligny, dandy and *bon vivant*, pities his former mistress Arsène, but also cherishes the memory of an unrequited love for Mme de Piennes. A marriage between the two had been thwarted by their respective families. Thereafter Max had consoled himself with courtesans like Arsène, and Mme Piennes with the rich, respectable and dull gentleman whose name she bears. Neither has tasted 'real' love, in contrast to the poor cocotte who alone has known what true love is like. So, when Max sadly asks the dying Arsène what happiness life has brought her, her last words are: 'J'ai aimé . . .'

It is of course not difficult to see why such a theme should be regarded by the established bourgeoisie as an affront. Mérimée is in fact singing the praises of spontaneous, emotional love while at the same time touting the emotional impotence and moral hypocrisy to which bourgeois virtue and piety give rise. Arsène's frivolity is partly excused on the grounds of her poverty. Mme de Piennes, a living monument to bourgeois morality, is portrayed as a hypocrite toward both Arsène and Max precisely on account of her good intentions. Driven by zealous piety, but secretly drawn to the forbidden world of sin and squalor, she finds it difficult at times to hide her jealousy of Arsène, while her feelings for Max become hopelessly mired in the swamp of bourgeois etiquette and formality.

In a revealing study, *Prosper Mérimée: Heroism, Pessimism and Irony*, Frank Paul Bowman (1962) makes a plausible case for regarding the motif of *Arsène Guillot* and other of Mérimée's novellas as direct reflections of Mérimée's ambiguous attitude towards his own social milieu. Bowman makes it clear how strongly Mérimée sympathizes with socially marginal characters like cocottes and dandies, and with the 'other world' of vagabonds and outlaws in the broadest sense. He identifies with these figures and through them criticizes his own established milieu. Arsène is directly modelled on his own earlier mistress Céline Cayot, the comedienne and singer, who also inspired Stendhal's Raymonde in *Lucien Leuwen*. While Max de Salligny is certainly no self-portrait, Mérimée has endowed him with several of his own most characteristic features. Mérimée's tragedy, argues Bowman, is that while he despises bourgeois and churchly morality because they suffocate every expression of strong feeling and block all forms of emotional contact, he is, in fact, a respected citizen who cynically adapts himself to the calcified rituals of 'le monde'. In spite of his social success he regards his life as a failure: in public the ironic, indifferent, distant dandy, in private a man with a vulnerable and volcanic emotional life which can only partly find expression in his literary work. Just as Mérimée is an Anglophile in his dandyism, so is he 'espagnolist' in his inner life — a mood which he shares with his old friend Stendhal. This duality also dominates his relationships with women: he can only enjoy sensual love with cocottes and *demimondaines* like Arsène/Céline while he reserves his deeper intellectual and emotional impulses for platonic friendships such as that with Mme de Montijo and her daughter, later the Empress Eugénie.

4. Mérimée's Carmen

Mérimée, the stranger–bourgeois, is attracted in his fantasy life to other strangers. While Arsène Guillot is still a marginal figure within his own social milieu, Carmen, the gypsy, seems to stand completely outside the familiar world. To a certain extent this is an illusion, since Carmen can in fact also be regarded as a symbolic radicalization of the same marginal type as Arsène. Even though the novella is situated in Spain, in the exotic world of gypsies and bandits, it is rooted in the same moral psychology which undergirds *Arsène Guillot*.[7]

Carmen 'enters' and confronts the traveller–narrator on the quay of the Guadalquivir in Cordoba, at the time of day when the *grisettes*, the factory girls of the city, bathe together in the river, while the men look on without being able to see much in the twilight. Carmen the gypsy possesses a strange and provocative beauty; her look is at once voluptuous and wild: 'The eye of a *bohémien* [i.e. gypsy], the eye of a wolf'. The narrator is clearly charmed and ends up following her to a house where she has promised to tell his fortune by the cards. Suddenly a man bursts into the room, whom the narrator recognizes as José Navarro, an infamous bandit whom he had met on the way and whom he helped escape from the police. This stroke of fortune now enables him to escape from the wiles of Carmen herself who had actually intended to seduce and then rob him.

When the traveller again stops in Cordoba on his way back several months later, it appears that José Navarro has been captured and put behind bars; his death sentence is to be carried out the following day. On his final evening, the bandit tells the narrator the story of his life. Originally a Basque nobleman, he had been forced to leave his homeland after killing a man in a quarrel. As his last hope of advancement, he had enlisted in the army and was detailed to Seville as brigadier. There he had met Carmen, who worked in a tobacco factory. Don José, who was already ill at ease among the sharp-tongued Andalusian women, had been defenceless against the wild Carmen.

The meeting between Carmen and Don José is depicted in the same terms as was that between Carmen and the narrator. Carmen 'enters' surrounded by the factory girls of Seville who, like their Cordoban counterparts, are depicted as carefree and unscrupulous; in the midst of these women the taunting and intriguing Carmen stands out as being a shade more self-conscious and independent. She takes possession of Don José by tossing him a flower, and when he is later forced to arrest her for her part in a knifing, he lets her escape; also, it seems, because she claims to be Basque, a lie which she can carry off because of her command of that language. As a result, Don José is demoted and has to spend a month in the stockade. At his release, Carmen organizes an intimate celebration-for-two during which she generously repays her debts. The next morning Carmen considers their accounts settled and she makes it quite clear to Don José that he need have no illusions because, though she does love him a little, it is clear that 'dog and wolf can't live together in harmony for long'.

But José is no longer able to leave Carmen, and the ensuing events only bear out her earlier warning that, in her, he has met 'the devil'. He goes from bad to worse and, in small but irrevocable steps, seals his fate as a member of the criminal fraternity. He first allows the smugglers' band to pass in exchange for a second night of amorous bliss with Carmen. But she is as capricious as the Basque weather and, not long after, José kills a lieutenant from his own regiment who has been taken home by Carmen. Because there is now a price on his head, he has no recourse but to become a smuggler, which also allows him to share Carmen's life and to live in the hope that he may finally come to possess her. In spite of her scorn for his jealousy, he obeys her every whim. When he commits another murder out of jealousy, Carmen senses that his possessiveness knows no bounds and that he will finally kill her as well. But she refuses to let this intimidate her and she faces death as she has lived her life: without a trace of fear. She no longer wishes to live with him, but neither will she submit to his threats. José begs her to stay with him and promises her everything he has. In desperation he pulls his knife, but she knows no fear and asks no mercy. After the murder José turns himself in, certain of facing the *garotte*.

Thus is the history of Carmen the story of the demise of Don José, who is unable to resist a demonic-seductive and utterly unyielding woman. As far as it goes, this theme clearly answers to the romantic myth of the *femme fatale* who irresistibly attracts men, uses them, and finally breaks them. Thus, the benevolent-feministic interpretation à la Berganza would seem to depend on a rather one-sided idealization. None the less, there is much in Mérimée's text to suggest and support such an interpretation. The structures of both characters and plot are so complex precisely because Mérimée is intent on depicting the conflict between José and Carmen as a conflict between bourgeois obedience and the will to freedom (Carmen: 'What I want is to be free and to do what pleases me') and on giving Carmen the features of a new sort of heroine. In contrast to Arsène Guillot, she is depicted as a forceful personage in whom a love of life and a stoic sense of fate are joined in an almost 'classic' manner. Moreover, Carmen and José are not radically opposite types in any simple sense. While Don José, with his military honour, his sense of duty and his male possessiveness certainly exhibits bourgeois features, he is also an outsider, a noble brigand, and Mérimée seems to sympathize with the anti-bourgeois features of *both* his protagonists.

None the less, it is clear that Mérimée is describing a head-on collision between two opposing mentalities: Carmen's, in which love is associated with freedom and uncertainty and José's, in which it is associated with permanence and faithfulness. In this sense, the two live in different worlds. Neither can live the life of the other without doing violence to him or herself, and ultimately also to the other. The man, driven by jealousy, finally destroys that which he cannot possess. The woman appears to call forth her own undoing by deliberately provoking the demon of jealous love. Both are thus the victim of an overarching tragedy that makes them fatal for each other according to an inevitable scenario which must run its full course.

It is this notion of inevitable fate which again betrays the extent to which Mérimée remains in the spell of a Romantic mysticism which regards true love as an unpredictable, sometimes annihilating emotion which creates a supernatural bond between man and woman. The intriguing thing about his Carmen is that she appears both to reconfirm this romantic image and to deny it. Thus, on the one hand, she is the 'satanic', 'fatal', woman who tramples all moral codes underfoot and who mobilizes love (or what she prefers to understand by it) cynically for her own purposes; while, on the other, she reduces love to more normal, more 'natural' proportions, no longer confuses it with security and eternal troth, rejects jealousy as mere foolishness, and in this sense is an unromantic being.

5. Bizet's Carmen

The premiere of Bizet's opera, in 1875, took place exactly thirty years after the publication of Mérimée's novella. The idea of adapting this story was Bizet's own. Upon reading it, he immediately saw possibilities for a production in the Opéra-Comique, the theatre for the lighter operatic genre. In his enthusiasm he sent copies of the novella to the famous librettists Meilhac and Halévy, who were associated with the theatre. In reply they warned him that the story as it then stood was far too risqué for a production in the Opéra-Comique, the latter being after all a theatre where, for example, a proper young man should be able to take his fiancée with no fear of embarrassment. The parties agreed that *Carmen* should be adapted in such a way as to fit into this tradition. The interesting thing about this adaptation was that, as a result of all kinds of interventions, the story was reframed within a simplified and much more explicit good–bad dichotomy while its graphically shocking elements were simultaneously repressed. Thus, with respect to Mérimée's treatment, the moral message was adapted in such a way that the figure of Carmen became more familiar, in so far as she lost some of her exotic cruelty, while at the same time, in her role of courtesan, she became increasingly effective as a 'terror of the bourgeoisie'. But even the sharp contrast between Carmen and her dramatic opposite, the archetypically naive and utterly decorous Micaëla (added to the cast of characters by Meilhac and Halévy) was insufficient to rob Carmen of all her ambiguity.

It is worthwhile once more to catalogue the differences between the opera libretto and the original story. First of all, the story is stripped of a dimension by the elision of the figure of the narrator and his adventurous meetings with Don José and Carmen. Subsequently, all the dramatic and moral gloom is dispelled to be replaced by an airy and strait-laced fantasy world in which all references to carnal pleasures are suppressed, murderous incidents cut back to a bare minimum and smugglers and gypsies are magically transformed into fairy-tale knaves who play the game of crime and punishment just as cheerfully as the tin soldiers who pursue them. The opera, incidentally, commences with a kind of fantasy-soldiering which is only conceivable in a nation as saturated with militarism as was France before the Dreyfus Affair. Throughout the entire opera, the garrison functions as a model of social normality and military honour as the apotheosis of moral respectability — an image which is underscored by the eulogy on the quasi-military virtues of the toreador Escamillo. Don José is deprived of all his unpredictable, anti-social features, and transformed into a withdrawn, naive and dutiful brigadier, who thinks often of his mother and his native village.

Moreover, at the beginning of the opera Don José's leading lady is not Carmen, but Micaëla. As the prototype of the retiring and obedient heroine, she functions as a complement to the dutiful figure of Don José and as an antithesis to the aggressive Carmen. The duet between Don José and Micaëla (she had come to bring him a kiss from his mother) is saturated with prudery and propriety and plays on the whole range of classical emotional symbols from mother-love and homesickness for the native land up to and including an arranged marriage with the orphan Micaëla. The ritual kiss seems to tie José to the respectable world and to protect him from the 'demon', the evil woman whom he has met just before.

The demon is Carmen, and she makes her entrance in the midst of the uninhibited cigarette-smoking girls of the tobacco factory, among whom the reticent José already has difficulties maintaining his composure. Singing, they compare love with smoke that rises up, that goes to your head but also disperses quickly ('Le doux parler des amants, c'est fumée . . .'). Carmen epitomizes this image of ephemeral and unfettered love in the famous Habañera whose most pregnant lines are these:

L'amour est un oiseau rebelle
Que nul ne peut apprivoiser
Et c'est bien en vain qu'on l'appelle
S'il lui convient de refuser . . .

L'amour est enfant de Bohême,
Il n'a jamais connu de loi;
Si tu ne m'aimes pas, je t'aime,
Si je t'aime, prends garde à toi . . .
L'oiseau que tu croyais surprendre
Battit de l'aile et s'envola . . . [8]

It is exactly this doubly exaggerated contrast between the haughty Andalusian girls of which lot the gypsy Carmen is clearly the 'worst', and the prudish, innocent pair José–Micaëla, which makes the moral confrontation between the bourgeois and anti-bourgeois ideals of love so effective. Carmen's aria is a eulogy on an erratic, unfettered and temporary love which is non-possessive and free of jealousy: a bird that escapes just as you try to cage it. This image of the caged and the free bird frequently recurs, for example when Carmen calls José a 'scared canary' because he feels compelled to obey the call to muster instead of staying with her. And when she proposes that he follow her into the unregimented gypsy life he is horrified ('Quitter mon drapeau . . . déserter . . . C'est la honte, c'est l'infamie. Je n'en veux pas!'). Carmen's own song of freedom is diametrically opposed:

Le ciel ouvert, la vie errante,
Pour pays l'univers, pour loi ta volonté,
Et surtout la chose énivrante,
La liberté, la liberté!

Meilhac and Halévy tended at times to go too far in their adaptation. Bizet took great pains to salvage as much of the original figure of Carmen as he could. The text of her Habañera was written by him personally and the accompanying music presented numerous difficulties which he solved in close co-operation with Célestine Galli-Marié who sang the first Carmen role. Thanks to the cross-purposes at which the composer and the librettists were working, the role of Carmen preserved some of the excitement and tensions of Mérimée's original. Even though her fatal characteristics were more strongly accentuated and her libertine candour is immediately catalogued as 'demonic', there was still room for a eulogy on free love which has since become classic. In spite of the fact that Carmen 'takes possession' of José by the cast of her eyes and her appearance, and of the repeated insinuation that she uses her charms as objects of exchange and blackmail, she none the less represents freedom over and against the jealous, security-obsessed, frightened man:

Jamais Carmen ne cédera,
Libre elle est née et libre elle mourra.

By the time the opera was finished, all the problems seemed to have faded into the past. In spite of Peter Brook's claim that his treatment comes closest to the opera as originally intended by Bizet, there is little evidence that Bizet was displeased with the final result. Elated, he wrote that the composition is 'suffused with clarity and liveliness, resplendent with colour and melody. It will be entertaining' (Dean 1975: 108, 119). But the premiere was a cold shower and deeply disappointing: the mood was not so much malevolent as icy. The reviews the next day were scorching, taking both libretto and score heavily to task. The characters were denounced as 'obscene' and 'antipathetic'; only Micaëla drew any sympathy at all. The only rave review flowed from the pen of the poet–critic Théodore de Banville. He praised Bizet for the 'living people' he set down in place of the usual operatic puppets, and called the music 'rapturous and irresistible'. A few composers, such as Massenet and Saint-Saëns, congratulated Bizet on his exquisite music.

Bizet was depressed by the dismal reception. He became ill and recovered poorly. The opera was retained in the repertoire, but largely as a 'succès de scandale'. One evening, when Célestine Galli-Marié was playing the scene in which Carmen saw her death predicted in the cards ('La mort! Encore! Encore! Toujours la mort!') she was possessed by an eerie premonition. When she came off stage she was clearly overwrought and called out: 'Bizet is dead! Bizet is dead!' That evening the composer had indeed died, only thirty-seven years of age. Grief at the failure of his opera had no doubt hastened his early end.

But only a year later *Carmen's* triumphal conquest began with performances in Vienna, after which successes followed in Brussels,

St Petersburg, London and New York. This was already the opera as reworked by Guiraud who, after the death of his friend Bizet, adapted *Carmen* for the 'grande opéra' primarily by replacing the spoken parts of the text by sung recitative. (This version has been virtually abandoned since 1964, after the discovery of Bizet's original score by Frits Oeser). At this time, Nietzsche began to count himself among the numerous notable admirers of the opera (including Brahms, Wagner, Gounod, Tchaikovsky, Puccini). In Bizet he found just the antidote he needed to neutralize the remaining influence of his former idol Wagner, after his violent break with him. At the time of his writing of the pamphlet *Der Fall Wagner* (1888) Nietzsche had seen *Carmen* no less than twenty times. He praised the light character of the music, but referred to it also as 'malignant' and 'refined'. Nietzsche was especially enthusiastic about Bizet's 'southern' sensibility, by means of which, according to him, the amoral character of Mérimée's novella had been preserved:

> At long last love, love retranslated into *Nature!* Not the love of an 'exalted virgin!' No super-sentimentality! But love as fate, as *fatality*, cynical, innocent, gruesome — and precisely thereby *Nature!* Love, which in its essence is war, and at base the mutual *mortal hate* of the sexes. (Nietzsche, 1984: 353).[9]

But the pessimism that wants to unmask harmonious and 'sentimental' love as a false dream-image and counterpose it to the raw martial instincts of 'nature' is so very much a direct inversion of established morality that it remains tied to its opposite number, hand and foot. Nietzsche and the bourgeois enjoy a meeting of minds in their common interpretation of Carmen as a *femme fatale* — in spite of the fact that where the one interprets her cruelty as a manifestation of an almost animal innocence, the other sees it as a personification of Evil. But the fascination of Carmen is that she seems perenially to confound such facile dichotomies; and that Mérimée as well as Bizet provide encouragement for a much friendlier and more optimistic interpretation, which has much greater affinity with the present-day feminist temperament and with the newer individualistic ideal of amicable and non-exclusive love.

6. *L'amour est enfant de Bohême* . . .

That it was Théodore de Banville who wrote the only positive review of Carmen at its premiere is hardly a coincidence. De Banville had belonged to the same Parisian *Bohème* in which the powerful civil servant and literary lion, Mérimée, camped out from time to time and which is indirectly and metaphorically reconstructed in both novella and opera. The French word *bohémien* derives from the name of the former principality of Bohemia, whose artists, intellectuals and musicians had diffused throughout Europe and who led largely peripatetic lives. The term carries the very specific meaning of 'gypsy', as well as the more general sense of 'tramp' or 'vagabond'; moreover, it can be and was generalized to refer to the new social phenomenon of the institutionalized margin, the subculture of (aspirant) intellectuals, artists, politicians and their respective mistresses such as began to take shape in the bourgeois society-in-becoming of nineteenth-century France.[10] These divergent senses are metaphorically fused in the novella and the opera, in such a way that exotic gypsydom also comes to represent the much more familiar vagabondage of the modern urban *Bohème* and the new lifestyles being invented within it.

Balzac was one of the first to speak of a '*vie de Bohème*' in this figurative sense. But it was Henri Murger who imprinted the idea of the romantic artists' life on the public mind through his serial publications in the *Corsaire-Satan*, the first instalments of which appeared in 1845, the year of Mérimée's novella. The anecdotes are more or less true to life, that is, to the lives of Murger and his friends, among whom can be counted luminaries such as Banville, Baudelaire, Nadar and Courbet. Murger's sketches, which had at first attracted little attention outside the world of the *petite presse* itself, became highly popular after they were adapted for the stage in 1849 (president and ex-bohemian Napoleon III attended the premiere) and collected in a book, *Scènes de la vie de Bohème* (1851) which much later provided the warp for Puccini's opera. Meanwhile, a slight orthographic nuance had crept into French (Bohême, Bohème) indicating which group — actual gypsies or the urban cultural fringe — was being referred to. The doubtless apocryphal story went that the artistic Bohème owed its *accent grave* to the deep *misère* of its existence (Baldensperger: 1927).[11] However this may be, the *bohémiens* resembled gypsies because of their rootless and nomadic lifestyle. Compulsory moves to new lodgings because of arrears in rent or in order to avoid paying yet other debts were an all too frequent occurrence (the peripatetic life of the older Baudelaire is one familiar example). The *bohémiens* preferred the public space of the boulevards, the *passages* and the pavement cafes to the enclosed space of the home, and thus diluted the sharp distinction between life *en public* and life *en famille*. They were, or at least pretended to be, familyless individualists, who established close friendships among themselves and shared their often meagre possessions in a spirit of brotherhood. Their sexual relations consisted in various more or less permanent forms of living together or in more casual *amours*, so that it could be said that they, at least comparatively speaking, practised a kind of 'free love'.

The *bohémien* shared this extra-legal and marginal status with a type of woman often called *grisette*, a misleading label considering that these 'grey' girls were frequently quite colourful types. Many of them, presumably, were working girls who had newly arrived from the countryside and thus lived in cheap lodgings away from the shelter and surveillance of the family home. In contrast to their lovers, they were virtually illiterate and exhibited no far-reaching ambitions. None the less, they did have jobs and independent incomes and were therefore — in contrast to cocottes and courtesans — relatively independent of their lovers' favours. As Seigel (1986: 39–41) notes, by the early 1840s an entire mythology had been woven around these *grisettes*, whose lives in the romantic fantasies of the middle class often seemed attractive, independent and free from restraint. Without doubt the fantasy image was also prone to confuse relative independence with sexual availability and prostitution (cf. Tilly and Scott, 1978: 121–3; Zeldin, 1979: 309–10 for some of the realities behind the myth).

August Forel, the famous psychiatrist, specified their position on the social ladder in the course of elaborating his classification of suspect female types or *femmes publiques* (i.e. women who indulged in non-marital sexual relations) in *La Question sexuelle* of 1905. The prostitute as such is ignored because she has nothing to do with 'free love', but in fact she is tacitly relegated to the lowest rung of the moral ladder. One rung higher we find the cocotte (also called *lorette* or *demi-mondaine*) about whom Forel is able to report that they do not 'cruise' and that they 'still exercise a certain choice'. And he continues:

> An ethically higher rung is occupied by the formerly well known *grisette* or *petit-femme* of the Parisian students and the like. One can compare their relationships with a kind of free and usually brief marriage, in which relative faithfulness is the rule. The *grisette* did not usually (just as many independent prostitutes) simply live off her lover. She was often a worker, a dressmaker, a seamstress, or a shop-girl and was, formerly anyway, of rather humble demeanour but none the less willing to be kept by a man, in order to live better and more pleasantly, with whom she lived and slept and whose household she often kept in order. (Forel, 1930: 270–1)

Thus, while the romantic image is no doubt overblown, the *grisette* may still figure as one of the first manifestations of the independent young woman in a social circle which is neither aristocratic nor bourgeois. Descriptions by contemporaries regularly emphasize her carefree nature in spite of the deprivations and insecurity which characterized her existence. Baldick (1961) draws portraits of several of them in his biography of Henri Murger, *The First Bohemian*. Even though Murger's fictional characters are sometimes composites of a number of real individuals, his portraits are, according to Baldick, quite realistic. The girls are described as jolly, cheerful and popular. They have a weakness for pretty clothes and know how to wear even the simplest dress with flair. But this doesn't prevent at least one of them from allowing herself to be transported about Paris in a rather spectacular fashion: hanging from carriages and wagons. They are promiscuous: one of them selects her lovers on the basis of their artistic reputation, while it is said of another that she changes lovers as often as she does her dresses. This latter woman is Marie-Christine Roux, a much favoured painters' model who was immortalized by, among others, Ingres. Murger, in *Scènes de la vie de Bohème*, turns her into Musette. Her friend Mimi is inspired by Lucille Jouvet, who worked in an *atelier* where artificial flowers were made, a trade quite injurious to her health. She died young of tuberculosis. While Murger praises her cheerful nature, he also describes her as someone with 'an almost wild brutality . . . very egocentric and without any sensitivity' (Baldick, 1961: 65; Seigel, 1986: 39).[12]

These young women irresistibly bring Carmen to mind. Mérimée, who had intimate ties with the literary and artistic *Bohème* in his younger years, was able to model Carmen on the *demi-mondaines* (among whom was Céline Cayot) whom he had encountered there. Mérimée, as we have seen, lets Carmen 'enter' twice among the *grisettes*, first those of Cordoba and later those of Seville. Her exotic gypsy identity can therefore also be understood metaphorically as a specification of the moral characteristics of the *grisette* or cocotte. It is, moreover, revealing to note that the Carmen-version of free love hardly existed among 'real' gypsies, and was simply ascribed to them by the artistic *Bohème* which projected its own lifestyle onto that of the other group. This romantic idealization of gypsy life is typical of Mérimée's generation and is also present in the work of Victor Hugo and George Sand. In actual fact, this idealization contains two layers. The artistic and intellectual *Bohème* rhapsodizes gypsy life (the wandering life) while the bourgeoisie in turn romanticizes the life of the artist. The *Bohème* is, after all, as much the antithesis of the bourgeois as his (fascinating) repressed self: the *bohémien* is (temporarily) permitted that which is forbidden to the bourgeois.

Bizet also had a real-life *bohémienne* in mind: Céleste Mogador, circus performer and actress, later countess and wife of France's ambassador to Australia. She bequeathed a phonetic French autobiography to posterity in which she also portrays her friendships with the *bohémiens*; Bizet, by the way, is described as relatively marginal in these circles. In this self-portrait she presents herself as in all respects immoderate, capricious and proud: 'Two faults of character which have always protected me'. Bizet's biographer adds: 'The repeated appearance of such characters in Bizet's music, from *La Coupe du Roi Thulé* to *Carmen* cannot be mere coincidence' (Dean, 1975: 62).[13]

But the *bohémienne* as 'little muse' was, in the end, not a partner for life. When Bizet, for example, married Généviève Halévy, a daughter of the *haute bourgeoisie* and a relative of the librettist, he forthwith put an end to his contacts with Céleste Mogador. Généviève's family initially protested against the proposed marriage on account of Bizet's former relationship with Céleste — a woman, after all, with 'a past', who in this milieu clearly had no future. In the unlikely event that a *bohémienne* did marry, it was often with a wealthy older man, not infrequently of noble blood. The *bohémiens* themselves were almost without exception of petit-bourgeois descent, a background not easily disavowed. The vagabond life was regarded as in principle a temporary business, a transitional phase between the parental milieu (often a provincial one) and the achievement of success as artist or intellectual in Paris. The *bohémien* was allowed a certain immaturity; after all, everything as yet was mere play and the grown-up world was waiting in the wings. But as soon as the young man had arrived as an artist, the understanding was that he would enter into a bourgeois marriage and leave the *grisette* behind. In this sense, the nineteenth century *Bohème* was a permitted, indeed functional, component of bourgeois society: it was an adventurous and dangerous twilight zone of morality, but also a halfway house, an experimental sanctuary, and as such the first veritable youth culture the Western world has ever known.

7. Carmen as modern myth

As we have already suggested, the ideal of romantic love has two faces, which belong together and presuppose one another precisely in their essential opposition. The good face is that of ruling bourgeois morality, that is to say, of an elite of bourgeois moralists; the evil face is given form by recalcitrant *avant-gardistes* who gravitate to the *Bohème* and take pleasure in posing as decadent anti-bourgeois. Both variants propagate normative clichés about the typically masculine and feminine, and about the ideal amorous relations between the male and female types as thus characterized. The conventional stereotype associates masculinity with activity, will-power, rationality and the public space; and the female identity with passivity, humility, emotionality and domesticity. Both masculine and feminine roles are socially functional and form a harmonious unity-in-diversity.

The 'decadent' stereotype not only tends to confuse these definitions, but also to turn them inside out. Thus, next to the figure of the irrelevant dandy and the anti-social artist, there also emerges the figure of the *femme fatale*, the sterile, futile and treacherous woman who, having become evil incarnate for both sexes of the bourgeoisie, is idealized by the *Bohème* for precisely this 'virtue'. But it is significant that this demonic type also exercises a fascination for the bourgeoisie, while at the same time the decadents cannot purge themselves of a certain commitment to the bourgeois-romantic ideal of love. In point of fact, both groups ultimately regard the woman as an untouchable idol and avow the evident 'truth' that men and women live in two utterly different worlds. For the one, essential inequality and natural distance is the basis for the harmonious complementarity of marriage, while for the other, the sexes are permanently at war with one another. Nietzsche's grim conception of 'love–hate' is as clear an example of the latter as is Baudelaire's thesis of the fundamental incompatibility of the sexes (cf. Zeldin, 1979: 291–2).[14]

The mores of bohemian and bourgeois also converge in their worship of love as (divine or devilish) *mystery*, and, even more fundamentally: in their characterization of love as exclusive and absolute, thus, as possessive and subjugating, in extreme cases literally 'all-consuming'. In the good variant, the man takes the initiative and becomes the dominant party, while in the evil variant this role is usurped by the woman. Thus, the element of fatality and destiny 'for life' is present both in official as well as in unofficial morality, and can be regarded as the emotional complement or product of the psychological distance between the sexes. But again it assumes the double aspect of, on the one hand, the *amour coup de foudre* which forever unites two predestined souls in blissful embrace and, on the other, of the equally unpredictable predestined meeting with the fatal woman whose embrace breeds nothing but death and destruction.

It is this antithesis which has for so long defined the two poles around which interpretations of the Carmen tragedy have tended to orbit. In both the novella and the opera, Carmen combines features which appear contradictory and upsetting to established morality.

The linking of femininity and emotionality on the one hand, with superior force of will and sexual exuberance on the other, readily qualifies her in the bourgeois operatic tradition as a 'public woman' in all senses of the word. In later editions her light-footed, humouristic aspects disappear and little remains of her forceful temperament but a kind of nervous and agitated fluttering. Or, alternatively, her wilfulness is portrayed as satanic and cruel — by Nietzsche, for example, who draws on the darkest passages of Mérimée's novella. Thus, the seductive and spellbinding gypsy Carmen either has her wings clipped and is caged like some exotic bird (now Carmen herself has become the caged, hysterical canary), or she is endowed with fearsome talons and idealized precisely because of her carnivorous nature.

The intriguing thing about most of the recent interpretations, by contrast, is that the figure of Carmen seems to escape both moral poles, and hence to leave both thesis and antithesis far behind. The germ of this new attitude is discernible in both Mérimée and Bizet, neither of whom simply invert conventional morality, but instead mix light and dark in such a way that a variegated and ambivalent *chiaroscuro* results. Nor can the female ideal of the *Bohème* simply be pasted onto the figure of the *femme fatale*, if only because there are obvious differences between the grim and gloomy approach taken by, for example, Nietzsche and Baudelaire and the lighter touch of writers such as Murger and Gautier. In contemporary portrayals of Carmen it is precisely this light-footedness and playfulness which is brought to the fore. Combined with the androgynous properties of the *canaille* or 'street-girl', these provide a model which in a number of ways bears little resemblance to the traditional type of the *femme fatale*. The modern *canaille* is more ordinary, and also possesses the caring and loving side which actually belongs to her opposite number, but which Mérimée's Carmen none the less displays when, for example, she nurses the wounded Don José.

While in the contemporary myth feminine provocativeness, frivolity and the desire to please are fused with 'masculine' attributes such as self-assurance and will-power, they no longer bear the romantic association with darkness and fatality. Quite the contrary: contemporary stars like Midler, Lauper, Benatar, del Sol and Migenes are sexy, but in a playful, ironic and relativizing manner. What seems to be disappearing, therefore, is precisely the mysterious *fatality*, the supernatural *mystery* which counts as the touchstone of true love in the romantic ideal. This emotional revolution is no doubt related to the gradual breakdown of psychological alienation between the sexes, which has been accelerated by the cultural revolution of the 1960s and the ensuing resurgence of feminism. Both have produced new male and female types whose cultural worlds are much less disparate, who are less afraid of one another, and who regard love less as a divine stroke of lightning than as a form of friendship which has somehow got out of hand.

It is therefore no accident that the Carmen revival catches on at a point in time when feminism is gradually abandoning the aggressive and puritanical combat mentality of its first decade and has begun to embrace new feminine styles. Originally, it was precisely the traditional image of the 'feminine female' which attracted much of the fire of the feminist campaign — a campaign in which strategic use was made of the anti-image of the masculine, combative, autonomous and therefore 'castrating' witch. Now that the bitterest struggles have been fought, the battle-dress can be buried, and, without ceding any of the newly-won assertiveness, a 'new femininity' can be discovered. A nice example of this is provided by an article in the May 1983 issue of *Marie-Claire* entitled 'Feministes et sexy', in which a number of veteran feminists are interviewed and photographed in their favourite outfits. The eight writers, actresses and journalists appear to be competing with one another over their capacity for expressing seductive, but simultaneously humouristic and relativizing femininity. This produces beautiful photographic typifications ('le sexy-chic', 'le sexy-choc', 'le sexy-théâtre', 'le sexy-canaille') in nearly all of which the Carmen syndrome is clearly recognizable.[15]

Also banished to the wings in the modern myth is the *possessiveness* or *exclusivity* which always accompanies the romantic ideal of love, and which is closely related to the idea of lifelong 'destiny' discussed above. Not for nothing is Carmen synonymous with the individualistic pursuit of freedom (*la chose énivrante*) which knows no laws or rules, does not let itself be blackmailed by jealousy and which views all affairs of the heart from the perspective of impermanence. This too corresponds nicely with the domestic lifestyles of the members of the contemporary intellectual and artistic elite, who experiment with 'open' marriages, friendship networks and communes, and who ultimately prefer to view themselves (male/female) as a kind of 'new bachelordom'. Typical is the conclusion of the sociologist Evelyne Sullerot, the author of a report on marriage and new domestic arrangements for the French Conseil Economique et Social, who is interviewed in *Marie-France* under the heading 'Le Mariage n'est plus à la noce' (Marriage is no longer in fashion):

I conclude . . . that situations considered up to now as difficult to maintain, marginal, vulnerable are becoming the voluntary options of the majority. We are truly entering into a new society, more individualistic and in which the pursuit of liberty and personal satisfaction are at a premium (*Marie-France*, August 1984).

But this new cult of individualism, amicable love and post-feminist femininity — shared by men and women — can only be placed in historical-sociological perspective by again interpreting it as a 'child of the *Bohème*'. Over the last hundred years, Murger's *Bohème* has expanded socially and internationally and it has, thanks to the redistributive mechanisms of the welfare state, achieved a kind of tenure within the social structure. The social fringe has become broader, more explicitly institutionalized, and better subsidized; as a result, not only has the transition to bourgeois 'maturity' been lengthened by the availability of numerous serially overlapping youth cultures, but at the same time, permanent subcultures have emerged within which one can grow old, engage in legitimate occupations and earn legitimate incomes. The *Bohème* has also become increasingly working class and increasingly feminized — without, of course, losing its traditional function as a field of recruitment for the new intellectual and artistic elite. Contemporary feminism too has contributed to the expansion of this subsidized social sanctuary, and (though hardly intentionally) also to the formation of this new elite.

Thus does the history of Carmen provide the first modern female myth possibly capable of outdistancing male myths like those of Oedipus, Narcissus or Don Juan and next to which traditional female images like those of Lilith, Salomé or Cleopatra appear to pale. The contemporary Carmen, measured against traditional moral standards, is in truth an 'impossible' being. As a 'comical vamp' she lacks not only the hysterical capriciousness of the *femme fatale*, but also the cruelty of the Don Juan figure. She is therefore not only someone with whom to fall in love, but someone to become friends with.

Reproduced by kind permission of the photographer, Cees van Gelderen, from
Avenue, **June 1984**

Reproduced by kind permission of the photographer, Cees van Gelderen, from
Avenue, **June 1984**

Reproduced by kind permission of the photographer, Cees van Gelderen, from
Avenue, **June 1984**

Reproduced by kind permission of the photographer, Cees van Gelderen, from
Avenue, **June 1984**

Notes

An earlier version of this chapter appeared in Dutch in *Maatstaf*, February 1986, and in English as a working paper at the Center for European Studies, Harvard University, 1987. Translation by Cornelis Disco. We should like to thank Benjo Maso for his careful commentary and the Department of Sociology, University of Amsterdam for making the translation financially possible

1. This line of thought corresponds to that of Catherine Clément in *L'Opéra ou la défaite des femmes* (1979); but unfortunately her title is more lucid than the rest of the book. One of the more comprehensible passages in this quintessentially French essay full of tortuous dramatic poses is the following: 'The opera is a women's affair. No, not a feminist version; no, not a liberation. Quite the contrary; they suffer, they scream, they die; this too they call singing' (p. 24). On Carmen ('the most feminist, the most headstrong among the dead') see pp. 94–104; on *La Traviata*, pp. 119–29, and on *La Bohème*, pp. 160–9.

2. See, for example, 'De Nieuwe Popvrouwen Barsten Uit Hun Voegen' (The New Pop-ladies Are Bursting Out All Over), *Viva* (May/June 1985) (adapted from *Newsweek*). Cyndi Lauper, nominated 'woman of the year' by the feminist magazine *MS*, is characterized in *Viva* as follows: 'A new-wave Betty Boop, with the heart of Janis Joplin, the lungs of Johnny Rotten, and the steeled spirit of a committed feminist like Germaine Greer'. Madonna, the 'material girl', would appear to be closer to the old-fashioned fatal, vampish type. See also interviews with Cyndi Lauper and Laura del Sol in *Viva* (58 and 65, 1984). *MS* (November 1986) portrays Sapho as yet another 'angry young woman' who escapes from the limited alternatives of 'either perfect, stupid, and passive virgins or bitch-whores', and quotes: 'La femme hystérique est historique'.

3. John Heilpern 'Carmen. Peter Brook', *Vogue* (March, 1984); W.F. Zuiderwijk 'Terug naar de Oer-Carmen' (Back to the Primeval Carmen), *Avenue* (June 1984); J. Kersting 'Das Spiel mit der Lust: wie Carmen Mode macht)' (The Game of Lust: How Carmen Makes Fashions), *Stern* (26 April 1984); 'Is There a Gypsy in Your Soul?', cover-story *Cosmopolitan* (English edn), June 1984). It is interesting that the German *Burda* (May 1985) which, in comparison with *Stern*, is more explicitly directed at a female readership, presented a much more decent version of the Carmen fashion: rather long skirts, the primmest of crew-necks, with, at most, bare arms.

4. In the autumn of 1985, Antonio Gades's company toured the Netherlands with the highly-acclaimed ballet *Carmen*. Once again, Gades economized on costumes and décors, used only fragments from Bizet's music, referred back to Mérimée basics, and presented Carmen not as the 'usual fatal and trifling coquette' but as 'a raw, untamed female animal' — thus closing in on Nietzsche's famous interpretation which we will discuss further on. Quotes are from a Dutch newspaper report (*NRC*, 29 October 1985).

5. Letter to Peter Diamand, in the text accompanying the DGG recording of *Carmen* directed by Claudio Abbado at the 1977 Edinburgh Festival.

6. A *Cosmo* story from September 1987 ('Meet the Feminist *Femme Fatale*') connects the rediscovery of womanliness with the new needs of 'serious careerist female executives', who wish to explore 'another kind of strength, another dimension to her already proven brain-power, muscle-power, business acumen'. The German *Vogue*'s cover-story of April 1988 ('Die neue Frau: sanfte Macht') likewise plays on the theme of power which is 'softened' by femininity and notes: 'Die Schönheit von heute hat Persönlichkeit'.

7. Cf. also Mérimée's story 'Le Vénus d'Ille' for a chilling portrait of the fatal woman in the unexpected guise of a marble statue.

8. Although one might object that the music to some extent counteracts or subverts the libretto, since it appears to emphasize Carmen's seductiveness rather than her 'free spirit', we are disinclined to think that there is any necessary tension here.

9. From our perspective, Peter Sloterdijk (1986: 133) would appear to be wrong in thinking that Nietzsche's judgement about the 'cynical' Carmen 'has been thoroughly confirmed by present-day mass audiences'.

10. Cf. the beautiful and comprehensive work by Seigel (1986), which was not available to us at the time of writing. Pp. 23-4 provide details on the metaphorical generalization of the term *bohémien* in the 1830s and 1840s.

11. Nevertheless, in the introduction to Murger's *Scènes* both spellings are used indiscriminately; he seems to have shed the traditional circumflex only somewhat later.

12. In the opera, Mimi and Musette are portrayed as much more contrasting types than in Murger's novel. However, it seems unlikely that the figure of Mimi will permit an artistic and moral 'transvaluation' which is in any way analogous to the Carmen revision. This is so despite the fact that Teresa Stratas' pitiful Mimi has recently received competition from the effervescent Mimi of . . . Linda Ronstadt, in Joseph Papp's new English language version of *La Bohème*.

13. On the *bohémiennes*, cf. Lapierre (1984) and Crébas (1985)

14. It is of course necessary to point out that large differences remained between the ideals of novelists and moralists and everyday practice. Among the bourgeoisie, the ideal of romantic love was accorded only such free play as remained after family interests and parental authority had had their say. And among the *Bohème*, 'fatal' love became the fate of only a very few — in general, one had to make do with the considerably less theatrical joys and sorrows of more or less illicit concubinage.

15. The Dutch *Volkskrant* (30 October 1985) has noted the same trend in reference to the last International Women's Festival: 'The fear of sexuality must finally be abolished . . . Feminists want their femininity back, want to be sexy. They want to wear high-heels and make-up. Women want to manifest themselves as sexually active beings, without feelings of shame'. Compare, however, Chapkis' (1986) critical view.

References

Baldensperger, Fernand (1927) 'Bohème et Bohème: un doublet linguistique et sa fortune littéraire', in J. Polivka et al. (eds) *Mélanges*. Prague.

Baldick, Robert (1961) *The First Bohemian: The Life of Henry Murger*. London: Hamish Hamilton.

Bowman, Frank Paul (1962) *Prosper Mérimée: Heroism, Pessimism and Irony*. Berkeley: University of California Press.

Chapkis, Wendy (1986) *Beauty Secrets. Women and the Politics of Appearance*. Boston: South End Press.

Clément, Catherine (1979) *L'opéra ou la défaite des femmes*. Paris: Grasset.

Crébas, Aya (1985) 'De Leerschool van een *femme fatale*', *Vrij Nederland*, (23 March).

Dean, Winton (1975) *Bizet*. London: Dent.

Forel, August (1930) *Het Sexueele Vraagstuk*. Amsterdam: N.V. Gebr. Graams.

Lapierre, Alexandra (1984) *La Lionne du Boulevard*. Paris: Robert Laffont.

Mérimée, Prosper (1973), *Romans et Nouvelles* (II) edited by Jean Mistler. Paris: Le Livre de Poche.

Murger, Henry (1851) *Scènes de la vie de Bohème*, Vols I and II. Paris: Librairie Grund.

Nietzsche, Friedrich (1984) *Der Fall Wagner* in *Werke* III edited by Karl Schlechta. Frankfurt a.M.: Ullstein.
Praz, Mario (1970, 1933) *The Romantic Agony*. Oxford: Oxford University Press.
Seigel, Jerrold (1986) *Bohemian Paris. Culture, Politics and the Boundaries of Bourgeois Life, 1830–1930*. New York: Viking Penguin
Sloterdijk, Peter (1986) *Der Denker auf der Bühne: Nietzsches Materialismus*. Frankfurt a.M.: Suhrkamp.
Tilly, Louise and Joan Scott (1978) *Women, Work and Family*. New York: Holt, Rinehart and Winston.
Zeldin, Theodore (1979) *France 1848–1945: Ambition and Love*. Oxford: Oxford University Press.

This chapter first appeared in *Theory, Culture & Society*, Vol. 5 (1988), 579–610.

15

THE MASK OF AGEING AND THE POSTMODERN LIFE COURSE

Mike Featherstone and Mike Hepworth

Postmodernity and the Life Course

During recent years there has been a good deal of sociological interest in the deconstruction of the life course. The term 'deconstruction' has been used by Derrida (1988) to point to the way in which the structure or 'architecture' of a phenomenon is built up in order to reveal the underlying principles of its construction. According to this mode of analysis the assumptions which underpin psychological models of universal stages of life development can be shown to be flawed. These weaknesses have been revealed partly by methodological criticisms of the interrelationship between the research and the researcher in the narrative framing of events and the retrospective construction of an ordered sequence of stages through which all individuals allegedly move during the course of their lives (Freeman, 1984). In addition, there has been a strong dissatisfaction with the absence of concepts of social structure from developmental psychological models which have a tendency to reduce complex notions of 'environment' and 'context' into simple 'variables' (Kohli and Meyer, 1986). The result is that individual development is artificially isolated from its social context, and the life course is not fully taken into account as a social institution in its own right interconnected with other parts of the social structure.

In contrast, it is argued, sociological analysis of the life course as a social institution makes it possible to demonstrate the ways in which this institution changes alongside other changes in social institutions associated with the process of western modernisation. In particular, it can be shown that during the course of this historical process a life form in which chronological age was much less relevant was replaced by an increasingly age-relevant one. As Ariès (1973), Elias (1978) and others have shown, the status of the family in pre-modern European societies was much more important than chronological age in determining questions of maturity, independence of action and power than in our present-day society where these elements tend to be firmly coded according to chronological age in socially constructed stages which include childhood, middle age and old age. With the growth of the state, industrialisation and the 'panopticon society' described by Foucault (1979), the life course was subjected to greater surveillance, control and normalisation, with the result that we now see a much more extensive institutionalisation of the life course socially structured into orderly sequences of psychosocial 'growth' and development.

The notion of the deconstruction of the life course, therefore, arises not merely from a heightened theoretical sensitivity but also in response to perceived social changes which are seen by sociologists of postmodernity to be producing a reversal in those processes of industrialisation and modernisation which brought about the institutionalisation of life stages to which we have referred (the prescription of, for example, rules concerning childhood and development, schooling, careers, marriage, retirement). Theorists of the movement towards a postmodern society point to an emerging de-institutionalisation and a de-differentiation of the life course, with less emphasis than in the past being placed upon age-specific role transitions and scheduled identity development. Postmodern change, it is argued, will lead to some blurring of what appeared previously to be relatively clearly marked stages and the experiences and characteristic behaviour which were associated with those stages. Meyrowitz (1984), for example, argues that in contemporary western society children are becoming more adult-like and adults more childlike. There is an increasing similarity in modes of presentation of self, gestures and postures, fashions and leisure-time pursuits adopted by both parents and their children, and some movement can be seen towards a more informal uni-age style. The so-called 'private sphere' of family life, especially in the middle classes, is becoming correspondingly less private and less authoritarian. Children are granted access through television to previously concealed aspects of adult life and experience such as sex, death, money and the problems besetting adults who are anxious about the roles and selves they present to children. Meyrowitz sees this movement towards a uni-age behavioural style as influenced by the advent of media imagery which adults had previously established over the kinds of information formerly believed to be suitable for children and the institutionalised processes of socialisation and education.

This sociological perspective on social change (which we must stress is seen as largely experienced by the middle classes) is increasingly evident in the body of postmodern theorising currently making an impact on a wide range of academic disciplines. It indicates a move away from universalism towards the tolerance of local knowledge (Lyotard, 1984) and the need to admit the 'other' as co-equal speaker in human dialogues. The de-hierarchisation and pluralism advocated by postmodern theorists, and detected as an emergent aspect of contemporary culture, point to the need to deconstruct development, to spatialise out and admit a multiplicity of variations under conditions of co-equality. Thus Friedman (1987: 35), writing as an anthropologist who has to work in a context in which his subject matter, the other, demands the right to reply and contest his interpretation, typically observes: 'Ultimately the life cycle can be understood as a panorama of cultures. What we are witnessing here is the collapse of an authority structure, one that defines the superiority of adulthood, of rational discourse, of standard linguistic usage.'

It must not be forgotten that such postmodern theorising is as yet far from being an everyday reality. At best these theories draw out attention to *emergent cultural tendencies* (Featherstone, 1988). At the same time it is also possible to show that they do gather some support from gerontological research which records evidence of the declining significance of age grades in contemporary social life in the West. One interesting example can be found in the increasing awareness of resistance to the notion of 'middle-age' and the current social exchange value of phrases such as 'mid-life', which normally refers to a very loosely defined age stage covering the wide chronological range 35 to 60, if not beyond. In addition, much of our contemporary cultural imagery of ageing is enlivened by heroes and heroines who vigorously deny the relevance of age-graded statuses. 'I don't think of myself as old-aged,' the film star Bette Davis recently observed; 'I don't feel old at all. Later years would be a more polite term from you' (*Sunday Times*, 20 September 1987).

Politicians such as Prime Minister Thatcher present themselves, and are presented, as anything but stereotypical grandparents. Near or past conventional retirement ages, they continue to deny the need to slow down, to rest, to take the back seat – responses traditionally associated with old age. It has, of course, often been pointed out that one's capacities to avoid retirement, or early retirement, depend upon the power resources one can muster; those at the bottom of the social class hierarchy have few resources to facilitate the choice of a 'positive' old age in terms of continued career/work, or a 'positive' and active retirement. Yet for those in the middle classes with the prospect of generous pension incomes, and who have planned for retirement, old age holds out the prospect of a prolongation of the plateau-like phase of adult life, with continued relatively high consumption of the pursuit of consumer-culture lifestyles, body maintenance and styles of self-presentation (Featherstone and Hepworth, 1990).

As far as body maintenance is concerned, an array of evidence continues to accrue which disproves the necessary decline of mental, sexual and physiological capacities in old age. Chronological age continues to be discredited as an indicator of inevitable age norms and lifestyles and a new breed of body maintenance experts optimistically prescribe health foods, vitamins, dieting, fitness techniques and other regimens to control *biological* age, which, it is argued, is the true index of how a person should feel. In effect they hold out the promise of turning the clock back and clearly have a strong appeal in the new middle-class markets for middle-aged and older people (Walmsley and Margolis, 1987).

In addition, therefore, to state intervention to promote an active, positive old age as a response to the demand to spread resources more thinly in the face of the old age population boom, there has been considerable impetus from the cultural sphere, where, as we have seen, the question of the deconstruction of the life course has been raised. Amongst the most significant features of 'postmodern culture', therefore, we must include:

1 the emphasis upon the cultivation of lifestyles or designer lives in which life and the consumer accoutrements which make it possible are constantly stylised and re-stylised to achieve a pleasing effect;

2 a playful, youthful and emotional exploratory approach to culture in which mass spectacles (Disneyworld), the media (MTV, videos), theme parks and post-tourism are paramount, and the knowledge that they *are* simulations does not interfere with their public acceptance or in any way reduce their pleasurable effect (Urry, 1988);

3 the emergence in the new social movements of post-scarcity values where women, nature, Third and Fourth World 'otherness', formerly excluded, are now admitted as valid partners.

Clearly, a strong generational factor can be detected underlying these values. They can be seen to represent cultural attitudes generated in the large post-Second World War cohort in western countries – the 'baby-boomer' generation which explored counter-cultural lifestyles in the 1960s and are now entering what used to be called 'middle age'. As they do so they are taking with them many of the values and cultural tastes of their youth (Hepworth, 1987), and to speak of the 'new middle age' (Hepworth and Featherstone, 1982) is in part to refer to a generational shift implicated in the emergence of a new cohort. As they work their way through into retirement and old age, new generations will continue to take with them many of their cultural tastes, values, preferences and sensibilities, and for any adequate analysis and understanding of these processes the life course must be firmly situated in this historical process and considered as a continual reconstruction as we move forward through historical and lived time.

Adult life, then, is a process – a process, we must emphasise, which need *not* involve a predetermined series of stages of growth. The stages or hurdles which are placed in front of people and the barriers through which they have to pass (age-specific transitions) can be shifted around and even discarded. Yet having said this we must be careful not to adopt a view of the life course in which culture is granted the overarching power to mould nature in any form it chooses. Human beings share with other species an embodied existence inevitably involving birth, growth, maturation and death. Our naturally endowed capacity to learn, to speak, to produce signs and symbols and to communicate knowledge through them should not make us neglect the unavoidable biological aspects of existence. To be an embodied person and to become a fully fledged member of society necessarily involves developmental sequences of biological growth; the body has to grow to produce the physiological co-ordination necessary to facilitate movement, facial and bodily gestures and other interpersonal responses. There is also the need for a certain amount of cognitive development and the acquisition of language, memory and communicative competence, as well as emotional development or the capacity to control and regulate the emotions. All are essential to becoming a person; yet the point at which it is assumed that development is complete will show considerable cultural variation. Different societies, for example, may require much lower levels of emotional and cognitive development, which require less than full biological maturation to grant quasi-adult status. An interesting example can be found in Ariès' (1973) research on childhood where he suggests that in pre-modern times the child was allowed to participate as an adult after the age of 7. In contrast, our present-day society formally demands a relatively high level of cognitive, emotional and biological development before human beings are treated as accredited persons. Yet as critics such as John Holt (1969) have pointed out, the chronological age at which we grant citizen rights to the child and make him or her an adult contains many contradictory and arbitrary assumptions. (Few would want to follow Holt and grant full citizen rights to all children, although we can point to some legal erosion of the formerly protected statuses of childhood.)

If the process of becoming an acceptable human being is dependent upon those developments, the loss of cognitive and other skills produces the danger of social unacceptability, unemployability and being labelled as less than fully human. Loss of bodily controls carries similar penalties of stigmatisation and ultimately physical exclusion. Deep old age is personally and socially disturbing because it holds out the prospect of the loss of some or all of these controls. Degrees of loss impair the capacity to be counted as a competent adult. Indeed, the failure of bodily controls can point to a more general loss of self-image; to be ascribed the status of a competent adult person depends upon the capacity to control urine and faeces. The sense of shame at the loss of control, Elias (1978) argues, varies historically with a greater sensitivity to the improprieties of bodily betrayals to our society. It can also be argued that it varies with social class. Individuals who have been brought up in an upper-class milieu may be more easily able to distance themselves from bodily betrayals and adopt a detached attitude towards them and experience less shame at the 'indignity' of being 'cleaned up' by lower-class persons. Members of the new middle class, whose class background and trajectory through life encourage many of the anxieties of the autodidact who is unsure of the appropriate behaviour in various contexts, may experience extreme shame and loss of self-image through their failure to live up to the perceived standards of others (Featherstone and Hepworth, 1990). The loss of bodily controls also impairs other interactional skills, and the loss of real social power through decline in these competences may induce others to feel confident in treating the individual as less than a full adult. Carers may, for example, feel secure in the belief that the 'person inside' will not be able to return and wreak any vengeance on them whatever their former social status or class background.

The Mask of Ageing

One of the most vivid examples of the contemporary dilemma of ageing occurs in a report of the experiences of Pat Moore, a young New Yorker who disguised herself as an elderly woman and went out into the streets of 116 cities in the United States to systematically observe the effects (Young, 1989). With the assistance of a professional make-up artist she transformed herself into 'Old Pat' whose sensory perceptions were blurred by steelworkers' wax in her ears and baby oil in her eyes. Her physical gestures and speed of movement were restricted by specially designed clothing, and she gargled with a paste of salt and water to ensure a rasping voice. So complete was the transformation we are told that fellow students in her gerontology class at Columbia University failed to recognise her. At the end of a period of three years she collapsed from nervous and physical exhaustion: the rigours of her double life had produced poignant evidence of the disturbing psychological effects that a negative reaction on the part of others towards an aged appearance may produce.

Lucie Young (1989), who described Pat Moore's research to readers of *The Guardian* newspaper, summarised her findings as follows:

1 the stigmatisation of 'Old Pat' was a routine everyday experience: negative
   reactions described by Moore included verbal abuse and exploitative
   behaviour like taking physical advantage of her apparent infirmity in bus
   queues;
2 on the personal level, the cumulative effect of stigmatisation was an increasingly submissive response expressed in the tendency to conceal or mask
   expressions of emotional and personal needs:

   'A lot of . . . researchers find the elderly have been lying to them. Telling
   them what they think they want to hear and not the truth. They don't
   want to be any trouble. They are frightened that if they tell the truth
   about what they have been eating and doing they will be locked away.'
   (Moore in Young, 1989: 17)

The strategy of concealing or masking inner feelings, motives,
attitudes or beliefs has been noted by other researchers into the
experience of old age. In her classic ethnography of the elderly
residents of a 'single room occupancy' hotel in a city in the
United States, Joyce Stephens discovered that although a number
of her subjects had children who would willingly take them into
the comparative physical comfort of their homes they preferred
to live in reduced material circumstances amidst the dangers of
the inner city. In this context one of the advantages of the single
room occupancy was that it allowed some of these elderly people
to enjoy pleasures such as drinking and sex which their children
would have found distasteful. A potential source of embarrassment and, of course, the real possibility of being deprived of
such satisfactions was avoided by clinging on to a separate
territorial and social sphere (1976).

The individual struggle to maintain a balance between the
external stereotypes of age-appropriate behaviour and the subjective experience of the self requires considerable energy, tenacity
and other resources. The majority of the men and women who
figure in Joyce Stephens's research are clinging on literally by
their finger ends. It does not take much – a sudden illness, a fall
– to disturb their equilibrium. There are other problems too: as
we have seen, the particular tensions in Pat Moore's research
resulted in mental and physical collapse. The strain of wearing
her disguise was intensified by the feelings of guilt she associated
with her ability to resume her youthful identity: 'I was always
painfully aware the disguise was just a shell for me' (Moore in
Young, 1989: 17). What is more generally significant is that
when she let some of the elderly people she met into her secret
she discovered that they also felt trapped in a shell: 'young

minds trapped behind old faces' (1989: 17).

In Gubrium's (1986) sociological analysis of the discovery and conceptual elaboration of Alzheimer's disease in the United States and the establishment of boundaries between 'normal' and pathological ageing, old age is also seen to be characteristically defined as a mask which conceals the essential identity of the person beneath. This view of the ageing process as a mask or disguise concealing the essentially youthful self beneath is one which appears to be increasingly popular (Featherstone and Hepworth, 1990). When asked at the age of 79 to describe what it felt like to be old, the celebrated author J.B. Priestley replied:

> It is as though, walking down Shaftesbury Avenue as a fairly young man, I was suddenly kidnapped, rushed into a theatre and made to don the grey hair, the wrinkles and the other attributes of age, then wheeled on stage. Behind the appearance of age I am the same person, with the same thoughts, as when I was younger. (Puner, 1978: 7)

In these examples it is the ageing mask which is pathological or deviant and the inner essential self which remains – even beneath or 'inside' Alzheimer's disease – as normal. Such a conceptualisation of ageing sets great store on the belief that ageing is a potentially curable *disease*, although several enormously expensive decades may pass before the desperately desired cure is discovered.

Other forms of traditionally age-related camouflage are also seen as barriers to person-perception. In her book *The Language of Clothes*, Lurie (1981) shows how conceptions of age-appropriate clothing confirm the association between physical ageing and decline. Lurie notes that the tradition of marking the transition from maturity to old age by a change of costume is well established. Certain garments such as the shawl come to be associated with old age partly because they may be worn for extra warmth. Other garments become associated with old age for reasons which are less obvious and linked to movements of fashion. Lurie observes a generational variation in fashion take-up:

> Even after pyjamas were widely available and had been popularised by such Hollywood films as '*It Happened One Night*' (1934), long nightshirts of white cotton or red flannel continued to be worn by conservative elderly men, especially in rural areas. (Until very recently they could be ordered from the Sears catalogue.) The wearing of somewhat outmoded daytime fashions is

another recognised sign of age – and of the possession of aged opinions and beliefs. (1981: 49)

Lurie also suggests, as a general principle, that if a garment is available in different lengths the longer version will be worn by older people. This applies to both men and women:

> At the height of the miniskirt boom . . . an American magazine published a guide to the proper hem length for women of different ages. A photograph showed three generations of smiling middle-class housewives in identical dresses. Grandmother's skirt clears her knees; Mother's is about four inches shorter; and Daughter's four inches above that. (50)

Clothes therefore transmit age-related messages, and when men or women do not dress to their age society may be offended. The source of offence or deviation here is not the fact of being old but the refusal to accept the state ('mutton dressed as lamb'), 'Extreme disparity of age and costume . . . is seen as disgusting or even frightening.' Some strong taboo, Lurie argues, is being broken – 'something forbidden is being said in the language of clothes' (1981: 57):

> The older woman who makes this error is especially apt to be castigated as 'mutton dressed as lamb'; but men are by no means immune. Cousin Feenix, the elderly beau in *Dombey and Son*, 'so juvenile in figure and in manner, and so well got up', is just as much a figure of fun as his relative the Hon. Mrs Skewton, though he does not inspire the same horror – perhaps because it is only she that we are allowed to see in private at her toilet: 'The painted object shrivelled under her hand; the form collapsed, the hair dropped off, the arched dark eyebrows changed to scanty tufts of grey; the lips shrunk, the skin became cadaverous and loose; an old, worn, yellow nodding woman, with red eyes, alone remained in Cleopatra's place, huddled up, like a slovenly bundle, in a greasy flannel gown.' (56)

Such images are considered ageist because they portray old age as an inevitable period of decline and, what is more, a period of decline which is at best laughable and at worst disgusting. Feminist writers have detected a strong sexist element in this theme. Fairhurst (1982) identifies the theme of decay as a socially constructed sexist stigma particularly limiting to women and adding terror to the menopause. The process here is a reflexive one where women (and men) evaluate the ageing processes of their bodies according to culturally validated ideas of physical attractiveness and age-appropriate behaviour. Fairhurst shows that, although physical attractiveness is 'not the exclusive concern of women', and both men and women 'believe they should make the "best of themselves"' (1982: 14), the ways in which they handle the problem vary according to the meanings they give to growing older. Significantly, the women she interviewed worried more about the images conjured up by the term 'old age' then about any supposed loss of physical attractiveness. Her interviews with a sample of middle-aged men and women in a northern English city reveal an important distinction between the physical body and the self. Changes in outward physical appearance are seen as separate from the self, which is considered to be more enduring. One man said: 'I think you'll find yourself that you reach a stage where you don't grow any older inside. Outside you do but you're perpetually 28 or something or whatever it may be – wherever you stop' (11).

This finding is not dissimilar to that reported by Kastenbaum et al., (1981), who show that most people have conceptions of ages other than their chronological one, and who distinguish between personal age (as revealed in self-reports of age status) and interpersonal age or the age status of an individual as evaluated by others. 'Consensual age' is the relation between the two. On the basis of a structured interview schedule given to a sample of gerontological students aged 20 to 60, and a matched sample of men and women following studies and careers involving personal interactions but not gerontology, they discovered that personal age appeared to be a separate concept from chronological age, and there was 'an increasing personalisation of personal age with advancing chronological age' (59). Personal age, moreover, tended to be younger than chronological age and to decrease with advancing years. Observers were more likely to rate age in terms of external appearance ('look age' compared with 'feel age'), and 'the present data imply that how old people *look* and *feel* (both from their own frame of reference) represent appreciably different aspects of their total personal age' (65). The age a person 'believes that she or he *looks* tends to be that aspect of personal age which is closest to chronological age' (61). Interestingly the authors observed that 'gerontologists do not appear to be immune to the challenge of age-oriented inquiry. Several gerontologists were among those who expressed the greatest amount of perturbation during and after the interview.' They also note that this confirms their impression that training in gerontology 'does not invariably prepare specialists to copy with age-related problems on a personal basis' (58).

It is instructive to compare concern over the stigmatisation of ageing and the 'age segregation' it can undoubtedly produce with the image of ageing as a mask which it is hard to remove. In the context of a postmodernist deconstruction of the life course, the image of the mask is a further sign of attempts to undermine traditional age-related categories. Beneath this imagery it is possible to detect three underlying issues and a closer look at these should provide a further indication of the possible direction of cultural change with regard to ageing.

First, the image of the mask alerts us to the possibility that a distance or tension exists between the external appearance of the face and body and their functional capacities, and the internal or subjective sense or experience of personal identity which is likely to become more prominent in our consciousness as we grow older.

Secondly, it indicates that an important deficiency of the vocabulary of ageing in its present forms is its limited potential for giving elderly people sufficient scope to express their personal feelings as distinct from stereotyped responses to inquiries about 'how you feel'. It seems to be very often the case that we fix elderly people – usually those without resources – in the roles which do not do justice to the richness of their individual experiences and multi-facets of their personalities. The sanitised one-dimensional benign stereotypes 'granny' and 'grandpa' are good examples of this ageist trap. The classic granny celebrity in the UK is of course the Queen Mother, typically described in tabloid newspapers as 'Our Super-Gran'.

The contrast between this stereotype and the reality as far as many of today's grandparents are concerned has been revealed by Cunningham-Burley (1985), who carried out intensive research on the ways in which people relate to the role of grandparents in Aberdeen. She points out that although the stereotype of grandparents is one of men and women who are chronologically elderly, the reality is that most people become grandparents in middle age, and would in fact be great-grandparents by the time they are old. But there is little sociological research which looks at the 'middle-aged nature' of grandparenthood. In other words, the reality of grandparenthood is ignored, as the British stereotype of the Queen Mother in the role of everyone's idealised super-gran testifies. The problem is, therefore, that because we *imagine* grandparents are old we don't *feel* 'like' them when in middle life we become grandparents ourselves. However, postmodern times are changing, and the publication of the magazine *Grandparents* is one move towards the destabilisation of traditional stereotypes.

The third issue is the matter of generational change, to which we have already referred. Whilst the image of the mask seems to remain the most appropriate as far as the present generation of the elderly are concerned, there *are* signs that, for certain sections of the population in entering *middle age* (in particular the middle classes), images and expectations are gradually beginning to change; a new language of ageing with a much greater expressive range has been gradually emerging. And the quest for a new public language to challenge and destabilise traditional cultural images of middle age for both women and men is a significant feature of the culture of mid-life as it has emerged in the West since the Second World War.

Positive Ageing and the Social Reconstruction of Middle Age

To put mid-life culture into a nutshell, during the last twenty to thirty years middle age has increasingly become a cause for concern. The public stereotype of middle age as a kind of 'mature' interlude with relatively unambiguous physical and psychological boundaries between young adulthood and declining old age has been replaced by an ideal of active, prolong mid-life which has more in common with youth than age. For the sake of convenience these changes can be broadly periodised as follows.

First, the closing decades of the nineteenth century through to the outbreak of the Second World War. These years saw an increasing concern with the elderly as a problem but, more particularly, the expansion of the concept of retirement both in Britain and in the United States. As, for example, William Graebner (1980) shows in his history of retirement in the USA, the professedly meliorative institution of retirement is itself the product of the desire to redeploy older workers. As such it is part of a process of age discrimination which has the effect of increasing age consciousness amongst both men and women.

Secondly, the post-Second World War period through to the 1970s. Both periods reveal the growing influence of *consumer culture*, but it is in the late 1950s and early 1960s in the USA where the elderly (or certain sections of the elderly population) are defined as a new market for consumer goods. As Calhoun (1978) puts it in his unwaveringly optimistic study of the 'emergence of the senior citizen between 1945–1970': there was 'an upgrading of the image and status of the elderly in American society' (33). There was also the first outcrop of popular books redefining middle age as a positive period of growth and development, though in the context of a movement through relatively fixed life stages. These books drew heavily, albeit selectively, on the increasing academic interest in middle age in the USA. Research into the menopause, for example, was highlighted, and tentative scientific speculations on the 'male menopause' received an airing..

Thirdly, the mid-1970s through to the present day. In the UK, as in the USA, the concept of the 'mid-life crisis' is by now taken much more seriously, and the popularity of such terminology alongside the word 'menopause', and even 'male menopause', reflects the legitimation of *a new vocabulary of motives* which places an emphasis on the positive value of greater flexibility and openness and a willingness to discard 'chronological bonds'. Such a view is confirmed by Stoddard (1983) in her study of the portrayal of women and ageing in American popular film, where she describes how the 1950s saw important changes in attitudes to women on the cinema screen. These were, she says, 'the years in which old age became part of a woman's life cycle to be avoided, physically and mentally, and the time that middle age began to turn in a period of crisis' (117). During the 1960s and 1970s, 'as the movie audience of the early sixties moved into an awareness of their own march towards early middle age in the late seventies, the film images became more and more sympathetic'. And by the early 1970s, middle age had become a crisis period for men as well as women and 'measured more in terms of self-fulfilment than terms of traditional social expectations' (121).

The use of the term 'mid-life' should not be taken to imply a complete break with the past on the part of a new generation of 'mid-lifers' but is a rather loosely arranged collection of ideals which intersect around the concept of youthfulness and its capacity for personal and social change and the irrelevance of chronologically determined age-related statuses. The significant reference point of the ideal imagery of the new middle age is the conception of the 'generation gap' which is expressed on two levels:

1 a sense of breaking with conventional images of age and what is sometimes described as 'loosening the chronological bonds' (Featherstone and Hepworth, 1984):
2 an appeal for the shared experiences of particular generations of men and women who are urged to discover a common identity and cause – the generation, born 1928–38, for example, who Rayner (1980) has described as the 'buffer generation'.

In this emerging and transforming context the culture of mid-life can be seen as one strand in the broader process, often described as the 'modernisation of ageing', which involves a distancing from deep old age – a distancing which is achieved through flexible adjustments to the gradually blurring boundaries of adult life. And this process of transformation has three significant characteristics:

1 Attempts to disconnect the cultural links that have been established since the latter decades of the nineteenth century between retirement and old age: this process involves appropriate changes in the imaging of retirement in terms which are positively youthful.
2 The social reconstruction of middle age, which becomes more fluidly defined as 'mid-life', or the 'middle years': there is a clear dissociation here from the dependence and powerlessness of deep old age. In 1894 Gardner defined the boundaries between middle and old age as follows: 'Some have said a man is old at forty-five; others have considered seventy the normal standard. Long observation has convinced me that *sixty-three* is an age at which the majority of persons may be termed old; and, as a rule, we may adopt this as the epoch of the commencing decline of life. Exceptions, of course, there are; but in a mixed company, few would fail to discern those who may fairly be pronounced old people, as distinguished from the middle-aged; and, we venture to say, most of them would be found, on enquiry, to have reached or passed sixty-three' (13).
3 The elaboration of the contemporary period of extended mid-life into a complex of states of 'being', 'development' and personal growth mediated by *transitional* states or crises: this elaboration of mid-life increasingly implies a flexible,

individualised, biographical approach which takes into account
human diversity.

As we stated in our discussion of postmodern deconstruction,
this flexible biographical approach is neatly accommodated by
the conceptual shift in gerontology from life *cycle* to life *course*
analysis. Unlike the term 'life cycle', which implies fixed
categories in the life of the individual and assumes a stable
system, the term 'life course' suggests more flexible biographical
patterns within a continually changing social system. It permits
a more dynamic approach to relations between the individual,
the family, work and others, and highlights the capacities of
members of differing generations to sustain reciprocal relationships over time. In his essay 'Ageing, Dying, and Death'. Turner
(1987) argues that we can theorise the stigma of both youth and
the aged with reference to a disengagement (expressed as a
relative absence of reciprocity) from the community. Turner has
devised a 'reciprocity-maturation curve' to demonstrate an
increase in social prestige as one moves into mid-life and
reciprocity and social integration increase. The community grants
esteem to such people for their services and for the value it has
for them. In line with disengagement theory, as people become
elderly and unable to reciprocate and perform responsibilities
they are forced to withdraw from powerful social roles and lose
prestige. Likewise young people score low on reciprocity because
it takes time to build up the skills and 'capital' that make this
possible – they are unable to reciprocate and to become involved
in the community. This model may go some way towards
explaining the low status of the old and children.

We would, however, like to supplement this in terms of our
previous discussion of postmodernity and ageing. First, it is
possible for different groups and classes to manage the decline
of reciprocity in different ways. While we agree with Bourdieu's
(1984) statement that ageing involves an accumulation of capital
(economic, cultural, social and symbolic), and a shedding of all
types of capital as one moves towards old age (in a similar
manner to Turner, 1987), the differential possession of different
amounts of capital in old age will allow varying classes to
manage the loss of status in different ways. With regard to our
previous discussion of the life course, and adult life as a process,
Turner's account should also be supplemented by adding an

analysis of the three types of control (cognitive, emotional and bodily) to which we have also referred. Clearly the timing and degree of the loss of these controls would result in a decline or ultimate loss of confirmation of full adult status. The decline of these competences could also produce a curve which is identical to Turner's reciprocity curve. However, it is possible, even likely, that these curves will *not* coincide, which will add a further series of combinations to our understanding of old age. We could, for example, have an inverted horseshoe reciprocity curve accompanied by incline and plateau shaped competence curves, and of course a range of combinations.

It is therefore important to have some sociological understanding and theorisation of the social construction of the life course in order to address the question of old age. Old age can only be understood in relational terms to (a) a discussion of the grounds for accounting for other stages of life; (b) a discussion of the previous life of the old people which acts as a background and context for their expectations and experience of old age; and (c) the relation of old people to the other generations following behind who may have their own cultural priorities which point towards either a 'caring' or a 'stigmatising' attitude towards the old. The cultural factors influencing generational experience are, of course, variable: the post-war 'baby-boomers', for example, will take into old age quite different values and resources from those who preceded them and from those who follow. And for the immediate future if looks as if it is this generation (particularly the articulate middle classes) which is at the forefront in the elaboration and expression of a public vocabulary of ageing in direct opposition to the traditional static model with which we have until recent times been more familiar.

Note

This is a modified version of the paper, 'Ageing and Old Age: Reflections on the Postmodern Life Course' which appeared in B. Bytheway, T. Keil, P. Allatt, and A. Bryman (eds) (1989) *Becoming and Being Old*. London: Sage.

References

Ariès, P. (1973) *Centuries of Childhood*. Harmondsworth: Penguin.
Bourdieu, P. (1984) *Distinction*. London: Routledge & Kegan Paul.
Calhoun, R. (1978) *In Search of the New Old: Redefining Old Age in America 1945–70*. New York: Elsevier.
Cunningham-Burley, S. (1985) 'Constructing grandparenthood: anticipating

appropriate action', *Sociology*, 19(3): 421-36.

Derrida, J. quoted in G. Rose (1988) 'Architecture to philosophy – the post-modern complicity', *Theory, Culture & Society*, 5(2/3): 357-71.

Elias, N. (1978) *The Civilising Process: The History of Manners*. Oxford: Blackwell.

Fairhurst, E. (1982) '"Growing old gracefully", as opposed to "mutton dressed as lamb"': the social construction of recognising older women'. Paper presented to The British Sociological Association Conference, University of Manchester.

Featherstone, M. (1988) 'In Pursuit of the Postmodern', *Theory, Culture & Society*, Special Issue on Postmodernism, 5(2-3): 195-215. Reprinted in *Postmodern and Consumer Culture*. London: Sage, 1990.

Featherstone, M. and Hepworth, M. (1984) 'Changing images of retirement: an analysis of representations of ageing in the popular magazine *Retirement Choice*', in D.B. Bromley (ed.), *Gerontology: Social and Behavioural Perspectives*. London: BSG/Croom Helm. pp.219-24.

Featherstone, M. and Hepworth, M. (1986) 'New lifestyles in old age?', in C. Phillipson, M. Bernard and P. Strang (eds), *Dependency and Interdependency in Old Age: Theoretical Perspective and Policy Alternatives*. London: BSG/Croom Helm. pp.85-94.

Featherstone, M. and Hepworth, M. (1990) 'Images of ageing', in J. Bond and P.G. Coleman (eds), *Ageing in Society. An Introduction to Social Gerontology*. London: Sage.

Foucault, F. (1979) *Discipline and Punish: The Birth of the Prison*. Harmondsworth: Penguin.

Freeman, M. (1984) 'History, narrative and lifespan developmental knowledge', *Human Development*, 27(1): 1-19.

Friedman, J. (1987) 'Prolegomena to the adventures of Phallus in Blunderland: an anti-anti-discourse', *Culture and History*, 1(1): 31-49.

Gardner, J. (1894) *Longevity: The Means of Prolonging Life after Middle Age*. London: Henry J. King.

Graebner, W. (1980) *A History of Retirement*. New Haven: Yale University Press.

Gubrium, J. (1986) *Old Times and Alzheimer's: The Descriptive Organisation of Senility*. Greenwich, Connecticut and London: JAI Press.

Hepworth, M. (1987) 'The mid life phase', in G. Cohen (ed.), *Social Change and the Life Course*. London: Tavistock. pp.134-55.

Hepworth, M. and Featherstone, M. (1982) *Surviving Middle Age*. Oxford: Blackwell.

Holt, J. (1969) *Escape to Childhood*. Harmondsworth: Penguin.

Kastenbaum, R., Derkin, V., Sabatini, P. and Artt, S. (1981) '"The ages of me": toward personal and interpersonal definitions of functional ageing', in R.Kastenbaum (ed.), *Ageing in the New Scene*. New York: Springer.

Kohli, M. and Meyer, J.W. (1986) 'Social structure and the social construction of life stages', *Human Development*, 29.

Lurie, A. (1981) *The Language of Clothes*. London: Heinemann.

Lyotard, J.F. (1984) *The Postmodern Condition*. Manchester: Manchester University Press.

Meyrowitz, J. (1984) 'The adult child and the childlike adult', *Daedalus*, 113(3): 19-48.

Meyrowitz, J. (1985) *No Sense of Place*. New York: Oxford University Press.
Puner, M. (1978) *To the Good Long Life: What We Know about Growing Old*. London: Macmillan.
Rayner, C. (1980) *Lifeguide*. London: New English Library.
Stephens, J. (1976) *Loners, Losers, and Lovers: Elderly Tenants in a Slum Hotel*. Seattle and London: University of Washington Press.
Stoddard, K.M. (1983) *Saints and Shrews: Women and Ageing in American Popular Film*. Connecticut: Greenwood Press.
Turner, B.S. (1987) 'Ageing, dying and death', in Bryan S. Turner (ed.), *Medical Power and Social Knowledge*. London: Sage. pp. 111–30.
Urry, J. (1988) 'Culture change and contemporary holiday making', *Theory, Culture & Society*, 5(1): 35–56.
Walmsley, J. and Margolis, J. (1987) *Hothouse People: Can They Create Super Human Beings?* London: Pan.
Young, L. (1989) 'The Incredible Ageing Woman', *The Guardian*, 1 August.

16

SOCIOLOGICAL DISCOURSE AND THE BODY

J.M. Berthelot

This chapter first appeared in *Theory, Culture & Society*, Vol. 3 (1986), 155–64.

Introduction

Although references to the body in the human and social sciences currently abound, a closer and more rigorous examination raises questions about their significance. Hence in the sociological field a detailed list of references (Berthelot et al. 1985)[1] for the period since 1945 based on over 500 texts reveals that sociology of the body in such a state of dispersion, evanescence, precariousness and discontinuity that the original question of orientation has to be reformulated: is there any meaning in a sociology of the body? (Berthelot 1982). Is such a sociology possible? (Druhle 1982). One could reply that the simple existence of such a field carried its own legitimacy. Therefore it might be better to formulate the problem in the following way: If we agree to designate as the 'sociology of the body' all the attempts to consider the body from a sociological point of view, what is the status of this sociology? Can it be considered as the embryo of a sociological domain such as work, the family or education? Does it have as its focal point, an object, the human body? Or is it something else? A counterpoint sociology as we have described elsewhere? (Berthelot 1983). But what does this term mean? And the term 'body' for that matter? In studying such an apparently familiar object, is there not the risk of drifting off in all kinds of directions? In the final analysis, to what precisely does the term 'body' refer in the expression 'sociology of the body'?

While our work[2] may help to provide the basis for an answer to these questions, we should not, however, overestimate the limitations of our investigation, for critical reflexion on the way sociology has approached the body is still in its early stages. This chapter can therefore be considered as a preliminary, and somewhat rudimentary, contribution.

The first difficulty to be faced is that the type of corporealism which has grown up since the 1970s has brought with it an excessive use of the term 'body'. The body would appear to be everywhere and, as a curious case of spontaneous and rational interference many researchers, who, in fact, don't deal with the topic in their work refer to it implicitly on every page. The basic approach has not, however, fundamentally changed even though the body is now exposed whereas before it was hidden and is referred to in various fields which have acquired scientific status such as diet, sexuality, beauty care, etc. The attention currently accorded to the body then is perhaps indicative of a fashion or even an intellectual movement which does not necessarily involve a step forward in knowledge.

What, in fact, is meant here by 'body'? Definitions are few and far between. The body seems to be taken for granted and by a sort of inverted spirituality, appears to constitute a self-evident fact and an obvious benchmark. Begging the question in this way is, in itself, highly significant. The body as the underpinning of all social practices can, *de jure* be referred to in all contexts even the most unexpected: intellectual and spiritual asceticism is unthinkable without corporeal discipline. The saint's ecstasy is rooted in a constrained and exacerbated corporeality and the illustrious creative man, of learning scribbles, manipulates, concentrates his body under his pen. In fact we are dealing here with a somewhat banal field of social knowledge. The real problem lies elsewhere: how can sociology conceptualize this entity which appears to be both present and absent, the necessary precondition for all possible practices yet devoid of theoretical existence? If the body's existence is, *de jure*, undeniable, how is this existence accounted for by sociology? How can social discourse take hold of this reality? What does it make of it? What is specifically sociological about the way it tackles the question and how does it differ from a mere intellectual fashion?

What does our work contribute to these questions? The encounter between sociology and the body takes place on three levels: social movements, social thought, and social sciences.

Social Movements

As far as social movements are concerned, the body, in the nine-teenth century was presented as an organic reality threatened in its very being by the arrival of industrial processes and their consequences. In fact, a whole traditional culture based on the notion of balance between the body and the world, tasks and resources, pleasures and difficulties, health and sickness was shattered by the battering ram of industrial capitalism.

What we observe first of all is the body attacked, mutilated, fallen from grace: the body considered as an *organic machine* was at the centre of the calls for enquiries into working condi-tions, for factory acts and the warnings sounded by the public health experts and the philanthropists. This was not of course the sole characterization of the body, it was also approached via conceptions of dignity, fraternity and charity. Nevertheless it did take a predominant place since, as Marx observed with great clarity, the invention of the machine-tool caused a definitive rupture in the timeless unity between capacity for work and means of working. Once the means broke free from the limits of the human organism and entered into an exclusively mechanical relationship with the object of work, a revolution occurred in the relationship between Man and his tools: from being master of his tools he became the object, the slave of the machine, broken by it, dominated by its rhythms, destroyed, mutilated.

In the medical and social literature of the nineteenth century, the industrial body constitutes the basis for the body considered as degenerate, sick or alcoholic (Rigaudias-Weiss 1930; Leclerc 1979; Leonard 1982; Perrot 1983).[3] The twentieth century, on the other hand, has tended to replace the notion of the body as a productive agent by the hedonistic body and its various manifestations. Between the two wars elements of both periods existed side by side (at one and the same time the body was seen as a mere element in the production line especially in the new media, as in Chaplin's film *Modern Times*. A definite foretaste of the period to follow also emerged with the birth of nudism, paid holidays, the notion of leisure and minority demands). This new social representation of the body established itself more firmly during the postwar period of economic growth, especially in the 1960s. The mono-functional body of the work process affected by the development of mechanization was replaced by a multi-functional spontaneous body which needs to exist as an integrated whole in order to be the source of knowledge, consciousness and nourishment. As Baudrillard (1970) remarks:

> At the present time everything would seem to indicate that the body has become an object of salvation. It has literally replaced the soul in this moral and ideological function.

Social Thought

Social thought has underpinned this social investment of the body through the prism of its references and ideological loyalties: the defence of the body threatened by 'degeneration' in the nineteenth century; the calls for authenticity, naturalness, the refusal to be manipulated, dominated and denied in the twentieth century. It would appear that with the development of industrial society and its techniques, the corporeal territory of the Ego has been considerably extended and, at the same time, weakened. It has now become a battleground, a source of tension between two opposing forces, that of the powers that be and of submission to social codes on the one hand, and that of lived experience and of concentration on the self on the other. The manipulation and abstraction of signs in order to construct media models on the one hand or self-expression and self-control of emotions in order to rediscover a corporeal ego on the other. The struggle for bodily integrity initially created by the condition of the working class which challenged the industrial organization of work seems to have taken a second place in social thought to a growing awareness of the social impositions and manipulations of the body and its representations. This can be interpreted in class terms as a middle-class discourse replacing one more proletarian in its inspiration. Or it may be expressed in terms of cultural values. In any case, this transformation may constitute an interpretative guideline common both to the demands for the free use of the body especially in sexuality and maternity and for the free manipulation of personal appearance by the individual. The nineteenth century saw the body restrained in strictly biographical limits and interpreted in terms of degeneration or racial inequality – social thought in the present period has tended to link it to the ego and to a somewhat narcissistic spontaneous base (Lasch 1979).

Social Sciences

The human sciences reflect the decline of the mechanistic model dominant in the nineteenth century and the rise of new preoccupations. They were initially obsessed by measuring the body[4] and analysing the various organic functions. Subsequently they moved on to other models as biology moved in the same direction. Psychoanalysis with its theory of conversion syndromes considers the body as a frame for the inscription of a discourse, which though rooted in the unconscious, nevertheless is expressed socially and spontaneously via the Id and the Super Ego. Psychology has struggled against reductionism and atomism by introducing the concept of bodily images and schema which permit the conceptualization of the body as a whole as opposed to the body-corpse inherited from Cartesian dualism. Finally and more recently a new fundamental perspective has emerged, in part from the ethological tradition, of the body as a means of communication: communication with the physical, ecological and social environment and communication with others on different levels of ritualization and expression. This contribution of the other human sciences has been more rapidly integrated into ethnology[5] than into sociology. The incredible diversity of ways in which the body is treated and the corporeal practices of diverse cultures gave rise to interpretations which psychoanalysis later overturned and diverted away from the aesthetic and ethnocentric sentimentality[6] characteristic of the beginning of the century: the body decorated, injured, extenuated or ritually paroxystic was interpreted as a text expressing the fundamental anxieties of castration and sexualization. Thus, what the various human sciences reveal, each following its own logic, is, above all, a complex social reality of the body, a reality which is neither reducible to the biological level nor synonymous with a two-dimensional, simplified vision of society. How has sociology apprehended this reality in its various forms of social emergence?

It might be thought obvious to reply to this question by starting from the problems discussed in the realm of social thought or by relying on the social dimensions of corporeality itself, as they have been rendered explicit by the various human sciences. We would answer the question in a different way. Of course, sociology should be sensitive to social movements and social thought. Different phases of social thought may, however, just as easily hide the body (the Durkheimian School) as recuperate it (French sociology since 1970). Moreover, the receptivity to neighbouring human sciences research on the body may be low especially when it is considered important to define oneself in opposition to one's rivals; conversely it may be extremely high when, as in the American tradition, the frontiers between sociology, anthropology and social psychology are practically non-existent. However behind these diverse frames of references there is the common question. What does the sociological interest in the body signify? What are the theoretical and epistemological stakes involved in stressing its importance? A possible answer would seem to be that the body arises in sociological discourse on the dividing line which separates the social sciences from the human sciences, at the point of friction between causal and structural rationality and a symbolic and intentional rationality which is expressed on a dual level in the relationships between structures and actors, codes and meanings.

What does this mean? It is well known that since its beginnings, sociology has been characterized by a multiplicity of inter-pretive models which concurrently come into conflict. It would be an over simplification to say that these can all be reduced to the basic opposition between explanation and understanding. Nevertheless a general dichotomy can be observed between apprehending social phenomena as structures (i.e. as various mechanical, functional, structural articulations of social elements defined as variables, segments or relative elements) and constituting them as meaningful constellations linked to meaning complexes created and interpreted in various ways by individual or collective social subjects.

In sociological discourse it would appear that the body was first introduced as part of a social symptomatology of which a good, though naive example is provided by the monographs of LePlay and his school.[7] This symptomatology which can also be observed in the work of the Chicago School is linked to a distinct way of approaching social reality. Using Windelband's classical categories to designate the tendencies mentioned above, we can say that instead of the nomothetic model typical of positivism and the natural sciences, it proposes an ideographic model aimed at middle-range generalizations built up from the description of particular characteristics. It discusses the 'marginal man' rather than 'marginality' thus totally inversing the

Durkheimian perspective which discusses 'suicide' rather than the 'individual who commits suicide'. This symptomatology is rooted in description and is used in ethnographic discourse and may thus retain an infrasociological status. In a similar fashion, breaking physical data down into measurable elements and constructing numerical indices may never manage to reveal a law and remain at the level of empirical accumulation. Criminological studies and Italian sociology which derives from them (notably Lombroso and Nicerforo) provides good examples of the tension which occurs when epistemic models are used on an infrascientific level: compiling heterogenous data, measurements of all kinds can be both revelatory of the perception of a conflict and of a total incapacity to express it.

This symptomatology which is closely associated with the ethnological and phenomenological approaches to social reality may thus remain on the infrasociological level if the social mechanism which legitimizes it is not made explicit. On the other hand, it can have the function of a secondary interpretation of a primordial and fundamental process of the inscription of the social dimension in the bodily *incorporation*.[8] The latter may, in turn, be conceptualized in a number of ways which depend on how it is linked to different levels of sociological theorization. Thus incorporation may be found in systems of thought belonging to either one or the other of the two tendencies described above. It depends on whether the system and its structural effect of symbolical imposition are stressed or, on the contrary whether the actor's interplay of adaptation and distanced symbolical appropriation are emphasized. But in both cases it is on the dividing line, on the line of tension between the two modes of logic, structural logic on the one hand, logic of action on the other, that the debate takes place. So much so that it may be wondered whether the perception itself of this dividing line as a theoretical stake does not itself foreground the question of the body to thus constitute it as a meaningful entity. That is certainly how the body appears in corporeal symptomatology: as a system of indices, the mirror of a certain condition, often the expression of a difference. However, the latter may lead to a change in perspective: the ethnological description of primitive body decorations may express the simplistic and sentimental idea of a desire to please or conversely it may be a more intellectually ambitious form of anthropological hermeneutics. The idea of incorporation not only allows rather naive aesthetic theories to be rejected it also enables the idea of the body as a mirror to be replaced by the idea of the body as a text or social operator. Thus the social by anchoring itself in the individual not only reveals its efficacy but is in itself realized as social or, as we might say from another perspective, as societal. Putting forward the body in this way as a secret operator reveals once more the cleavage described above. In the work of Bourdieu (1979, 1980, 1982) for example, we have a structural dominance where incorporation is considered as the naturalization of a rule is also the necessary condition for the realization of what is instituted. On the other hand from Maffesoli's (1982a, 1982b) perspective we have the dominance of agency in which sociality would disintegrate without the intense interplay of affects which underpins it and whose 'confusion of bodies' is the paroxystic expression of the underlying tragic dimension. On the one hand we find the body of order, of the norm, the practical and theoretical operator of social rules, on the other we observe the body of disorder and effervescence, the practical and theoretical operator of a fundamental dimension of the social aggregate.

We can thus understand the ambiguities of corporeal symptomatology even when supported by a theory of the body as a social operator. The latter is, in fact, more often than not designated primarily as a mirror and thus inserted into various orders of meaning: the order of indices where, through the interplay of cause and effect the body reveals social conditions of its functioning (the relaxed, expressive body of the athlete, the deformed body of the manual worker, the degenerate body of the tramp); the order of non-verbal communication where in the incessant though discontinuous whirl of individual interactions, gestures, postures, attitudes, looks, distances are integrated into what Goffman called 'the ritual idiom': the order of the signs of personal appearance which can be inserted either into a logic of appearance or into an economy of signs; the order of signs of belonging not reducible to that of indices in so far as it associates signs and the use of signs and reveals, via corporeal hexis, the class and group properties which both determine them (cause–effect relationship), constitute them (the signifier–signified relationship) and mobilize them (emitter–receiver relationship); finally the order of symbolic associations which link the body and any of its aspect and forms to the image-forming dimension which solidifies into media stereotypes, or, in certain cases, break out into varied images.

If, then, in addition to the resulting ambiguities, sociology proposes several ways of inserting the body into a signifying order, it is because the body is the particular site of an interface between a number of different domains: the biological and the social, the collective and the individual, that of structure and agent, cause and meaning, constraint and free will. But this interface only emerges in sociological discourse because it is at the same time the objective counterpoint of the internal tension existing between the social and human science and because it is materialized in an irreducible, unique being: the individual who is both object and subject, product and actor, structure and meaning. In the nineteenth century this entity was first of all apprehended according to the norms of the dominant spiritualism of the period: the body was firmly placed in the biological domain, in the order of mechanical causes and vital functions; the spiritual was separated out around the categories of thought, consciousness and representation. Thus, in opposition to anthropology which concentrated primarily upon the body as a physical entity and made strenuous efforts to give meaning to an accumulation of measures and indices, sociology reacted by reversing this perspective by considering the corporeal base as secondary to representation and ideas.[9] From which came the body's strange destiny with it more often than not present only implicitly, especially when a particular field highlighted one of its roles, with it generally tending to disappear into the functioning of the system or into the semiotics of the code. Only Mauss with his great culture and intellectual honesty stressed its taken-for-granted nature even if he only accorded it the status of a by-product of anthropological observation.[10]

Thus through the various uses of corporeal symptomatology and the various attempts to sustain or go beyond it, the body appears to have a particular status in sociology: not that of an object but rather that of an epistemic index. It appears in a precise and somewhat paradoxical way as an indicator of the *refusal of a certain type of reductionism*: it was rejected by the Durkheimian School not so much for its existence as 'body' but for its role as another point for biologism, organicism, and anthroposociology. It was restored by Mauss, the Chicago School and finally by contemporary sociology as an index of the inadequacy of a certain type of exclusive structural paradigm or in the case of the deterministic sociologies as the point at which the social becomes inscribed on the individual.

In all these cases, the approach to the social existence of the body thus appears to be highly over-determined: caught between social movements reflected to a greater or lesser extent in social thought and the epistemic problems of sociology, the body could only be taken into account at the expense of considerable distortion. This would explain why, in our view, particular aspects of corporeality were stressed at different times without any attempt at a global approach. Moreover, these aspects were in most cases not so much linked to corporeality as to a system of signs which made use of them or to form a social reality which expressed itself through them. In short, it would appear that sociology only dealt with the body to break it down while expressing the connotative or illustrative character of its unity on another register.

Conclusion
If this is the fundamental status of the body in sociological discourse, what can we conclude about the way in which this discourse accounts for the social reality of the body? There would seem to be four dominant characteristics.

a) Many of the social dimensions of corporeality are only briefly sketched out. Although the body at work is englobed by a symptomatology whose purpose is to reveal its operational conditions, in the final analysis this perspective is more characteristic of social thought than of sociology. The latter, by stressing the symbolic order tends to neglect the materiality of the body as this dimension were of a purely biological nature.[11] Whereas the life sciences, medicine, demography, biometry, ergonomics and other disciplines study the somatic effects linked to environment, especially the social environment as if each one had global importance. The social production of bodies and the effects of economic and technical changes on this production seems to be a blind spot for sociology which leaves it to the imagination of science-fiction writers to invent possible corporeal futures.

b) A corporeal practice can always be apprehended from the point of view of the social, institutional, cultural context in which it takes place. Sociology is fairly experienced in this field and thus often tends, even in areas where the body would appear to be dominant to ignore it in preference to studying the structural, institutional or cultural mechanisms with which it is familiar. The sociology of sport is a good example of this case.[12]

c) The sociological conceptualization of corporeality remains essentially limited and dependent upon part sociological or non-sociological theorizations. Apart from the notion of incorporation which needs greater theoretical exploration, the concepts used remain rather general: corporeal techniques, corporeal symbolism, the social image of the body, body language, the social representations of the body are all part of a general taxonomy and do not amount to an attempt at a specific theorization of the social reality of the body.

d) Finally, the body as a social being, the result of the interplay, of the fashioning of the organic by the social, and the appropriation of the social by an organic being gifted with consciousness. The articulation of agency and structure, causality and meaning, rationality and imagination, physical determinations and symbolic resonances, remains beyond an indeterminate horizon which programmatic attempts at global apprehension have not yet managed to reach (Barthes 1982; Berthelot 1983).

This brings us back to our first question: is a sociology of the body possible? If, as we hope to have shown, sociology only deals with the body when placed in the most difficult and uncomfortable epistemic position, is there not a considerable risk that all sociology concerned with results and efficiency might avoid dealing with the question entirely? In fact recent approaches have tended to oscillate between various positions which relegate the sociology of the body to a mere annexe of a more powerful branch of sociology: the sociology of modernity, the sociology of domination and symbolic imposition, the sociology of interaction, the sociology of the imaginary.

Even this status as an annexe, however, can be considered as the result of the inadequacies of those more powerful sociologies. In fact whether it is a question of sectoral sociologies linked to a field of social activity or transversal sociologies attempting to render explicit a fundamental social dimension, the role given to the body appears as a way of taking up a position at a privileged place for understanding the social dimension; at precisely the place where the social dimension can be grasped not only by means of a particular symptomatology but also via one of its most secret conditions of perdurance. For if the socialized body so often conceals the organic body in the spectacular display of its characteristics is it not in the depths of the organic body, at the articulation of the spontaneous and the symbolic that the social dimension finds its resources?

Doubtless, a sociology of the body will remain a secondary sociology for as long as a scientific approach to the body has not managed in a detailed study of the different processes to grasp the articulation between the various disorders which meet there and fuse. We can only, at this stage, sketch out the perspective of a counterpoint sociology which finds its epistemological vector in the body considered as product and producer, the place of pain and pleasure, alienation and reappropriation, inscription and affect.

Notes

1. Published in *Current Sociology* 33: 2, 1985 (Sage Publications Ltd) under the title 'Les Sociologies et le Corps'. This study was carried out by the 'Corps et Socialisation' team of the 'Centre de Recherches Sociologiques' at the Université de Toulouse-Le Mirail (a laboratory affiliated to the CNRS). The present text is based on the author's conclusion.

2. An analytical grid was applied to texts which mentioned the body which were selected in the following manner:

a) By separate, individual probes for the period before 1945 in order to grasp the way the body emerged in 'classical' sociology. Two tendencies and two periods were studied in particular: the emergence of the body in the social thought of the nineteenth century and its practical repression in Durkheimian sociology; the role played by the body in the sociology of the Chicago School and the way it was gradually left aside by culturalism and functionalism.

b) In a systematic manner after 1945 and especially after 1970. The latter date is coincidentally the point of departure of the corporealist movement in sociology and the starting date for available computerized bibliographic material on the CDSH FRANCIS catalogue (Maison des Sciences de L'Homme. Paris).

3. By way of example and to give the tone of this literature here are two extracts:

The reader only has to walk through the poor streets of the East and South districts of London. If he is of average height he will be a head taller than those he meets on his way; everywhere he will come across pale faces, stunted silhouettes, weak and feeble bodies, narrow shoulders and all the external signs of a lack of vital force! (Lord Brabazon, quoted in Jones [1977]).

Certain industrial tasks afflict the human species with deformities and create a race apart, quite different from the one God put on earth. To what can we reasonably attribute the under-developed aspects of the 'canuts' of Lyons, the weak and suffering air of the silkworkers of Spitalfields, the deformities of the handloom weavers if not to the influence of the calling they have followed since their childhood? (Buret 1840).

4. Body Measurement in the nineteenth century constituted a surprising movement: deriving from physical anthropology, armed with various instruments, encouraged by the development of statistical positivism this current practised the accumulation of factual data. The latter instead of giving rise to any real attempt at theorization were used to supply arguments and alibis for the most contradictory forms of Social Darwinism and also nourished the humanistic thought of scholars such as Broca or Quetelet, the revolutionary anarchism of Malato (1907), the social racialism of Ammon and Laponge's 'anthropo-sociologie' as well as the criminal anthropometry carried out in France under the auspices of Bertillon and in Italy by the Lombroso School. For further information on this movement see Gould (1983), Kremer-Marietti (1984), Berthelot et al. (1985).

5. For our inventory of texts and the constitution of our corpus we chose to exclude ethnology, and especially the ethnology of exotic societies, for the following reason: even more than in sociological discourse, the body in this field is an ambiguous term: a bibliographical inventory based on a computerized catalogue gave 1800 references for this field as against 300 for sociology during the same period. A cursory examination revealed that many references were linked to the functioning of the body not as a concept but as a convenient category for recording data. The size of this catalogue on the one hand, and the particular function of the key word on the other, led us to concentrate on the principal ethnological texts only.

6. Although the authors, travellers, ethnographers, observers of the end of the last century showed interest in the way the body was treated in their descriptions of the term 'dress' ('parures' in French) used to account for such usages as face painting, cosmetics, tattoos, incisions, mutilations, etc. . . . lead explicitly to an aesthetic form of interpretation. They were seen as reflecting a 'desire to be beautiful'. This interpretation was easily integrated into the type of naive evolutionism well expressed in this conclusion of Letourneau's (1880): 'The more man progresses and his reason develops, the more the intelligence dominates in his mental life and the more he renounces adornments of all kinds and brilliant colours.' In the same tradition Lombroso (1896) interprets tattoos on criminals as an atavistic phenomenon; commenting on the smaller proportion of tattooed women and the more restricted variety of their themes he writes: 'The atavistic explanation which we have given can also be applied here since savage women tattoo themselves less than males and make simpler designs.'

7. Under the heading 'hygiene and health service', these monographs give a physical description of the subjects observed in which the characteristics noted can, according to each case, be purely factual or be integrated into a meaningful social portrait. For example: 'The worker is of small stature (1 m 62) and of a bilious temperament; in spite of a frail appearance he has only suffered from the usual childhood illnesses, he can stand, without difficulty, the strains of his profession as well as those of hunting'. (Tinsmith, monograph no. 10 significant factual data.)

Nearly all the members of the family are distinguished by highly developed physical strength and robust health: the head of the household is 1 m 75 tall and his wife 1 m 65. Though 74 years old, the former still shares in all the tasks and can, if need be, climb the neighbouring mountain. The older daughter, aged 18, can easily carry loads of 88 kg on her shoulders. The fertility of the women which is *one of the consequences of the purity of the customs* and one of the principal causes of the prosperity of the families, must also apparently be attributed to the fact that the girls only marry when they have reached their full physical development.

(Pyrenean peasant monograph no.3. Note the use of factual data as a symptom, implicitly of the beneficial influence of the rural world and explicitly of the purity of the customs. Perhaps, in the author's mind, the one is linked to the other.)

8. The term is used both by the theoreticians of the Chicago School and by Bourdieu and J.M. Brohm.

9. Thus Durkheim (1912), when speaking of tattooing, uses the following reduction: tattooing is 'the most direct and the most expressive means whereby the communion of consciences can be asserted'.

10. At the beginning of his well-known article 'Les Techniques du Corps', Mauss (1973) writes:

In the natural sciences at their present stage of development, one always comes across an ugly heading. There always comes a moment when the science of certain facts not having yet been reduced to concepts and these facts not having been grouped organically, the work of ignorance is stamped upon these facts in the word: 'Others'. That is what we need to penetrate. We can be sure that truth is to be found there: firstly because we know that we don't know and because we are acutely aware of the quantity of facts. For many years in my classes on descriptive ethnology, I had to teach and take responsibility for this disgrace, this opprobrium called 'others' (especially on a point at which this heading 'others' was truly heteroclite in ethnology) I knew full well that walking, swimming and many other activities of this type are specific to particular societies of this type. That Polynesians don't swim like we do, that my generation didn't swim like the present one. But what kind of social phenomena were these? They were 'others' and since this heading is a horror, I have often thought of this 'others', at least every time I have had to mention it and on many other occasions too. Please excuse me if in order to give form to this notion of techniques of the body I have had to bring up the times when and how I have been able to express clearly the general problem!

11. In the habitual distinction between nature and culture we can detect in the work of many sociologists the relegation of the body to the biological order, even in the approach of the initiators of a sociology of the body. Thus Boltanski (1971) in his well-known article 'Les usages sociaux du corps' writes:

Social determination never influences the body in an immediate way through actions which have a direct effect on the biological order, but is rather transmitted by the cultural order which retranslates it and transforms it into rules, obligations, interdicts, repulsions, desires, tastes and disgusts.

12. The sociology of sport has been highly developed in the USA. Its main interest has been in economic, juridical, institutional, and psychological questions.

The study of sport as a social phenomenon has generally focused on the market analysis, and the interactions which take place inside small groups. The body itself is left to the disciplines which deal with it rationally: anatomy, physiology, pathology . . . It has, however, become the object of a wider sociological interrogation through a politically committed approach where it is viewed as a sporting body. This approach has been developed by both academic researchers and practitioners of physical education (cf. *Partisans* No.13, 1968, Culture and Repression: and the revue *Quel Corps?* founded and animated by J.M. Brohm).

References

Barthes, R. (1982) 'Encore le corps', *Critique*, 423–4.

Baudrillard, J. (1970) *La Société de Consommation*, Paris.

Berthelot, J.M. (1982) 'Une sociologie du corps a-t-elle un sens?', *Recherches Sociologiques*, 1–2, pp. 59–65.

Berthelot, J.M. (1983) 'Corps et société, problèmes méthodologies posés par une approache sociologique due corps', *Cahiers Internationaux de Sociologie*, 74, pp. 19–32.

Berthelot, J.M., Druhle, M., Clément, S., Forné, J. and M'bodj, G. (1985) 'Les sociologies et le corps', *Current Sociology*, 33, 2.

Boltanski, L. (1971) 'Les usages sociaux du corps', *Annales ESC*, 26: 1, pp. 205–33.

Bourdieu, P. (1979) *La Distinction*, Paris: Minuit.

Bourdieu, P. (1980) *Le Sens Pratique*, Paris: Minuit.

Bourdieu, P. (1982) 'Les rites comme acte d'institution', *Actes de la Recherches en Sciences Sociales*, 43, pp. 58–63.

Buret, E. (1840) *De la Misère des Classes Laborieuses en Angleterre et France*, Paris.

Druhle, M. (1982) 'Une sociologie du corps est-elle possible', *Recherches Sociologiques*, 1–2, pp. 53–7.

Durkheim, E. (1912) *Les Formes Élementaires de la Vie Religieuse*, Paris.

Gould, S.J. (1983) *La Mal-mesure de l'Homme*, Paris.

Jones, G.S. (1977) 'Le Londres des Réprouvés', *Recherches*, 29.

Kremer-Marietti, A. (1984) 'L'Anthropologie Physique et Morale en France et ses implications ideologiques', in B. Rupp-Essemreich (ed.), *Histoire de l'Anthropologie XVI–XIXème Siècle*.

Lasch, C. (1979) *The Culture of Narcissim*, NY: Norton.

Leclerc, G. (1979) *L'observation de l'Homme. Une histoire des enquêtes sociales*, Paris.

Leonard, J. (1982) *La Médicine entre les Pouvoirs et les Savoirs*, Paris.

Letourneau (1880) *La Sociologie d'après l'Ethnologie*, Paris.

Lombroso, C. (1896) *La Femme Criminelle et la Prostituée*, Paris.

Maffesoli, M. (1982a) *L'Ombre de Dionysus*, Paris: Méridien-Anthropos.

Maffesoli, M. (1982b) 'La forme dionysiaque expression du corps collectif', *Actes et Recherches en Sociales*, 1, pp. 19–27.

Malato (1907) *Les Classes Sociales au Point de Vue Zoologiques*, Paris.

Mauss, M. (1973) 'Les techniques du corps', in *Sociologie et Anthropologie*, Paris: PUF (orig. 1936), translated as 'Techniques of the body', *Economy and Society*, 2: 1.

Perrot, M. (1984) 'Les Bonneff et l'enquête sociale au début du xxème siècle'. Preface to re-edition of L.F. Bonnet, *La Vie Tragique des Travailleurs*, Paris.

Rigaudias-Weiss, H. (1930) *Les Enquêtes Ouvrières en France entre 1830 et 1848*, Paris.

INDEX

abortion issue 77, 78, 94–5
absolutism 27, 30, 257, 259
abstract, tyranny of the 77–8, 84, 89, 91, 92
action theory of the body 38, 47–54
adolescence 52–3
advertising 170, 172, 173–6, 179, 190
aesthetics 12, 274, 275, 278, 302, 318–19
age 11, 372, 374, 376, 381
ageing: contemporary imagery of 372–4; defeat of process 19, 178, 186, 202; the mask of 377–83; of population 21–2, 168, 170; positive 383–7; stigmatisation of 192, 378, 382, 387
agency 7, 257, 260, 271, 275–8, 396–7, 400
Aikido training 84, 209–24
analytical theory of the body 36–90
animal behaviour 103–7, 108, 114, 117, 121, 125
animism 299, 301
anorexia nervosa 127, 150–1
anthropology 1–6, 310, 398
anxiety, politics of 24
aporia 90
appearance 170, 178–81, 186, 187, 189, 393
appetite, civilizing of 126–56
appropriation 77, 89, 93–5
archaeology 226–7
architecture: of butchery 289–96; postmodern 282
art: of the body 281–96, 318; oppositional 18–19
asceticism 44, 46, 47, 50, 52, 53, 56, 58–60, 158–9, 182, 303, 309, 391
autonomy 212–17

Bacon, Francis 19, 29, 282, 284, 289–96

baroque, and postmodernism 24–30
Belle dame sans merci, Carmen as 339–43
bio-politics 18, 225–55
biography: and ageing 386; authenticity in 326–7, 335; boundaries 325–38
biologism 7, 106–7
Bizet, Carmen 339, 344, 351–5, 358–9
blood symbolism 78, 83–4
bodies, and their resources 270–5
body beautiful 19, 170, 199
body image: and appetite 128; slim 146–51
body language 12, 55, 190–1
body maintenance 182–7, 202, 374
body metaphors 9
body techniques, social 48–50
body weights 147–9, 185
body without organs (Deleuze) 268–70
Bohemianism 355–9
bourgeoisie 18–19, 144–5, 164–6, 191–2, 339, 347–8; see also middle classes
budo 209–11, 211–17, 223
bulimia 127
bureaucratization 30, 190–2
butchery, architecture of 289–96

cannibalism 134, 152
capital: cultural 68; physical 68
capitalism 14–21, 25, 28–9, 94, 228–30; advanced 248–9; and oedipalisation 268, 269–70; and the spirit of medicine 164–6; and welfare 236–9, 244–50
carceral archipelego 233, 234
care 58, 60–1, 88–9, 191, 245
Carmen myth 339–70

castration anxiety 71
cerebral dominance 108–9
charisma, routinization of 299–301
Christ, body of 5, 53, 62
Christianity 15, 18, 19, 44–5, 273–4, 310, 311
Church, and constraints on appetite 135–7
cinema 179–81, 342, 384
class: and ageing 377; and disease 165; and eating habits 141–2, 149–52
class theory 10, 11, 42, 66–8
classificatory system, body as a 4, 5, 9–10
clothing 177, 189, 380
comic strips 197–208
commodification 44, 173–4, 189, 230
communicative body 37, 53–4, 79–89, 91–6, 315–16, 394
communism 15, 26
competitiveness 214, 216
computerization 94
conflict, human 218–19, 221–2, 223
consciousness: body's of itself 91–6; language as embodied 50–1, 91–2; and relaxation 220; use of bodies 50–4
consumer culture 18, 51–5, 61–8, 94, 170–96, 197, 200; and ageing 383–4
consumerism 7, 19, 175, 230, 374
contingency: and alignment 91–6; of dominating body 72; dyadic 79–80; and the hyperreal 92–3; and response to blood 78
control 51, 55; biological agencies of 124–5; loss with ageing 376–7, 386–7; see also regulation
corporeality 49, 50, 59–60, 296, 391
cosmetics 170, 180
courtly love 46, 302
critical theory, on the dialectics of love 314–19

cuisine 142–5
cultivation of the body 209–24
cultural ideals 28, 45–7
culture, and nature 2, 4, 8, 13–23

dance 79, 80–5
death 22, 66, 186, 232
decay, theme of 380–1
decentring 242
decisionism 30
deconstruction 371–2, 386
democratization 16, 19, 30
department stores 52, 173, 189
desire 8, 51–2, 55, 62–5, 76, 257, 260, 264, 265, 266–70, 277, 319
dialogue 231
diet 57, 61, 68, 157–69, 170
dietetics 159, 160–3, 167
differentiation 305–8, 317
discipline, and the body 157–60, 228–9, 232
disciplined body 37, 53–4, 54–61
discourse 48–9, 59–60, 91, 259, 276, 281; of postmodernity 281–96
diseases 23, 43, 44, 165
display 173, 187
dissociation 52, 56, 72–3
dissolution, fear of 76–7, 86
dominating body 53–4, 69–79
domination: mediated by taste, 66–8; technologies of 56–61

eating disorders, pathological 127–8
economics 7, 249–50, 252
education 218–19
emotions 13, 45, 103–25; expression of 118–20, 124–5; hypotheses about human 107–17
epidemics 22, 132
eroticism 17–18, 19, 28, 30, 297, 301–5, 310–11, 318, 319, 321
ethics: of the body 39, 90–6; and medical technology 22
ethnography 4, 11, 378
ethnology 4, 103, 394
ethnomethodology 46
eugenics 7, 167
events 264–5
evolution, and social development 105–7, 114–17
evolutionism 7, 9, 165
exercise 61, 68, 181, 182
existentialism 9, 17, 189, 307

expert cultures 317
Expressionism 288–9

face, human 120–4
family 372; nuclear 297, 305
famines 131–5
fascism 69–79, 94
fashion 312–13, 341, 342–3, 379–80
fasting 58–9, 129–30, 135–7
fatness, fear of 146–51
feasts, and fasting 129–30
feeling component of emotions 13, 116–17
female body 50, 83, 276–7
female identity 360
female sacrifice, persistence of 75–6
female sexuality 23, 79–80
femininity, ideals of 179–80, 345–6, 362–3
feminism 10–11, 18, 20–1, 40–2, 77–8, 84, 95, 276–7, 362–3, 380
femme fatale 339–42, 344–6, 350–1, 355, 360–1
fertility 41, 77
films, see cinema
fin de siècle bodies 24–30
fitness 19, 68, 183
food: entitlement relationships 132–4; quantity and quality 139–45
force 54, 55–6, 69–79
force relation 231–5, 250–2
Freikorps, German 69–73, 75, 77, 79, 86
functionalism 9, 43–4
functionalization of love (Parsons) 308–11

gastronomy, and moderation 145–6
gender, and classification systems 4, 10–11
gender relations 20–1, 95; see also sexuality
genealogy 226, 227, 256–80, 314
generality 212–17
generation 11, 382, 385
'George and Lynne' 197–208
gerontology 373, 381, 386–7
global crises 24, 26–7
gluttony 145
Gnosticism 52–3
Greeks 51, 209–10

'habitus' 67–8, 276
health education 183
hedonism 19, 65, 171, 186–7, 392

hermeneutics 46–7
history 8, 104, 226
Hollywood 179–81, 189, 326
homosexuality 23, 235
human sciences 103–5, 229
hunger, and appetite 127–8
hyperreality 65, 92–3

identity models 192
ideologies 45–7
illness: and the communicative body 85–9, 93; tax burden of 166
images of the body 93, 170, 177–81
impression management 187–93
incorporation 396–7, 400
individualism 362–3
information technology 94
institutions 43, 44, 49, 59–60, 91
instrumental rationality 8, 15, 16, 24, 158–9

Japanese culture 209–24
jogging 170, 185

Kaiser, Georg 284–8
kinesics 190
kitsch 28
knowledge: bodies and 270, 272–3; and power 157–9, 167, 212, 225, 242–4

labour, embodied 94–5
labouring body 166–8
lack: masculinity and sense of 55, 69, 71, 73–5, 76; physical 86–8
language, and nature of human beings 109–15
law 7–8, 20–1, 229
learning: biological propensity of humans for 108–17; nonverbal 209–24
leisure ethic 19, 172
liberal education 209–24
Liberalism 249–50
life expectancy 22, 132
lifestyles 19, 185; mid-life 197–208
'lived body' 9, 269
love: dialectics of 314–23; differentiation as base of 305–8; erotic 301–5; functionalization of (Parsons) 308–11; Platonic 298–9; reduction of social complexity by body-presence and 311–14; and religion 299–301,

love *contd*
313–14, 320; sociology
of 297–324
love-and-learn process
112–17
love-hate relationship with
the body 15–16

machine metaphor 182
magic, repressed 299–301
male bodies, appropriation
of 95
male domination 39–42,
69–79
male ideal 180–1
male sexuality 79–80
malnutrition, and
mortality 131–5
marriage 303, 309
martial arts 209–24
Marxism 1, 8, 10, 15, 16,
20, 22, 25, 26, 39, 41,
64, 94, 176, 189,
241–2, 244–50, 258,
297, 392
masculinity 69, 71, 76, 360
mask of ageing 371–89
mass culture 16, 29–30
media 170, 172, 174,
183–4, 192, 373, 375,
393
medicalized body 37
medicine: and ageing
population 21–2; and
capitalism 164–6; and
constraints on appetite
138–9; 'contrary'
162–3; high-technology
22, 93; preventative
183; social power of
138, 228
megaera 301, 314–15, 319
memory 258–9
menopause 380–1, 384
Merimée: *Carmen* 339,
344, 346–51, 355, 358,
361
metonymy 267
middle age: images of
197–208; social
reconstruction of 375,
383–7
middle classes 12–13,
373–4, 393; *see also*
bourgeoisie
midlife culture 197–208,
373, 383–7
mind–body relations 218,
219–24
mirroring body 53–4,
61–8, 397
modernism 12, 24–30,
39–40, 176
monadism 27, 55, 61, 64
Mondrian, Piet 282, 284–8
Monroe, Marilyn 325–38
moral responsibility 22,
165–6
mortality 131–5

movement, and thought
85–8, 92
myth, feminine 339–70

naked body 197, 199, 392
narcissism 63, 178, 187,
192, 202, 393
narration, and sensation
293–4
narrative, and illness 87–9
nationalism 25, 77, 78
nature: and culture 2, 8,
13–18, 20–2; hinge
with non-nature 104,
110–15
needs 229, 239
negotiating self 190–2
neurosis 13, 14, 15, 23
normalisation 228–30, 239,
241
nutrition, physiological
effects on psychology
130

obesity 138, 147, 149–50,
151
oedipalisation, and
capitalism 268, 269–70
ontology 1, 104, 281
organic metaphor 9, 46,
164–5, 392
organic processes 270–2
Other, body of the 288–9
other-relatedness of body
52, 55–6, 61–2, 73
ownership of bodies 76 7

pain 63, 86–7, 88, 220,
258–9, 261
panopticism 14, 40, 44,
58, 157, 231, 233, 242,
372
paralysis 85–8
passivity 257–66
patriarchy 20, 44
performance social theory
79–85, 93
performing self 187–93
personality, emotional
economy of the 130–1
personality handbooks
188–9
perspectivism 27, 29,
272–3
pessimism, classical and
modern 257–60
phallocentrism 267, 277
phantasms 264–5, 269
physiology 49, 258, 261
policing 237–9
politics: art and 283; of
the body, power and
the 230–5; and organic
metaphors 46
pornography 83, 321
postmodernism 8, 16–18,
40, 82–5, 278, 281–96;
and the baroque
24–30; and the life

course 371–7; and the
mask of ageing 371–89
power: from sovereign to
bio-power 244–52; and
knowledge 57–61,
157–9, 167, 225, 229;
and the politics of the
body 230–5, 276; and
sexuality 22–4, 319
process, body as 47, 79,
89, 96
process model of sociology
103–25
production 234, 247,
248–9
progress 176, 282
Protestantism 13, 14, 23,
27–8, 127, 164, 188
psychiatry 157
psychoanalysis 16, 24, 45,
70, 230, 266–8, 284,
310, 394
psychology 103, 394

rape, gang 74–5
rationalization 302–5, 317
reason 8, 48, 124
recognition 54, 79–89
reenchantment industries
317–18
regulation 23, 43, 45, 47,
54–61, 160, 232, 233–5
reification 173–4, 193, 317
religion: civil 309; love
and 299–301, 313–14,
320; sex and 301–5,
309
representation 43, 45, 285,
288–9; social of the
body 392–3
reproduction 42, 43, 44–5,
64; and contingency
79–80; expanded
271–3, 274, 277–8;
technologies as male
control of 78, 94
resistance, knowledge and
intervention 242–4
restraint 43, 44, 135
retirement 374, 383, 385
rituals 6, 221, 397
romantic love 312, 320,
339, 359–62

schizodynamics 266–9
scientific management 172
secularization of the body
182, 186
self, and ageing 378–9
self-image 106, 120
self-preservation 170,
186–7
self-relatedness of the
body 50, 52–3, 56
self-surveillance 135, 182,
184
sex, and religion 301–5,
309
sexism 20, 192

sexual body 37
sexual inequality 20–1
sexual liberation 16, 21, 277
sexuality 17–18, 73–5, 182; commercialization of 19; and instrumental rationality 16–18; and power 22–4, 227–8; and sociocultural requirements 4, 13, 14, 235, 250–1
shopping 173
simulation 288, 375
slave moralities 273–4, 275, 276
slimness 151, 183, 184–5
smiling 121–4
social body 232–4
social complexity, reduction by love and body-presence 311–14
social control 157–9, 258, 268; love and 308–11
social differentiation 107
social economy 240
social interaction, distance in 218
social movements 392–3
social policy 225–55
social sciences 104–5, 394
social stratification 10–11, 312
social system theory 48, 308–11
social theory: the body in 12–18; status of love in 297–8
social thought 393
sociobiology 4
sociology 4–5, 26; and the body 36–8, 390–404; classical 6–12; and male domination 41–2; and Marilyn Monroe 325–38
sociology of the body 18–22, 36–102, 390–404
somatism 39

space, restructuring of social 192
speech: capacity for 111–14; as embodied consciousness 50–1, 91–2
sport 68, 400
starvation 134–5
state: and constraints on appetite 137–8; control of health standards 165–6; role in medical ethics 22, 94; social expenditures 246
state agencies 232–5
state formation, and security of food supplies 130–1, 141
state intervention 226, 236–9, 242–4; and ageing 374–5
structure 11–12, 48–50, 395
styles of body usage 53–89
suffering 85–9, 92, 93, 95–6
sumptuary laws 137–8, 142
sun tan 180–1
surrealism 18–19
surveillance 14, 23, 173
symbolic interactionism 11
symbolism 6, 267, 299–301, 311–14, 397
symptomatology, corporeal 395–9
synergy 223

taboo, incest 2–3
tasks, in social systems for bodies 43, 48
taste 11, 66–8, 142
tattooing 6
technologies of control 228–30, 232–5, 242, 243
technologies of the self 14, 95
technology, and appropriation 94
text, body as a 394, 397

theology 5, 275
theory of the body 1–35
thermodynamics 167
thought, disembodiment of 85–6
training the body 166, 209–24
truth games 56–9
tutelary complex 233, 234
typologies of the body 42–54, 95

unconscious, the 275–8
urbanization 23, 162

violence 13, 14, 73–5, 219–20, 294, 303–4
vitalism 251–2

war 73, 132, 166, 167, 246–7, 304
welfare: in capitalism 236–9; Foucault on 225–55; political economy of 244–50; social role of 240–2
western philosophy 4, 5, 17, 52, 218
will to power 260, 263–4, 268, 271, 273, 274
women: in advertisements 178–9; appropriation of bodies 94–5; choice for 77; emancipation of 298; fantasy of 346; and housework 172–3; medieval holy 50, 52, 53, 58–60, 63, 92, 93–4; pathologizing of 235; political orientation of 21, 41; role in family 308–9; and social theory 321–3; thin 184–5
work ethic 14, 19, 302
working class 19, 167–8, 192, 198

youth, idealization of 183